a natural high

Millwall Football Club's two years in the First Division

MERV PAYNE

A Natural High – Millwall Football Club's two years in the First Division

A Natural High – Millwall Football Club's two years in the First Division

Copyright © 2019 Merv Payne

All rights reserved.

ISBN: **9781798006290**

1

The Second Summer of Love

August 1988. The second Summer of Love. The UK wasn't basking in a heatwave, but the euphoric mix of acid house, rave and psychedelia meant that most were completely oblivious to the weather anyway. A year that had started like any other had blossomed beneath a feel-good factor not experienced since the sixties. Love was in the air, house prices were up, unemployment was down…and Millwall were in the First Division.

The Lions' appearance at football's top table for the first time in their 103 year history is probably best compared with Punk than Rave culture. Exploding on the scene and sticking two fingers up to the establishment, shocking their way to the top of the pile before being chewed up and spat out and disappearing as quickly as they had arrived. But this was 1988 not 1976 and while their somewhat unwelcome arrival was no less dramatic and explosive than the opening chords to Anarchy In The UK, there was a little bit more class about these boys as they slotted into the high life to the assured but no less revolutionary backing track of Voodoo Ray. It wasn't just over Cold Blow Lane that the planets had aligned. Football had, it seemed, licked its wounds and dragged itself up from the doldrums of dwindling crowds in the early eighties and disasters of Heysel and Bradford in the middle of the decade. It still bore the scars of course. It had taken loss of life on catastrophic, unacceptable levels to shake the game into action to address its failings on the terraces. It couldn't be done without pain, it couldn't be done overnight and, tragically it wouldn't be done without one more tragic lesson learned.

But for now, in August 1988, all was right with the world. Millwall's rise from Second Division promotion hopefuls to Champions in just a few weeks at the end of the 87-88 season had shocked many in the football world – and not in a good way. The footballing hierarchy was still coming to terms with perennial trouble-makers Millwall gate-crashing their elite top-flight party when they were dealt another bloody nose.

Unfashionable Wimbledon, just ten years after being elected to the league's Fourth Division and in only their second top flight term, defied all the odds by beating Liverpool in the FA Cup final. Liverpool were the team of the eighties. Only briefly relinquishing their Division One crown to Aston Villa and Everton and chasing a second league and cup double in three seasons. The sheer cheek of Wimbledon to whisk the famous old trophy from under their noses rocked the sense of entitlement that the game's elite enjoyed. As the decade began to draw to a close, the climate was noticeably changing. As dear old Motty famously proclaimed after that cup final upset, the Crazy Gang had beaten the Culture Club. The tables were turning, the peasants were revolting.

A Natural High – Millwall Football Club's two years in the First Division

Watch out Barnes, Aldridge, Gascoigne, Waddle and Lineker. Hurlock, Cascarino and Sheringham had arrived.

Like a merry charabanc on a jolly boys outing rocking up at a gentleman's club, Millwall flung open the First Division door with a drunken "Tadaaaaa" – and promptly took it by storm.

But, in true Millwall tradition, even after actually winning the Second Division title, receiving the trophy and having their place in the game's top division for the first time etched in the annals, it almost ended before it began. Perhaps it was the apparent threat of the game's proletariat that sparked it. Maybe the Manchester Uniteds, Arsenals, Evertons and Liverpools could feel the increasing threat from the likes of Luton, Wimbledon, Norwich, Southampton – and now perhaps even Millwall? The revolution had reached their front door and they weren't that confident they'd be able to keep them out, so they plotted a cowardly counter to stop them in their tracks: The Super League. Proposals were hurriedly drawn up to outline a brave new footballing world. An elite league, one with no horrible trapdoor into the abyss of the Second, Third or Fourth Divisions, a private members club where only the very best need apply. No new money, just old war horses with their medals of battles won in 1970s cup finals. Money was of course at the root of this new evil – and, just as it is today, the strings of this puppet show were being held by television.

Football on television was very different back in the 1980s. In 1983 we were treated to our first ever live league match when Spurs played Nottingham Forest in a First Division match and it was a move that was met with a mostly negative reaction. It was boring. There was no appeal to the neutral, nothing to play for except three points, no trophy, no glory. ITV and BBC persevered with the format, but live football on television only seemed to be acceptable to armchair fans tuning in to FA Cup finals, European Cup finals and World Cups. Football and television remained awkward bedfellows. Fans were often the victim as industrial dispute and jostling for contractual position between the TV networks saw them go without their regular Saturday evening or Sunday afternoon fix.

The argument of the 'big' clubs was that they should be at the forefront of any TV deal and get the lion's share in proportion with their profile, pulling power and box office value. Their argument was that people were more likely to watch a match on television featuring Manchester United than Wimbledon – even the though the less illustrious of the two were arguably the better team on current performance. That didn't matter and it was felt that the only way this disproportionate distribution of the television purse could be resolved was for them to break free from the rest.

It was announced that a group of teams had planned to give notice to the Football League that they would be leaving its 92 team structure and forming their own league under the auspices of the Football Association and with the ITV television deal exclusively for them – leaving the Football League's remaining clubs out in the cold to thrash out their own deal – if indeed anyone wanted to offer them one.

The BBC had done a deal to rebrand their beloved Match of the Day to cover the FA Cup and in an era where only the Beeb and ITV regions had any broadcasting power, there seemed to be virtually no takers.

For many First Division clubs this was very worrying. For Millwall it was catastrophic, but oh so typical. After 103 years of waiting, after finally earning their right to play the top teams in the land, it looked as though it was to be cruelly snatched away from them.

A Natural High – Millwall Football Club's two years in the First Division

Peter Mead was a director at Millwall at the time. He had been part of the revolutionary new board formed alongside the sponsorship agreement with Lewisham Council. They helped to bankroll the unprecedented investment in the squad in the summer of 1987 which led to the magical promotion which now seemed to be slipping away from them. Mead remembers hearing of the plans straight from the horse's mouth – head of ITV Greg Dyke:

> *"The chairman Reg Burr was on holiday at the time and because I was in advertising Greg Dyke rang me and said this is going on. They didn't want us in the First Division anyway the toffee-nosed sods, and we had to do a lot of work. Reg did in his normal belligerent way, and made sure that we fought our corner. It was the ultimate class system, they were footballing snobs"*

The list of suspects was never officially revealed – but you could take it as read that it included Liverpool, Manchester United, Everton, Tottenham and Arsenal. All the teams that Millwall's fans – and players – had dreamed of facing as the champagne corks popped along the Old Kent Road just a few weeks before. Each of these teams could point to their long-standing top flight tenure and trophy haul as justification for their place at the new top table. But what about the other five?

Rumours spread and stories leaked about who would make up the final treacherous team line-up. Arguments broke out and the cracks began to form. In a bun fight that resembled the scramble for Willy Wonka's precious golden tickets, the new Super League seemingly had more applicants arguing their eligibility for the new competition – freshly-relegated Chelsea allegedly among them – than the 20 team First Division. Which clearly completely defeated the object.

It was this greed-motivated clamour that was to be its fitting downfall. Time was against the conspirators. They wanted to start immediately, mainly because ITV with its millions ready to splash on a new live league TV deal was impatiently drumming its fingers waiting for a resolution. As the clock ticked down and the deadline for fixtures to be published for the new season approached, a compromise was reached. The rebels relented and agreed to remain in the Football League's 20 team top division, with a proviso that the TV chips were stacked very much in their favour.

The sigh of relief could be heard right across the country – and loudest in SE16. I've no doubt many football fans who faced missing out on seeing their team lock horns with the Liverpools, Manchester Uniteds, Tottenhams and Arsenals of the world were ready to take to the streets and smash the harmony of this second summer of love in demonstrations not seen since the storming of the Palace of Versailles. National disaster averted folks, it's all going to be OK, as you were.

Back in 1988 the vast majority of the country had access to just four television channels and with no 24 hour rolling Sky Sports News, no Internet and no social media, the impact of these machinations on the various clubs and fans up and down the country wasn't felt on a wide scale. It was talked about in the pubs and workplaces, but only of course with a local perspective and how it might affect Millwall. The Millwall fans had little or no idea of what the club was thinking of it all and how it might have been affecting their preparations for what they all hoped would be that historic first season in Division One. Writing in his programme notes for the first match of the new season, Chairman Reg Burr perfectly captured the typical mood of Millwall fans at the time and gave only the merest of hints of what had been going on behind the scenes:

A Natural High – Millwall Football Club's two years in the First Division

"At the end of last season, once promotion was finally assured, one of our supporters told me: 'I don't believe we will ever play in Division One. I expect World War Three will break out and stop us'. As Bill Shankly might have said it was more serious than that for, at one stage, it looked like war had broken out over the structure of the League itself. Your directors have worked long and hard to encourage moderation and good sense and I am pleased that finally matters were resolved in such a way as to maintain the integrity of the League. Thus I am able to welcome you back to The Den for the start of our first ever season in Division One."

It's hard to adequately describe to any football fan that has only lived through the Premier League era what that excitement was like for a team embarking on a top flight season for the first time – or even making a return after a prolonged absence. Promotion to the Premier League these days is obviously considered very big news but you can't escape the fact that the romance of it all – the prospect of playing host to and visiting some of the biggest names in world football – is drowned out by the booming voice of the bean counters. "It's the most valuable game in world football" or variations on that theme accompany the build-up to the Championship play-off final.

Visiting Anfield and Old Trafford is barely mentioned. After all, even if you can afford to spend over £100 million after winning that final, trips to the big boys are merely a process of having your Premier League passport stamped at another destination of heavy defeat on the 19-date tour of struggling to survive. Back in 1988 it was very different. So with the spectre of the Super League banished, the long-awaited fixtures announcement was probably another, albeit much less, disappointment to Millwall fans. A season opening trip to Aston Villa – who had been promoted with The Lions of course – then a Den debut against Derby (who had been promoted as Second Division champions the season before Millwall) was underwhelming to say the least. That was followed by the short trip to Selhurst Park where Charlton were ground-sharing with Crystal Palace to face a Charlton side that had been promoted two seasons before. It was almost as if the Football League had decided Millwall had to first face-off against some of their fellow newer members of the elite club before enjoying the privilege of facing the establishment.

That particular treat would come soon enough though as, back at The Den after the Charlton match, Millwall would face an Everton side that had two First Division Championship titles and a Cup Winners Cup victory to their name from the previous four seasons.

There were two ways of looking at these opening matches. On the one hand, Millwall fans could be happy that their side would be eased into life in the top flight. They were very much split into two camps before the fixtures had been released anyway. Some felt that, without huge investment in new players (something the club and especially manager John Docherty had made clear wasn't going to happen) they would be well out of their depth and find themselves relegated early.

Others felt, as Docherty publicly stated, that the team that had won the club its historic promotion fully deserved to have a crack at the top flight, but that may well have been more because his hands were tied financially, as captain and, what appears to be unofficial shop-steward Les Briley recalls:

'We spoke to John [Docherty] and all asked for new contracts, he said 'no, you haven't proved yourselves yet'. But John was really good and

he relied on me an awful lot. I was the go-between, being captain, and I wasn't greatly liked by everyone because I was forever in John's office. Not because I wanted to be but that was the relationship he wanted. I was the most experienced player at the club and he wanted me to relay information from the team. Not grassing people up, but checking things were OK. It was my job to look after everybody and hopefully I did that".

It was an old-fashioned way of doing things, but it worked and was pretty much the norm for 1980s football. It would be laughed at in the current era – as would the notion of the players approaching the manager to discuss contractual demands and being told 'you haven't proved yourself yet'. Imagine that conversation between Pogba, Sanchez and Mourinho?

As Docherty alluded to, investment in the team was minimal and unspectacular. Two major signings were made, one for squad strengthening and one out of necessity. Neil Ruddock arrived from Spurs for a reported £300,000 – which would have been a club record at the time had that fee been confirmed. But Ruddock was certainly no new boy. He had come through the youth ranks at The Den a few seasons before and been spotted by Spurs' scouts when Millwall were in desperate need of financial assistance. A towering athletic centre back, Ruddock struggled to claim a place in the north London side's title-chasing teams and was happy to return to his old stomping ground to fight Alan McLeary and Steve Wood for a place at the centre of the Lions defence. Joining him was left back Ian Dawes from QPR. His signing was as a straight replacement for the desperately unlucky Nicky Coleman who had seriously injured his knee in a behind-closed-doors pre-season friendly – ironically against QPR.

It was tragic for Coleman, a home-grown prospect and lifelong Lions fan who had established his place in the team and overcome a certain amount of negativity from the terraces to win over the Millwall crowd and put in some solid performances in that vital promotion run-in.

Dawes was well-known as a solid defender and his signing along with that of Ruddock was welcomed by Millwall fans, even if they had perhaps hoped for a little more excitement in the summer after the spending spree twelve months before.

Today, the cost of assembling a team good enough to stay in the Premier League runs into the hundreds of millions. In 2018 Fulham were promoted via the Championship play-offs and spent £105m. They were relegated with five games to spare. Back in 1988, the Millwall players that spent most of season in the top five and eventually finished tenth was put together as follows:

Player	Fee
Brian Horne	£0 – youth team
Danis Salman	£20,000 – Brentford
Ian Dawes -	£155,000 – QPR
Keith Stevens	£0 – youth team
Alan McLeary	£0 – youth team
Steve Wood	£90,000 – Reading
David Thompson	£0 – youth team
Sean Sparham	£0 – youth team
Darren Morgan	£0 – youth team
Terry Hurlock	£95,000 – Reading
Les Briley	£0 – Aldershot
Wes Reid	£0 – Arsenal
Jimmy Carter	£15,000 – QPR
Paul Stephenson	£275,000 – Newcastle
George Lawrence	£150,000 – Southampton

Teddy Sheringham	£0 – youth team
Tony Cascarino	£250,000 – Gillingham
Kevin O'Callaghan	£85,000 – Portsmouth
Steve Anthrobus	£0 – youth team
Dean Horrix	£75,000 – Reading

Total: £1,235,000

Many of these transfer fees were 'undisclosed' at the time, but the reported figures won't be a million miles away from the true sum. These are the players that started at least one league match for Millwall that season which is why Neil Ruddock (who cost up to a reported £300,000 at the time) has been left out. It should also be noted that Paul Stephenson, whose transfer fee makes up virtually a quarter of that team's value, started just 11 league matches.

Obviously a lot has happened to the game in 30 years. The £2million Everton paid for West Ham in a British record transfer in the summer of 88 is similarly laughable but wasn't trumped too greatly in the ensuing four seasons before The Premier League.

Up until 1992-93 it was possible for any team to build a squad capable of challenging for a place in the top division without jeopardising its very existence or placing its wellbeing in the hands of a foreign megalomaniacal billionaire. Whilst fans can still dream today that their team will reach the promised land of the Premier League, it is very much a case of staring into the abyss for most. The real dream, the true romance of this aspect of the game, died forever in 1992.

If Millwall fans were hoping for an encouraging preview of their team's First Division credentials, they were in for a bit of a disappointment with two winless Den friendlies against Brighton and Crystal Palace. Whilst nothing should ever be read into such practice games, the way in which Palace outmaneuvered Millwall with slick pacey football in their 2-1 win must have given Lions fans some cause for concern as they were to face far more power and pace when hostilities began for real.

The Den itself was undergoing some changes in for the new season. A family stand was being constructed on the corner terrace that adjoined the halfway line and Cold Blow Lane ends. It signalled the end of an era for many fans who had enjoyed that rather unique vantage point that many stadiums with four separate stands do not provide.

The open terrace with its walled walkway and clock was replaced with shiny blue seats and a rather awkward-looking angled roof to provide a more comfortable place for families to watch the match. Pre-match entertainment was even provided in the shape of the Bargain Bucket Theatre Company who put on madcap shows at the foot of the terrace before each match. It was a nice touch by the club and not for the first time, a gesture that was made a considerable time before other more illustrious teams followed suit.

Finally, a close-season that had felt like an eternity was coming to an end. Final preparations were made and the English Football League prepared to raise its curtain for the 101st time – this time with Millwall at its top table. The players, management and fans were ready for the First Division. The big question was, was the First Division ready for Millwall?

2

A Good Tradition

"For me, going to Aston Villa on the first day of the season wasn't like being in the First Division because we'd already played them twice the previous season and taken six points off them..." Reg Burr, Millwall FC Chairman 1988.

It's fair to say that Villa Park is considered by fans of most clubs to be a 'proper football stadium'. All-seater legislation has meant that the sight of the huge Holte End terrace packed to its capacity and swelling like an eternal ocean of fans is consigned to the archives, but it never ceases to impress. Today traditional architecture and modern structure sit side by side but in 1988 it was every inch a stately place to watch your football. So Aston Villa away would have been a fitting curtain-opener for Millwall's top flight bow, but for one small detail that chairman Reg Burr was eager to outline when he revealed his own personal emotions about that historic day.

It's probably just as well that quote was taken later in the season as part of the club's Christmas video because it would have surely served as extra motivation for a Villa side who were no doubt just as indignant about having their First Division return passport stamped by these south London upstarts. Just seven years previously Villa fans were celebrating being champions of England – and 12 months later conquering Europe as European Cup winners. So the palpable contrast in enthusiasm between the two sets of supporters as kick-off drew near was understandable. The weather – a very untypical opening day mixture of grey skies and drizzle - also seemed to drain the enthusiasm from half empty home enclosures, and put the focus on the 7,000 plus travelling Millwall hordes.

That mood must have filtered down to the pitch and players as Millwall got off to a flying start with winger George Lawrence having the first chance of the game as The Lions attacked the famous Holte End, his left foot shot from 25 yards skewing inches wide of Nigel Spink's left hand post after just 75 seconds. Villa's robust Scottish striker Alan McInally posed the hosts' first threat when he spun Millwall's rookie centre back David Thompson, but Lions 'keeper Brian Horne was relieved to comfortably gather the shot. Thompson was a home-grown prospect of Geordie descent and his inclusion in this historic fixture was the only major surprise to Millwall fans. He replaced Steve Wood who John Docherty named as one of his two substitutes, Darren Morgan being the other. It was something of a surprise to Millwall supporters – especially given the rock solid central defensive partnership that Wood had built with Alan McLeary and the summer arrival of Neil Ruddock but despite that early scare, Thompson acquitted himself well as Millwall settled in to the game.

Another surprising omission was that of Jimmy Carter. The pacey winger had a delayed start to the promotion-winning season after deciding to take up a bizarre build-up diet which involved eating bunches of bananas. Manager John Docherty discovered Carter's holdall full of the things one day and realised this was the reason behind his mysterious loss of pace which was the hallmark of his game. Carter recalls both the banana episode, an ignominious substitute appearance and his spectator role in that famous first game very well:

> *"We were playing Leyton Orient in the cup at home and by then I was eating fifteen bananas a day to try and beef myself up a bit. I'm sub for the Leyton Orient game and George Lawrence is playing on the right wing. I think he pulled his hamstring so The Doc says: 'warm up, you're going on'. Fifteen minutes after coming on I look over to the dugout and see my number being held up. It's the ultimate humiliation in front of my home crowd to sub the sub!"*

This was back in the days when regular league matches still only permitted the use of one substitute, but as an experiment in time to be rolled out for all matches the following season, League Cup matches such as this one against Orient were trialing the use of two. This meant that Carter was almost certainly the first substitute to be subbed in the English League at least. On returning to the bench, Carter recalls The Doc's frosty response to his brief and unimpressive cameo appearance:

> *"So fifteen minutes after being sent on I'm back on the bench sat next to The Doc and he doesn't say anything, doesn't look at me, just puffs away on his cigar. Finally he says, without looking at me, through a big cloud of cigar smoke, in this really thick*

Glaswegian accent: 'you've got to get off those bananas son'. It took me a good two months to get the two stone I had put on with the banana diet off and get back to full fitness and my first game back was at Villa Park where we won 2-1"

Carter didn't look back after that and his lightning speed and trickery down the right flank helped to fire Millwall into the First Division and made him a firm favourite with the fans.

Back at Villa Park in the top flight however, Carter found himself out of the fourteen-man squad altogether and his memories of that famous day were more of being a spectator than a player, but that would soon change.

Millwall's stay in the First Division would quickly draw comparisons with Wimbledon for their direct style, but it was a largely unfair and lazily applied accusation. Docherty did indeed deploy a certain directness where the plan was clearly to play their football in their opponent's half as quickly as possible, but there was a variation on this 'in your face' theme that was very pleasing to the eye.

It was one such move where a searching ball forward had been cleared by a Villa defender that almost led to the first goal. The ball was intercepted by Ian Dawes close to the half way line on Millwall's left and played in to Sheringham who had made a run for Dawes with his back to goal. Instinctively he pinged the ball wide to the left for the waiting Lawrence who attempted to bustle and shrug his way through two defenders in the same way that John Barnes had made his hallmark.

Whilst this foray broke down, Villa were clearly rattled, and it was they who seemed to be resorting to long balls out of defence. The ball was once again sprayed neatly around the width of the pitch between McLeary, Salman and then Hurlock who played Briley in beautifully behind the defence to shoot goalwards. Spink was able to save on that occasion but the attack raised the decibel level of the visiting Millwall fans who felt that history was about to be written. They were right.

In the 20th minute Millwall were awarded a corner. O'Callaghan's out-swinging cross found Cascarino on the penalty spot who stooped to head home beyond a bemused Villa defence and send the visiting fans wild. Villa looked to have been caught cold, it was as if they weren't ready for them. Villa Park was echoing to the sounds of "EIO", the now well-established Millwall post-goal celebration chant and as a shell-shocked home side centred up to restart the match, celebrating arms pumping up and down to the mantra could even be seen among the home fans close to the dugouts.

Docherty's tactics were finely honed for such a smash and grab job on the road. Millwall had a long history of being hard to beat at The Den but frustratingly inefficient on their travels. It had taken several fruitless trips to find their first three points during the previous season's Second Division title winning campaign but once that first victory came away to Sheffield United, The Lions at times looked more ruthless on the road than at home in SE16. Their haul of ten away victories equaled a club record and was a direct result of how they were able to turn defence into attack so quickly and hit teams with quick-fire attacks – and goals. It was their variation on the tempo and how direct or intricate they chose to be that seemed to catch teams out. No-one could accuse them of being one-dimensional. Like a pace bowler in a test match varying his run up and pitch, cajoling the batsmen into a certain shot before hitting him with a surprise delivery, Millwall were about to hit Villa with a very quick plan B.

Two minutes later Hurlock, dominating the centre circle as he did so well, laid the ball off to Thompson who aimed his long ball in the direction of the same Villa corner that had produced the first goal. Sheringham gave chase but Villa veteran Allan Evans had several yards head start on him and appeared to be marshalling the ball to safety.

But once again they appeared to be dozing as Sheringham robbed Evans as he attempted to turn with the ball and send it back upfield and Ian Dawes appeared from nowhere just inside the 18 yard box on an intelligent overlapping run. Dawes took one touch before cutting it back to Cascarino who was again occupying an unmarked position twelve yards from goal and he jabbed home the second with the inside of his left boot.

With Millwall fans already in full voice and still celebrating that historic opening goal with a chant of "Champions", the noise levels from the away sections at the Witton Lane end of the stadium had now reached new levels and there was probably just as much surprise in their celebrations as joy. Villa fans meanwhile could only stand dumfounded at how history was not so much being made but repeating itself after Millwall had performed a similar quick-fire assault in the corresponding fixture the previous November.

Chants of "Easy, easy" were of course to be expected and mostly shouted with tongues firmly in cheeks. The realty was that Villa had almost 70 minutes to claw their way back into the game and once they had regained their composure there was a very distinct route for them to take.

Aston Villa winger Paul Birch was no stranger to Millwall fans. Two years previously he had visited The Den with his Villa team still in the top flight for an FA Cup replay. The Millwall faithful subjected the speedy wide man to a chorus of wolf whistles and cat calls every time he touched the ball – a gesture aimed at his bright blonde curly hair. He was eventually switched to the opposite wing but when this failed to quell the attention he was getting which was clearly distracting him, he was subbed and Villa went on to lose the tie. Appearing far more comfortable and no doubt stronger for the experience back at Villa Park, Birch's swift, tricky runs were starting to trouble Millwall and it was one such foray in the 30th minute that saw his cross catch the Lions' new look central defensive pairing flat footed. As midfielder Andy Gray bore down on goal, Lions 'keeper Horne made a desperate attempt to gather the ball as it entered the area before Gray could clip it goalwards, but only succeeded in felling the ex-Palace man. Penalty to Villa, emphatically converted by Andy's namesake Stuart, and game very much back on.

Millwall were an agonising 90 seconds away from taking that same slender lead that they had beaten Villa with both home and away the previous season into half time when disaster struck. A long ball forward into the Millwall half eluded Thompson who was caught too far forward. McInally once again got the better of the young centre half and set off on a three way race with Dawes and Horne – who had galloped several yards out of his area. Had Horne remained in his area, Dawes may have won that race and been able to clear the danger or return the ball to his goalkeeper.

As it was, with Horne in a centre back position and running into the quickly retreating Dawes, the pair managed to become entangled, allowing the ball to ping clear for McInally to race onto and slide gleefully into an empty net. After such a ruthless and accomplished start it was desperately disappointing for both the Millwall team and fans to see half time arrive with the scores level.

Hopes the tempo could once again be raised after the break were quickly quelled as the second period almost seemed to pass without either team making many efforts to regain the lead. It was almost as if an agreement had been reached to call it quits at 2-2. Despite the first half capitulation, it was hard for Millwall fans to be despondent as they headed back towards London that evening. Dissecting both goals conceded, they could have pointed to Docherty's decision to give young Thompson his debut and the forced inclusion of Dawes. Both did well and looked solid for most of the game but had they been able to field the same back four that had appeared for most of the previous season it may have been enough to cling on. Thompson's baptism of fire facing the pace and power of McInally that would stand him in good stead for the rest of his career and Dawes – with the exception of that brief misunderstanding with Horne for the second goal – looked assured both defensively and going forward.

Such was the mood among players and fans, it was impossible to be despondent and the journey home was as upbeat and joyous as the trip to the midlands for both, as Millwall fan Ronnie remembers:

"We went on a coach from the Horseshoe Pub on Tower Bridge Road. On the way home in traffic it pulled up alongside the Millwall team coach! They were laughing at us E'd up and dancing away!"

Millwall had plenty to dance about. Sure it had only been one match, and just a single point against a team they had beaten twice at the lower level the previous season, but this was a new Millwall, a glass-half-full club now. Genuine positives were taken from everything. This was their time, they had waited over 100 years for this. Fans had born and died standing on the terraces at The Den having never seen their team in the First Division. Now wasn't a time for dissecting matches and nit-picking. Looking back at those opening weeks, Les Briley can clearly remember the magic extending beyond the terraces and into the dressing room:

"The atmosphere around the club after the Villa game was electric, absolutely electric, and as we went through those first few games, we even came off the pitch saying: 'was that us?'"

Wes Reid was a young prospect who had joined the club from Arsenal during the summer of 1987 when the club made its unprecedented investment that secured promotion. Despite his Highbury footballing origins, Wes was a true Millwall man and has vivid memories of the atmosphere at that time and gives an insight into how the club got under the skin of not just the fans:

"I'm a Peckham lad born and bred, I still live just off The Old Kent Road and went to Peckham Manor School. Getting promoted gave not only the club but the whole area, that part of south London a lift. You would walk down The Old Kent Road and you could just feel it, I can't describe it, everyone was happy, success breeds success you know? I spent ten years travelling from Peckham to Arsenal and I knew some of the Millwall players like Darren Morgan, Mickey Marks, Sean Sparham and Trevor Booker but I obviously never knew Millwall from the inside as a club. When Bob Pearson signed me for Millwall, the day I signed, it sounds funny but it just felt like I'd come home. I'm a south Londoner and going to Highbury in north London is totally different but I didn't realise how much until I signed for Millwall."

Reid's Millwall career was unfortunately restricted by a bad, long-standing knee injury which hadn't been detected which meant his appearances were few and far between but his hard-work, loyalty and the affection with which he still talks about his time as a player at the club speaks volumes and he's very philosophical about why, even when fit, his first team opportunities were limited:

> *"You had the likes of Les [Briley] and Terry [Hurlock] and they were great, great players and I think about a quote from Zola who was Maradona's understudy: You can't knock on the manager's door and say 'can you get rid of Maradona so I can play', you just have to learn and keep working and my proudest moment in football was making my full debut at Anfield in 1990."*

It had to be said that the fixture list had been kind to Millwall. Similar defensive naivety against one of the division's big hitters such as Liverpool, Arsenal or Everton – for whom English record signing £2 million Tony Cottee had scored an opening day hat-trick – could have seen a demoralising thrashing. As it was, The Lions had emerged unscathed from their historic first top flight match, against a team they had beaten to the Second Division summit. Now it was time to face the team who had passed their Division Two crown to them: Derby County, for the long-awaited first ever First Division game at The Den.

3

A Groovy Kind of Love

This was it, the culmination of a dream shattered so cruelly 16 years before. For a few beautiful seconds in May 1972, Millwall fans basked in the glory of finally winning promotion to Division One and allowed themselves the luxury of looking forward to seeing The Den welcoming the game's elite, only for those dreams to be shattered. Now it was finally here...

If anything could take the shine off Millwall's big day it was the rather sorry state of The Den. With work not yet complete on the new family stand, just a thin strip of terracing was available in front of large yellow-painted hoardings which protected the scaffolding. It meant that two of the ground's more famous terraces – the Halfway Line and Cold Blow Lane end behind the goal – were even more tightly packed providing a great atmosphere for Lions fans in them, but overall, The Den's wall of noise generated by its bowl of terrace wrapped around almost three sides of the pitch was fragmented. The Ilderton Road terrace behind the other goal was still designated members only – a sanction forced on the club following various crowd disorder incidents, and one that was vehemently opposed by fans who didn't want to go to the inconvenience of filling out forms and providing photographs to obtain a membership card in order to buy tickets in advance. These fans sacrificed their favourite end and joined the Cold Blow or Halfway, leaving a sparsely populated terrace on what should have been a packed stadium. The real sadness must have been felt by Millwall's older generation of long-suffering fans. They had endured lean post-war years and the bleak fifties in the Football League's newly-formed basement division.

Throughout those seasons of struggle against the likes of Workington, Rochdale and Hartlepools, The Den was an impressive arena which regularly attracted attendances of 20,000 or more for a regular Fourth Division match and the place absolutely rocked to its rafters with over 45,000 in attendance for a 1957 FA Cup visit of the then mighty Newcastle. Had you been able to deliver top league football to that Millwall era so many more fans would have been able to enjoy it and, who knows, it may have provided a foundation for an established top flight Millwall.

13,040 were in attendance on September 3rd 1988 at a Den bathed in late summer sunshine - an idyllic afternoon for football. Derby were no mugs and arrived with an established team of experienced First Division players including England internationals Peter Shilton and Mark Wright and striker Paul Goddard. The latter would feature again in a very different chapter of Millwall's First Division story. A tight encounter was decided by Teddy Sheringham's first half tap-in after a goalmouth scramble. Millwall comfortably saw the second half out to etch an indelible entry into their history archives: the first ever First

Division match at The Den was won 1-0 and, for all that it mattered so early in the season, the league table showed Millwall in sixth place of English football's top division.

As has always been the case at Millwall, results and league position were often overlooked by the media who, despite a period of relative calm throughout the game where crowd trouble was concerned, were still keen to put the boot in. Manager John Docherty's programme notes for that historic first game at The Den carried a defiant message in response to an article which had appeared in the London Evening Standard during the week before the match. Boxed off from his usual piece welcoming fans and opposition and sharing his hopes and aspirations for the new season, and headlined: "Sacrificial Lamb or Scapegoat?" The Doc pulled no punches:

> *"The season was barely four days old when a "distinguished" ex-Superintendent of the Metropolitan Police, Fred Lush, writing in the Evening Standard made the scurrilous statement that we, the players, management and supporters of Millwall encourage violence and obscenities. We all know that this is not true. Some of you, like me, must have wondered how a man whose apparent characteristics could reach such high office in the Metropolitan Police – thankfully he has now retired. These remarks are a warning to us that there are people in high places who, seeking an easy solution to a problem in society, have selected us (amongst other candidates) as a suitable peg to hang the blame. We must not allow this to happen. Over the next three to four years we are determined with your help to build Millwall to a position where our talents on the field and our facilities will equal, if not surpass the very best. We must all remember that*

each and every one of us represents Millwall and it's upon this that the world will judge us. We must all work together to ensure that in no way do we give anyone the opportunity to point a finger against us however unjustly. Keep up your magnificent support which we all greatly value but let's make sure no-one presses the self-destruct button. Let's have no own goals at The Den or elsewhere no matter what pressure may exist."

It was a quite remarkable outburst but, when you examine it more closely, was a very cleverly worded variation on an old theme. Episodes of crowd trouble that followed Millwall – especially since that infamous night at Luton three years before – had driven an understandable wedge between club and fans. Discord between a football club and its supporters wasn't unique to Millwall, but you could go back half a century to the pre-war years when Charlie Hewitt managed the team and had various fall-outs with the newly-formed supporters club. Millwall belonged to the fans, it was *their* club. It is a belief that supporters of the majority of clubs across the country held but one that fell away through the years as money played a greater part in the game. Football clubs became businesses and supporters customers who were held at the same arm's length as patrons of a high street store. Millwall is one of the few clubs where that traditional club/fan ethos still exists today.

No manager or player comes to the club and enjoys any level of success unless they recognise the fact that they have to adapt to the Millwall fans' expectations – and not the other way around. After a meeting with the Millwall Supporters Club, Hewitt famously tried to put them in their place by indignantly stating that "The tail should not be allowed to wag the dog", but this wasn't a dog's tail he was dealing with, it was a lion's – and once he had pulled that the writing was on the wall for what could have been the most successful manager in the club's history.

The club regularly used its match day programme to berate its fans following incidents of unrest. In the sixties it levelled its ire at the younger element of the support, assuming that it was cheeky young upstarts responsible for crowd disorder and urging older fans to take them to task. The reality was obviously very different but this appeared to be a somewhat weak attempt at preserving a certain amount of harmony between supporters and club. In the seventies, Gordon Jago, a coach years ahead of his time, had ambitious plans for Millwall. He brought the first black players to appear in a Millwall shirt to the club in Trevor Lee and Phil Walker and they were an instant hit with the fans.

But at a time when football hooliganism was starting to dominate the headlines, Jago's trusting well-meaning ambitions were shamelessly abused by the media. A Panorama programme focused entirely on Millwall's hooligan element, giving nationwide publicity and notoriety to some of its fans as perceived career thugs and sent the club spiraling.

Jago was sold a very different programme and the club were powerless to stop it being aired. One section of it showed Jago chatting to fans about his plans for the club and what he expected of them and whilst their respect was evident for their club's manager, it was quite awkward at times to see the disparity between Jago's dream of a family-friendly Millwall and the supporters who were keen not to overdo the good PR by losing their unique reputation which, while they agreed did sometimes overstep the boundaries, was an essential part of supporting Millwall as long as it was kept within the law.

Panorama spelt the end for Jago and he realised his vision in the US.

Crowd trouble at The Den before an FA Cup quarter final with Ipswich in 1978 appeared to prove the media witch-hunt correct and a heavily-sanctioned Millwall saw attendances drop, relegation and an exodus of good players. It was understandable that the club would be bitter towards those responsible for making life difficult for them in what were already testing times.

The relationship between club and fans reached its nadir in the mid-80s when, still reeling from post-Luton sanctions, further crowd trouble when Leeds visited The Den for the first time in decades saw the club take unprecedented steps. Once again it used the match programme, but this time it named and shamed individuals under the headline: "You were warned, now you're banned"

Slowly the club rebuilt its bridges with the supporters and a community scheme run brilliantly by Gary Stempel and Ron Bell helped to heal some old wounds. Promotion to the First Division, a new era of youth culture and the fact that most of those involved in serious incidents were now either banned or locked up saw a previously unseen calm.

Docherty's message to fans, whilst it would have read like a refreshingly defiant condemnation of yet more mud-slinging and promoted a new solidarity of Millwall Football Club and its fans, was much the same as previous ones: "Please don't mess this up for us lads", but the mood around the club was very different to any time in the club's recent history. For once, club and fans seemed to be in total harmony and the results of this were there for all to see.

The rays of that second summer of love were stretching well into September and truly shone down on Millwall when they took over Selhurst Park the following week. Charlton, who were ground-sharing with Crystal Palace, had defied the odds yet again to remain in the top flight for a second season. Their fans must have felt a similar regret to their Millwall counterparts that they were unable to enjoy First Division football when their home ground was at its best. The Valley was capable of holding around 70,000 fans at its peak and had hosted concerts by The Who. Now they were left to borrow the stadium of their bitter rivals Palace. At least Millwall could console themselves with the fact that they were still playing at their natural home.

The way that Millwall brushed Charlton aside belied their status as top flight rookies. A first minute opener by Teddy Sheringham who looped his header from a Terry Hurlock free kick over stranded Charlton 'keeper Bob Bolder gave The Lions the perfect start and they dominated the match at a swaggering pace. The game was over with the second goal on the stroke of half time – a Cascarino strike from the edge of the box after Sheringham had seen two attempts blocked. The Second Division title-winning strike force were picking up where they left off and appeared to be unstoppable.

The win was crowned with a spectacular Les Briley thunderbolt from fully thirty five yards mid-way through the second half. As Millwall fans celebrated the goal from what appeared to be all four sides of the stadium, the only surprise was that the win wasn't achieved by a greater margin than 3-0. If Millwall needed a confidence-booster before the visit of Everton to The Den a week later they certainly had it with seven points from nine in their three opening games and a lofty fourth place in the table. Had you told Millwall supporters just over a year before when Everton had been crowned Champions of England and Millwall had just managed to cling on to their Second Division place that the two would be meeting in a top four First Division clash in less than 18 months' time they would have quite rightly advised you to seek expert help.

But that was the situation on a drizzly Saturday at The Den on September 17th. Sitting on top of the table was the equally unbelievable Southampton and Norwich with maximum points from their first three games. Norwich away would be Millwall's next match, a game which, quite staggeringly, could have been an early battle for the top of the table. There was a very different atmosphere around The Den when Everton's golden carriage rolled into Cold Blow Lane. This was footballing royalty now, no makeweight promotion companions, no recently elevated second season wonders or perennial strugglers. This was where the hard yards would start, the ultimate scrutiny. Would Millwall be up for it? Would coming up against a true top flight warrior finally find The Lions out for the second rate pretenders some feared they were? Did Millwall fans care? Nope.

The carnival backdrop had long since been torn down. This was English football at the sharp end: drizzly rain, a sodden pitch which was a minefield for errors and an opposition that would prove the ultimate test of Millwall's top flight credentials. Everton's team was packed with medal-laden internationals. Southall, Ratcliffe, Watson, Steven, Van den Hauwe, Bracewell, Nevin, Sheedy, Sharpe and of course, record £2 million signing Tony Cottee.

From the first whistle Millwall tore into their opponents. The strategy was clear: an aggressive high tempo start with the tried and trusted tactical blend of direct football and using width to put Everton under pressure from Kevin O'Callaghan and George Lawrence crosses to the menacing Sheringham and Cascarino. It's a risky tactic and one that often backfires – especially against a team as experienced as Everton who had won league titles and cups both home and in Europe in the face of far more complex game plans. For this to work Millwall would need to turn it in to first half goals.

Everton's slick football looked to have caught Millwall on the hop midway through the first half as they took possession from one of The Lions many forays down the wings. A few neat passes later and Cottee was released with a piercing through ball but thanks to the well-drilled defensive partnership of Alan McLeary and Steve Wood the two-million-pound man was flagged offside.

Looking to grasp the initiative straight back – and slightly rocked at how easy Everton could turn defence into attack, the free kick was launched from just inside their own half towards George Lawrence on the right hand corner of Everton's penalty box. Lawrence missed out on the aerial duel to win the ball but Sheringham was typically alert to it and spotted Lawrence peeling off to the right, in anticipation of the lay-off from Sheringham. Lawrence's instant cross caught the Everton defence flat-footed and seemed to hang in the air for an age before coming down to be met by the head of Cascarino who had been waiting in his customary place on the penalty spot. His header looped up and over the despairing Southall and nestled gloriously in the back of the net to send most of the 17,000 Den crowd wild.

Millwall were rampant. Everton visibly rocked back on their heels. Moments after that first goal a brilliant first time ball from Lawrence was perfectly weighted to put Cascarino through. Showing a skill and speed that completely belied his often awkward looking, rangy frame, he nodded the ball down and sped into the Everton area, turning the full back he hit his shot goalwards but as the crowd screamed "GOAL!" Southall pulled off a miraculous reaction save with his left hand.

Everton had absolutely no clue how to deal with Lawrence who appeared to be playing with a Jedi-like instinct. Latching on to another second ball from an midfield aerial battle he turned and fed

Sheringham who had switched to Lawrence's right wing berth in one silky smooth movement which again left Everton's defenders off the pace. Lawrence continued his run and Sheringham spotted him bursting into the area. Instantly clipping the ball over the advancing Southall the crowd again erupted into expectant celebrations as they waited for the net to bulge only to see the ball bounce back into play off the far post. "Yes" became "Ah" a then "YES!" again as Cascarino was first to the loose ball to gleefully prod home his – and Millwall's second goal in ten minutes.

The Den was literally rocking now. It was the sort of ground where even with small crowds the volume could easily be cranked up and amplified way beyond the actual attendance. That may sound obvious and apply to all football grounds, but there was something about the combination of that unique, compact little ground with its sweeping bowl of terrace hugging the pitch and the menacing, almost constant backdrop of the "Miiiiiiiiill…" 'monks chant' that the fans used to keep the team revved up when they were chasing a crucial goal or looking to complete a late comeback that made the roar of a goal somehow even louder. That was with 3,000 in there more often than not earlier in the eighties. Now, with more than 17,000 enjoying watching The Lions take apart the recently dethroned twice league champions and baying for more goals, it literally had the place reverberating with the noise as if Concorde was swopping across The Den in a low-level flyby.

Understandably, the breakneck speed at which Millwall had started the game meant that the pace could not be prolonged. The gamble had paid off handsomely, but as Millwall learned at Villa Park on the opening day, 2-0 is often a very precarious lead and can quickly be erased. Determined to take their advantage to the half time break, Millwall eased off the gas and spent the remaining half of the first half ably containing Everton who themselves it seemed had decided to get to half time in order to regroup. Their manager Colin Harvey would almost certainly send them out for the second half fired up and determined to ruin the party.

Everton did indeed emerge more determined and the old Villa Park spectre once again loomed when pressure in the 54th minute forced Alan McLeary to score an own goal. But these Millwall supporters were well-versed in watching nerve-jangling 2-1 leads held on to. That had been a hallmark of their successful Second Division championship-winning run-in and it was encouraging to see that, even at a higher level, this team of Millwall warriors were just as solid in the crucial closing stages. The only thing we hadn't seen so far that was so regularly in evidence during that famous late season surge was a Kevin O'Callaghan penalty and it would prove interesting to see just how much harder it was for Millwall to win a spot kick in the top flight than the Second Division.

In previous years, starting a season in any division with three wins and a draw would usually see you sitting at the top of the table. Not that it really mattered of course. Millwall fans had certainly had their fair share of seasons starting at the very top of the Third or Second Divisions and ending, if they were lucky, in mid-table obscurity. But this was different. Had you been able to speak to every Millwall supporter in August 1988 I'm sure the consensus would have been that they didn't really expect (or care for) survival in the top flight, they were just there to enjoy the ride. Even with the remarkable start they made, many were, I'm sure, waiting for the magic to wear off and for the wind to quickly evaporate from their sails before the inevitable descent back to whence they came. So if you'd offered any Millwall fan the chance to see their beloved Lions at the top of English football for just one week however early in the season – even if it meant eventual relegation – I'm pretty sure they would have taken it. It was a little frustrating then that after such a good start they had to be satisfied with third place behind Southampton and Norwich.

Southampton had started the season in much the same vein as Millwall but Norwich had quite rightly earned their early pole position with a perfect record of four wins from four. Reigning league champions Liverpool – who had missed out on a second league and cup double in three seasons only by that shock FA Cup final defeat to Wimbledon, were in fourth place. Behind Millwall! So the fifth week of the 1988-89 First Division season provided the perfect set of fixtures with second placed Southampton hosting fourth-placed Liverpool and third-placed Millwall travelling to Norwich.

Barclays League Division One
(Up to and including 17th September 1988)

	P	W	D	L	F	A	PTS
1. Norwich City	4	4	0	0	8	3	12
2. Southampton	4	3	1	0	9	3	10
3. MILLWALL	4	3	1	0	8	3	10
4. Liverpool	4	2	2	0	6	2	8

Lions fans will have worked out that, had they been able to hold on to all three points on that opening day visit to Villa Park they would be visiting East Anglia on top of the pile by virtue of a better goal difference. In the space of just seven days they had gone from wondering if they could keep up to being ready to cheer their team on to a rightful place at the top of the First Division. What they were to witness was another 2-2 draw which was every bit as thrilling in a very different way.

Norwich, managed by the relatively unknown Dave Stringer, were already earning a reputation for playing attractive attacking football, but they also had the ability to go direct when required, similar in many ways to Millwall. Back in the eighties, the tactical side of football wasn't dissected anywhere as near as much as today – and certainly not as forensically, but if it was, the experts with their computers, stats and fancy giant touch-screens may have concluded that Norwich's direct/passing-game ratio was smaller than Millwall's. As it was, back in late September 1988, fans were just looking forward to a fascinating match-up of two of the season's unlikely early-season upstarts.

After a tense first half in which neither side seemed keen to test the opposition, the game exploded into life in the second minute after the break when Ian Crook placed a brilliant free kick out of Brian Horne's reach from 25 yards. Forget Everton at home, this was Millwall's first real top flight test right here, falling behind for the first time, how would they react?

Their noisy band of travelling fans didn't have long to wait. Literally from the restart, O'Callaghan laid the ball off for Ian Dawes just inside the Norwich half on the left hand side. Dawes placed a perfect cross onto the head of Sheringham who had made a run to the edge of the Norwich area. Aware that his strike partner would be making a similar run behind him, his deft flicked header found Cascarino who calmly took the ball on his thigh before slotting past Bryan Gunn for an immediate equaliser.

The game settled again and seemed to be heading for a 1-1 draw until the 73rd minute when Norwich were awarded another free kick, this time to the right midway into Millwall's half. It was Crook again who this time delivered a perfect ball into the box for Norwich's own target man Robert Rosario to rise above the Lions' defence and plant a header beyond the despairing reach of Brian Horne. With fifteen minutes left, this had surely knocked the stuffing out of Millwall? Despite the scoreline, Carrow Road seemed to be filled with chants from the visiting Millwall fans and, spurred on almost as if they had just taken the lead rather than fallen behind for a second time, Millwall hit straight back again.

Following the restart, Keith Stevens took a throw-in to Sheringham who played the ball back to Stevens. He found Cascarino making a run to the right-hand corner of the Norwich penalty area but the Eire international was now closely guarded after his earlier strike. Shielding the ball brilliantly with his back to goal he turned his marker and crossed to the opposite corner of the area where Kevin O'Callaghan had made a hopeful late run. O'Callaghan met the ball perfectly on the run with a left foot volley that swerved into the bottom left corner of the Norwich goal to make it 2-2 less than a minute after Norwich had again taken the lead. The Millwall supporters went berserk, hardly believing the character and fighting spirit that they were witnessing in their team, even though it was what they demanded. To see it at this level under this kind of scrutiny was inconceivable.

The game ended 2-2 and with Southampton losing 3-1 at home to Liverpool, the fact that Millwall had ended the only perfect record in the division was tempered somewhat by the fact that they still had to settle for third place – this time behind Liverpool. What was almost as remarkable about that Norwich game as the immediate response to falling behind twice was the manner of the goals. Norwich, as I said earlier, had a reputation for playing attractive football but also had the direct tactic in their locker which they used, it could be argued less than Millwall who could also play a bit too. The fact that Norwich's goals had both come from set pieces and that Millwall's equalisers had both resulted from neat, patient football was encouraging for Lions fans – even if the match had perhaps revealed a slight weakness from free kicks.

September had been everything that Millwall fans could have dreamed of – and more. October would bring more fixtures that fans could now consider winnable matches with QPR and Nottingham Forest visiting The Den and trips to Coventry and Middlesbrough. The old heads among The Den faithful however knew how quickly they could be knocked from their perch but for now, every single Millwall fan was basking in the glory.

4

One Moment in Time

What did Millwall fans expect from that first season in the First Division? Relegation? A brave but ultimately unsuccessful battle to avoid dropping back into Division Two? Maybe consolidation, a dramatic last day survival, but not this, never this in a million years this...

The carnival atmosphere returned to The Den on the first day of October. An incongruously warm and sunny afternoon made for a pre-match atmosphere more in-keeping with the opening day or final match of a season. The buoyant mood on the Cold Blow Lane, Halfway Line and Ilderton Road terraces and in the stand was reminiscent of that idyllic afternoon in May when the fans witnessed that glorious coronation of their Second Division title-winning heroes. Many there that day acknowledged that it would be unlikely they would experience such an afternoon for many years – but they would only have to wait a few months.

Top flight success had brought with it the usual marketing ingenuity that follows football. The Cold Blow Lane unofficial merchandisers were pedalling a new range which included t-shirts showing Fred Flintstone exiting his cave with the words: "Not now Wilma, I'm off down the Millwall", the now omnipresent smiley face associated with the Acid House craze announcing: "Millwall make me happy", and claiming: "I don't need acid, I'm high on Millwall". These somewhat tacky Ts were snapped up and were part of the shirt-sleeved Den crowd shielding its eyes from the early autumn sun that was starting to drop behind the South Stand as Millwall kicked off against QPR and a match that would be forever etched in Lions history. Every Millwall supporter of a certain age remembers the day The Lions sat proudly on top of the league.

Terry Hurlock was already a crowd favourite at The Den but this was the match that officially inducted him into the Millwall Hall of Fame. It was a fairly routine start with Millwall dominating play and taking an early lead when Tony Cascarino headed beyond ex-Lions custodian Nicky Johns after Hurlock crossed following an indirect free kick. QPR hadn't read the script though and were soon level thanks to their aging but lively player manager Trevor Francis. Rocked for a few minutes, Millwall composed themselves and then began the Terry Hurlock show. Bullying his way through the midfield he dispossessed a Rangers defender attempting to play his way out of trouble and unselfishly squared the ball to the waiting Cascarino to roll home and put Millwall back in front. It was a goal out of nothing, created entirely by Hurlock. While the cries of "There's only one Terry Hurlock" still rang in the air to celebrate The Lions' second goal, he repeated his smash-and-grab raid on a shell-shocked QPR back four, this time unleashing a skidding shot that flew past Johns for number three which sparked a crescendo of pandemonium on the Den terraces.

It could have been more but a fourth just before half time was ruled out for offside and Francis' battered team must have been relieved to hear the whistle to provide some respite from the battering they were receiving.

The second period had one more twist. QPR scored what appeared to be nothing more than a consolation, and they never looked like getting themselves back into the game. Then out of the blue, a hopeful attack saw Mark Stein stumble in the area and to the horror of the home fans, the referee pointed to the spot. Veteran Francis stepped up to save an unlikely point for QPR but his kick was brilliantly saved by Horne and as the final whistle blew and Millwall fans applauded their team down the tunnel, a perfect day was made complete as results elsewhere were announced over the stadium public address system. It was a familiar routine that most Millwall fans either missed exiting the ground quickly to find their cars or make their train home or ignored, being oblivious to scores elsewhere unless they were affecting a late-season promotion or relegation battle.

But the announcements on Saturday October 1st 1988 were of more significance than any announced arguably since that fateful day in May 1972 when fans celebrating what they thought was promotion to the top flight after a victory over Preston were told they had in fact not gone up. On that day, needing a win and for promotion rivals Birmingham to slip up to clinch glory, word had incorrectly gone around The Den that Birmingham had lost 2-1.

With Millwall beating Preston, the final whistle saw wild celebrations and pitch invasions and even some of the Millwall players believed they had been promoted to the First Division for the first time, before the stadium announcer confirmed the awful truth that Brum had in fact won 2-1. They completed the job of robbing Millwall of the last remaining promotion place with a win in their final game at Orient. It was a chain of events that lived long in the scarred memories of 'Wall fans who were there to witness it.

In the build up to the QPR match Millwall fans were well aware that there was a chance they could see their team top of the First Division by five o'clock that afternoon, but they were realistic. For that to happen, both Norwich and Liverpool who sat above them in first and second place respectively had to slip up at home. Norwich faced struggling Charlton and Liverpool hosted Newcastle – both were in the bottom five of the league table with just one win between them. The Den terraces often emptied quickly, whatever the score, and the announcement of results was by no means a regular formality. More often was the playing of Fleetwood Mac's Albatross by way of a calming influence following a defeat or Kool and the Gang's Celebration to mark a victory. This day was different.

There appeared to be very little movement on the terraces, even after the players from both sides had long since departed. Fans chatted amongst themselves almost as if it was half time and even those that did make their way to the exits at the top of the terraces did so with an almost deliberate reticence as if they were waiting for something to happen. There didn't appear to be any knowledge of scorelines from Anfield or Carrow Road from fans as they stood almost surreally waiting for something to happen. Then it did. The public address system crackled into life and an excited voice made the following announcement:

"So here are a few full time scores… Liverpool 1, Newcastle United 2 and Norwich City 1, Charlton Athletic 3, those scores mean Millwall are TOP OF THE FIRST DIVISION!".

It was almost panto-like, but totally befitting the Millwall fairy tale that was unfolding in 1988. The fans it seemed had somehow sensed there was something worth waiting behind for. A few had given up, assuming that even the stadium announcer had gone home and Liverpool and Norwich had earned their expected home victories to stay ahead of Millwall and yet the large amount that stayed were able to celebrate not only another brilliant Millwall victory but history being made:

Barclays League Division One
(Up to and including 1st October 1988)

	P	W	D	L	F	A	PTS
1. MILLWALL	6	4	2	0	13	7	14
2. Norwich City	6	4	1	1	11	8	13
3. Liverpool	6	3	2	1	10	5	11
4. Southampton	6	3	2	1	10	6	11

Les Briley, who had now played for the club at the bottom of the Third Division and the top of the First in his four year Den career admits that even the players were struggling to take it all in:

"I had friends coming up to me after that QPR match saying: 'you're top of the league, how'd you manage that?' and I replied: 'I don't know!' Even as players we shocked ourselves really. We weren't getting big-headed, but the way we adapted to the First Division was incredible."

If it was possible to find a downside to this remarkable achievement, then it would be that Millwall fans would be denied the opportunity to attend one of their most eagerly awaited top flight matches as league leaders. The hotly anticipated journey to Highbury to see Millwall face

A Natural High – Millwall Football Club's two years in the First Division

Arsenal in a league match for the first time ever was postponed, meaning they could only sit and listen to Norwich regain top spot without a challenge with a 1-0 win away to Derby. Liverpool surprisingly lost again – this time to Luton – which meant that The Lions travelled to Coventry a week later and kept their incredible unbeaten record intact with a hard fought goalless draw and remain the only unbeaten team in the First Division. A staggering statistic for a team making its top flight debut going into the last ten days of October.

The match programme for Nottingham Forest at home on October 21st showed Cascarino's imperious headed opener v QPR with the league table at the end of the match inset into the picture. It was a priceless keepsake for any Lions fan and very apt for the day's visiting manager. Brian Clough had tasted unprecedented success at domestic and European level and yet always maintained that the most important thing for any football club was to be champions of their league. There was an eager anticipation of the visit of Cloughie and his Forest team. Even though they weren't the same all-conquering side of the late seventies that had won a league title and back to back European Cup finals, they were still an attractive side to watch and Clough, well, he was just Brian Clough. Seeing such a celebrity of the game in his trademark green sweater striding onto The Den touchline and taking his place in the dugout was another moment to savour for Millwall fans.

He looked genuinely touched by the generous welcome he received from Millwall fans sat in the South Stand behind the managers' benches as he took his place, but as his slick Forest side took control of the game, Lions fans seemed to be getting their first lesson – and first defeat – in First Division football from one of the experts.

Trailing to two Steve Hodge strikes either side of the interval, Millwall had been forced to attack the Ilderton Road end in the second half which made them look particularly out of sorts. Football is filled with superstition and 'favourite ends' is a big part of this. Millwall always preferred to attack the Cold Blow Lane end in the second half – even though their fans were situated behind both goals. Whilst others disregarded Millwall's threat, there's no doubt that Clough, being meticulous in his preparation and treating Millwall away in exactly the same way as a trip Manchester or Milan, will have had it well documented to him about The Lions' preferences and known that even the slightest disruption could work in his side's favour.

As the match moved into its final ten minutes, Millwall threw everything at Forest in a direct assault on their goal. Forest goalkeeper Steve Sutton made two smart saves from what looked like goal-bound blockbusters from Hurlock and an 83rd minute Sheringham header appeared to be no more than a consolation, but the introduction of substitute Neil Ruddock would prove to be a master stroke by manager John Docherty. As the final minutes ticked by, Millwall's relentless battering on the Forest door finally paid off. A Ruddock header found Sheringham on the right and after a swift interchange of passes with Keith Stevens and Terry Hurlock, he found the perfect angle to deliver a deep cross which was met by Ruddock who powered home his header low into Sutton's right hand corner.

Ruddock peeled off in hysterical celebration and was dragged to the floor after Danis Salman leapt onto his back as The Den once again shook to its foundations and incredibly, as play resumed, rather than sit back and protect an unlikely and hard-earned point, Millwall pushed for a winner. It wasn't to be but after another thrilling 2-2 draw, the sight of Brian Clough, one of the most decorated club coaches in the game, acknowledging the undoubted contribution of the Lions fans with his customary brief hand clap to all four sides of the stadium as he made his way to the players' tunnel spoke volumes about the character of this Millwall team.

There was something ironic and so typically Millwall that their first defeat of the season would come against a team that had been promoted with them. The final match of October took The Lions to Middlesbrough and whilst Ayresome Park had never really been a happy hunting ground for Millwall, it did seem for a brief spell that they would beat that hoodoo and remain unbeaten. Bernie Slaven gave 'Boro a first minute lead which was quickly cancelled out by two goals in ten minutes by Sheringham and Cascarino to give them a 2-1 half time advantage. The second half however saw the first signs of fatigue in Docherty's men. With Cascarino, O'Callaghan and Wood already carrying knocks, Middlesbrough swept in three goals without reply to leave Millwall defeated for the first time in the First Division against a side that had followed Millwall into the top flight via the play-offs and who The Lions had taken four points off during that promotion campaign.

Of course the unbeaten run had to end eventually and whilst it must have stung a little for it to have come in the manner that it did, there was a certain sense of relief amongst Millwall fans that they had perhaps got the monkey off their back in time to regroup for November where Luton would visit The Den before the one fixture that virtually every Lions fan had looked for first when the fixtures were announced back in June: Anfield and champions Liverpool away.

5

First Time

The match programme for the home game with Luton on November 5th was dominated with talk of the following Saturday's historic trip to Anfield where Millwall would play Liverpool for the first time this century. The only previous meeting was an FA Cup clash back in 1896 when Liverpool were just four years old and had taken over residence of Anfield from neighbours Everton. The home side beat a slightly older Millwall Athletic who had been formed seven years earlier 4-1. 92 years later things would be just a little different…

Demand for the relatively small allocation of tickets offered to The Lions by the Merseyside club meant that thousands of fans were disappointed. In a bid to ensure as many fans as possible could see the game live the club arranged for it to be beamed back to The Den on giant screens erected on the pitch. It proved a successful venture during the promotion run-in for Millwall's midweek trip to

Bournemouth and a bumper Den crowd was expected. There were few fireworks in Millwall's straightforward Guy Fawkes Day 3-1 victory over Luton, with goals from O'Callaghan, Sheringham and a superb long-range effort from Ian Dawes - his first goal for the club. The swagger with which Millwall brushed aside what was a well-established First Division side in Luton to bounce back from their first defeat of the season at Middlesbrough seven days before gave Lions fans the belief that they could go to Liverpool with high hopes of pulling off a shock. They were certainly getting under the skin of the opposition with Luton manager Ray Harford dismissing The Lions in the post-match press conference, suggesting that their 3-1 victory was flattering.

The build-up to the historic trip to Anfield was unlike anything the club had seen before. What made it all the more surreal was a midweek match at home to Barnsley in the Simod Cup. Well over 3,000 turned up at The Den to watch a slightly weakened team win 3-1 on penalties after a 1-1 draw. It may not sound like a good crowd for a first team game but it was a match no more attractive than a reserve fixture that would previously attracted less than half that attendance. These were exciting times and the fans simply couldn't get enough. The following day Millwall announced a new signing. There had been no speculation that Docherty was on the lookout for new faces but the team had been starting to show some signs of fatigue and the defeat at Middlesbrough was a classic example of where a stronger squad may have got them all three points. So when it was announced that Paul Stephenson would be joining from Newcastle and going straight in the squad that would travel to Anfield, Millwall fans felt, probably for the first time, that the club had genuine ambitions to not only make a token appearance in the top flight but to establish themselves there with a First Division-quality squad.

Stephenson, along with Paul Gascoigne and Ian Bogie had been considered three of the brightest prospects in the game. As part of Newcastle's successful youth team, Bogie was actually considered the pick of the trio but it was Gascoigne who blossomed first and was already making a success of his big move to Spurs. Newcastle were struggling and were looking to buy their way out of trouble with the money received from Gascoigne's sale so when Millwall offered what was then close to a record fee of £275,000 they were only too willing to allow him to move down south.

For Millwall fans arriving at the famous stadium, to see their team take to the Anfield pitch was the stuff of pure fantasy. Of course it was the London derbies with Spurs, Arsenal and West Ham that they were looking forward to just as much, but for any fans that had been glued to their televisions in the seventies and eighties watching a Liverpool team sweeping both English and European opposition aside in front of a packed swaying Kop, to be looking across the lush green Anfield turf, glistening from the chilly November drizzle from their packed corner of the Kemlyn Road stand as You'll Never Walk Alone began playing was truly goosebump stuff. No sooner had the first notes of Gerry and the Pacemakers started echoing around the stands, the famous old number was drowned out by Millwall's own anthem No-one Likes Us, to a backdrop of a spine-tingling "MIIIIIIIIIIILLL…"

Millwall fan Chris remembers his trip to Anfield that day being almost as surreal as the match itself:

"I was 16 at the time and was planning to go with a good mate of mine and a couple of his pals, brothers who lived on Barry Road in Peckham. We thought we'd be clever and just get tickets for the match. Travelling on the football special trains was grim

at the best of times and we knew there'd be a special welcome shall we say from the Merseyside Police. So we paid extra to get regular Inter City tickets from Euston to Liverpool Lime Street a week or so before the match. We noticed that one of the brothers bought two train tickets but wouldn't say why. My mate decided to drive to Euston early Saturday morning. The brother with the extra ticket asked him to go a certain way and to pull over just after we'd crossed the river. Suddenly a bloke appears from nowhere and gets in the back with. I was still half asleep and not sure what was going on but the others all seemed OK with it. The back seats of my mate's old Escort was quite a comical sight as the two brothers were big lads and this other fella was squashed in. I made eye contact with him and he didn't seem too happy. He was a short stocky dark haired bloke and was wearing a black Harrington jacket. As we pulled away he clapped his hands together and in a broad northern Irish accent said excitedly: "YESS this is it lads, the big one!" He never spoke again. When we arrived at Euston and attempted to get on the regular passenger train for Lime Street we were stopped by station staff and, after clocking my mate's Millwall badge on his jacket ushered to the next platform. We tried to protest that we were supposed to be on the nice new train with a proper buffet, lights and heating but they were having none of it and we ended up travelling on just another crappy old train. We were a bit naïve I suppose as it appeared hundreds of 'Wall had exactly the same idea and were quickly rumbled. When we arrived at Lime Street the police numbers were ridiculous, and they were carrying *these massive sticks. We were all searched as we left the train before being herded together outside the station for the escort to Anfield. As the last of the Millwall fans were searched and joined the escort we looked around and noticed our Irish travelling companion had vanished. None of us had seen him go and we never saw him again. I later learned that he was an old friend of one of the brothers and had been released from prison the previous day after serving 15 years inside for his part in an armed robbery. Apparently his first wish was to see Millwall at Liverpool. Whether he made it to the match or not I don't know as he wouldn't have had a ticket, none of us ever heard anything about him again."*

Even today, images of that match seem unbelievable. Liverpool's famous red shirts alongside the blue of Millwall with their Lewisham shirt sponsor have many wondering if they're nothing more than an elaborate photographic hoax, up there with the conspiracy theories over images of the moon landings. But it was real and Millwall arrived one point and one place above fourth placed Liverpool in the First Division table which thankfully was enough for them to somehow treat this like any other game. Millwall played towards the famous Kop in the first half and after nine minutes Sheringham found new signing Stephenson on the right hand side of the Liverpool penalty area. He hit the ball first time and it flew into the top corner of Mike Hooper's net. Liverpool had been ready for a war. Still smarting from their shock defeat to Wimbledon in the FA Cup final six months earlier, they were determined not to be bullied by what they would have considered to be another tin-pot bunch of London upstarts. Yet here they were once again getting a bloody nose from what was on paper, compared to their illustrious squad of medal-laden internationals, a pub team. That wasn't the case of course, yet the only teams who had really shown The Lions any respect were two that knew them already – Aston Villa and Middlesbrough – along with Clough's Nottingham Forest. They were arguably the only three teams that had really given Millwall any problems.

Now Liverpool were forced to show them the respect they deserved and had earned and they came back with a vengeance. A 30th minute equaliser from Steve Nicol seemed inevitable as the home side laid siege to Brian Horne's goal and Millwall were struggling to contain the wing trickery of John Barnes. What they also struggled with was aggression levels that they had possibly never encountered before. That they held on through the second half as Liverpool attacked their beloved Kop end was testimony to The Lions' spirit – not least because they did it in the face of some horrific challenges by the Liverpool midfield. One in particular left a huge open gash on the leg of Kevin O'Callaghan.

The fact that Millwall fans were a little disappointed to come away from Anfield with a 1-1 draw, knowing how close they had come to watching a famous win summed up perfectly how far the club had come in its short top flight existence. Over 5,000 fans watched from The Den on the big screens and there's no doubt that, had it been possible to accommodate more than the 41,000 in Anfield that day, every single ticket would have been snapped up.

Millwall-supporting director at the time Peter Mead has very different memories of the historic first trip to Anfield:

> *"We walked into the Directors' Room and John Smith who was then Chairman of Liverpool was there. The first thing he said to us was: 'it must be so nice for people like you to come to places*

like this'. I felt like saying: 'go fuck yourself', there obviously was a class system. If you're a Millwall supporter you're reviled before you even start."

That said, Mead does have fonder memories of the visit to football's aristocracy when they made the shorter journey to Highbury, but not so much at their other London rivals:

"Going to Arsenal was the most congenial of memories, so kind, pleasant and welcoming and going to Chelsea with Ken Bates was just the reverse. It was slightly surreal, little old Millwall who I had been going to see since I was eight, in the First Division, just crazy."

What Millwall were learning with each passing week at their new higher level was how you had to adjust from preparing to play a Liverpool one week and a Luton the next. Managers and players talk of taking each game as it comes and treating them all exactly the same but at no time in their history had Millwall had such experience of playing such varying pedigrees of opposition. That's not meant to be as disrespectful to Luton as it probably sounds, but it's hard to accurately convey in words the buzz that emanated from The Den during this period. The place was literally glowing and fans were counting down days and looking ahead to key fixtures. The demand for tickets also meant that even more focus was placed on games such as Liverpool away with early morning queues stretching down Brocklehurst Street. Keeping the players as focused for the visit of bottom of the table Newcastle as they were for the trip to Anfield was the key task for manager John Docherty and his assistant Frank McLintock.

A Natural High – Millwall Football Club's two years in the First Division

Despite their lowly position, Newcastle was still an attractive opponent and a fascinating one for Millwall to pitch their blossoming top flight skills against. They had been part of the First Division furniture for several seasons and invested heavily in the likes of Dave Beasant and Andy Thorn from Wimbledon's successful FA Cup winning side and Brazilian international Mirandinha – who was intended to fill the Gazza-shaped hole in the Geordies' squad. These were the type of signings that Millwall could only dream of, and yet here they were, sitting comfortably in third place in the First Division table with pretty much the same side that had won them the Second Division title six months earlier. Once again a Millwall home match was dominated by talk of another game to come. For most Millwall fans, it was *the* game: West Ham at home.

The two bitter rivals hadn't met for almost ten years when events off the field unsurprisingly dominated. The anticipation of Millwall v West Ham in English football's top division was almost too tantalising to describe and with the match just two weeks away, it hung in the air all around The Den while the match with Newcastle seemingly a sideshow. It didn't take long however for Millwall fans' attention to be grabbed when an uncharacteristic 20 yard volley from defender Alan McLeary gave The Lions the lead and set them on their way to a crushing 4-0 win. Goals were being spread around the team. Cascarino scored his tenth of the season, and Hurlock and O'Callaghan – both of whom had recovered with their battle scars from Anfield – also weighed in. If the rest of the First Division were waiting for this Millwall bubble to burst, they were being disappointed week in week out. Of course the bubble that every Millwall fan wanted to completely destroy was that of West Ham, but they had a tricky trip to Southampton first. The Saints had, along with Millwall and Norwich, been the surprise package of the season and were still in fifth place in the table – just a point and two places below The Lions.

Another large contingent of travelling Millwall supporters filled the Archers Road terrace to watch yet another thrilling 2-2 draw. Kevin O'Callaghan played a starring role, seemingly enjoying the stick he received from Southampton supporters in recognition of his time with local rivals Portsmouth. After falling behind, goals from O'Callaghan and then Sheringham looked to have given Millwall three very impressive away points but a late goal from Baker settled what was, on reflection, a fair share of the spoils.

Something that came out of that trip to Southampton was another first for Millwall. A scandal surrounding the players at the hotel they stayed at before the match actually made it on to the front pages with several players named amid scurrilous accusations of the type of bad behaviour that usually follows a touring rock band. This was new territory for Millwall, whose fans were no strangers to seeing both front and back pages dominated by sensationalised, hysterical coverage of their own misdemeanors over the years. Whether or not there was any substance to the story wasn't really up for discussion. What was of more concern was whether or not this first negative to come out of this season, however humorous or insignificant it may have appeared, would have an adverse effect on the team, especially with West Ham at home to come next. In a season of firsts and fans' wishes being surpassed, this was the one game that they wanted to win – and win well – the most.

6

Cat Among The Pigeons

If there was one match Millwall fans wanted to win more than any this season it was West Ham, with Spurs probably a close second. December brought the chance to do both in the space of a week to set up a very happy Christmas, but in typical Millwall fashion, it wasn't to be…

While football's various warring fan factions had called a truce, there are certain rivalries that can never be at peace and Millwall versus West Ham was the perfect example. The Simod Cup clash at Upton Park just over a year previously was nothing more than a charade compared to the long-awaited first ever top flight league clash on December 3rd 1988. There was a very different atmosphere in and around The Den leading up to kick off. A packed Den usually buzzed with excitement and anticipation, but this was different. It was more of a low menacing hum, the kind that emanates from a dodgy nuclear reactor that was just about to blow. Nerves had never been more evident, even during those tense promotion run-in matches the previous season. This was a very different Den.

Millwall fans had every right to be confident though. They were still in third place, 16 places above The Hammers who had mustered just two wins all season. Surely The Lions would find three points here as easily as they had done against a similarly struggling Newcastle two weeks before?

The Den saw its first attendance over 20,000 since the equally anticipated clash with Chelsea back in 1976. The previous league meeting between the two sides came nine years before when already-relegated Millwall won an end-of-season Second Division encounter 2-1. A crucial factor in boosting the crowd was the controversial decision to allow visiting fans to use a section of the Ilderton Road terrace behind the goal. This area, usually reserved only for members (a scheme which most Lions fans still stubbornly refused to join out of protest of its sanctioning by the FA) was allocated to visiting fans when demand required. This meant that, for the first time in that historic season, The Den was truly filled on all four sides – with of course the exception of a rather crucial empty space on the right hand side of the Ilderton Road end to keep both sets of fans apart!

One thing that only one other team had managed to do that season was to play Millwall at their own fast-out-of-the-traps, high-tempo game. That team was Middlesbrough and the plan worked with an early goal and all three points. West Ham manager John Lyall was an experienced coach who had pretty much seen and done it all and it was clear from the kick-off that he had told his team to push the pace of the game from the first minute. They obviously didn't need any motivation in a derby like this one but the tense air around the home sections of supporters began to thicken as the first few minutes played out. For the first time Millwall were second to every midfield battle and fifty-fifty or second ball. Their usually decisive passing and patient build-up from wide positions looked clumsy and over-thought and even though the first clear cut chance of the game fell to them when a Keith Stevens header flew inches over Allen McKnight's bar, it was apparent that the tension surrounding this game may well have seeped from the terraces to the Den pitch and the Millwall players.

It was another uncharacteristic Millwall moment that led to West Ham's 17th minute goal. Alan Dickens robbed Terry Hurlock in his usually assured centre circle territory and while Leroy Rosenior was unable to pick up Dickens' pass the seemingly wasted opportunity suddenly came to life again when the usually faultless Ian Dawes played the ball back to Horne in the Millwall goal without checking first for danger. That danger was clear and present, and it was in the shape of both Dickens again who had continued his run and Paul Ince. Dickens' slid in with Horne to win the ball and got his foot to it first leaving Ince with the easiest of tap-ins into an empty Cold Blow Lane end goal. Spurred on by this, West Ham went in search of a second goal and for vast periods of the remainder of the match appeared more like the team in third place. Millwall's frantic attempts to claw back an equaliser resulted in nothing more than a handful of crosses that were met every time by a West Ham head and the last shot of the match was Ince's once again as his shot from twenty yards fizzed just wide of Horne's right hand post before referee Wiseman signalled the end of the match. Millwall had lost the one match that the majority of their fans had wanted to win more than any. It's highly likely that, if you'd offered every Lions supporter before the game a thumping victory in this match and the return at Upton Park in the spring as Millwall's only two wins for the rest of the season they may well have taken you up on the offer.

A Natural High – Millwall Football Club's two years in the First Division

It was of course hard for Millwall supporters to feel aggrieved – as much as that West Ham defeat hurt. It was December and yet, for the first time in their inaugural First Division season, they had lost a match having never really been in with a chance of winning it. For the first time that season, questions began to be asked. Had they been found out? Was their paper-thin squad on which injuries had been so kind but tiredness an inevitable factor, starting to creak? As was the way in English football's top division, the next stern test would only be days away, this time in the shape of a visit to Tottenham.

Spurs too were struggling at the wrong end of the table with just three wins so far that season and on a four match winless run. Their team was bursting with flair players such as Paul Gascoigne, Chris Waddle and Paul Stewart but they had struggled for any consistency. It was the flair that would prove to be the difference between the two sides however and a first half strike from Waddle followed by a trademark long range free kick from Gascoigne, who struck while the Millwall defence looked uncharacteristically disorganised, settled the match with Millwall rarely troubling their north London rivals.

In his programme notes for the next match at home to Sheffield Wednesday, Millwall manager John Docherty admitted that two or three players had been below par for the trip to Spurs but that the dressing room was not despondent after losing two on the spin for only the second time in 1988. The fact that he had to say that suggested that perhaps the harmony that was so evident right across the team since the turn of the year had perhaps started to falter or that weariness was beginning to take its toll. The First Division pace was as relentless as Millwall could have imagined. There was no way to grind out a win against a lowly outfit if a few players were carrying knocks as they could in the Second or Third Divisions. Even the teams at the opposite end of the table had quality running through their team that could turn a game in an instant. Rumour on the Den terraces however was that the team had seemed completely unrecognisable since the Southampton hotel scandal, yet it was hard to pinpoint why that could have been as all parties had remained tight-lipped about the incident since the story broke. Off the pitch the club were desperately trying various business initiatives to bolster the club's financial position in order to be able to strengthen the squad and compete, but these would turn out to be catastrophic. For now, Millwall had to regain their focus and composure on the pitch with three points against Sheffield Wednesday before the hectic festive period which would take them to Wimbledon and Derby and start the New Year at home to Charlton. On paper, here were four winnable matches to go some way to easing the concerns that had started to emerge following those derby defeats to West Ham and Spurs.

Wednesday were indeed beaten, by a solitary Sheringham strike in the 88th minute, but it wasn't a convincing win and there was certainly still an air about the team that something wasn't quite right, as if the magic was starting to somehow wear off. There was little surprise when Millwall slipped to their third defeat in four games – all against London rivals – when they timidly submitted to a dour 1-0 defeat to The Dons of Wimbledon on Boxing Day. There was a theory among London football fans at the time that the lack of success of the capital's teams in winning the league title was down to amount of local derbies they had to play and unpredictable nature of such games.

Millwall could certainly subscribe to that view. Of course, despite still occupying third place and just six points from leaders Norwich, no sane Lions fan actually believed they could sustain their early season form and mount a serious tilt at the title, but they had first-hand experience of how much harder they had found matches against West Ham, Spurs and Wimbledon than other teams from outside the capital. All three of those teams were in the bottom four of the league table at the time they played The Lions and yet it appeared that an entirely different Millwall team had turned up. Was it the 'derby effect'? Were other factors responsible? Or was it just a combination of them all: fatigue, getting found out, scandal and the pressure of a local derby.

Millwall's history-making year would end with a Derby – the one in the east Midlands. Arthur Cox's experienced team had found some form since that sun-drenched day at The Den back in September when they became Millwall's first ever First Division win and as the two teams brought the curtain down on the year with a Baseball Ground tussle on New Year's Eve, lay in fourth place – just a point behind The Lions. Much to the relief of the fans that had decided to spend the first half of their Hogmanay watching their team, it saw a return to The Lions of old as Millwall battered away at The Rams in search of a rare away victory. Winning on the road had long been Millwall's Achilles heel. They'd had to wait until mid-September for their first away victory during the previous promotion-winning season and you could track similar point-squandering homesickness right throughout their history.

As it turned out, their eventual total of ten away wins during the 87-88 season equalled a club record and was no-doubt instrumental in their Second Division championship triumph. Their sole win away from The Den this season had been that emphatic 3-0 victory at Selhurst Park over Charlton way back in their third match of the season and whilst, as I said, no Millwall fan could truly expect The Lions to mount a serious title challenge, had they managed more than just that solitary three point haul who knows? As the last shadows of 1988 fell over Derby's famous old stands, Millwall threw yet another assault at Peter Shilton, the highly-decorated England international goalkeeper who had, not for the first time, been the Millwall strikers' nemesis. Keith Stevens took a 77th minute free kick on the right just inside the Derby half. It hung in the air for an age before coming down on the head of Sheringham who planted his header to Shilton's left corner. The ball seemed to fall way short of its intended target and comfortably into Shilts' grasp but he inexplicably fumbled it and it continued its comically slow path into the net to send the travelling Lions fans on the terrace behind it berserk.

1988 had ended pretty much as it had begun, with a hard-earned single goal victory over a team from the east Midlands. On January 1st 1988 Millwall's adventure had truly begun with a 1-0 win over Leicester City at The Den. By December 31st 1988 a First Division Millwall were ending the year as one of the top three teams in England. Could 1989 really top that?

Barclays League Division One
(December 1988)

	P	W	D	L	F	A	PTS
1. Norwich City	17	9	6	2	26	18	33
2. Arsenal	16	9	4	3	34	18	31
3. MILLWALL	17	8	6	3	10	5	30

7

Good Life

Millwall's television appearances had been restricted to a few grainy goal highlights on Sunday lunchtimes. It'd be fair to say that the footage of flying orange seats at Luton in 1985 that the television news programmes seemed to enjoy replaying so much far outweighed any footballing airtime for The Lions. But that was about to change. Don't adjust your sets, this is Millwall, in their full, live glory, not once, but twice. They had really arrived...

The new year began with two home games in the space of five days with Charlton visiting The Den the day after New Year's Day and Luton coming back for the second time in two months – this time for an FA Cup third round tie. The programme for the derby clash with Charlton announced that, for the first time ever, a Millwall match would be given live TV coverage. Part of the huge television deal that ITV had struck with the First Division in the wake of the ill-fated 'Super League' row the previous summer was a new-look way of showing English football on television. Gone were the three matches picked at random in the hope that they would be the best of the weekend's action. Now, ITV brought us 'The Match', with a new anchorman in Elton Wellsby. This regular Sunday afternoon show had full live coverage of one top flight match with all of the goals from the other games shown afterwards. At the time it was revolutionary, a small peep into the future and Sky Sports' coverage of today, but of course they still didn't have the luxury of their own channel and were restricted to a timeslot alongside all other Sunday programming. Pundits would analyse the action and both managers and players were grabbed straight after full time for their reaction to the match and the now familiar man-of-the-match award.

Millwall's match at home to Norwich at the end of the month had been chosen, with both teams going into the new year as surprise title challengers and it would end up being dubbed one of the greatest live matches to have been shown. In all fairness there wasn't that much competition at the time but it was a fantastic match.

Also in that programme was a plea from chairman Reg Burr to oppose the Government's new plans to introduce a national membership scheme. The proposals, fronted by Sports Minister Colin Moynihan, would make it compulsory for anyone who wanted to attend a football match to have a membership card which would have to be applied for and ratified with the holders' details and photograph. Given that Margaret Thatcher's Conservative Government had just rejected proposals for a national public identity card scheme on the basis that it was an infringement of the public's civil liberties, Burr quite rightly pointed out that this was a shocking display of double standards. The reality was that Millwall were striving to generate new revenue streams to enable them to compete at their new found level. In the days when TV money was nowhere near the sum it is today and would barely cover the club's running costs, such a membership scheme, should it be forced onto the club, could be catastrophic. Previous sanctions by the Football Association following crowd trouble involving Millwall often involved making matches all ticket or the recently imposed compulsory members' area at The Den. Both had an impact on Den attendances with fans wanting to exercise their right to choose to go to the match at the last minute and stand where they wanted to. An all-ticket ruling following trouble when Millwall played Leeds in 1985 saw home attendances plummet to the 3,000 mark and harm the club financially almost to the brink of ruin. Burr asked Lions fans to lobby their local MPs in a combined effort to make Thatcher's seemingly football-hating administration rethink their madcap membership plans. It was a fight that would go on for some time.

Before the excitement of a first trip to Old Trafford to play Manchester United since the early seventies and their live TV debut, Millwall had the task of facing a struggling but stubborn Charlton side who frustrated Millwall until the dying minutes when a David Thompson header settled the match with the only goal of the game. Thompson had emerged as the go-to back-up for Wood and McLeary during that season with Ruddock conspicuous by his absence. His only involvement that season had been his late heroics after coming on as sub in the comeback against Nottingham Forest and a few League Cup and Simod Cup appearances. Understandably rumours as to why Ruddock wasn't being used began to circulate, from Docherty wanting to play him in an unfamiliar midfield role to other more scurrilous tales of unrest in the dressing room.

The truth was that with Wood, McLeary and Thompson playing so well at the back and the continued consistency of Briley and Hurlock in midfield, there was very little opportunity for Ruddock, so only those hardy souls that bothered to watch Millwall in this second season of the Simod Cup got more than a glimpse of him. This season's Simod adventures had taken Millwall past Leeds again and then eliminated away at Everton at the third round stage. Unsurprisingly, it was a competition that had not captured fans' imaginations and wouldn't stay around for long. The attendances for Millwall's home ties against Barnsley and Leeds were 3,000 and 4,000 respectively which may not sound good but the fact that less than 4,000 bothered turning up at Goodison five days before Christmas told you all you needed to know about the credibility of the tournament – despite the promise of a Wembley final.

One competition that Millwall fans were certainly interested in this season was the FA Cup. With seemingly no relegation battle to concern themselves with, while talk of a title challenge may have been wide of the mark, it wasn't quite so unrealistic to fancy The Lions' chances of at least bettering the club's previous best performance and reaching the Wembley showpiece final. They had similar hopes in the League Cup but these were ended at the second stage with a somewhat timid 1-3 defeat at Aston Villa. The match had started well with Neil Ruddock scoring a stunning volley in one of his rare cameos from that season but Villa striker Alan McInally was quickly becoming their nemesis and settled the tie.

Millwall's high-tempo football was suited to cup ties and, with a bit of luck in the draw, there was every chance that they could possibly emulate Wimbledon the previous season and upset the establishment. Now, more than ever, they felt they could beat anyone on their day and as they raced into an early lead against Luton in their third round Den clash, the feeling around the club was that this really could be their year. Luton, who themselves had a good cup pedigree, fought back and with the game poised at 3-2, more drama threatened to derail their Wembley ambitions. As the game moved into the dying stages and it seemed as though The Lions had held off Luton's fightback, the floodlights flickered and died in one corner of the ground leaving a section of the pitch in darkness. Referee Mr. Martin had little option but to lead the players off and Luton's travelling fans began celebrating an unlikely reprieve with the game seemingly headed for abandonment. Behind the scenes however, Millwall's stadium maintenance manager Colin Sayer was working against the clock to fix the faulty floodlight and save the tie for The Lions. After about 20 minutes the lights burst into life and Millwall were able to return to the pitch to complete the job to a backdrop of "There's only one electrician" from The Den's relieved home fans.

For decades, Millwall supporters following their team in the Third and Second Divisions had been desperate for a big home tie in the FA Cup. On many occasions as a third tier club, The Lions had battled their way through two rounds of plucky non-league opposition only to land a dud third round tie and miss out on the excitement of hosting a top flight side at The Den. The previous season had seen a change however, with them being drawn away to Arsenal, but with Millwall minds very much preoccupied by promotion, it didn't have the same appeal somehow. After disposing of Luton and making it to the fourth round, now more than ever, Millwall fans fancied an easy tie to help them progress further in the competition. All was going to plan when their number was pulled out of the velvet bag first to give them home advantage. What came next was typical of Millwall's luck. After years of wanting to get one of the big boys at home in the cup and failing, now, the one year that their fans felt they had a genuine chance of reaching the FA Cup final, who would they face? Liverpool. Obviously Millwall fans couldn't claim to be disappointed to be drawn at home to perhaps the biggest name in the game at the time, and it was instantly picked by the BBC to be Millwall's second ever live appearance on TV and second in a week, but there was a distinct sense of irony that, if Millwall were to make 1989 as remarkable as 1988 with FA Cup glory, they'd have to get past one of the favourites at the early stages.

The trip to Old Trafford proved to be another bloody nose for Millwall. A comprehensive 3-0 defeat saw them look truly outclassed for probably the first time in over a year as United's youngsters blew them away with a display of pace and power. Manager John Docherty took exception however to post-match press conference suggestions that Millwall's bubble had burst and they had the perfect opportunity to show the whole country that it hadn't eight days later when Norwich – and the ITV cameras – visited The Den.

That Old Trafford match was one of the fixtures that Millwall fans looked for when they were published back in June and whilst they weren't the powerhouse that they had been, playing Manchester United in a league match was what really epitomised the dream of reaching Division One. Making his debut for Alex Ferguson's side that day was a young winger by the name of Giuliano Maiorana. His ascent to the big time, like Millwall's, had been sudden and eye-catching. Just a few weeks before he took to the pitch that day in front of over 40,000 fans he was playing for Histon in his home town of Cambridge. He recalls the whirlwind weeks that led up to that first match against The Lions – and a rather interesting trip home afterwards:

> *"I was playing for Histon in front of about 50 fans and earning £10 a week. I was invited up to Manchester United to play in a testimonial match and before I knew it I had signed for United for £30,000 and was training with the likes of Norman Whiteside and Mark Hughes"*

"That day was a bit of a blur for me really, but one thing I do remember is I had to get the train home because I was still living in Cambridge. It was only after I sat down that I realised the train was packed full of Millwall fans on their way back to London!"

"I thought I'd be OK as they seemed happy enough and I speak with a southern accent anyway, but I went over the names of the Millwall players in my head – just in case anyone asked me"

"Luckily they all got off at Sheffield."

The following week Maiorana played a starring role in United's match with Arsenal and the usual comparisons were being made with George Best. He was one of a crop of bright youngsters including Russel Beardsmore and Tony Gill who had helped dismantle Millwall in that match. He was in the United team for the return match at The Den in April, where he remembers more close – but good-natured – encounters with Millwall supporters:

"You were so close to the fans at The Den, I was sub that day too and was sent out to warm up. As I jogged up and down in front of the stand, some of the Millwall fans started singing 'Shaddup Your Face!"

While Millwall's established squad players had been relatively lucky with injuries, new signing Paul Stephenson had suffered an ankle strain in the year's opener against Charlton. Lightning-fast winger Jimmy Carter had been brought in to replace him and made a goal-scoring comeback in the cup victory over Luton. Carter was to play a starring role in this television classic – but not before Millwall's defence made a catastrophic live TV debut. Millwall fell behind to an early Ian Butterworth strike after failing to clear the danger from a corner. It was another corner that led to Norwich extending their lead minutes later. Horne fumbled a shot and the resulting goalmouth scramble eventually saw Canaries' defender Mark Bowen make it 2-0 after just eight minutes. This wasn't the Millwall that Docherty was expecting to show off to the watching millions at home on their armchairs. It certainly wasn't the Millwall that Lions fans had been watching for most of the season, although the 4,500 that witnessed their defensive capitulation the previous week at Manchester United will have recognised these rather concerning cracks that seemed to be appearing.

Jimmy Carter remembers how keen the Millwall players were to show their new larger audience what they were made of, something which perhaps dwelled on their minds and was partly responsible for that shocking start:

"It was a big thing for the club and a big thing for us players as well trying to prove ourselves in the top division. It did feel different, it was all new to us. There was a full house at The Den and millions watching at home."

It was certainly a far cry from Carter's debut less than two years before when he came on as a sub at home to Oldham in front of 3,370 fans struggling to stay awake for a 0-0 bore draw. Millwall was absolutely rocking now and setbacks such as this one against Norwich only seemed to make them come roaring back stronger.

Millwall had attacking power of their own in abundance. On eleven minutes a Norwich attack down the right hand side was broken down and O'Callaghan burst clear. Out-running the Norwich defence he found Cascarino on the edge of the area who composed himself before burying a smart shot beyond Gunn in the Norwich goal. The play now swung backwards and forwards like a basketball match with both teams peppering the opposition goal and having, it seemed, no intention of defending. Carter and O'Callaghan were tormenting the Norwich back four down either wing and youth prospect Darren Morgan was having the game of his life deputising for skipper Les Briley. As a breathless first half came to an end, Millwall mounted one more attack in an attempt to go into the break level. A mazy Morgan run on the left hand side saw him break into the Norwich box and, after a neat one-two with Sheringham, he crossed to find Carter who had made an intelligent late run and met the ball first time to thump it into the net and send the teams in at the break tied at 2-2. Any neutrals watching at home who thought, along with the press corps at Old Trafford, that Millwall's bubble had burst after that dodgy opening ten minutes were now licking their lips at the prospect of another sparkling half of no-holds-barred football.

Millwall started the second period as they had ended the first and it seemed to be just a matter of when rather than if they would go on to win the game – and how many they would score. Unfortunately for them, two Scotsmen on the Norwich team would have the ultimate say in the outcome of this amazing match. The first was Norwich goalkeeper Bryan Gunn who proceeded to thwart Millwall's every attempt on goal. Two Hurlock blockbusters that looked goal-bound as soon as they left his boot were brilliantly saved by Gunn and when he was beaten, the frame of the goal came to his rescue. Norwich looked gone and happy to reach the end of the game with a point and as they survived what had to be one last Millwall onslaught, winger Mike Phelan ran the ball to safety down Millwall's left had side. With The Lions' defence playing catch up, suddenly Phelan was in an advanced attacking position but as Hurlock raced across to stop his run he appeared to weakly play the ball across to the safety of Millwall full back Salman to clear. Instead, Salman's left-footed clearance was sliced up into the air and from the resulting header Norwich striker Robert Fleck catapulted a stupendous bicycle kick past the despairing hand of Horne and into the top corner of the Millwall goal.

Almost immediately referee Vic Callow brought the game to a close and back in the studio, the pundits were agreeing with legendary commentator Brian Moore that they had just witnessed by far the best match of the season's coverage so far. This was little consolation to Millwall's fans or players who had seen what looked like a certain victory snatched from them. Somehow they would have to pick themselves up for the visit of Liverpool in the cup a week later.

Another bumper Den crowd squinted in the winter sunshine to see if their team could pull off a cup shock and whilst it wasn't quite the Crazy Gang attempting to once again topple the Culture Club, there was a quiet confidence that, if they could shore up their defence and stifle the threat of Barnes, Rush, Aldridge and co and produce the same attacking threat that had torn Norwich apart for large parts of the previous week's thriller, they might just do it. As expected, the match started at a frantic pace with Millwall doing much of the attacking.

After ten minutes, Lions fans thought they had been given the perfect start when referee George Courtney seemed to point to the penalty spot after a foul in the area on Les Briley. Amid the confusion in which even some of the players initially thought a spot kick had been awarded, it transpired that Courtney had actually awarded a free kick inside the area for what could only have been obstruction when it appeared Briley had been fouled. The free kick came to nothing and

Liverpool began to impose themselves on the game. Carter was again impressing with his tricky runs and pace but Millwall's defence had no answer for the slick play of Barnes and Beardsley and early second half goals by Aldridge and Rush ended Millwall's FA Cup hopes for another year.

8

Keep on Movin'

Was the dream starting to fall apart? Had Millwall been sussed out? Could they get that 1988 mojo back? Of course they could, these Lions were ready to roar right back...

It would have been very easy now for Millwall's season to collapse. Out of the cups and, for virtually the first time all season, out of the top four, February could have been the start of the decline with two matches against title favourites Arsenal to face.

Millwall's fans were of course licking their lips at the prospect of hosting George Graham's Gunners at The Den and then travelling to Highbury two weeks later. Nothing would have given them greater pleasure than to put a spanner in their Championship-winning works – and they so nearly did it too. First there was the small matter of a trip to another London rival – QPR – to try and draw a line under the disappointment of a January that had promised so much but delivered almost nothing. What was becoming a worry was the sudden leaking of goals. After conceding four in December's five league matches (three of which were defeats) The Lions' usually reliable back four shipped ten in five league and cup matches in January.

In typically poetic form, manager John Docherty spoke about his side's morale-sapping month before and their resolution to put it behind them in the tabloids that Millwall fans read on their way to Loftus Road that day:

> "The Lion has been wounded, but it will lick its wounds and come back roaring stronger than ever".

Robbie Burns himself would have been pleased with that one.

To the relief of the travelling supporters, Millwall served up a disciplined and ruthless performance to beat QPR far more comfortably than the 2-1 score line suggests. The stand-out player was Jimmy Carter who set up Cascarino for one of the goals and helped himself to the other. Teams were struggling to cope with his pace and trickery and, almost two years to the day since he signed for Millwall as a virtual unknown from QPR, he was starting to attract the attention of other clubs.

It was a performance particularly pleasing for Carter for one main reason as he explains:

> "I was pumped up because QPR had let me go. They also put their asking price up for me at the last knockings. It was only going to be a £5,000 transfer fee then they put it up to £15,000 at the last minute and I sort of held that against them so going

back there was good and whenever we played at QPR our fans always made a tremendous noise and created a great atmosphere. It was very satisfying because we dominated the game."

Matches at The Den at the start of 1989 never seemed to be short on incident or controversy. From the power cut drama of the Luton Cup tie, the all-round madness of that live match with Norwich to the penalty that never was against Liverpool, Millwall supporters were certainly getting full value for their £4 terrace ticket. Arsenal at home was to prove no exception, although the true controversy wasn't fully revealed until long after the game had ended.

Another bumper Den crowd of over 20,000 turned up to watch the first ever league encounter between the two sides and George Graham's title chasers were clearly out of their comfort zone early on. Millwall were now back in third place, two places and nine points behind Arsenal but looking more like the confident, fluent team that started the season. Cascarino hassled Tony Adams off the ball close to the left hand corner flag at the Cold Blow Lane end, then took the ball into the Gunners' area and coolly picked out the on-rushing Carter in the centre of the six yard box and the winger powered a diving header past the despairing Lukic to give Millwall the lead. It was a goal that Arsenal themselves would have been proud of, but as Carter admits, was probably more luck than judgement:

"I was coming in just behind Teddy and all I remember was the ball coming across and a deflection took it away from Teddy. I'm about four yards out but I'm rubbish at headers, I never practiced them as a kid, I was like a tortoise, if you so much as tap my head it goes in its shell! I'm four yards out and thinking 'I can't miss this'. It seemed to happen in slow motion. John

Lukic was in goal on the near post and as the ball comes across I can see out of the corner of my eye he's dashing across his line. If I head it properly he'll probably save it, in the end I pretty much closed my eyes, headed it into the ground and it bounced over the line. While I was celebrating with Teddy I knew that, even though I had a few years left in my career it would probably be the only goal I scored with my head and it panned out that way."

Chances to increase that lead were spurned but nevertheless The Lions went into the half time break with their slender lead intact. As expected, Arsenal came out in the second period determined to grab control of the game and a screamer from Brian Marwood levelled the scores early on. With Paul Merson now dominating the midfield and orchestrating attack after attack from Arsenal, it was another Marwood shot that deflected off Steve Wood into the path of Alan Smith who poked Arsenal into a 2-1 lead.

But it was antics off the ball that became the talking point days later. It turned out that referee David Elleray had been wearing a hidden microphone for a current affairs television programme which monitored his interaction with various Arsenal players during the match. Not Millwall. Why? Because Millwall's players had been told about the 'secret' recording, while Arsenal's hadn't. Elleray explains that both clubs were informed of the 'experiment' but Arsenal "forgot" to tell their squad. What followed was a bizarre pantomime of Arsenal players being reprimanded and giving plenty of cheek back to Harrow Schoolmaster Elleray, and Millwall's squad staying suspiciously schtum. It all boiled over when Arsenal felt they had scored after an almighty goalmouth scramble. Elleray is surrounded by protesting Arsenal players appealing for the goal to be given while the ref repeatedly tells them to "play on". Tony Adams, who had felt for all the world that he had netted a rare but vitally important goal charged towards Elleray screaming in his face that the ball was over the line, finally crossing it altogether by calling him a cheat.

The game ended 2-1 to Arsenal but there was still time for George Graham – no stranger to the referees' changing rooms at The Den – to almost fall foul of the hidden microphone himself. Interrupting their post-match cuppa, Graham appeared at the door of the small dressing room under The Den stands to ask for a few words with the officials. Spotting that the cameras and microphones were still very much on, he smiled and hastily retreated. It's unthinkable for something like this to be done in the modern era and you can only imagine the sort of mischief social media would have with it. Replays later showed that Adams' goal did indeed cross the line and, were it not for that lucky deflection from Marwood's shot that led to Smith's winning goal, it would have proved to be a decision that ultimately cost Arsenal the title. But there was still time for some more drama on that score…

Docherty was desperately trying to get Millwall back to the basics that had formed the foundation of their Second Division title triumph and incredible start to their first ever season in the top flight. A big part of that was being hard to beat at The Den and grinding out results based on a miserly, well-drilled defence. There was ample opportunity to put the disappointment of that Arsenal defeat behind them with two very winnable looking games at home in the next two weeks. Bruce Rioch's Middlesbrough were the first visitors in a midweek encounter and a comfortable 2-0 victory with a goal from Les Briley and an own goal provided welcome revenge for Docherty's men for that first league defeat of the season back at the end of October. The match also provided an impressive First Division debut for young left back

Sean Sparham. Four days later, in atrocious conditions, a late Cascarino goal sealed the points against Coventry in as typical a Millwall performance as fans could have hoped for and the ideal preparation for the midweek trip to Highbury.

With Arsenal's title-winning nerve slipping slightly, Millwall could sense the chance of an upset but they had to endure an almost constant onslaught of Arsenal attacks as the home side looked to get the job done and secure three more priceless points. Wood and McLeary were immense at the centre of The Lions' defence and repelled everything that Arsenal threw at them. Midway through second half Millwall started to get into the game and a flicked header from Cascarino skimmed Lukic's right hand post. Moments later Millwall were awarded a free kick midway into the Arsenal half on the left hand side. O'Callaghan lofted the free kick into the packed Arsenal area and it was headed clear but only as far as Les Briley on the edge of the area who unleashed a stunning volley into the top left corner of the goal.

As the Clock End, packed full of Millwall fans, erupted, Briley wheeled away and celebrated his second spectacular strike of the season, arguably better and certainly more significant than his wonder goal at Charlton back in September. Only when he turned to face the goal did he see that it had been disallowed for offside. Replays showed that the trademark Arsenal defensive efficiency in clearing their lines had gone exactly to plan and whilst it wasn't quite as clear who had been caught out, it seems that Sheringham was the one left close to the penalty spot on his own. Under today's rules of course the goal would have stood and, had the match finished 1-0 to Millwall, Arsenal would have ultimately been denied their first league title in almost two decades.

Briley understandably remembers the 'goal' vividly:

"I smashed it in the top corner and we were celebrating, then someone said 'he's disallowed it, the linesman's flagged' so I went chasing the referee while they take the free-kick and play it long, I'm still chasing the referee, still in his ear asking him why he's disallowed it and not concentrating on the ball. It was definitely a goal for me and even George [Graham] after the game came over and said: 'Les, that was a goal'."

Despite that disappointment, Jimmy Carter sees that Highbury performance as a major point in Millwall's First Division journey:

"That game was quite a defining game for us as a team. The season before we'd gone to Highbury in the FA Cup third round and we didn't perform, we all froze. They outclassed us. We didn't have any chances, they won it two-nil in second gear and that was a real disappointment to us. The next time we went to Highbury was that night, we drew 0-0 and at times we battered them. After the final whistle I remember Frank McLintock being on the pitch and he hugged every one of us as if to say: 'you became men tonight', and that's how it felt."

9

Good Thing

It's a foolish football fan that looks too far ahead. Taking one game at a time maybe a footballers' cliché, but one that supporters would do well to follow too. But we don't do we? Where's the fun in that? Millwall were heading for a top two finish, a formality surely…

Millwall were quickly learning that life in England's top division was harsh and unforgiving. The challenges came at you relentlessly and there was little time to feel sorry for yourself. The contrasts were quite bizarre too.

One day The Lions were competing against a title contender in front of almost 40,000 at one of the most famous stadiums in the country with the noisy vocal backing of their army of loyal supporters and the next they were trying to bounce back on a plastic pitch in the tight confines of Luton's little Kenilworth Road ground – with no away fans to cheer them on amongst the paltry 7,000 attendance.

Millwall made the short journey to Bedfordshire sitting nicely in third place:

Barclays League Division One
(Up to and including 4th March 1989)

	P	W	D	L	F	A	PTS
1. Arsenal	27	16	7	4	52	25	55
2. Norwich City	26	14	8	4	39	28	50
3. MILLWALL	26	12	7	7	38	30	43
4. Coventry City	26	11	7	8	34	26	40

Luton's controversial away fan ban was still in force and it meant that Millwall fans were forced to watch their team on a big screen beam-back at The Den. Docherty's side's resilience was there for all to see again though as they comfortably won the game 2-1 with Jimmy Carter grabbing both goals in a much more sedate atmosphere than the last time Millwall had visited Luton almost four years to the day. The season was quickly ticking down now and the focus was on finishing as high up the table as possible.

Third place was cemented with an easy 2-0 victory at home to Aston Villa courtesy of goals from O'Callaghan and Hurlock and when Sheringham stooped to head home a first minute goal at Everton following a fantastic flowing move it looked like runners-up spot was a realistic ambition. From a defensive position on the left hand side in their own half, Hurlock went on a typical marauding run through the midfield and found Carter cutting in from the right, his deep cross was headed back across goal by Cascarino and Sheringham was there on the edge of the six yard box to finish the move. It proved too long for Millwall to hold on however and Everton were controversially awarded a penalty midway through the second half to send Millwall back to SE16 with that now familiar feeling of injustice after facing one of the First Division's top clubs.

Forty-eight hours later on Easter Monday Wimbledon were the visitors and continued to prove something of a jinx team for The Lions. In a typically scrappy and bad-tempered game, Sheringham was red-carded and Wimbledon snatched the points with the only goal of the game. Sheringham's three match ban would prove a bridge too far for Millwall's paper-thin squad and the slump was just around the corner.

If Millwall's sensational start to their First Division lives had been born in the summer of love, the honeymoon was now well and truly over and storm clouds were starting to gather above Cold Blow Lane. It wasn't obvious at first, after all, Millwall were 5-4 favourites for relegation at the start of the season and even many of their own supporters suspected the top flight would be too much for their team to handle over the course of a 38 game season. During that season, the one constant was their ability to bounce back – long before the term 'bouncebackability' had been coined, Millwall had it in abundance, it was part of both the club and fans' DNA. By April however, a long season was starting to take its toll.

10

Requiem

April 1st 1989 was so much more than just a heavy defeat for Millwall away to Sheffield Wednesday. It was to be the first of two events that would inexorably link Millwall Football Club with one of the biggest tragedies in football, not by way of actual involvement of course, but certainly emotionally…

From the first minute Ron Atkinson's Wednesday sliced through the Millwall defence at will and the final score of 3-0 really should have been at least two or three more.

With the majority of Millwall fans situated mainly in the upper seated area at the Leppings Lane end of the stadium, I was one of a handful or so stood on a virtually empty terrace in the same section of terrace directly behind the goal where so many Liverpool fans would perish just 14 days later. It's hard to comprehend the horror of that day and the fact that, as we trudged out of the stadium after the final whistle, despondent at something so trivial as seeing our team lose a game of football, we would be among the last football fans to ever exit that terrace alive.

To say the spice of a visit from Manchester United had been taken out somewhat by Millwall's poor recent showing against Wimbledon and Wednesday was probably taking things a bit too far, but the club must have been a little disappointed with the eventual 17,000 crowd for the all-ticket affair. The goalless draw was played out almost in a pre-season friendly or testimonial atmosphere. The problem was, with Millwall still fairly secure in fifth place, an impressive final placing was almost guaranteed no matter what happened in the final seven matches, but there was no doubting that the spark of the team had most certainly vanished and without Sheringham, they posed virtually no attacking threat.

Consecutive home matches against Manchester United and Liverpool is what it was all about though and many fans were still rubbing their eyes in disbelief as they made that familiar walk down Cold Blow Lane to enter the stadium, buy a programme and a burger and take their place on The Den terraces with signs above their head advertising the fact that two of the most famous names in world football were the next attractions at this humble but extremely proud little football club.

Liverpool had moved through the gears since that FA Cup win at The Den back in January. Their inevitable path to the FA Cup final was seemingly set with Hull and Brentford brushed aside on their way to the last four. The return of Dalglish's men to SE16 only served as a bitter reminder to Millwall fans, and to quote one of the most popular TV shows of the time, Bullseye, of what they could have won. Lions fans knew that Liverpool had been there for the taking in that fourth round match and with Nottingham Forest awaiting them in the semi-final at Hillsborough, a first ever FA Cup final appearance was a definite possibility, but ultimately chance missed.

The original date for Millwall's home league match with Liverpool was set for Saturday April 15th but brought forward to Tuesday 11th in order for Liverpool to play their FA Cup semi final with Forest on that day instead. A clear spring evening bathed the packed Den terraces in a dazzling sunset, the buzz was certainly back as Liverpool arrived looking to continue their late surge up the table to catch Arsenal and grab a second league and cup double in three years. At the Cold Blow Lane entrance the Liverpool players arrived and were greeted by dozens of young Millwall autograph hunters, awestruck at coming face to face with these stars they had only previously seen on their television screens or sticker books. Most of the Liverpool squad pushed their way through the throng of small hands holding up pieces of paper, pads and pens, ignoring their pleas for a signature. John Barnes on the other hand stopped, not only to sign but to chat happily with children and parents. It was a pleasant, heart-warming scene that contrasted with the cauldron of noise building on The Den terraces. That noise sent the needle off the scale after fifteen minutes when Danis Salman arrived late on the left hand side and fired Millwall ahead.

Following some great hold-up play by Dean Horrix, who was in his second spell at the club and deputising for the suspended Sheringham, Hurlock scuffed his shot into the path of Steve Wood who tried his luck, only for his strike to hit Steve Nicol. The ball ran lose to Salman who made no mistake from the corner of the six yard box. Barnes showed his class on the pitch as well as off it with a dominant display that led to him levelling the scores with a neat header and it was his shot that rebounded back off Brian Horne's post to fall perfectly for John Aldridge to stab home the winner.

The second half almost brought Millwall level with one of the most spectacular goals The Den is ever likely to have seen. An acrobatic scissor kick from outside the area by Horrix slammed against Bruce Grobelaar's crossbar and left it still shuddering minutes later but yet again, the fine margins between success and failure for The Lions against the league's elite that season were all too evident and Liverpool saw out the match comfortably after that.

Four days later, some of those Liverpool fans that had been at The Den to watch their team may well have travelled to Hillsborough to see their team in an FA Cup semi-final and never return. Ten days after Millwall fans had taken their places on a sparse Leppings Lane terrace to be the last fans to watch a football match from that tragic vantage point, it was Millwall that proved to be the last time some fans saw their team play. Two teams that, until that season had only met once before in the previous century, were somehow bound by a terrible tragedy. Suddenly, football fans questioned how safe they were standing on the concrete steps behind high fences that they had simply taken from granted as the way you had to watch your football.

The Hillsborough tragedy naturally sent ripples throughout the entire game at every level. It was one of those terrible moments that highlighted how trivial football actually is. Suddenly, almost every football fan began thinking back to several experiences either at or on their way to a match when they had been caught up in crowd congestion which, just for a scary second or two, felt like it might turn into a serious incident. Then, almost as quickly, it would subside, and it was forgotten about. Until now. In the days and weeks that followed that awful afternoon in Sheffield, fans' minds were no longer preoccupied with end-of-season run-ins and whether or not their team would escape relegation, make the play-offs, or secure promotion. As those horrendous television footage scenes and images were played out again and again, you couldn't help thinking how close we had come to this so many times over the years and never heeded the warnings.

The harsh reality of football is of course that it has to go on and, even in the face of this terrible tragedy, fans and players alike made their way through the turnstiles, onto the terraces and out into the field of play once more just days after the horror of Leppings Lane. Understandably some, closer to the event itself, never set foot inside a football ground again.

Millwall travelled to West Ham for another eagerly-anticipated top flight derby and it was one that they must have felt could get their quickly faltering season back on track. The Hammers were ten points adrift of the safety point at the bottom of the table with just two league wins since that 1-0 victory at The Den almost five months before. Just 16,000 fans witnessed the first ever top flight West Ham v Millwall derby at The Boleyn, and it ended in an instantly forgettable 3-0 defeat for The Lions, comfortably West Ham's easiest league win of one of their poorest ever top flight campaigns. It's safe to say that Millwall supporters would have happily taken a repeat of the previous season's 2-1 Simod Cup victory there as the last points to be claimed of the season as they dropped to seventh, the lowest league position since the opening day. There was little doubt that the jaded Lions were missing the suspended Teddy Sheringham who would sit out the last of his three match ban at The Den a week later when Tottenham were the visitors.

The match programme for that Tottenham match suggested possibly the first signs that all was not well off the pitch at Millwall. Hillsborough was obviously still very much in the minds of everyone and John Docherty's manager's notes were preceded by a message from chairman Reg Burr. A collection before the match was organised and, along with offering his condolences to the families and friends of those affected by the tragedy, he appealed for Millwall supporters to give generously – which of course they did, raising £2,634.20. Unfortunately, Burr's message also contained an apology and rare acknowledgement of criticism of a section of Millwall fans which must have been hard for him as a staunch defender of the decent majority that were often demonised by the media. He wrote:

"We have taken some 'stick' in the press these past few days – rightly for once – some of our so-called supporters let themselves and the club down badly at Upton Park last Saturday and for this we apologise".

Burr is remembered fondly by the vast majority of Millwall fans, but at the time, despite him backing the supporters on countless occasions when incidents were blown out of proportion and sensationalised by the tabloids, just the merest of criticisms such as this was enough to unsettle a small section of the support. A good example being the cup match at Arsenal at the start of 1988. As more and more Millwall fans were allowed to flow through the Clock End turnstiles for the pay-on-the-door tie, the huge terrace quickly filled. Even at 1.30pm it was uncomfortably crowded as fans began to edge towards the perimeter, not under their own steam but by the gentle but menacing force of still more fans arriving at the top of the section. There were no fences at Highbury, which proved merciful as the surge sent fans over the low wall and onto the track around the pitch behind the goal. The instant reaction of police was that this was a pitch invasion attempt rather than merely fans seeking safety from the increasing crush. As home fans in the smaller left-hand section of the Clock End terrace were moved to the adjacent stand to allow Millwall fans to spread across the full width of the Clock End the incident subsided. The newspaper headlines the following day were of course full of stories of a Millwall riot – just days after they had claimed 'a Millwall hooligan group' were plotting to steal the famous clock. There were of course a few unsavoury scenes as Police attempted to forcefully intercept fans looking to escape the crush, which gave the photographers the perfect, if wholly inaccurate snapshot of the day.

The club and fans had shared an unprecedented bond throughout 1988 that led the team to the glory of a Second Division title and taking the top flight by storm. Like a newly-wed couple, all was perfect bliss with not a cross word between them.

The apparent absence of any violence or unrest inside football stadiums all over the country at that time certainly helped to cement this bond. After all, if the fans were behaving, the club could get on with its business of playing – and winning – football matches and continuing its excellent – and soon to be award-winning work in the community. The truth was that the violence hadn't gone away, but had been driven further underground.

The second Summer of Love had given way to a chilly autumn. Both Millwall Football Club and its fans were starting to come down from the euphoria of 1988 and the honeymoon was well and truly over.

In his programme notes, Docherty made a quite startling admission about the previous week's 3-0 defeat at West Ham:

> *"Our direct style of play won us the Second Division Championship last season and has helped us to make a big impact during our first ever season in the top flight. At West Ham I thought we looked the business for the first 15 minutes,*

but after that — for reasons best known to themselves — the players decided to adopt a different style of play. We were overelaborate and we played all our football outside the penalty area. The result was we hardly had a worthwhile shot at goal — and that's not like us.

"We had one or two words about it afterwards and hopefully we will put things right against Spurs this afternoon..."

Docherty's hope was in vain.

Spurs were rampant as they brushed Millwall aside in a 5-0 drubbing. It was hard for Lions fans to be angry — or even disappointed. After all, a more realistic cross-section of the support suspected this would be the case from day one and the previous seven months of over-achievement had to be put into perspective. What stung most for Lions fans though was the way Spurs strolled through the usually resolute and impregnable Millwall midfield and defence as first half goals from Paul Walsh and Paul Stewart set them on their way. Stewart completed his hat-trick in the second half, sandwiching a Vinny Samways effort, inflicting Millwall's heaviest home defeat since the 6-1 FA Cup drubbing by Grimsby in 1982.

11

Baby I Don't Care

Millwall's season may have been winding down to a slightly disappointing end, but how could Lions fans possibly not be proud of what their team had achieved in this historic first season? There can't have been many times in the club's history where such a bad run of results had been unable to dampen the mood at The Den...

After conceding just six goals throughout February and March in a run that had seen them in a great position to challenge for runners up spot, Millwall had shipped an incredible 13 goals in their last five matches and were hurtling towards mid-table. A 4-1 midweek reverse at Nottingham Forest four days later suggested more unrest in the dressing room but this was an era where speculation remained between a handful of fans on the terraces and in the pubs and football specials rather than millions of social media users, and so the public face of the club kept things in perspective and remained proud of its achievements in this first season which ended with a home match against Southampton. The final away game came at already-relegated Newcastle. Millwall took the lead with a stupendous effort from Sheringham who collected the ball waist-high on the left hand corner of the Newcastle penalty area with his back to goal. Flicking the ball up with his right foot he turned and sent a looping shot into the roof of the Newcastle net in one slick movement. It was a goal that even drew applause from the sparsely-populated Gallowgate End where it had gone in. Newcastle equalised later on to deny The Lions a first win in nine, but at least the rot had been stopped.

Southampton arrived at The Den on May 13th having had a very similar season to Millwall. As one of the early and unlikely pacesetters alongside The Lions and Norwich they too had fallen away, even more so than Millwall and sat in 13th position, safe but just six points above the drop zone. Glenn Cockerill gave The Saints the lead just before half time which was cancelled out by a Sheringham goal ten minutes from time. The game was understandably played out in a testimonial-style atmosphere with the crowd of barely 12,000 suggesting that perhaps the First Division was a novelty that may very quickly be wearing off.

The single point dropped Millwall a further two places to tenth – their lowest at any stage that season. In the ten matches since a 2-0 home victory over Aston Villa in March The Lions had tumbled seven places and amassed just four points, scoring five goals and conceding 21. When you factor in the hard-fought but ultimately unproductive months of December and January it amounted to virtually half a season of struggle. Had Millwall been found out? If so, did the players decide to take matters into their own hands at West Ham with Docherty maybe in denial? Cascarino had inexplicably lost goalscoring form and Sheringham - who had sat out three of those matches suspended following his dismissal in the Easter defeat at home to

A Natural High – Millwall Football Club's two years in the First Division

Wimbledon, and spent one on the bench as a non-playing sub – was finding the net but appeared to be ploughing something of a lone furrow. Youth prospect Steve Anthrobus had been given his first top flight start at Forest and stayed in the side for the final two matches in place of O'Callaghan who was another injury casualty.

Another product of the Millwall youth system, Sean Sparham, was also featuring more and more and impressing with his displays at left back. Whether the absence of some of the squad's senior pros in favour of youth was merely – and most likely – Docherty's way of taking advantage of the club's safety from the threat of relegation or being involved at the top of the table to give them vital experience, or more hints of unrest in the dressing will probably never be known.

One thing that was certain was the contrast in mood at The Den as fans walked away for the final time that season compared to twelve months earlier. It should have been just as buoyant as that gloriously sunny day when they celebrated winning the Second Division title. Little old Millwall, after 103 years in the footballing wilderness had claimed their spot as tenth best team in the country. Fatigue will certainly have been an issue as they struggled to replicate their high tempo game every week against bigger squads.

Les Briley recalls the mood around the club at the time:

"We'd been on such a high for all of the season and I just think the season took its toll on us and we tailed off the last few games. But finishing above Man United was quite good for us!"

One aspect of that late season fall away may also be the lack of European competition for English clubs. Following the Heysel riot in 1985, all English clubs were banned from European competition and there was little indication from UEFA when the ban would be lifted.

Five years earlier, had Millwall been in third place going into the last ten games of the season, with second placed Liverpool heading for a FA Cup success, the prospect of a UEFA Cup place would have been a very real possibility. Having seen the quixotic early season ambitions of winning the League Title at the first attempt and the disappointment of not having a more realistic tilt at the FA Cup disappear, bringing European football to The Den for the first time may well have provided just the impetus needed to breathe new life into their season.

Of course, finishing as high as possible should have been enough, but sometimes you need that little extra incentive to push you over the line. It would have been an incredible way for this squad of players to write yet another chapter in the club's history but it was not to be. Millwall fans would see their team in an FA Cup final – and in the UEFA Cup – but they'd have to wait the same 15 years that Lions supporters had been made to wait for First Division football after coming so close in 1972.

During the previous decade, Millwall had ridden the rollercoaster somewhat more than most. They narrowly missed out on promotion to the top flight in 1972, finishing third when only the top two were promoted. Two seasons later the rules were changed to boost excitement in the ailing game and from the 1973-74 season three teams were promoted – and relegated. The glee that Lions fans enjoyed watching rivals Crystal Palace slip into Division Three in that inaugural season of three up, three down (one season after The Eagles had been in the top flight) was short lived.

In 1975 it was Millwall that dropped into the third tier in that new demotion berth. Meanwhile Norwich, one of the two teams that had denied them promotion to the First Division three years before regained their top flight status by finishing third. The footballing fates could certainly be cruel and Millwall felt they were often against them.

Under Gordon Jago – considered one of the best coaches in the game – Millwall bounced straight back and, for a brief spell in the 76-77 season, looked a very good bet to make it back to back promotions and finally take their place in Division One. But the fates once again conspired against them and things unravelled quickly following the damaging Panorama programme. Extensive crowd trouble before, during and after Millwall's televised FA Cup quarter final match with Ipswich tipped them over the edge. Jago left and 12 months later Millwall slipped back into the Third Division, disgraced and in debt.

The silver lining to this cloud was a brilliant youth team that beat Manchester City in the FA Youth Cup final in 1979. Yet despite most of that victorious squad graduating into the first team, manager George Petchey was unable to find a winning formula and new boss Peter Anderson inexplicably replaced almost all of that youth team with aging pros, sending the team to the brink of oblivion.

It felt like an inescapable cycle for Millwall, they couldn't seem to swim against the tide of success which brought crowd trouble which then hurt the club financially, leading to it sell its greatest assets and start over.

Desperate to break this cycle, Chairman Reg Burr, seemingly free of the financial shackles of FA punishment after the general good behaviour of Millwall fans for the previous three seasons and now sat at the top table was desperate to take advantage of this unique situation in the club's history.

What First Division status brought of course was the burden of paying your players a wage commensurate with their peers. This was easy for the Manchester Uniteds, Arsenals, Evertons and Liverpools who enjoyed regular home crowds of between 30,000 – 40,000 and the commercial benefit that brought. Millwall's average home attendance had jumped from around 8,000 during their promotion season to over 17,000 but it wasn't enough.

The truth was Millwall were struggling to monetise their lofty status in the way they might have hoped. Burr had been shrewd enough to take out an insurance policy against winning promotion the previous season. A clever move but just one, a mere drop in the ocean. The summer of 1989 brought the necessity to build the squad and that would mean trying to compete financially on a bigger scale.

Admittedly the figures back in 1989 are miniscule compared to those of the modern day, but Millwall were still operating virtually a market stall on Knightsbridge rather than Rye Lane, Peckham as they had been used to for decades before and they needed to upgrade, and fast.

Millwall had never had a commercial sponsor. Their first, The London Docklands Development Corporation and current one – Lewisham Council – had both been partnerships with the club based on good PR rather than cold hard cash. While their First Division colleagues enjoyed a healthy revenue stream from the electronics and brewing giants of the day, a Sharp, JVC or Holsten did not seem to be interested in having their instantly recognisable brand on The Lions shirts. With the Lewisham agreement ending in 1989, this should have been a good opportunity for Millwall to lay down their first financial foundation stone to catapult them to the next level. But it didn't happen. Speculation has often concluded that Millwall's lack of commercial appeal sits squarely with their hooligan reputation – and it's hard to deny. It would be churlish to drag out the old maxim 'all publicity is good publicity', try telling that to the Marketing Director of Panasonic or Hitachi when their logo makes the front pages of the tabloids as part of a pitch riot. The money men will always play it safe and in football they have many suitors to choose from.

Director Peter Mead makes no bones about the task of securing a good deal for Millwall when it came to sponsorship, even in his position running one of the most successful advertising agencies in the UK:

> *"Getting shirt sponsorship for Millwall was almost impossible because of the club's reputation. I spoke to almost all my clients and they all shied away."*

Incredibly, despite the club not being involved in any major crowd trouble incidents for several seasons, Mead cites the ill-fated Panorama documentary that was aired more than ten years before as providing a lasting obstruction to the club's attempts to secure crucial financial backing. The big brands had long memories it seemed. Mead also confirms there is no truth in stories circulating at the time that the reason Millwall's shirt deal with Lewisham was ended two seasons short of its original four year term was that a deal had been struck with Continental Airlines which then collapsed bizarrely because the logo wasn't clear enough on the shirt! It was all par for the course down at Cold Blow Lane, so understandable how such a false tale could become perceived as true. Millwall's failure to secure a lucrative shirt sponsorship deal was catastrophic but kept under wraps. On the surface, they had many more irons in the fire that were sure to bring the club the revenue boost it needed. The reality was they were taking huge gambles in ventures they had little experience or knowledge of.

In the Autumn of 1989, the club stunned fans with its announcement that they were to float the club on the stock exchange. In a move unprecedented for a club of Millwall's size and stature, the flotation was a two-pronged strategy to enable it to stay in the ring with the financial heavyweights. Initially it would help to inject a cash sum into the club's coffers, long term it would enable them to attempt to grow through acquisition. The pitfalls were also clear, the club being open to takeover was the main concern, but that was put to one side given the current apparent rude health it was in.

Millwall joined Tottenham – who floated in 1983 – as the only two clubs to sell shares. Spurs had clearly benefitted from the exercise, outlined by their ability to beat Manchester United to the signatures of Paul Gascoigne and Chris Waddle. The difference was of course that Tottenham, as an established top flight team, had the infrastructure at board level to pull it off. Millwall, despite the undoubted business acumen of Burr and commercial nous of director and fan Peter Mead of leading UK advertising agency Abbott, Mead and Vickers, the club very still much in unchartered territory where mistakes could be fatal.

Mead perfectly sums up the frustration and harsh reality that Millwall were facing in trying to compete at the top level for a second season and was the first real steps that the club took toward leaving their beloved Den four years later:

> *"Running a small club like Millwall is like trying to put out financial forest fires with tumblers of water. We simply couldn't do anything with the ground, every time you tried to do something or build, a gaping hole would appear".*

The season had started with manager John Docherty insisting his Second Division title winners deserved to taste First Division football. Fans were apprehensive about this, but The Doc had been proved right. However, a tough season had taken its toll and squad strengthening was surely essential during the summer of 1989 if Millwall were to compete again. As the squad jetted off for a well-deserved end-of-season break and the UK basked in a mini-heatwave, the first wisps of storm clouds were beginning to gather over Cold Blow Lane.

12

Back to Life

After what felt like a year-long party, the music had finally stopped and tired bodies needed time to recover from the euphoria of two unforgettable seasons of football at Millwall. The question now was, how bad would the hangover be and when would it actually kick in?

If Millwall fans were expecting a summer of transfer activity akin to the one in 1987 that catapulted them into the First Division they were in for a big disappointment. A quiet June gave way to the usual tabloid transfer speculation as players reported back for pre-season training in July. While Terry Hurlock made his England B debut in a three match tournament at the end of May (scoring in his second match) speculation was growing that Docherty was keen to sign another midfielder, Tottenham's Paul Allen. Fans followed daily newspaper speculation which proved to be entirely groundless and Allen remained a Spurs player.

Ironically he would pull on a Millwall shirt in the First Division, but only at the twilight of his career almost ten years later. By that time the top flight had been rebranded The Premier League, the Second Division was The Championship and the third tier was now Division One. Docherty eventually got his man but, with all respect to the player involved, it was hardly a signing to excite the fans as the weeks ticked down to the new season opener.

Gary Waddock was a highly-regarded midfielder for QPR in the early eighties but a knee injury appeared to curtail his career prematurely. He managed to resurrect it with Belgian outfit Charleroi and, suitably convinced of his fitness, Millwall made him their first – and only – signing of the summer.

In his programme notes before the first home match of the season against Charlton, Docherty explained the complex nature of the Waddock transfer and empathised with fans' possible disappointment at the apparent lack of further investment:

> *"Gary Waddock's transfer from Belgian club Charleroi was one of the most complicated I have ever been involved in. As well as Charleroi we also had to negotiate with an insurance company and satisfy the Football League that everything had been done correctly, before finally getting the go ahead to sign him. Our chief executive Graham Hortop did a great job wading through the endless paperwork, and I am confident that all the hard work and complicated negotiations will turn out to be worthwhile. Gary is an exciting, highly experienced player and I am sure that he will fit in well and develop into a very useful acquisition for the club. He made over 200 appearances for Queens Park*

Rangers and was a regular in the Republic Of Ireland squad before picking up a serious knee injury. The doctors reckoned he was finished and an insurance company paid Q.P.R. £300,000 in compensation, but Gary battled back to full fitness and after two successful, injury free years in Belgium I found out he was looking to come home. We agreed to pay Charleroi £130,000 for his services and will be paying the insurance company back in year instalments, providing Gary keeps playing. Some of you may be disappointed there wasn't more transfer market activity during the summer, but I am only interested in the right player at the right price — and some of the recent fees have been quite ridiculous. It makes you look at your own squad and realise how lucky you are. The players have proved that they are capable of competing at the highest level and I'm confident we can consolidate on what we achieved last season. At the start of the 1988-89 campaign only three of the players had ever kicked a ball in the top flight, now 19 of them have and the experience they picked up last season will be invaluable."

In the same programme, chairman Reg Burr outlined further ground improvements that had been invested in over the summer. Understandably in the wake of Hillsborough, most of these were focused on the safe movement of fans into and out of The Den and new procedures had been put in place where exit gates in the high perimeter fences were installed and stewarded, being opened at the first sign of any problems. Burr also touched on the lack of transfers and stressed that it was 'important not to confuse activity with progress', citing the fact that key players had been kept at the club with the extension of contracts. The more cynical and long-in-the-tooth Lions fans however will have almost certainly read this as being the 'same old Millwall looking to save money again'. The difference between what really goes on behind the scenes financially at a football club and the perception of its fans was as hugely disparate then as it is now. What wasn't revealed was the £2million bid that Manchester United put in for Tony Cascarino at the end of 1988, which was immediately turned down.

Burr was right about the positives of the summer's business and that was the lack of traffic *out* of The Den. Not holding on to their talent was so often the club's downfall. Given the incredible first season they had enjoyed, it would have been understandable for bigger clubs to have courted several Lions star performers, but there was only one departure, and he left barely noticed, but not without huge speculation.

Neil Ruddock's second spell at Millwall had been unremarkable to say the least. Struggling to displace either Steve Wood, Alan McLeary or young Dave Thompson at the centre of defence, Ruddock was tried in a more advanced central midfield position. High points were few and far between and punctuated by niggling injuries. He scored a stunning long-range volleyed goal at Villa Park in the League Cup and his cameo that saw him head the last-minute equaliser and seal the comeback from 2-0 down at home to Nottingham Forest suggested there was perhaps a place for Ruddock in the team where he had started with Teddy Sheringham as a youth player. The fact that his season virtually began and ended with that thrilling Forest match, during a campaign where Millwall were crying out for some extra energy, suggests that all was not well with player and club.

Millwall fans were left scratching their heads as to why he had been allowed to leave for Southampton for a similar fee to that which they had paid Spurs twelve months earlier. It was a transaction made with minimal comment from either club or player, further fuelling the gossip on the terraces as Millwall began their pre-season campaign. Transfer talk quickly took a back seat however when The Lions took to the pitch for their home friendly against Wolves.

The Midlands side were worthy opponents in an entertaining 3-2 win for Millwall, but the players' demeanour had some fans wondering if all was well, although it could have been down to the stifling conditions on a hot August Saturday afternoon. There appeared to be very little interaction between teammates, even when a goal was scored. What was more enthralling was that the players appeared to be kitted out in what can only be described as the sort of bog-standard shirts you find at the bottom of the bargain box in your local independent sports shop or a dodgy market stall when holidaying abroad. A basic blue shirt with plain white collar and very little other detail suggested that perhaps the somewhat late big reveal of the new season's kit had been further delayed and this was merely a training shirt cobbled together at the last minute – especially as there was no sponsors logo on the front either. But, as it turned out, this was to be The Lions new kit for their second season in English football's top division. There was no explanation from the club in the local press as to why the four year £70,000-per-season shirt sponsorship deal with Lewisham Council had apparently been ended and, for the first time since 1980, Millwall were playing without a shirt sponsor in the most high profile league in the world with increasing television coverage.

13

Fool's Gold

If anything, this Millwall team appeared even better than the one that had begun the previous season in such impressive form. It seemed to be business as usual, picking up where they had left off before they lost their way. But as Millwall fans were about to discover, all that glitters...

The fixture computer pulled the predictable opener away to Southampton, where Neil Ruddock made his debut against his two-time former employers. A Les Briley effort gave The Lions a half time lead, but typically it was Ruddock who scored what looked to be a point-saver for The Saints – until Cascarino popped up with a last-minute winner to send the packed Millwall travelling army wild on the Archer Road stand of Southampton's unique Dell ground. There was more late drama as local rivals Charlton visited The Den for Millwall's first home league game. Looking far from the hapless outfit that

Millwall had effortlessly taken six points from the previous season, Charlton took the lead after thirty minutes through Paul Mortimer. They looked to have secured a rare victory over The Lions when Paul Williams made it 2-0 with just five minutes remaining, but an instant reply from Sheringham set up a frantic finish and Ian Dawes grabbed a dramatic last-minute equaliser. It had been a worryingly lacklustre performance by Millwall for most of the match however and there were some equally troubling signs of the same defensive raggedness that had haunted them in that awful run-in the previous season.

Nottingham Forest were the next visitors to SE16 and once again Millwall left it late when an 81st-minute Jimmy Carter strike clinched an impressive 1-0 win and second place in the table. Carter was really beginning to look the part now and a buzz went up as soon as he received the ball. Less impressive were the attendances for those first two matches. Just under 15,000 for a midweek derby at home to Charlton and barely 12,000 for the visit of Brian Clough's Forest must have been extremely disappointing for the Millwall board. Surely the novelty of top-flight football wasn't wearing off already? Especially with such a fine start again. Despite the Charlton blip and the strangely bland kit, Millwall were looking every bit the same unlikely challengers as in their debut season and were now showing an encouragingly resilient side with their ability to score late goals in either half. Youth graduate Steve Anthrobus scored his first goal for club, cancelling out Carlton Fairweather's ninth minute opener just before half time in The Lions' next match away to Wimbledon and, despite the setback of Alan Cork restoring The Dons' lead within ten minutes of the restart, another late goal – this time from Cascarino – was enough to save a point and preserve Millwall's unbeaten start. Suddenly, summer fears of a second season of struggle due to lack of investment seemed unfounded.

Next to arrive at The Den were John Sillett's Coventry, whose similarly impressive start had seen them win three of their first four and arrive at Cold Blow Lane in top spot. Millwall were handily placed in third, with Norwich in second, completing a top three of unfancied teams once again, as was the case twelve months earlier.

A rain-drenched Den saw Millwall get off to a flyer when a booming first minute header from Dave Thompson was flicked on by Cascarino to fall perfectly for Sheringham on the edge of the area to fire sweetly past Ogrizovic in the Ilderton Road End goal. A little over ten minutes later and Ogrizovic was beaten again by Sheringham from a similar distance when his free kick took a slight deflection. Anthrobus scored his second in successive matches on the stroke of half time to give The Lions an impressive 3-0 lead at the break. Millwall's football was noticeably less direct during these opening matches – and especially so in the opening half of this clash. Cascarino, showing a new dimension to his more familiar role as part of the two-pronged attack up top with Sheringham, worked himself a brilliant opening on the right hand side and sent over a perfect cross for the impressive Anthrobus to head home. Coventry were looking anything but table toppers as Millwall blew them away with a ruthless first half display.

The second half saw the diminutive figure of David Speedie in the Coventry goal, replacing the injured Ogrizovic. The ex-Chelsea man was given an understandably warm welcome from the Cold Blow Lane terrace as he took his place between the sticks and the sodden Den crowd were licking their lips at the prospect of even more goals.

Typically, it was Coventry who scored next when tricky left winger David Smith ended a brilliant run down the left flank with a smart finish past Brian Horne. Although Millwall's lead was never in any danger they were frustrated by Coventry's stubbornness to allow them to get anywhere near Speedie's goal.

The fourth goal did eventually come when Ian Dawes played a lovely overlap with Les Briley before cutting inside and planting a sweet right foot shot out of the reach of Speedie's despairing right hand an into the top left corner for yet another late Millwall goal. Six of Millwall's ten goals scored in those first five games had been scored in the last ten minutes and there seemed to be more stamina and a noticeably steadier pace to Millwall's play when compared to the high tempo style which ultimately appeared to run out of steam in the 88-89 term. The result was enough to see Millwall move back to the top of the Division One table – a month earlier than they had managed the feat the previous season although once again the attendance of just over 12,000 was disappointing, but with things seemingly going well on the pitch that was sure to improve soon and Millwall fans had every right to feel confident as they headed for Old Trafford to face Alex Ferguson's Manchester United.

Barclays League Division One
(September 1989)

	P	W	D	L	F	A	PTS
1. MILLWALL	5	3	2	0	8	3	11
2. Everton	5	3	1	1	9	6	10
3. Norwich City	5	2	3	0	9	5	9
4. Coventry City	5	3	0	2	6	7	9

Determined to put the disappointment of last season's 3-0 Old Trafford defeat behind them, Millwall got off to a solid start and should have taken an early lead when neat interplay between Sheringham and Carter saw the winger burst into the United box and shoot just wide of Jim Leighton's right hand post. Moments later however the home side took the lead when a long clearance from Leighton found Mark Hughes who muscled himself some space to shoot and sent a rocket into Brian Horne's top left corner from 20 yards. United dominated most of the remainder of the half but despite bombarding the Millwall defence were unable to add to their lead. Three minutes before the break a Keith Stevens free kick was only partially cleared by Leighton and, with the United 'keeper scrambling to get back to his line to deal with a looping ball back in from Briley, Sheringham was first to reach it to head home the equaliser. It didn't last long though and Hughes was once again The Lions' tormentor, evading challenges in the Millwall box before find Bryan Robson to fire into the top corner and see Manchester United somewhat fortuitously ahead at the half time whistle.

Despite making a steady start to the second half, any hopes Millwall had of regaining parity were blown away when Lee Sharpe made it 3-1 in the 60th minute and Hughes went on to complete his hat-trick. The 5-1 scoreline was harsh on Millwall, but they simply had no answer for the swash-buckling Hughes and pace of Ince and Sharpe.

A 1-0 midweek League Cup defeat at Stoke followed and it would take Sheringham, Cascarino and extra time for them to overturn the deficit in the second leg to set up a tricky away tie at Tranmere. Back in the league, Gary Waddock made his first start in a morale-boosting 2-0 win at The Den over Sheffield Wednesday. Second half goals from Carter and Cascarino settled a match where Millwall always looked comfortable and Waddock looked assured in the Lions' midfield alongside Hurlock as the Millwall metamorphosis from direct style to more of a passing game seemed to be moving on apace. It was Waddock's composure and inch-perfect ball from the left to find Carter who finished first time with a fierce volley that gave Millwall the lead and Cascarino rose to power home one of his trademark headers to put the gloss on a win that took Millwall back into third place but in front of yet another disappointing crowd of just over 11,000, a figure that will have worried the Millwall board and had them scratching their heads. If a second consecutive season of top three First Division football wasn't going to pack The Den and bring in the revenue required to build the squad, what would it take? September ended with a slightly more encouraging crowd of over 13,000 typically witnessing the first home defeat of the season. The rather drab and disappointing 1-0 submission to Norwich had none of the drama of that live televised goal-feast from eight months before, but all of the disappointment.

14

The Road to Hell

Football has always had a knack of kicking you when you're down and turning against you when you least expect it. One week every attack seems to end in a goal and every fifty-fifty ball falls at your players' feet. The next, you're starting to wonder where the next win is coming from…

All Millwall needed to lift their season was a rare run in the League Cup, and with Third Division Tranmere standing between The Lions and a place in the fourth round, what could possibly go wrong? A two-week break from league action seemed to have revitalised Millwall as they led courtesy of an 18th minute goal going into half time at Everton. But more defensive frailties, coupled with some questionable refereeing decisions led to the Merseysiders grabbing an equaliser against the run of play from the penalty spot and then, to the travelling fans' dismay, a late winner courtesy of Norman Whiteside.

It wasn't the best way to prepare for the first ever top flight local derby with Crystal Palace. Selhurst Park had been an unhappy hunting ground for Millwall during the eighties – certainly where the quest for league points was concerned. The 1985 FA Cup replay win aside, Millwall had left Selhurst Park empty handed on all three of their previous visits. In 85-86 and 86-87 they had led only to lose 2-1.

It was Millwall who scored first again in this latest meeting after a speculative back-pass from Palace defender Jeff Hopkins, who was attempting to deal with a ball forward by Waddock in the sixth minute, looped over the despairing Perry Suckling. The electronic scoreboard behind the goal where the ball was now nestling comically displayed frowning stick men and the words: "OH DEAR!" as the travelling Lions fans celebrated Hopkins mishap. But by half time the Welsh defender's Palace teammates had more than redeemed his gaffe. Millwall had absolutely no answer for Palace's pace in attack. A sloppy pass from Waddock as Millwall went on the attack was picked up by Palace defender Pemberton who powered his way forward leaving Hurlock in his wake, his cross found Wright who was able to control the ball and poke it beyond Horne from ten yards out. Five minutes later it was two for Palace and Wright who found himself unmarked at the near post from a corner and he easily steered home. More woeful defending – this from a Palace throw a minute before the break saw Mark Bright get in on the act as Millwall fell apart and went into half time 3-1 down with the fans fearing a humiliating defeat.

Thankfully The Lions came out fighting and within five minutes had pulled a goal back. Some neat play between Sheringham found Dawes on overlap on the left side of the Palace area and his cross found Cascarino to head home. Millwall grew in confidence and in the 75th minute Sheringham found Carter in space on the right midway in the

Palace half. Making one of his typical runs to the edge of the area, his perfectly weighted cross found Anthrobus who had made a brilliant late run to the edge of the six yard box and the youngster powered home a sensational diving header to level the scores in front of the delirious Lions fans. As Millwall continued to cause Palace problems down the right hand side there appeared to be only one winner but Suckling pulled off a string of fine saves to deny The Lions. Just as it looked like Millwall were going to have to settle for a well-earned point, Thompson lost out in a duel for a loose ball with Palace midfielder Andy Gray. As the young Millwall defender tried to regain possession, Gray appeared to block his path as the ball broke to Wright. Wright sped towards the Millwall area before releasing Bright on the right hand side who blasted home first time to seal a last-minute winner for Palace. Millwall were rightly crest-fallen. Yet again they had squandered a lead and not even been able to salvage a point.

Keeping their heads was vital – especially with the trip to Tranmere in the third round of the League Cup two days later. The Wirral club were going well in the Third Division but shouldn't have posed too great a threat for Millwall. They took a first half lead through McCarrick but Hurlock equalised eight minutes later and it was Hurlock again as Millwall took the lead early in the second half. Both were typical Hurlock goals similar to the ones that Lions fans had enjoyed at Leeds and Bournemouth during that famous promotion run-in and at home to QPR on the day The Lions went top of the First Division for the first time.

But that sunny day just twelve months before seemed like a world away as Tranmere hit back. More nervy defending saw Wood scuff his clearance which let Steel in to level and the entire Millwall defence were pedestrian as Bishop helped himself to the winner after finding himself completely unmarked in the penalty area. Millwall were out, humiliated and once again had surrendered a lead after fighting their way back into a match.

The fact that the attendance for that Monday night match at Tranmere was higher than the crowd that turned up at The Den for the visit of Luton five days later was little surprise. Elstrup cancelled out Ian Dawes' opener before half time and whilst a point was a welcome respite from three shattering defeats, the fact that Millwall had led in all four of their previous games and yielded a solitary 1-1 draw from any of them spoke volumes.

The optimistic Millwall supporter scanning the up-coming fixtures as they walked away from The Den a month earlier after that 2-0 victory over Sheffield Wednesday may well have looked at the next sequence of four league games against Norwich, Everton, Crystal Palace and Luton and understandably expected a decent return of points to help cement their top three place. They'll have also no doubt been excited at the prospect of moving into the last 16 of the League Cup. To have come out the other end with just a single point, hurtling down to tenth place in the league and being dumped out of the cup by a Third Division team will surely have knocked any bonhomie he may have had left right down the Old Kent Road. Especially when having a further inspection of the upcoming fixtures: Chelsea away, Arsenal at home, Liverpool at home.

These are the sort of matches that Lions fans were so desperate to see after gaining promotion to the First Division surely? Perhaps, when the Millwall machine was at full throttle and a match for anyone, but right now they appeared to have been thrown into reverse and were careering out of control.

The clash at Stamford Bridge was eagerly anticipated as the first league meeting between the two sides in over ten seasons. If Millwall were to pull themselves out of the same nosedive they found themselves in going into the last few games of the previous season, they were going to have to do it against a London rival. With so many teams from the capital in the top flight, including an unprecedented all four representatives from south London, local games came thick and fast and tended to throw the form book out of the window. Not so for Millwall unfortunately, who had managed just four wins from their 13 top flight derby games so far.

After a steady start, a familiar pattern emerged. Kevin Wilson beat The Lions defence to a through-ball and blasted home from the edge of the area on 24 minutes. Almost immediately Millwall had a golden opportunity to get back into the game. A great run from Carter through the Chelsea midfield got him into the penalty area on the left hand side and his cross found an unmarked Cascarino on the edge of the six yard box with the goal at his mercy and Beasant stranded, yet he somehow managed to get tangled up in his own feet and squandered the chance. Just 60 seconds later Lions goalkeeper Horne was caught off his line as Dixon lobbed home unchallenged and in an identical move ten minutes later Wilson made it 3-0. Game over. Dixon completed his brace with a neat strike twenty minutes from time to leave The Lions wounded from their second mauling in as many months.

What was particularly disconcerting about this performance was the overall demeanour of the players. As each goal went in, every member of the team trudged disconsolately back to their restart positions with no colleague within five yards of them. No player took it upon themselves to rally the troops, no encouraging pats on the back or even heated discussions about conceding took place. A solid unit of eleven that had stood shoulder to shoulder and regrouped almost as enthusiastically when they lost a goal as when they scored one twelve months earlier had now become eleven disparate zombies sleepwalking their way to another spirit-sapping defeat.

There was brief respite – and a healthier crowd – at The Den seven days later as Teddy Sheringham cancelled out Michael Thomas' Arsenal opener on the stroke of half time but there was a familiar feeling of inevitability about Quinn's winner on the hour. The early season fight that saw Millwall grab so many vital late goals had evaporated.

Just over 13,000 attended for the second successive home game – a televised clash with Liverpool. An error by Thompson let John Barnes in to head the visitors in front in the 37th minute but he redeemed himself with the equaliser just a minute later. A 70th minute strike from Ian Rush was enough to condemn Millwall to their sixth defeat in seven league games but they could count themselves extremely unlucky having given the league's two main title contenders a real run for their money yet again. The harsh world of top flight football is totally unforgiving and an anemic goalless draw away to QPR the following week with Millwall desperately missing the suspended Hurlock and injured Briley in midfield, completed a depressing winless November, extended that sorry record in London derby games and left The Lions in 16th place in the table. Panic hadn't set in just yet, after all a winless return from Chelsea, Arsenal and Liverpool was hardly a shock and one or two bad months could be survived especially as only a third of the season had been played. December would have to be different though. With winnable matches against Southampton, Charlton and Aston Villa to come before tough festive visits to Spurs and Manchester City, it was time for Docherty's wounded Lions to find their fight again.

15

Getting Away With it

The 1980s had been a typical rollercoaster ride for Millwall. After flirting with relegation to the Fourth Division for the first time in almost 30 years, they had finally made it to the top flight, but was the new decade about to start with another big dip?

The QPR match may have restored a little confidence with a first clean sheet in two months, but it also exposed Millwall's paper-thin squad. Teddy Sheringham was forced off after less than half an hour with a twisted ankle and Docherty was forced to push winger Paul Stephenson into his striker berth to partner Cascarino. Meanwhile Nicky Coleman made a welcome return to first team action after the unfortunate injury (sustained coincidentally against QPR) that had prevented him from playing a part in the historic first season's opening matches, in an unfamiliar midfield role. It was little surprise then that a single point was the best they could manage and when Paul Rideout gave Southampton the lead with an 18th minute strike at

The Den a week later, fans were concerned how their side could battle back without the talismanic Hurlock and strike threat of Sheringham. Fortunately a quick reply from Cascarino – his first in over a month – and a Stephenson goal midway through the second half seemed to have revived Millwall's fortunes and given them their first win since the 2-0 Den victory over Sheffield Wednesday ten weeks before.

Just when it looked like Millwall would complete the double over The Saints, referee Tom Fitzharris awarded them a penalty with just three minutes remaining. Matt Le Tissier duly dispatched the spot kick and two precious points had been snatched away from the unlucky Lions.

Self-pity is usually the beginning of the end for any football team, but Millwall could have every right to feel the fates were against them when they travelled to Selhurst Park to face a Charlton side that were once again spending the season camped in the bottom three. The Lions were now of course moving steadily downwards to meet them so the award of a first half Millwall penalty was the perfect opportunity to kick-start their ascent. As it transpired, Bob Bolder's spot-kick save was just the incentive Charlton needed and within seven minutes of the second half starting they led through a Scott Minto goal.

A season of struggle can be a toxic environment for young players to progress but that didn't seem to be the case for Steve Anthrobus who appeared to enjoy playing at Selhurst Park. He matched his equaliser that he scored against Palace with another goal to draw his side level but they couldn't find that all-important second strike and the winless run was extended into double figures.

The injury list was starting to grow too with Steve Wood now also out, joining Hurlock, Sheringham and O'Callaghan. Hurlock made his welcome return in the Zenith Data Systems cup match at Swindon four days later however and the 2-1 defeat was taken with a large pinch of salt. After all the last thing this Millwall team, which was being stretched to the very limits of its fitness, needed right now was more matches.

Of far more interest than that meaningless cup exit in Wiltshire was the staging of an England international at The Den 24 hours earlier when the B squad faced Yugoslavia. A healthy crowd of almost 9,000 braved the bitter December evening to see goals from Dennis Wise and Mike Newell settle a 2-1 victory – which the full squad replicated the following night at Wembley. The majority of the attendance were of course Millwall supporters, no doubt marvelling at the novelty of seeing an England team (albeit the Bs) on The Den turf. Unfortunately, another stark reminder of the injury crisis that Docherty's squad found themselves in was the absence of two Millwall players that would almost certainly have both played some part – if not all – of the match.

Terry Hurlock and Alan McLeary had made their B team debuts that summer but with Hurlock only just returning from injury and Millwall unable to risk losing the second of their regular centre back pairing, neither made the squad. It has to be said that Sheringham's injury almost certainly deprived Millwall fans of seeing possibly three of their players in an England shirt that night. For now however, with just one match left before Christmas, the focus at The Den was fixed firmly on getting three points against Aston Villa the following Saturday.

With Hurlock fit again it was a more familiar-looking Millwall side that lined up against Graham Taylor's in-form Villa who were emulating The Lions' top three challenge of the previous season which now felt like a distant memory. After a cagey first half, a quickfire double inside the first ten minutes of the restart from

Cascarino and Stephenson gave Millwall that long-awaited victory. Stephenson was now back in his customary wide position after temporarily filling in for the still-injured Sheringham. Making his debut up front alongside Cascarino was another youth prospect in Steve Torpey. Similar in stature and gait to Cascarino, his full top flight league debut came after he had previously made just one appearance, coming on as a substitute during the League Cup defeat at Tranmere. It was a win that restored some confidence and the glass-half-full brigade on The Den terraces could point to the fact that whilst it had ended a ten match winless run, the unbeaten streak was now four with the defence finally showing some signs of the resilience that had served them so well the previous season. It would need to be, with a Boxing Day trip to Tottenham next.

Millwall clearly struggled to rouse themselves for the 11:30 kick off at White Hart Lane and found themselves 3-0 behind not long after the clocks had struck midday. A second half Cascarino goal was little consolation for a shell-shocked Millwall who had now conceded thirteen goals in three top flight meetings with their north London rivals.

The year – and decade - ended in similarly bleak fashion with a 2-0 loss away to Manchester City. The newly-promoted Maine Road side were second from bottom and yet the ease with which they won the match with a goal in each half from David White must have been of grave concern for Millwall's managerial duo of John Docherty and Frank McLintock. The fact that the hardy souls who had travelled up to the north west to witness such a feeble submission greeted the award of Millwall's first corner of the game in the dying minutes with the same rapturous celebrations as if they'd just witnessed a last minute winner was testimony to their sense of humour. This was no laughing matter now however, their side were now firmly entrenched in a relegation scrap. Charlton, who The Lions had struggled to overcome two weeks before, were now rock bottom and only a point now separated Millwall and the bottom three. The one plus point from that Manchester City defeat was the return of Steve Wood, but it would obviously take time for him to get back to the same form that he found with defensive partner McLeary before his injury and time was not something that Millwall had going into the New Year. With Derby visiting The Den just 48 hours later, the last thing Millwall needed was distraction from the vital task of winning league points. The FA Cup draw meant that they would be making their second trip to Manchester City in a week, but that was just the start of the saga. Those first few days of the 1990s brought a record signing - and more drama.

16

Could Have Told You So

Millwall fans were about to get a late Christmas present, but unfortunately it wouldn't be long before some were asking if the club had kept the receipt...

Matches against Derby County seemed to have a habit of being significant for various reasons. It was against The Rams that Millwall played their first ever top flight match at The Den, celebrated with a 1-0 victory on a warm sunny September south London afternoon. That felt a million miles away when the two teams met on a chilly New Year's Day to mark the start of a new decade. Derby were also the last opposition of what will surely go down in the long and varied history of The Lions as their single most successful calendar year. A late goal that had given Millwall another win at The Baseball Ground on New Year's Eve 1988 was now also consigned to the happy memory banks.

Now, a year and a day later, things were very different. 1989 had been far more turbulent than Millwall fans could have imagined it would be. Hopes of FA Cup glory were dashed by the only time in living memory that the club managed to snare a prize home draw against Liverpool on surely the one occasion they'd have preferred not to, and early season promise dissolved into late term disappointment. The new season had got off to the best possible start but faltered badly and now The Lions were hoping that they could wipe the slate clean and start the 1990s with renewed vigor and get that roar back, but most of all to pull themselves out of a worrying nosedive:

Barclays League Division One
(Up to and including 26th December 1989)

	P	W	D	L	F	A	PTS
16. MILLWALL	19	5	6	8	27	33	21
17. Luton Town	19	4	8	7	21	25	20
18. Sheffield Wednesday	20	5	5	10	15	29	20
19. Manchester City	19	5	4	10	21	34	19
20. Charlton Athletic	19	3	7	9	15	25	16

Derby arrived at The Den to mark another red letter day in Millwall's history – the unveiling of their new record signing. In a strange twist, he was listed in the Derby line-up on the matchday programme having been snapped up by John Docherty completely out of the blue just a few days before. The continued absence of Teddy Sheringham prompted The Doc to smash the club's transfer record in shelling out £800,000 for 30-year-old striker Paul Goddard. The ex-West Ham favourite was to find out exactly what wearing the blue of Millwall entailed having previously donned the claret and blue of The Hammers even before the whistle had blown to mark the start of his debut.

During the warm-up The Lions' new record capture, who the club hoped would repay their investment by scoring the goals to help retain their precious top-flight status was told in no uncertain terms that his past would not be ignored.

Jimmy Carter remembers Goddard returning to the dressing room following the pre-match routine:

"Paul walked in and he said: 'I've just been massively abused. I'm the club record signing, I've just gone out for a warm-up and I've been battered. I've just been told to go back to West Ham!' We just said don't worry about it, just do your job and you'll be OK".

It wasn't the best of welcomes, and his rather quiet debut was probably more down to the speed at which his shock signing had come about and the bizarre nature of it coming against his former teammates rather than the lack of red carpet treatment he received from the Millwall faithful.

The concern on The Den terraces was that Goddard's arrival was the signal that there would be a major name going in the opposite direction. With rumours of interest in many of their star players usually rebuffed with the club doing so well, now that they had begun to struggle and signs of unrest in the dressing room seemed to be appearing, the vultures were circling. Had Sheringham not been injured it's highly likely that, at the very least, he'd have been the target of at least some Christmas window shopping by the big clubs.

The match with Derby ended in familiar frustration with Millwall's early lead courtesy of Ian Dawes cancelled out, leaving The Lions with just a point yet again after looking good for three. Just a week after their timid 2-0 submission at fellow strugglers Manchester City, Millwall were back at Maine Road for their third round FA Cup tie where they played out an equally boring goalless draw. Cup replays were not what Docherty's men needed right now, although the extra games would have probably been welcomed by The Lions' new signing Goddard in his quest to get the fans on side – and it very nearly worked.

Goddard's arrival was officially announced in the programme for the FA Cup replay with Manchester City:

Record signing Paul Goddard is convinced that Millwall have got the character, and more importantly the class, to pull clear of the First Division danger zone. Lions' manager John Docherty treated himself to the perfect late Christmas present when he paid First Division rivals Derby a cool £800,000 for the stylish striker's services. And although Goddard admits the transfer came `right out of the blue' he has already got his sights set firmly on winning a major honour with the Lions. "It was quite a shock when Arthur Cox called me in from the training ground and told me that he had accepted a bid from Millwall, explained the 30-yeard-old marksman. "Things had been going really well for me at Derby. I was happier with my game than I had been for a long time and I certainly wasn't looking for a move. "In fact when I told my wife she nearly dropped the phone! "But when I spoke to John Docherty I was impressed by how ambitious he was. He actually signed me for QPR when I was 14 so I knew him slightly and that certainly helped: "His views on the game are very similar to my own. We talked about the way he wants to play, how he saw me fitting into the side, and even what effect the club going public might have. "It gave me a good overall picture of the club and after talking to John I decided that the move would be good for myself, and for my family. "I had made a lot of good friends at Derby and leaving was a wrench, particularly as it meant breaking up a really good partnership with Dean Saunders. "But these things happen in football, and the flip side is that I am very excited at the prospect of playing with Tony Cascarino and Teddy Sheringham. "I like to play most of my football on the ground, Tony is great in the air and Teddy can do a bit of both, so I think we could develop into a very effective partnership. "If you want to be successful in the First Division you have got to mix things up. Liverpool are the masters at varying things and that's why they are so difficult to play against. "We have got to start picking up a few wins soon, and I can guarantee the fans that we will be giving it 110 per cent in order to put things right as soon as possible." The Lions' latest recruit admitted that making his Millwall debut against his old Derby team mates was 'a very, very strange experience.' "I only met the Millwall lads at their hotel on the morning of the match, and in the thick of the action I was struggling to remember some of the names. "I hadn't trained for about four days before the game and I certainly felt it during the last 20 minutes or so. "We made life difficult for ourselves by giving away a sloppy goal, but we fought back quite well and in the end we were disappointed not to win. "I know I can play a lot better and equally the rest of the lads know that they can play *to me a lot better. "But I am convinced that there is too much quality and character in the side for this disappointing run of results to continue much longer."*

A Jimmy Carter opener was cancelled out by a late Colin Hendry goal in a feisty draw, played in front of an encouraging crowd of nearly 18,000. It was a puzzle for the Millwall board who were desperate to get similar figures for league matches to boost the coffers and provide more squad-strengthening funds and they would have been encouraged by a similar attendance for the second replay six days later – also played at The Den by virtue of Millwall winning the right to stage it after winning a coin-toss at the end of the first replay stalemate. Boosted by the return of Teddy Sheringham who had scored on his first match back from injury in the 3-1 league defeat at Nottingham Forest 48 hours before, Docherty fielded an attacking line-up with Goddard and Cascarino also in the starting eleven. Cascarino was played slightly wide with Goddard playing off Sheringham in the centre as Millwall tried to utilise these extra matches to evolve their playing style into one that would not only finally see them through to a winnable home tie with Fourth Division Cambridge, but also gain the points required for surviving in Division One.

Millwall went on the attack from the first whistle and The Den erupted when Goddard prodded home the opening goal after just 90 seconds. It was a far from spectacular strike, appearing to scuff off his shin to bamboozle City 'keeper Dibble and squirm into the net, but it was enough to allow most of the Millwall faithful to forget – for a while at least – Goddard's West Ham baggage.

After nine minutes Sheringham made it two goals in two games and 2-0 to The Lions who were now in complete control. A Paul Lake strike just after half time temporarily let Manchester City back in the game but another Sheringham strike just after the hour sent Millwall through to round four at the third time of asking. It was an encouraging performance and created hope amongst fans that this new-look strike force of Sheringham and Goddard could be the catalyst for Millwall's rise back up the table. The last team you want to face when you're desperate for a morale-boosting win is Wimbledon and Bobby Gould's Dons frustrated The Lions efforts to get that elusive three points in a goalless Den bore draw before the visit of John Beck's Cambridge in the cup. Wimbledon should have provided the perfect warm-up for the similarly direct onslaught that Millwall faced in the early stages of the match with Docherty's old side. Also facing his former team was goalkeeper Keith Branagan who had taken over from the injured Brian Horne since that New Year's Day Derby draw. Their fourth-tier opponents were proving a handful and it was with some relief that Cascarino gave The Lions the lead two minutes before half time. Undeterred, Cambridge came out for the second half in even more determined mood and soon got a deserved equalizer. As unrest spread around the terraces, Cambridge sniffed a shock and came close on several occasions to dumping Millwall out of the cup. At the final whistle they were certainly more happy than Millwall to be heading back to The Abbey Stadium for a replay three days later.

January had been a tiring month for Millwall's injury-ravaged, wafer-thin squad and they lined up for the FA Cup fourth round replay at Cambridge on January 30th for their eighth match of the month. A typically cagey match saw the home side batter Millwall with long balls and roughhouse tactics. Just as Docherty seemed to be attempting to tweak The Lions' own direct style which had brought so much success but seemed to be too one-dimensional for top flight survival, the same tactics seemed to be unsettling them in a typical David and Goliath cup scrap.

After ninety goalless minutes extra time again loomed. With Bristol City awaiting the visitors, a quarter final place was very much up for grabs and despite their lowly league position, Millwall will have fancied a cup run now with Wembley enticingly close. Extra time played out to a similar pattern with Millwall appearing to just about keep Cambridge's battering ram tactics at bay and with the final two minutes winding down it seemed The Lions were heading for their second successive second replay and the toss of a coin to decide its venue.

Making one final foray into The Lions' half, an over-hit Cambridge pass toward the Millwall right back position was intercepted by Lions defender Thompson, with the home attacker in hot pursuit, the Geordie stopper played the ball back to the safety of his goalkeeper, only to put far too much pace and angle on the pass. Branagan was caught flat-footed and could only watch in horror as the ball rolled towards his left hand post. His attempt to claw the ball back from the line was in vain and Millwall had gifted their bottom-tier opponents a shock victory which, on the balance of play over two matches including extra time had barely been a surprise at all.

17

How Am I Supposed to Live Without You?

Millwall's season was quickly turning into a runaway train, speeding downhill with no-one able to slam on the brakes. Chunks were falling off it with every bump in the road and it was only a matter of time before drastic times called for drastic measures, but nobody saw it coming...

A cup-less February was probably just what Millwall needed to refocus on survival, but the calamitous manner in which they crashed out at Cambridge will have been giving both players and fans nightmares in each of the four days they had to wait to make amends. A trip to Hillsborough to face fellow-strugglers Sheffield Wednesday was an ideal way to pick themselves up but the few travelling Lions fans who made it (most were stranded on a broken down train and never saw the match) must have feared the worst when David Hurst gave The Owls a sixth minute lead. One bright spot from a new year that had yielded just two points – albeit in only three league games with the FA Cup getting in the way – was the immediate return to form of Sheringham who bagged his third in five with a ninth minute equalizer but once again Millwall were unable to turn one point into three and the winless league run now extended to almost two months with the visit of Manchester United looming. Far from being the ominous prospect that facing The Red Devils should have been, United were also struggling. That 3-1 defeat at Forest had finally dumped The Lions in the bottom three but Manchester United arrived just one place above them with manager Alex Ferguson under increasing pressure and only their continued involvement in the FA Cup seemingly keeping him in the job.

Barclays League Division One
(Up to and including 4th February 1990)

	P	W	D	L	F	A	PTS
17. Manchester United	24	6	7	11	28	34	25
18. MILLWALL	24	5	9	10	30	40	24
19. Luton Town	23	4	10	9	25	33	22
20. Charlton Athletic	23	3	7	13	18	34	16

On a bright spring afternoon, Millwall fielded two of their young guns to face Fergie's fogies. Twelve months earlier all the talk had been of Fergie's fledglings with several exciting youngsters making the breakthrough at Old Trafford but injury had deprived many of game time and now, with the proud old club slipping alarmingly towards the Second Division trap door, Ferguson was putting faith in more established stars such as McClair, Hughes, Anderson and Phelan. After a feisty opening twenty minutes on a ploughed field of a pitch, it was Millwall's youngsters that drew first blood. A mazy Carter run and cross down the left hand side was partially cleared but picked up by Darren Treacy. The flame-haired youth prospect had been brought in to replace the injured Hurlock. His neat dinked ball into the area was met by youth team-mate Darren Morgan who belied his small stature by rising with the towering United defenders to win the aerial battle and somehow flick the ball into the Ilderton Road End net past a despairing Jim Leighton. It was a brave attempt and Morgan was down for some time after scoring with a head injury, but it was typical of the battling spirit the diminutive midfielder had always showed in a Millwall shirt and was quickly endearing him to The Den faithful.

Millwall held on to their lead for just over an hour, with numerous chances to increase their advantage squandered, and just as a chorus of "Going down, going down, going down" rang out to goad the travelling United supporters, Danny Wallace prodded home a 65th minute equalizer after Hughes had been denied a very similar headed goal to Morgan's first half effort. Hughes had been a thorn in Millwall's side every time the teams had met and it was the Welsh striker that struck the winner with seven minutes left to leave Millwall, not for the first time that season, feeling extremely hard done by. Once again they had squandered an advantage, missed chances to add to their lead and found themselves losing by the odd goal. Injuries were also taking their toll once more. Sheringham was again missing and coupled with the absence of Hurlock, the squad simply wasn't strong enough to suffer losses to key players that made up the spine of the team.

For all the gallant efforts of the rising stars of the youth team such as Treacy, Torpey, Anthrobus, Sparham and Morgan, the side was crying out for top flight nous. Docherty had hoped that this would be provided with the arrival of Goddard but he had failed to add to that early goal he scored in the cup win against Manchester City and looked lost without Sheringham - with Cascarino seemingly an incompatible strike partner. Millwall's record signing was substituted in the 51ˢᵗ minute of the United defeat, replaced by Dean Horrix, another prospect of the Millwall youth set up from another era - and it would tragically prove to be Horrix's final appearance for The Lions. It would also be the end of John Docherty's Millwall managerial career. On Sunday February 11ᵗʰ, 24 hours after narrowly losing at home to Manchester United, Docherty was sacked.

As sackings go, no-one really saw this coming. There were very few calls from the Den terraces for The Doc's head. Patience was wearing thin, but there were no massed chants of "Docherty out", unlike the early days of his tenure when it only took two home defeats in his first three matches in charge at the start of the 86-87 season to have virtually the entire Millwall support angrily baying for him to be fired. Back then he took it all in his stride, almost as if he knew everything would work out in the end – which of course it did. But there are no happy-ever-afters in football, just new seasons and the renewed challenge of matching or bettering your successes of previous years, or pulling your team out of a slump. For a few months it seemed that Docherty had worked his magic again and reversed the downward momentum of that disappointing finale to the club's first season in the top flight. The Doc was certainly no mug, he had the experience and coaching knowledge to understand that he had to adjust the way the team played, but resources made his job virtually impossible and he paid the ultimate price.

Les Briley recalls how the players were as surprised as the fans by the sacking of The Doc:

"Things were OK. We never really saw it coming. There was nothing untoward as far as we were concerned, a meeting was called and it was: 'John's gone'.

Docherty's replacement was as much as a surprise as his departure. Bob Pearson was promoted from Chief Scout and took charge as caretaker manager for the shell-shocked Lions' trip to Coventry where Sheringham was back and hopes were raised when Cascarino gave The Lions a sixth minute lead but Millwall's resilience was now as brittle as glass and they found themselves 1-3 down by the 50th minute and tumbling to a second successive defeat after taking the lead.

Pearson's home managerial debut against QPR had a huge chunk of irony about it. The previous season Millwall Football Club arguably enjoyed the highest point of their 103-year existence when Rangers visited The Den. The euphoria of winning to go top of a league after yearning to reach it for generations and playing in it for just a few weeks was impossible to describe in mere words. Literally every single element about the club had clicked right into place. Supporting Millwall had touched perfection, it was the ultimate high, but as with all highs, there has to be a come-down. QPR revisited SE16 and a club in complete turmoil. Fans who had been cynically scratching their heads at the arrival of Paul Goddard and had been knocked back on their heels by the sudden sacking of Docherty were now incredulous that the task of saving Millwall's top-flight skin was to be placed in the hands of a man with absolutely no managerial experience whatsoever. He was held in high esteem by Lions fans who knew of his scouting work, but for most, a scout – or even a chief scout – is nothing more than the bloke who trawls around the parks of south London watching football matches and hoping to unearth the next rough diamond.

That was of course a harsh and wholly inaccurate description of any scout, let alone Pearson, but it was clear that the dissatisfaction of his appointment had not been kept under wraps. Cracks had started to form in the wafer-thin veneer of unusual harmony that had existed between club and supporters. The fanzine market had exploded and Millwall's first publication enjoyed a good relationship with the club after the initial suspicion of fans selling The Lion Roars outside the ground passed. A programme note soon after the first editions appeared in 1987/88 warned fans not to purchase it as it was not the official programme, but once their motives as a purely fan-produced mag were made clear the club withdrew their opposition. It was of course easy to get along with them when everything was going well. The truth was these home-made publications grew quickly as a voice of disgruntled football fans and their dissatisfaction with the way they were treated by various factions of the game – and the government. Prime Minister Margaret Thatcher had tasked her Sports Minister Colin Moynihan with introducing a controversial membership card scheme in the wake of the numerous instances of crowd trouble through her time in charge of the country. She had beaten the Miners and the Unions, now she felt beating the football fans would be just as easy, but she was wrong. Fanzines provided a vehicle to mobilise fans into successfully playing their part in defeating the move to force all fans to carry an identity card to attend a football match.

The announcement had come that the scheme was finally dead once and for all at around the time Millwall announced Pearson as caretaker-manager and by then, another Millwall magazine had appeared – No-one Likes Us – and the professional production and well-written editorials of both that and The Lion Roars pulled few punches on issues that fans took with the way their club was being run.

At around the same time, a new supporters club was set up. The Independent Millwall Supporters Club – IMSA – was never really intended to be a militant fans' union, although one of its founders Barry O'Keefe made no bones of their intentions to take club to task if they felt their voice wasn't being heard. Its main activities in its short existence was to organise subsidised away trips, quiz nights and meetings at its Champion Hill HQ – the home of local non-league side Dulwich Hamlet.

So with the voice of the fans now louder than ever – even without the omnipresent opinion of social media, both chairman Reg Burr and newly-appointed temporary boss Pearson made it clear in their programme notes for the visit of QPR that they knew of the bewilderment of the decision. First Burr explained the decision to sack The Doc and make his surprise appointment:

> *Many of you will be sad, as I am, at recent events. We all recognise John Docherty's achievements in getting us into the First Division for the first time in our long history, but unfortunately we can't live in the past and our record over the last 40, or for that matter 20 games speaks for itself. Reluctantly, and possibly belatedly, the board of directors decided that in the best interests of Millwall FC changes were necessary. With the most vital 12 games in our history to play, we felt that those interests were best served by making appointments from within the club. Bob Pearson may not have any previous managerial experience, but he has been at the club for 15 years and he is Millwall through and through. That's important. Millwall is a very close knit community and the directors felt that bringing someone in from outside would have caused unnecessary disruption. Appointing Bob wasn't a 'soft option' as some people have suggested. He has picked up a wealth of experience working under many different managers during his football career and he*

knows the players well. Now I am appealing to you all to get behind Bob, his assistant Frank Sibley and the team for the last three months of the season. Your support really can make a big difference. Thank you.

The message was accompanied by the now familiar image of Burr looking very serious but possibly more comical was the picture that accompanied Bob Pearson's opening managerial notes on the facing page. Dressed in blue slacks and black shoes and wearing a dark tank-top that would become as iconic as Gareth Southgate's World Cup waistcoat, 'Tank Top Bob' as fans would quickly dub him was shown entering the ground via its blue iron gate with the white 'MFC' letters at the top. His expression was understandably apprehensive, similar one imagines to that worn by the newly appointed Archbishop of Canterbury by Henry VIII.

He was saying all the right things though:

There's no disguising the importance of this afternoon's game. If we are going to get out of trouble we need to win most of our home matches - and one or two away ones as well. It's going to be tough, but I can assure you that we will battle every inch of the way to keep this club in the top flight. There's plenty of character and commitment in the squad, and although the players' confidence has taken a bit of a battering they are all determined to beat the drop. I learnt a great deal from last weekend's 3-1 defeat at Coventry and we will be changing our style of play slightly for the rest of the season, It's a gamble, but it's a gamble I felt I had to take because if I had kept things the same, I simply couldn't see us picking up enough points to get out of the relegation zone. Unfortunately I haven't got a magic wand, and I don't expect this change in style to put things right overnight, but it's something I felt we had to try. The players are all happy about it, they feel it's the right thing to do and hopefully all the hard work they've put in on the training ground during the last few days will pay off this afternoon. There's no way I can guarantee that we will stay in the First Division, but we are certainly going to give it a damn good try. I know my appointment surprised some of you, and I can understand that. I was quite surprised myself, but I accepted the job because the alternative would have been someone coming in from outside and frankly I think that would have been a shot in the dark. Okay, so I haven't got any managerial experience, but I have been here 15 years, I know the players well and I am confident that Frank Sibley and I can do a good job. Whatever you feel about my appointment, the important thing is that for the next 12 games everybody gets behind the team. The fans who travelled up to Coventry last weekend gave us some great vocal backing and if you can repeat that sort of support over the next few weeks I certainly won't have any complaints. We are all working towards the same end. It took this club 102 years to get into the first division and it would be a tragedy if we got relegated after only a couple of seasons. I think the relegation issue will go all the way to the final Saturday of the season and I honestly believe that we are good enough to pull clear of the bottom three. Hopefully we will take a step in the right direction this afternoon.

Unfortunately those words were to prove somewhat empty. QPR quickly assumed control of the match with goals from Barker and Wegerle. A Cascarino goal briefly gave them hope of salvaging at least a point but the ease with which Rangers held on to their 2-1 victory was worrying for Lions fans – especially with the prospect of a trip to Liverpool for the next match.

In a chaotic start at Anfield, Lions 'keeper Keith Branagan was caught in possession trying to roll the ball out in front of The Kop and as Steve Nicol crossed to the unguarded goal, John Barnes was bundled over and the referee pointed to the spot. Fortunately for Millwall Peter Beardsley sent his spot kick over and into the packed Kop crowd. Sensing some rare luck, Millwall held strong and went into the break at 0-0. Midway through the second half Millwall were awarded a free kick on the right hand side. Wes Reid, making his full debut for the club, remembers it well:

"I remember Jimmy crossed the ball and I saw Cas rise. It was something I had seen for the last two or three years, and I just thought: 'one-nil to us', I had no reason to think any other way, once Cascarino lifted, two feet off the ground, it was a goal."

Instead, the ball crashed back off the bar and moments later Liverpool defender Gary Gillespie headed home the only goal of the game from a Beardsley corner and Millwall fell to a fourth successive defeat – three in a row for Pearson. Reid's full Millwall debut had been a big plus however and his development to come through to support Briley and Hurlock could have proved vital to the team. Unfortunately, soon after, Reid's knee injury flared up again and his Millwall career was once again derailed. Yet again The Lions could feel they had been dealt a tough hand by the fates of the game, but events off the pitch were about to take a far more tragic turn to remind everyone just how insignificant mere goals and points were. Towards the end of the previous season, Liverpool visited The Den just days before the Hillsborough tragedy. The devastating scenes from that day put supporting football into perspective. Just under a year later, Millwall were to suffer a tragedy of their own just days after playing Liverpool.

Striker Dean Horrix had left the club in February. His opportunities had been limited since Sheringham's return to fitness and the arrival of Goddard. He had however proved a valuable member of the squad for the 12 months he spent at The Den during his second spell at the club. He had been part of the 1979 FA Youth Cup winning squad and enjoyed a successful goal-scoring career, netting 19 goals in 72 appearances for Millwall before moving on to Gillingham and Reading after leaving the club in the early eighties. His last match for Millwall had been a typically hardworking performance in that 1-2 defeat at home to Manchester United and soon after that he signed for Bristol City who were chasing promotion from Division Three. On March 11th, just hours after helping his new club cement their place at the top of the division with a 1-0 win at Shrewsbury, Horrix died when the car he was travelling in, driven by his wife Carol, crashed into trees on a main road close to their Basingstoke home. Carol was seriously injured.

The news shook the club from top to bottom. Horrix had been synonymous with the Millwall way. Breaking through from the youth team, the Slough boy wasn't a local lad but understood what it took to represent the club and knew exactly what the fans demanded. He was at the club for two of its proudest moments in its recent history – the 1979 FA Youth Cup victory and that unforgettable promotion to the top flight during his second spell at the club. It was particularly hard for Pearson to take. He had known Horrix since those Youth Cup winning days having snapped him up from Slough Rockets and seen him blossom as a player both at The Den and elsewhere. A promptly-arranged Friends of Millwall Dinner raised over £11,000 for the fund set up to help support Horrix's widow and two young children and an end-of-season testimonial was planned. Once again, as in the previous season, tragic events had shown how little numbers on a football league table really mattered, but the harsh reality was that life – and football – had to continue. Less than a week after the tragic news, Millwall had to pick themselves up to make the trip to Norwich to continue the fight to stay in Division One.

Jimmy Carter remembers the shockwaves that reverberated right through the close-knit Millwall family on hearing the shocking news about Horrix:

"That really affected the players."

He recalls with palpable emotion in his voice.

"The boys were in tears on the day and then we had a testimonial and the boys were in bits. Before the game both Deano's boys walked in to the changing room and that was tough, really tough."

The players could have been forgiven for completely going to pieces, but Millwall seemed to have a renewed fight about them and this looked to be enough to earn Pearson his first win when a 59th-minute Sheringham goal looked to be earning The Lions a surprise away win and a possible first step out of the bottom three. Once again though Millwall squandered chances to make the game safe and conceded a late Andy Townsend equalizer which left them second from bottom. Missing from that Millwall squad at Norwich was Tony Cascarino. The striker had left for Aston Villa for a reported fee of over

£1million shortly after the defeat at Liverpool but his departure, despite coming as both a surprise and great disappointment to Millwall fans obviously paled into insignificance in the light of the Dean Horrix tragedy.

Cascarino's departure was a great blow though. Not least because this was the start of the break-up of that legendary side that had won the Second Division title back in 1988, but also because he had matured into so much more than just a big target man at Millwall.

Cascarino's move turned out to be a closely-guarded secret and far from the arrival of Paul Goddard a few months earlier being support for the Republic of Ireland international, it appears he was a replacement as Briley explains:

> *"We didn't know at the time, but when we signed Paul Goddard, I think Cas' transfer was already a done deal. Cas didn't say anything, it was all a big secret but it all went through much later."*

To his credit, Cascarino gave his all in the matches he played in between that deal supposedly being done and it going through some months later and Briley was always full of admiration for him:

> *"He was a big loss. A huge loss to the club and to us as a team, he was a great guy, a great personality, he put his head in and put his heart in everything. He did everything he could for the club and we missed him."*

The atmosphere for the midweek visit of Everton was understandably subdued. It was the first time the news about Dean Horrix had chance to sink in to the assembled Den regulars and the common opinion was that talk of being relegated being described as a 'tragedy' really didn't wash anymore. The mood briefly turned light-hearted when Paul Goddard's second goal for the club gave The Lions a 40th minute lead. Comments of him costing "just four hundred grand a goal" wafted around the Cold Blow Lane and Halfway Line terraces for the two minutes that Millwall protected their lead. Goals either side of half time earned Everton a 2-1 win and three days later, defeat by the same score at Luton saw Millwall hit rock bottom. The Millwall board's motives for the managerial position were not clear. Was Pearson appointed for the remainder of the season whether they escaped the drop or not? Escape was now looking increasingly unlikely. Were they in negotiations with a new manager? When would he be appointed? Would they leave it until relegation was confirmed or make the move in the summer?

18

This is How it Feels

Millwall were on the lookout for a new manager, Director Peter Mead knew exactly who to go for…

There was little speculation about who, if anyone, would replace Pearson, but one option, put forward by director Peter Mead, would have shocked the game right across the world let alone in SE16 had he been able to convince his fellow directors to go along with the plan.

Mead explains, looking back at the spell when the board were considering a new boss:

> "I wanted us to go for Brian Clough. I felt it was better to pay big money for a good manager who could work with our young players than give a manager money to spend. I guessed Clough

would have been on no more than £250,000 a year which I think we could have bettered."

Obviously that never happened and Pearson was still in charge for the third 2-1 defeat in a row at home to Crystal Palace. Palace controlled the game, taking a 2-0 lead early in the second half before Millwall produced an immediate response from their new signing Malcolm Allen. Allen had starred for Norwich in recent seasons and his signature was seen as something of a coup – if a little late in the day for Millwall's cause. If The Lions were heading for the Second Division, with players undoubtedly leaving, he could prove to be a huge asset in the second tier.

It provided little antidote for the ignominy of being bottom of the pile – so soon after being on top of the world:

Barclays League Division One
(Up to and including 24th March 1990)

	P	W	D	L	F	A	PTS
18. Manchester City	30	7	10	13	31	45	31
19. Charlton Athletic	31	6	9	16	26	43	27
20. MILLWALL	31	5	10	16	36	53	25

The 1990s had seen the feel-good factor of that second Summer of Love less than two years before well and truly cool. Thatcher's administration, defeated by football fans in their quest for an identity card scheme were on a new crusade, with the introduction of the Poll Tax. A series of demonstrations across the country on the same day as that defeat to Palace erupted into violence, the worst being in Trafalgar Square. Police made 339 arrests and over 100 were injured in scenes reminiscent of the Miners' strike battles a few years before.

The following day, prisoners at Manchester's HMP Strangeways rioted and took control of the jail, starting a rooftop protest that would last 25 days and see one prisoner killed. 47 prisoners and 147 prison officers were injured and £50million-worth of damage was done to the prison which had to be virtually rebuilt.

The mood amongst Millwall fans however was slightly more upbeat – and certainly surprisingly so given their imminent relegation. A first half Dave Thompson goal gave them the lead in the next home game against fellow strugglers Manchester City who were nine points ahead of The Lions in fourth-bottom position. But City claimed a late draw and with just 15 points left to play for and matches against Arsenal and Tottenham to come, the end was almost at hand. Millwall travelled to Derby on April 14th knowing that defeat would mean relegation.

Derby, the side that had provided Millwall with their first ever First Division win, had been their opponents that ended that remarkable year of 1988 with a brilliant 1-0 New Year's Eve away victory and had been the team from whom Millwall purchased and gave his debut against to their record signing would now be the team to end the fairytale.

The result was never in any doubt, Derby controlled the game from start to finish and won far more comfortably than the eventual 2-0 scoreline suggests. Far from being disconsolate, Millwall's travelling fans treated the match as a celebration of their brief time in the top flight. Steve was there that day and his memories of it were far from morose, and bizarrely not particularly about the match:

'I remember we were pretty much singing right from before the game until well afterwards. No-one was bothered that we were

going down, we sang "The Football League is upside down" in celebration of us being bottom and "Going down, going down, going down", I don't think the Derby fans knew what to make of it. Then at half time, Barbara Windsor appears on the pitch to do some sort of prize draw or presentation. So we all start singing: 'where's your Ronnie gone', taking the piss out of her ex Ronnie Knight. My lasting memory of Millwall getting relegated from Division One was taking the piss out of Babs Windsor from the Carry On films. Mad."

Relegation confirmed, Millwall took the opportunity to make a fresh start and sitting in the Baseball Ground stands was their new manager, Bruce Rioch. Known in the game as a strict disciplinarian, the Millwall board felt the experienced but still relatively young coach was an ideal candidate to whip the now Second Division Lions into shape and the last four matches of the season was the ideal opportunity for him to assess the job ahead of him in what would be a busy summer.

A single Gary Lineker goal was enough to give Spurs a 1-0 win at The Den for Rioch's first game in charge on Easter Monday. Coming just 48 hours after the Derby defeat meant that the programme had already been produced and Bob Pearson's managerial notes appeared in it and there was of course no mention of The Lions demise. Next up was a 1-0 defeat at Aston Villa where Millwall faced Cascarino for the first time, and the travelling fans made their feelings towards the striker very clear throughout. This was followed by a 2-0 loss at Highbury. Once again though, the travelling Lions fans could see the funny side. More chants of "The Football League is upside down" rang out from the Clock End and outgoing Gunners' custodian John Lukic was playfully ribbed about his imminent departure and replacement by David Seaman. Lukic turned to applaud the Millwall fans at the final whistle and received a warm response to his gesture. This was relegation, but not as it had ever been experienced before.

It was Bruce Rioch's fourth match before he was able to finally address the fans in the programme for the final match of the season against Chelsea. It was also the opportunity, once again, for chairman Burr to explain the recent events, including the revelation (which he did not elaborate on) about the problems starting during the previous close-season:

> *We have come to the end of a most disappointing season. Looking back with 20:20 vision, our problems occurred pre-season but out of misplaced loyalty which I deeply regret, I failed to take the appropriate action. Unfortunately, the results are clear for all to see—the fault was mine and I am truly sorry. You, our fans, have supported us magnificently to help us achieve our dream. The dream is not over, merely interrupted. All our efforts and our energies will be devoted to regaining our rightful place in Division One.*
>
> *Depressing though it is, we must put the immediate past behind us. It would be wrong of me not to express our appreciation to Bob Pearson for all his efforts during a most difficult period. Bob will continue his task of finding and developing young and exciting talent as he has done so successfully for so long. We will be entering into Season 1990/91 with a new management team of Bruce Rioch and Ian McNeil. I need hardly tell you of Bruce's career which covered all the Leagues, reaching a pinnacle as Scotland's World Cup Captain. I am sure you will join me in*

welcoming Bruce to the Den and that you will give him and his team your usual magnificent support. I look forward to seeing you in August for what hopefully will be an exciting and successful season. Thank you for your support. Have a good Summer.

Fans could only speculate that the 'problems' were the lack of investment available, but the 'misplaced loyalty' comment suggested to some that perhaps Docherty's tenure was shaky from perhaps even before the end of that first season. At the start of the First Division adventure Docherty announced that they would be giving every member of that historic promotion-winning side a chance to play for the club in the top flight.

Some fans may have been disappointed at the lack of investment and perhaps would have hoped to see a few big names wearing the shirt. But that was soon forgotten when Millwall made that magnificent start and the players really did prove they were worthy of their new division.

The problem perhaps came when, having proved themselves and quite understandably gone back to the club for better deals, they were told that the funds weren't available. Had Docherty made a promise that he had no right to? One that the board of directors, desperately trying to fund a First Division club on Second Division attendances couldn't possibly keep?

Financially all was quiet. The club were still without a shirt sponsor and news of the share issue had gone suspiciously quiet – as had the investment in Tavern Leisure, an ailing pub chain which the newly-formed Millwall PLC had purchased in the hope to create a new revenue stream.

A Natural High – Millwall Football Club's two years in the First Division

In another odd twist to Burr's message, printed in a small outlined box just below where Burr had signed off was the following:

> *Quotes by Tony Cascarino*
> *Aston Villa Official Matchday Magazine — April 21st 1990*
> *"I enjoyed my time with them but things were not going too well this season so there was no way I could turn down the chance to move to a club who were competing with Liverpool for the Championship."*

It was a rather bizarre thing to reproduce, something which again, fans could only speculate about the motives for. Far more straightforward was Rioch's first message to fans on what would be the last time Millwall Football Club would play a match in English Football's top division:

> *First of all I would like to thank everybody at the Den for the warm welcome my assistant Ian McNeil and I received when we were appointed three weeks ago. Relegation had become a reality just 48 hours earlier, and I know from experience how disappointing that must have been for everybody connected with the club. Despite that disappointment all the staff and supporters I met after the Spurs game went out of their way to be friendly and offer Ian and I their best wishes for the future—it was much appreciated. I've also been pleased with the reaction and attitude of the players since I took charge. During the last four months they have had to work under three different managers and I know that can't have been easy for them. They have been through a lot this season and it had clearly affected their confidence, but*

A Natural High – Millwall Football Club's two years in the First Division

I've got no complaints about their spirit or commitment. The four games I've seen so far taught me a lot about the strengths and weaknesses of the present squad, and there is obviously a lot of hard work to be done. Part of the problem is that the side is badly unbalanced. We have only three left footed players at the club, and unfortunately two of those are injured at the moment. That lack of balance makes us very predictable. I thought we played some quite nice football against both Aston Villa and Arsenal without ever really troubling them where it matters, in the penalty area. The players who got this club promoted and did so well during their first season in Division One have now to prove that they can rise to the challenge and do it all again. There is a good base to build on here—and some very promising youngsters. I want to piece together a side which is capable of playing bright, attacking, entertaining football, and being successful at the same time. I'm not going to make any rash predictions about how long it will take. Obviously our aim is to get back into the First Division as quickly as possible. It's a big challenge, but it's one that I am really looking forward to and hopefully we'll be able to take a small step in the right direction by ending the season with a win this afternoon. Thanks for coming, and thanks to all the supporters who travelled to Villa Park and Highbury.

Just over 12,000 watched Millwall lose 3-1 to Chelsea, a match that, under any other circumstances, would have seen a sell-out at The Den. It was perhaps quite fitting that the last goal to be scored in a top flight Millwall match would come right at the end of the final match and by Millwall. Malcolm Allen's 88th minute effort in response to Kerry Dixon's perfect hat-trick for Chelsea gave Lions fans the chance to cheer a First Division goal for the final time. Just like the first, The Lions' second top flight season had been eventful to say the least., with many twists and turns, highs, lows and of course terrible tragedies that far exceeded the trivialities of a game of football. One constant during that ultimately unsuccessful second year however was that the team simply wasn't good enough. Another simple explanation is provided by Briley:

"Teams find you out, it happens today, it's always happened. We tried to change the playing style but injuries to key players in a small squad is also a factor too."

Millwall had simply had their fifteen minutes of fame. No-one was really that bothered, in fact Millwall's relegation that season was probably the least mourned demise in football history – certainly by other club's and fans but by their own too. For all the rumours of dressing-room unrest and financial shortcomings, that was the bottom line. There was no scandal or underhandedness that brought about the ultimate downfall, it was just football. Teams win promotion, teams suffer relegation, and then it all starts again from zero a couple of months later. It is this eternal cycle that allows us to enjoy the game and to quickly learn that, as football fans, it doesn't do to dwell too much on the bad times, but to make the most of the good and squeeze every bit of enjoyment out of it, because you don't know when the party will end and the hangover starts to kick in. It was perhaps a lesson that extended beyond football over those two years, borne out by the tragic events involving Liverpool fans at Hillsborough and Dean Horrix.

Sometimes it really is just a game.

All Our Yesterdays

Football's aristocracy, finally rid of the hoi polloi, brushed itself down, re-plumped the cushions and tidied up as if having seen off a naughty child who had come to visit for a few hours and trashed the place. Millwall, with a new manager on board enforcing a strict regime which wasn't to every player's liking, were desperate to regain their place in the First Division but it wasn't to be. A Play-off semi-final defeat to Brighton would be Teddy Sheringham's final appearance in a Millwall shirt. His 38 goals in that ultimately unsuccessful season had alerted the game's elite and ironically it was he that ended up playing for Brian Clough – only at Nottingham Forest rather than Millwall. Terry Hurlock had made a pre-season move to the Scottish top flight where Rangers' manager Graeme Souness obviously appreciated the midfielder's twin qualities of strength and skill and he quickly became an Ibrox favourite. It's hard not to agree that Cascarino, Sheringham and Hurlock were the key driving force in what was a very good team from one to eleven. Sheringham's departure saw the last of the holy trinity depart.

Thirty years after Millwall played in the First Division for the first – and only – time in the club's history, most of that squad are still in touch and meet quite regularly. Wes Reid explains a unique bond of not just ex-pros, but friends that would almost certainly not be replicated by any of this season's promotion-winning teams three decades in the future:

"From the elation of going up and the sadness of going down, it still resonates amongst us all now that we made in history in two ways. Firstly by going up but also by being the only team to have gone up in our history. In a way it's heartbreaking that we're still the only team"

Reid's passion for Millwall now is still evident, he talks enthusiastically about the club, the local community and the fans. For him, the dream of another Millwall squad etching its own name in the club's history and reaching The Premier League is still very much alive, and his pride at being part of the only squad to manage it thus far is warm and genuine.

As are the memories of the fans that were there of course. Nick Hart was involved in the *'No-One Likes Us'* fanzine toward the end of the club's stay in the top flight and currently produces the popular podcast *Achtung! Millwall:*

Sometime around 4:45pm on October 1st 1988, Millwall went to the top of the First Division, thanks a 3-2 home win over Queens Park Rangers.

It still seems odd to write those words. It remains the most outlandish event in my 47 years of following the Lions, topping even the FA Cup final of 2004 and the bizarre qualification for the UEFA Cup as a consequence.

One of the hard truths about age is the way in which your life, the precious memories that seem like only yesterday, very rapidly become 'history'. What seems so fresh in your mind, quickly takes on the same fragile yellowed quality of the Sunday morning News of the World league table page that I kept - and still have to this day.

Rather like one of the Venerable Bede's pages from the Anglo-Saxon Chronicle, it's a fact that goals from Tony Cascarino and two from Terry Hurlock took us to the number one position in the Football League. Yet now seems to mesh myth and reality together in a strange dream.

As far from logic as it may know seem, Millwall really could consider themselves title contenders as late as March 1989. And for that, the Lions' greatest team ever will always hold a special place in my heart.

Yes the photos of the time, with their swaying packed terraces, too short shorts and 1980s casual hairstyles all now look as far away as a Charlie Chaplin silent movie, certainly in the eyes of subsequent generations. But if I close my eyes ... I can still hear the guttural roar of the Cold Blow Lane end as we scored the opening goal at home to Derby, Everton and the late, late comeback versus Brian Clough's Nottingham Forest.

Suddenly the Lions were competing with the game's very best and were more than holding their own. The 1988-89 season remains Millwall FC's great gift to me as a fan. Something for which I will remain grateful to the end of my days.

As ever though, come the 1989-90 season, it turned out that the gift was in fact only a loan and in true Millwall style, it turned out that football wanted it back - and so we fell back into the second division never to return. Well no-one ever followed the Lions for the glory, did they?

Sometimes however, reality can out-match even your wildest dreams.

A Natural High – Millwall Football Club's two years in the First Division

As is the case with fans of all football clubs, the older generation will always bang on about 'the good old days'. I've no doubt the young fans of today who know no different from soulless breeze-block and plastic stadiums, half and half scarves, drums and music to accompany goals being scored perhaps tire of Uncle Albert-style tales of yesteryear, but at the same time I know for a fact that the current crop of Lions fans aged 25 and under are hungry for stories of the original Den and the time when Millwall were top of the pile.

People outside the club who lazily lump all Millwall supporters with the stereotype that the media has so readily attached would probably be surprised to hear the depth of feeling and appreciation of their past when it comes to what amounts to a Saturday afternoon pastime. As the words of the Everton standard rightly proclaim: "If you know your history, it's enough to make your heart go…".

BermondseyBoy, a Twitter regular and lifelong Millwall fan sums up what so many fans feel not just about Millwall Football Club, but what has become known as 'The Millwall Family':

I was born in 1967, my grandad, a docker, would tell me stories about a packed-out Den. It was the early 1970s before I started going with my dad and grandad. Until later blowing them out to stand behind the goal of the CBL end with my mates. It doesn't matter who you support, it becomes part of you, and that's what happened with me and Millwall. The early 80s brought dwindling crowds, the thought of playing in Division one seemed like a unattainable dream for a unpopular club from a rundown part of South London. Even the school I went to in Peckham, all the kids supported Liverpool. (Who were the popular choice at the time) Only me and a few other kids were 'Wall. We of course had promotions and relegations between the lower leagues and Cup upsets. Beating

A Natural High – Millwall Football Club's two years in the First Division

Chelsea 3-2 in the cup at Stamford Bridge in 1985, being a standout memory, with one of my favourite players at the time, John Fashanu scoring. I remember being absolutely gutted when we sold him. Then in 1986, a man named John Docherty, 'The Doc', had taken over from George Graham, who had left for Arsenal. My first reaction was "WHO?" If only I knew what a rollercoaster of a ride he would take us on. In his second season as manger he made Millwall history by taking us up as champions to Division one. I was 21, and have to say though we spent only two seasons there, they are some of my favourite times supporting Millwall. Briefly top of the league, drawing away 1-1 at Anfield and out-singing The Kop. With the likes of Sheringham, Cascarino, Hurlock and Briley we were feared by teams, reputations meant nothing to this Millwall team. The funny thing is, I remember seeing the same kids who laughed at me at school for supporting Millwall, now stood on the terraces at The Den. Almost 30 years on since being relegated from the old Division one, "Premier League" to the kids, and even though Millwall have achieved much since, an FA Cup final, a place in Europe, play-off wins, and numerous visits to Wembley, those two seasons under 'The Doc' travelling around the country with mates, I still see now at Millwall, will stay with me forever."

Social media and the Internet has allowed fans separated by hundreds of miles and detached from following their team for whatever reason to come together and share opinions and memories in the way they used to on the crumbly terrace steps or over a few pints in the local. It has its bad side too of course. I often find myself trying to defend Millwall on Twitter. It's pointless really.

More so than arguing the toss about Brexit, and that's saying something. I'm not pretending that Millwall hasn't had more than its fair share of trouble over the years and much of the harm the club has been done by way of fines and sanctions by the football authorities and being unable to attract players and lucrative sponsorship deals because of the reputation it has for violence and racism has been self-inflicted. Yet no other club in the country has done more for its local community and to rid itself of the societal problems that have attached themselves to all football clubs at one time or another. They have done it for over 40 years, long before it was seen as the trendy thing to do or to produce some nice-looking posters or sound bites for good PR. Try telling that to the latest 'expert' on Twitter however and they'll often come back with: "Well that just proves the problem is worse at Millwall then doesn't it?". Others will say: "I thought you didn't care that no-one liked you?". They have a point I guess. Why sing 'No-one Likes Us, We Don't Care' if we're going to take offence?

The truth is Millwall fans *do* care. Not so much what anonymous Twitter trolls accuse them of, but it's evident when you chat to the supporters – especially those who followed the club through the 60s, 70s and 80s – how important the club as a part of their local community as much as a football team is to them. It's *theirs*. So many other football clubs have lost this, they have become detached, isolated, fearful of familiarity with their fan base – and then they scratch their heads and wonder why the atmosphere on match days is more like a wake. Pre-match light shows and grown men in face paints and masks (the footballing-equivalent of wearing socks and sandals) won't do it. Pre-rehearsed songs and elaborate banners won't do it either. You can't fake that indescribably unique and unconditional bond between a football club and its fans. The modern era is erasing that because it's not good for the business plan. I say you can tie your business plan up in your half and half scarf and shove it up your arse. I want my football to be real, raw, spontaneous, and I thank the footballing Gods on a regular basis that my dad made sure Millwall was my team, because that's what they deliver time and time again.

I remember being a passenger in my mate Steve's Capri and pulling into Cold Blow Lane one midweek morning, we were probably picking up some match tickets. It was at the height of the club's success in 1988. As we parked up a brand new Escort XR31 drove out of the blue iron gates of the stadium. Behind the wheel was Millwall goalkeeper Brian Horne. Without even hesitating as we passed him on our way into the ground, we acknowledged him as if he was a close mate. It was a warm morning and his window was down and he looked across, winked and said "Alright lads" as if he knew us.

It sounds like nothing doesn't it, but we didn't acknowledge him like he was the famous footballer for our favourite team and we were just fans. We nodded to him as if he was one of us. He might have thought "Who do they think they are the cheeky sods", but I honestly don't think he did.

That was how the club worked then, and to a certain extent, still does today, and I don't think you get it at any other club.

Millwall still struggle to attract lucrative sponsorship and I have it on good authority that some player agents advise their clients not to sign for Millwall because of the fans. The modern day footballer who can set himself up for life with one or two decent contracts or transfers doesn't need to be told by a handful of supporters in the front few rows to 'liven the f*** up you lazy c***'. There are still a few though who thrive on the challenge of satisfying the exacting standards of Millwall supporters because, when it is earned, it must be the most satisfying feeling in the game.

When I set out to write this book I was excited at the prospect of unearthing some juicy tales. Perhaps of scandal or unrest or of some similarly previously unrevealed detail that led to the delicate house of cards that was Millwall in the First Division to collapse. I quickly discovered that wasn't the case, but far from being disappointed, I found even more enjoyment and pleasure in hearing about how time hadn't coloured the memory favourably as it often does, 1988 at Millwall Football Club *really was that good*.

I was 16. Life was good, and for the thousands of Millwall supporters lucky enough to share those golden days, it was the very best of times. Nothing can take away the happy memories, the buzz we got from seeing our team finally make it. For me at least, no drug or drink came close, but even for those that fuelled their party with Ecstasy or alcohol, these substances couldn't fog the magical memories.

If you were there, you *will always* remember it.

Acknowledgements

I would like to thank Millwall FC for their help and support with this book, especially Mark Litchfield. Also thanks to Wes Reid, Jimmy Carter, Les Briley, Peter Mead, Giuliano Maiorana, Nick Hart, BermondseyBoy, Big Chris, Ronnie Ball for their time and memories!

Also by this author:

Because My Dad Does – Me, Dad and Millwall.

A true story of growing up in the 70s and 80s, the murky world of junior football and how supporting Millwall forged a bond between father and son. Available at Amazon.co.uk and at www.anaturalhighmillwall.co.uk.

Made in the USA
Columbia, SC
11 May 2019

MIXED MEMOIRS

An Account of his Life and Business

by

Leslie G. Harris

Revised and extended by

Andrew D. Harris

Published by L. G. Harris & Co. Ltd

Text copyright Mrs E. M. Harris
and Andrew D. Harris

For information on the copyright of the photographs
please contact the publishers

First Published in 1985
Revised and Extended Edition Published in 2003
by
L. G. Harris & Co. Ltd
Stoke Prior, Bromsgrove, Worcs B60 4AE, UK

Printed by Arron Print Ltd, Redditch

CONTENTS

CONTENTS 3
PREFACE 6
PREFACE TO THE SECOND EDITION 7
MY ANCESTORS 10
MY FAMILY 15
    My Mother's family 15
    My Brothers and Sisters 22
MY LIFE STORY 32
    The White Star Line 35
    My Own Business 40
    Stoke Prior 43
    The War 47
    Engagements and Marriage 54
OUR FIRM AFTER THE WAR 61
    Our New Factory and Offices 61
    The Leslie Harris Employees' Trust 63
    Machinery Manufacture 68
    Other Activities in the 1950s And 1960s 72
    The Aerlec Site 73
SALES ORGANIZATION 79
    Show Material 79
    Our Sales Force 83
    Advertising 91
OVERSEAS FACTORIES 94
    South Africa 94
    Ireland 97
    Kenya 99
    Ceylon (now Sri Lanka) 103
    Portugal 107
    Turkey 108
    West Germany 110
    Singapore 110
FORESTRY 113
BRISTLE – OUR NEXT VERTICAL INTEGRATION PROJECT 123
PAINTERS TOOLS, HOUSEHOLD BRUSHES AND OUR NEW FACTORY (1974) 135

    Household Brushes 137
    New Despatch and Warehouse 139
    New Handle Production Line 139

JOINT CONSULTATION and THE INDUSTRIAL PARTICIPATION SOCIETY .. 140
    Trade Unions 142
    Industrial Co-partnership Association (later Industrial Participation
    Association) 143
    Management Research Groups 145

MURAL PANELS IN THE FACTORY 149

THE STOKE PRIOR BRUSH WORKS ARTS FESTIVALS
(Contributed by Mr George Chance, Festival Director) 155

PRISONS – AND REHABILITATION HOSTELS 175
    The Margery Fry Memorial Trust 181

FEDERAL UNION 188

AVONCROFT MUSEUM OF BUILDINGS 195

EDUCATIONAL AND RELIGIOUS INTERESTS 206
    Fircroft College 206
    Sibford School, Sibford Ferris, Oxon 208
    Birmingham University 209
    Society of Friends 209

HOUSE BUILDING AND HOBBIES 213
    Ridge End 213
    Golf 219
    Walking 219
    Music 219
    Theatres 219
    Photography 220
    Cars 220
    Travel 220

EPILOGUE 222

PART 2 224

MY FATHER'S LAST YEARS 225

SUPERMARKETS AND DIY 228
    B&Q 230
    Environmentalism 233
    Wickes 235

    Central Distribution 241
    Focus Do It All and 'own brand' 241
    U-Build and Retailers' margins 243
    Texas, Homebase and Great Mills 244

L. G. HARRIS & CO. LTD 1985 – 2002 246
    The Tea Break Dispute 248
    Our Sales Structure 250
    Our Pension Scheme 253
    Our Commercial Property 257
    Our Financial Results 1995 – 2002 265

OUR COMPETITORS 274
    Hamilton Acorn 274
    Addis 276
    Mosley Stone/Stanley 276

IMPORTS 279
    Our Chinese Factory 282

MY COLLEAGUES AT WORK 284
    Peter Harrison and Geoff Fox 284
    Glyn Lowe and Gary Jordan 285
    National Accounts, John Love and Stuart Hobbs 287
    Henry Reiner and Derek Starr 288
    Frank Redfern and his staff 290
    Douglas Wride and Paul Chandler 291
    Henry Wynekin, Brian Middleton, Geoffrey Braithwaite and David
    Cooper 292
    Dick Deeley and Robert Brooks 294
    Ramsay Eveson, George Chance and Ethna Harris 294

PREFACE

It has sometimes been said that to write one's autobiography is the 'ultimate vanity'. I have read many autobiographies over the years. They have nearly all been written by distinguished people of one sort or another: and very interesting I have found them.

I do not claim to be in the least distinguished. My autobiography and family history is not likely to be of any interest to people outside my immediate relatives, and possibly not even to them.

Why, therefore, write it? I have two excuses. The first is that in the genealogical tree of our family there have been at least one or two people whose lives I would like to have known more about. My ancestor William Harris (1802-1885) seems to have been a man of parts. We still have a very good painting which he did in 1832 of his father Joseph Harris (1775-1844). He also wrote a number of guide books in the 1840's - 'Halesowen', 'Clentine Rambles', 'Hagley Hall', and 'Dudley Castle' which are still extant. And William's brother Thomas Harris (1809-1890) is referred to in 'The Halesowen Story' by L. Schwarz, as owning in 1848 "The largest and most efficient button factory in the country, surrounded by flower gardens".

But today, we know practically nothing about William and Thomas's personal lives. If either had written his autobiography, it would have been very interesting to us 150 years later.

My second excuse is that I have lately been reading the autobiography of a rural curate in Herefordshire, written in the early 1870s. He was certainly undistinguished. But the account of his daily doings in the early Victorian period has provided us with a fascinating record of country life in those times.

So perhaps - who knows? - in a hundred years' time, members of our family may like to read about the life of one of their forbears.

Leslie Harris

PREFACE TO THE SECOND EDITION

I have long been interested in local history, and I know how valuable original family records are. National and international events are well documented, but local and family stories are not recorded anything like so well, and once those directly involved have gone, there is often a vacuum which is filled with hearsay and speculation. This can apply to quite recent events, as I know myself from having tried to discover some aspects of the recent history of my local village, which I have been researching. So I agree entirely with what my father wrote in his preface, and think the value of this record of his life, which he first published in 1985, is that it sets out the history of the company which he founded, and which in the sixty six years since it moved to Stoke Prior has played an important part in the life of the community. All those involved in building up the company in the early post-war years have now passed on, and, particularly in recent years, the company has changed considerably. Such is the pace of time, that I now often find myself the only person who can remember events from my early years with the company in the '60s and '70s. So I make no apology for bringing my father's book up to date and correcting a few mistakes while at least some of those involved are still able to tell the tale.

My father only printed a small number of copies of his book, badly underestimating the number of people who had shared his various activities and interests and who wanted a copy, so for many years original copies have been few and far between. The idea of republishing it first came to me in 2000, and I thought that at the same time I would bring the story up to date as, by the time it is published, nearly 20 years will have passed since he wrote it. Having re-read the book I think there are some omissions, particularly about some of my father's colleagues, and I have tried to put this right.

My greatest problem was how far to stick rigidly to my father's text. As the project has unfolded it became clear to me that it would not be right to repeat the original slavishly. Firstly, the text contained a number of errors, mostly about dates, which I have obviously tried to correct. Secondly, I felt that some of my father's literary characteristics obstructed its readability, so I decided to adjust his excessive capitalisation, the occasional rather erratic punctuation, and generally tidy up the text. I also felt that it would be a pity not to make the book available to a wider public by offering it for sale, so I decided to omit the rather long chapter on foreign travel and holidays (unillustrated in the original), also the section on his children, which the family felt was rather personal. Other than this I have made no substantial changes, but in a few places I have brought the events he describes up to date in square brackets. The original was lavishly illustrated, although the quality of many pictures was not brilliant. I have been able to locate nearly all the original photographs, and, using my own 'digital darkroom' scanned them in and tried to improve them where necessary. I have been a little more free with the pictures and their captions than with the main text. I have tried to position the pictures in a more logical and relevant sequence, and, to save space, put them in line of text rather than on separate pages. Many are also somewhat smaller than in the original, but I hope this will not detract from the finished result. For various reasons I have omitted a few of the original pictures, but I have used some new ones as well where I felt they added to the story. I have also rewritten many of the captions, in an effort to make them more informative.

Finally, I would like to thank my mother for her help with the text and the photographs – her memory of the events in this book since before the war is prodigious.

Andrew Harris, November 2002

Photographs in the preface: my father as a young man; wedding to Mary in 1942; speaking at a dinner for employees marking the 50th anniversary of his company in 1978; with his American niece Diane and friends; receiving a forestry award in 1981.

Chapter One

MY ANCESTORS

We have always had a family tree. But my wife Mary has unearthed a lot of additional information about our ancestors by studying wills and other old documents in Public Record Offices. Most of the details we have been able to discover are appended on the genealogical trees which will be found in this book. There has always been a tradition in our family that we were in some way connected with the famous Abraham Darby family, the third of whom built the first iron bridge at Coalbrookdale, Shropshire, in 1779 over the River Severn. Earlier Darbys had been responsible for other achievements of the first magnitude such as the application of coke as fuel in iron smelting, and the substitution of cast iron for brass in the early steam engine cylinders. Their fame has been perpetuated by the establishment of the Iron Bridge Gorge Museum, which attracts many thousands of visitors a year.

We have been able to trace that my great-great-grandfather Joseph Harris (1775-1844) married Mary Darby, daughter of William and Esther Darby of Green Hill, at St Martins Church, Birmingham, on October 13th 1801. William Darby's father William (1708-86) was the son of Edmund (1670-1746) whose grandfather Thomas was the brother of Edmund (d. 1668) who we believe was the ancestor of the Coalbrookdale Darbys. His great-grandson was the first Abraham Darby (1678-1717), whose success in smelting iron paved the way for the entire industrial revolution. The Harris relationship to the Darby family does, therefore, seem somewhat remote. Nevertheless, our family pride in the connection was evidenced by the naming of my grandfather William Darby Harris, and our elder son Andrew Darby.

My great-great-grandfather Joseph Harris taken from a painting done in 1832 by his son William (1802-1885), my great-grandfather.

Joseph Harris's wife Mary Darby Harris (1773-1848) from a print of 1841. (Below) My grandfather William Darby Harris (1842-82) in 1875.

The above Joseph Harris, with his wife Mary, not only produced some exceptional children, but also finished up a comparatively wealthy man, owning no less than 44 houses, according to his will made in 1842. It may be that his father Joseph (1747-1804) who kept the inn known as the 'Plume of Feathers' in Church Street, Halesowen, had laid the foundations of the family fortune; and some no doubt came from the Darbys. Very little of it came down to us in the 1940s!

Joseph's eldest son William Harris (1802-1885) was my great-grandfather and married Sarah Drinkwater on November 2nd 1829 at St Swithin's Church, Worcester (a fact which we have confirmed from the Church register). He was firstly a schoolmaster at Stourport, then wrote a number of guide books in 1844-46. These were to local places such as Halesowen and Clent. He was also a printer, and printed the books himself! We have four of these little books, which have been preserved in excellent condition. In addition he was quite a capable artist, as is evidenced by two paintings which have been handed down to us. Later he joined the firm of Rabone Brothers of Birmingham, now Rabone Petersen Ltd, as a designer and salesman, and we believe represented them at the Crystal Palace Exhibition in 1851. Truly a man for all seasons!

William was married twice, first to Sarah Drinkwater (d.1872) and secondly in 1874 (at the age of 72) to Hannah Salt, who was a member of a family related to a minor poet of that time, William Salt. His first marriage produced nine children between 1832 and 1842: eight

My grandmother Elizabeth Anne Harris, née Burgum (1846-1916) in (right) 1875 and (below) 1914.

daughters, then finally one son, my grandfather William Darby Harris (1842-1882). One of the daughters was my great-aunt Ada Lucy (1847-1942). Well known in her day as a concert singer, Ada Bellamy, she was a delightful old lady, and visited us at Mill House in 1940 in her 93rd year. We still have a beautiful crocheted tablecloth which she gave us.

William Harris's will, written in 1882, contains some interesting clauses. He left his second wife all his real estate, "provided that she remains my widow and lives a chaste and prudent life". The will went on to direct his Trustees that his widow should "make provision of food, clothing and lodging for my daughter Selina Ellen Harris while she remains unmarried". If it was found that "my said wife and daughter cannot agree to live amicably together", his widow was directed to make Selina an allowance of five shillings per week. In the event of her refusing or failing to comply with the stipulation, the trustees were directed to take over the income from the estate and pay Selina her five shillings a week, the rest going to the widow. Evidently, William anticipated some trouble as his second wife Hannah was five years younger than his daughter. The original will left "three dwelling houses situate at Black Lake, Hill Top, West Bromwich", to William's son William Darby Harris (my grandfather). Unfortunately, after my grandfather predeceased his own father in 1883, a codicil was added to the will directing that only one-sixth part of William Darby's legacy should be divided among the latter's four sons, of which my father was one. So this explains why our generation didn't inherit the Harris wealth! William's brother Joseph Harris (1805-1872) who married another Darby, Ann Elizabeth a niece of Mary Darby, carried on the family trade of button manufacturer at Halesowen and St Paul's Square, Birmingham. Another brother, Thomas (1809-1890) achieved the distinction of being referred to in a book 'The Halesowen Story' by Lena Schwarz, as "the most efficient button manufacturer in the country" in his factory at Halesowen. His factory was ultimately absorbed by James Grove & Sons Ltd of Halesowen, a firm which still exists. Thomas's son William (b.1834) was also a button manufacturer, carrying on his father's business at Spring Hill, Halesowen. In the Worcestershire directory of 1876, he is described as employing 4 men, 10 women and 15 children. It seems that button manufacturing ran in the family's blood.

My father's father, William Darby Harris (1842-82) had been in partnership with a man named Smith in a stamping and piercing business in Birmingham. When he died, my father, who was studying engineering and only 18 at the time, joined Mr Smith in the small firm, while continuing his engineering studies. Before he received his appointment with the Birmingham Education Department in 1892, my father was apparently carrying on business as a die sinker, toolmaker, stamper and piercer, at 7 Caroline Street, St Paul's, Birmingham, according to an old business card in our possession. He married my mother, Florence Ann Deakin (1863-1943) at St George's Church, Edgbaston in 1893.

A family outing – my father (back row with cap), my mother holding baby Elsie. My uncle William Deakin is with a pipe, his wife Selina with daughters in front. Their sons Herbert (holding bike) with Ernest. My cousin Ada left of my father.

At 112 Oak Tree Lane, Selly Oak in 1913. Frank, Mabel and Elsie at the back, with mother, myself and father in front.

Chapter 2

MY FAMILY

My father (1866-1935) was the eldest of four brothers. Harry John Harris (1868-1943) at one time carried on a nursery business in Enfield, Middlesex. I believe one of his sons went to Rhodesia (Zimbabwe). A daughter, Sybil Olley, is still alive at the time of writing (1984), living at 65 Victoria Road, Woking, Surrey. Another daughter, Gwen, is also still with us.

Frank Herbert Harris, my father's second brother (1872-1947), emigrated to British Columbia in 1920. He ran a successful apple growing farm in the Okanagan Valley, near Vernon, B.C. His son Donald, who died in 1975, practised as a chiropractor. With our sons Andrew and Richard I visited him and his wife Maud in 1960 in their delightful house on the side of a lake, near Oyama, B.C. Donald's daughter, Barbara, married Bill Cashen, an engineer. They had four children, Don, Chris, Robbie, and Wendy. In 1983, their address was R.R.2, Bethany, Ont. Barbara's sister Marion had two children, and Barbara and Bill had visited us at Mill House when Bill was working in England. She was living in Ottawa when we heard from her in 1982. Frank Herbert Harris had another son Dick with whom we lost touch.

My father's third brother Alfred Harris (1880-1952) also emigrated to Canada, making his career as secretary/accountant to Imperial Oil Ltd, Calgary. He visited us in England with his wife Muriel in 1952, but died shortly after his return to Canada. His widow died in 1966. They had one child, a daughter who was physically infirm and died young.

My Mother's family

My mother's grandfather John Deakin (1773-1870) owned Fast Pits Farm, Yardley, Birmingham. We have a photograph of an old painting of him seated in the kitchen of the farmhouse (see p. 17). We believe that Deakins Lane, Yardley, was named after him. His son William Henry (1819-1912) (my mother's father) started a small presswork business carried on in 1880 at 140 Hampton Street, Birmingham. This was afterwards continued by his son, my uncle, also William Henry (1860-1918). His firm, William Deakin & Co Ltd, which was later transferred to George Street, Parade, Birmingham, became very prosperous, and

(Above) My father William George Harris aged 22 in 1888 and (below) aged 47 in 1913. (Right) My mother Florence Ann Deakin aged 19 in 1882 and (below) later in life.

(Above left) My maternal grandfather William Henry Deakin (1819-1912) in 1869. (Above right) My mother's brother William Deakin (1860-1918). (Below) My maternal great-grandfather John Deakin (1773-1870), from a painting of him in the kitchen of his farmhouse.

William was one of the first motorists in Birmingham, owning a 'De Dion Bouton' car in the early 1900s. I remember that he used to call for our family and take us rides in his car, which had seats facing each other, entered from a gate at the back. The family lived in a large house in Wentworth Road, Harborne, Birmingham. They were our rich relations, and maintained a chauffeur and domestic staff.

My mother, Florence Ann Deakin (1863-1943) was the youngest child of the family of four sisters and two brothers. Her elder sister Sarah (1845-1916) was married three times. Her first husband was a Mr Harding, of the firm of Heaton and Dugard Ltd, Birmingham. Secondly she married a Mr Joyce, and thirdly a Mr Devall. She became a wealthy lady and lived in her later years in City Road, Edgbaston, where she kept domestic staff. She had an imperious bearing and was known as the family battle-axe! Her daughter Ada (my cousin) married a man named Walter Bott,

1905 - the Harris family outside 29 Beech Rd, Bournville, Birmingham. Mother holding baby Leslie and (left to right) Frank, Mabel and Elsie.

who worked for a firm of maltsters in Lincoln. Ada's daughter Dorothy married a Professor Brooks of Hull University. Another daughter, Enid, who was the wife of Leslie Whitehead of Farnborough, Hants, died in 1975. Their daughter Jane, was at Cambridge University with our son Andrew in 1964. Jane now lives in Marlborough (1984) and is on the staff of Bristol University.

My mother's sister Kate Deakin (1857-1946), who married a man named George Hill, had one son, William, and two daughters, Florence and Miriam, both beautiful ladies. Florence, my cousin, married a Dr Reynolds, who was chief chemist at Reckitt and Colman, Hull, and was the inventor of the antiseptic Dettol. Their daughter Gladys married Rev Edward Stanford, a Methodist Minister. Florence Reynolds had two other children, Greta and Jack, neither of whom married. Her sister Miriam (also my cousin), who died in about 1947, married Francis Harrison, who had inherited his father's manufacturing jewellery business, Jas. Harrison & Sons Ltd, Tenby Street, Birmingham. His sons Trevor (born 1903) and Peter (born 1910) both went into the family business, but Peter soon left it and joined my company L. G. Harris & Co Ltd in Stoke Prior, as sales

The Harris family in 1922. Frank and Leslie at the back, mother, father and Mabel in front. Frank was aged 25 in 1922, the year before he emigrated to the United States, working for the American Smelting and Refining Co. in Baltimore, Maryland.

manager in 1938. He retired after a long and pleasant association with the present writer in 1975. The younger brother James went into the family's optical concern, his wife Joan dying after a long illness of multiple sclerosis, about 1978. He married again in 1984 Eugenie, the widow of Robert Danielsen.

I hope all these details do not seem too tedious. But I am setting down the facts as I have known them. They may be interesting to others who undertake more family research.

Turning now to my own immediate family, my father William George (1866-1935) was employed for the main part of his career by the Birmingham Education Department as Heating Engineer and Inspector of School Caretakers (a joint appointment). He was a kindly man, devoted to his family. Very interested in the Adult School movement, he used to play the organ on Sunday mornings at the Adult School held at Fircroft College, Oak Tree Lane, Bournville. He was

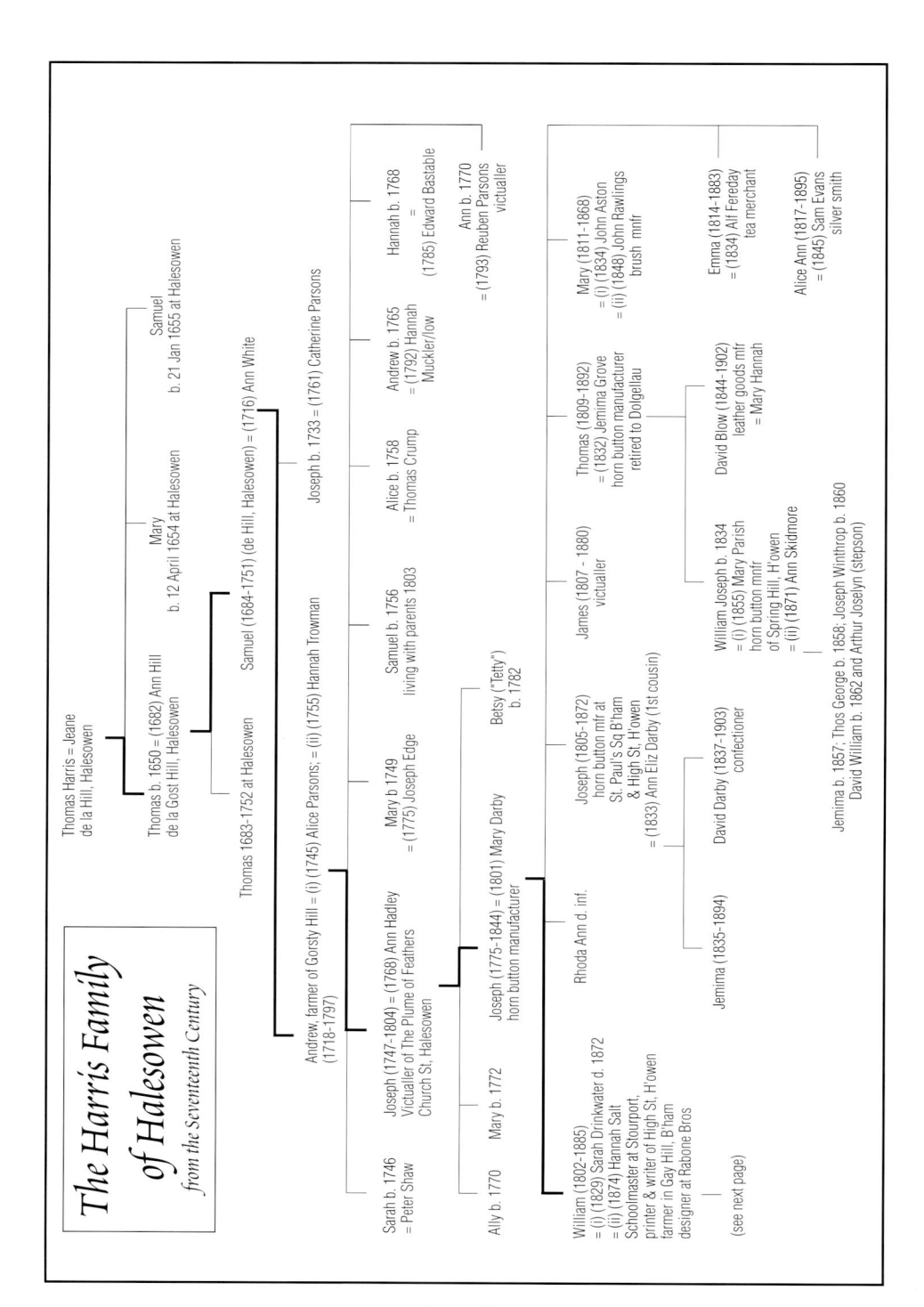

The Harris Family of Halesowen

from the Seventeenth Century

Thomas Harris = Jeane
de la Hill, Halesowen

┌─────────────────────────┬─────────────────────────┐
Thomas b. 1650 = (1682) Ann Hill   Mary   Samuel
de la Gost Hill, Halesowen   b. 12 April 1654   b. 21 Jan 1655
                                    at Halesowen   at Halesowen

Thomas 1683-1752 at Halesowen

Samuel (1684-1751) (de Hill, Halesowen) = (1716) Ann White

= (i) (1745) Alice Parsons; = (ii) (1755) Hannah Trowman   Joseph b. 1733 = (1761) Catherine Parsons

Andrew, farmer of Gorsty Hill
(1718-1797)

- Sarah b. 1746 = Peter Shaw
- Joseph (1747-1804) = (1768) Ann Hadley, Victualler of The Plume of Feathers Church St, Halesowen
- Mary b. 1749 = (1775) Joseph Edge
- Samuel b. 1756 living with parents 1803
- Alice b. 1758 = Thomas Crump
- Andrew b. 1765 = (1792) Hannah Muckler/low
- Hannah b. 1768 = (1785) Edward Bastable
- Ann b. 1770 = (1793) Reuben Parsons, victualler

Joseph (1775-1844) = (1801) Mary Darby
horn button manufacturer

- Ally b. 1770
- Mary b. 1772
- Joseph (1775-1844) = (1801) Mary Darby
- Betsy ("Tetty") b. 1782

Children of Joseph & Mary Darby:

- William (1802-1885)
  = (i) (1829) Sarah Drinkwater d. 1872
  = (ii) (1874) Hannah Salt
  Schoolmaster at Stourport, printer & writer of High St, H'owen farmer in Gay Hill, B'ham designer at Rabone Bros
  (see next page)
- Joseph (1805-1872) horn button mfr at St. Paul's Sq B'ham & High St, H'owen = (1833) Ann Eliz Darby (1st cousin)
- James (1807 - 1880) victualler
- Thomas (1809-1892) = (1832) Jemima Grove horn button manufacturer retired to Dolgellau
- Mary (1811-1868) = (i) (1834) John Aston = (ii) (1848) John Rawlings brush mnfr
- Emma (1814-1883) = (1834) Alf Fereday tea merchant
- Alice Ann (1817-1895) = (1845) Sam Evans silver smith
- Rhoda Ann d. inf.

Children of Joseph (1805-1872) & Ann Eliz Darby:

- David Darby (1837-1903) confectioner
- Jemima (1835-1894)
- William Joseph b. 1834
  = (i) (1855) Mary Parish horn button mfr of Spring Hill, H'owen
  = (ii) (1871) Ann Skidmore
- David Blow (1844-1902) leather goods mfr = Mary Hannah

Jemima b. 1857; Thos George b. 1858; Joseph Winthrop b. 1860
David William b. 1862 and Arthur Joselyn (stepson)

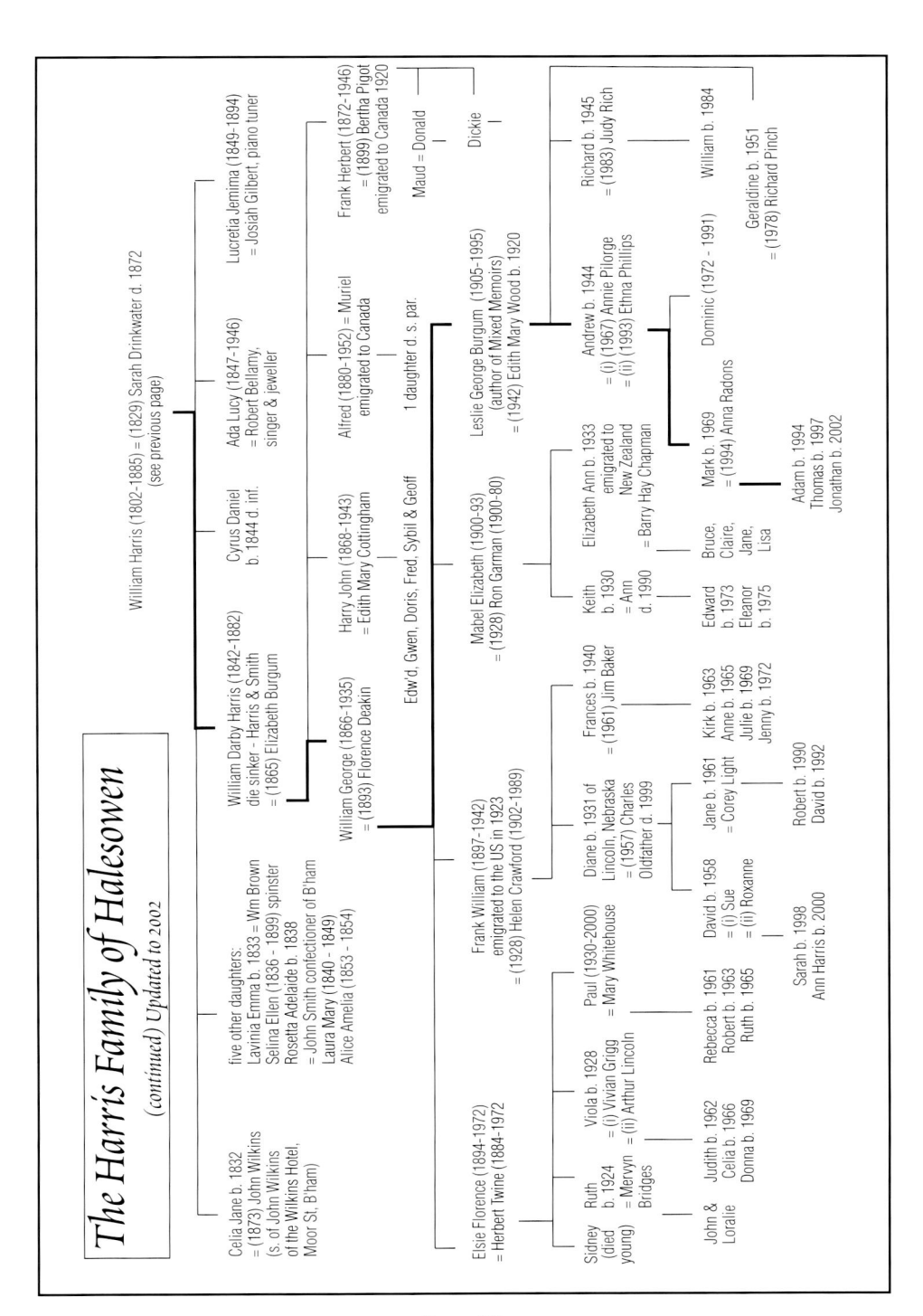

The Harris Family of Halesowen

(continued) Updated to 2002

William Harris (1802-1885) = (1829) Sarah Drinkwater d. 1872
(see previous page)

Children of William Harris and Sarah Drinkwater:

- Celia Jane b. 1832 = (1873) John Wilkins (s. of John Wilkins of the Wilkins Hotel, Moor St, B'ham)
- five other daughters:
  - Lavinia Emma b. 1833 = Wm Brown
  - Selina Ellen (1836 - 1899) spinster
  - Rosetta Adelaide b. 1838 = John Smith confectioner of B'ham
  - Laura Mary (1840 - 1849)
  - Alice Amelia (1853 - 1854)
- William Darby Harris (1842-1882) die sinker - Harris & Smith = (1865) Elizabeth Burgum
- Cyrus Daniel b. 1844 d. inf.
- Ada Lucy (1847-1946) = Robert Bellamy, singer & jeweller
- Lucretia Jemima (1849-1894) = Josiah Gilbert, piano tuner

Children of William Darby Harris and Elizabeth Burgum:

- William George (1866-1935) = (1893) Florence Deakin
- Harry John (1868-1943) = Edith Mary Cottingham
  - Edw'd, Gwen, Doris, Fred, Sybil & Geoff
- Alfred (1880-1952) = Muriel emigrated to Canada
  - 1 daughter d. s. par.
- Frank Herbert (1872-1946) = (1899) Bertha Pigot emigrated to Canada 1920
  - Maud = Donald
  - Dickie

Children of William George Harris and Florence Deakin:

- Elsie Florence (1894-1972) = Herbert Twine (1884-1972)
- Frank William (1897-1942) emigrated to the US in 1923 = (1928) Helen Crawford (1902-1989)
- Mabel Elizabeth (1900-93) = (1928) Ron Garman (1900-80)
- Leslie George Burgum (1905-1995) (author of Mixed Memoirs) = (1942) Edith Mary Wood b. 1920

Children of Elsie Florence and Herbert Twine:

- Sidney (died young)
- Ruth b. 1924 = Mervyn Bridges
- Viola b. 1928 = (i) Vivian Grigg = (ii) Arthur Lincoln
- Paul (1930-2000) = Mary Whitehouse

Children of Frank William and Helen Crawford:

- Diane b. 1931 of Lincoln, Nebraska = (1957) Charles Oldfather d. 1999
- Frances b. 1940 = (1961) Jim Baker
- David b. 1958 = (i) Sue = (ii) Roxanne

Children of Mabel Elizabeth and Ron Garman:

- Kirk b. 1963
- Anne b. 1965
- Julie b. 1969
- Jenny b. 1972

Children of Leslie George Burgum and Edith Mary Wood:

- Elizabeth Ann b. 1933 emigrated to New Zealand = Barry Hay Chapman
  - Bruce, Claire, Jane, Lisa
- Keith b. 1930 = Ann d. 1990
  - Edward b. 1973
  - Eleanor b. 1975
- Andrew b. 1944 = (i) 1967 Annie Pilorge = (ii) 1993 Ethna Phillips
  - Dominic (1972 - 1991)
  - Mark b. 1969 = (1994) Anna Radons
    - Adam b. 1994
    - Thomas b. 1997
    - Jonathan b. 2002
- Richard b. 1945 = (1983) Judy Rich
  - Geraldine b. 1951 = (1978) Richard Pinch
  - William b. 1984

Children of Ruth and Mervyn Bridges:

- John & Loralie
- Judith b. 1962
- Celia b. 1966
- Donna b. 1969

Children of Viola:

- Rebecca b. 1961
- Robert b. 1963
- Ruth b. 1965

Children of Frances and Jim Baker:

- Jane b. 1961 = Corey Light
  - Robert b. 1990
  - David b. 1992

Children of David:

- Sarah b. 1998
- Ann Harris b. 2000

also a member of the Bournville Village Council. We have a photograph of him (right) with other members of the Council in 1906, when Mr George Cadbury junior was Chairman. My father is at the back on the right, next to George Cadbury.

My father had strong socialist sympathies, and I remember he used to subscribe to a Labour periodical known as The Clarion, edited by Robert Blatchford. Although, as a Birmingham Council official, he had no need to be a member of a Trade Union, he nevertheless belonged to one (I think it was the Engineers) and one of my jobs as a boy was regularly to take his Union dues to the Secretary, Mr Tallis, who lived in Northfield. My father was a fine figure of a man, tending to become stout in his later years. Sadly, in 1931, when he was about to retire, he suffered a series of strokes. For the last three years of his life he lost the power of speech, and was physically helpless, looked after devotedly by my mother. He died in 1935.

My mother Florence (1863-1943), who retained her good looks until late in life, was known by most people who knew her as a sweet lady, devoted to her family. After my father's death in 1935, I lived with her in our house at 112 Oak Tree Lane, Selly Oak (my brother and two sisters having married and left home) until 1939, when we moved to a large Victorian house in the grounds of the Mill which I had taken over as a factory at Stoke Prior, near Bromsgrove. My mother's sister, my Aunt Kate, later joined us for a time in this house but left to live with other relations and finally in a nursing home. My mother, who became increasingly frail, went to live with my sister Mabel where she died in 1943.

My Brothers and Sisters

My eldest sister Elsie (1894-1972) had several accomplishments. After studying for a year in 1911 at the Pupil Teachers Centre in Bath Row, Birmingham, she spent two years at Exeter College, receiving her Teaching Diploma in 1914. The Principal of the College at that time was Miss Amy Walker, a cousin of my

The Deakin Family of Yardley, Worcs

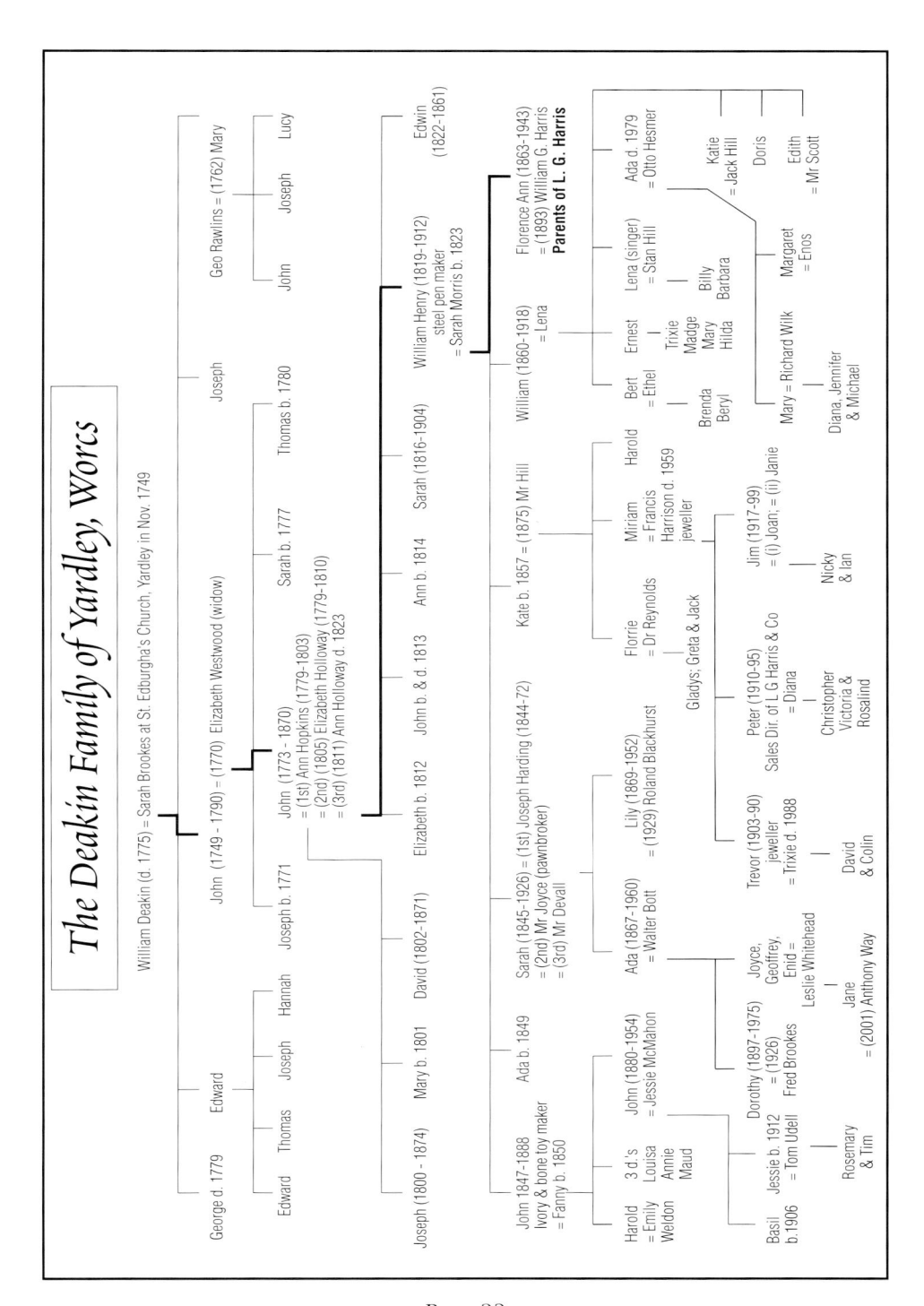

William Deakin (d. 1775) = Sarah Brookes at St. Edburgha's Church, Yardley in Nov. 1749

John (1749 - 1790) = (1770) Elizabeth Westwood (widow)   Joseph   Geo Rawlins = (1762) Mary

George d. 1779   Edward   Thomas   Joseph   Hannah   Joseph b. 1771   John (1773 - 1870)   Sarah b. 1777   Thomas b. 1780   John   Joseph   Lucy
- (1st) Ann Hopkins (1779-1803)
- (2nd) (1805) Elizabeth Holloway (1779-1810)
- (3rd) (1811) Ann Holloway d. 1823

Edward   Mary b. 1801   David (1802-1871)   Elizabeth b. 1812   John b. & d. 1813   Ann b. 1814   Sarah (1816-1904)   William Henry (1819-1912) steel pen maker = Sarah Morris b. 1823   Edwin (1822-1861)

Joseph (1800 - 1874)   Ada b. 1849   Sarah (1845-1926) = (1st) Joseph Harding (1844-72) = (2nd) Mr Joyce (pawnbroker) = (3rd) Mr Devall   Kate b. 1857 = (1875) Mr Hill   William (1860-1918) = Lena   Florence Ann (1863-1943) = (1893) William G. Harris **Parents of L. G. Harris**

John 1847-1888 Ivory & bone toy maker = Fanny b. 1850   Ada (1867-1960) = Walter Bott   Lily (1869-1952) = (1929) Roland Blackhurst   Florrie = Dr Reynolds   Miriam = Francis Harrison d. 1959 jeweller   Harold   Bert = Ethel   Ernest   Lena (singer) = Stan Hill   Ada d. 1979 = Otto Hesmer

Harold = Emily Weldon   3 d's Louisa Annie Maud   John (1880-1954) = Jessie McMahon   Dorothy (1897-1975) = (1926) Fred Brookes   Joyce, Geoffrey, Enid, = Leslie Whitehead   Trevor (1903-90) jeweller = Trixie d. 1988   Peter (1910-95) Sales Dir. of L G Harris & Co = Diana   Jim (1917-99) = (i) Joan; = (ii) Janie   Brenda Beryl   Trixie Madge Mary Hilda   Billy Barbara   Margaret = Enos   Katie = Jack Hill   Doris   Edith = Mr Scott

Basil b. 1906   Jessie b. 1912 = Tom Udell   Jane = (2001) Anthony Way   Gladys; Greta & Jack   David & Colin   Christopher Victoria & Rosalind   Nicky & Ian   Mary = Richard Wilk

Rosemary & Tim   Diana, Jennifer & Michael

Page 23

father's. Elsie was also a good hockey player and a talented pianist, playing Chopin and Beethoven Sonatas with fluency. She taught first at Stirchley School and later at Floodgate Street, a poor quarter of Birmingham. Brought up in local Society of Friends circles (although not actually a member), she became friendly about 1918 with Herbert Twine, under whose influence she joined the Anglo Catholic section of the Church of England. She then went to live with his family before marrying him in 1921. This caused considerable unhappiness to my mother and father, and it was several years before the breach was partially healed. Herbert Twine (1884-1972) was 10 years older than my sister, and had been married before to a wife who died young. He was an official in the Birmingham Corporation Tramways Department, and later rose to the position of Chief Cashier. They lived in a pleasant fairly large house in Linden Road, Bournville. After Herbert's retirement in 1949, he and his wife went to live in a house they had built in Sidford, near Sidmouth, Devon. Both of them enjoyed good health until 1970, when Elsie contracted cancer, dying in February 1972. Her husband passed away in October of the same year. Their first child Sydney (b. 1923) died aged 8. Ruth (b. 1924) joined the Womens Royal Naval Service during the second world war. In 1945, while serving in Germany, she met her future husband, Mervyn Bridges. After discharge from the RAF, Mervyn worked for a few years as a travelling representative for L. G. Harris & Co Ltd. Later the couple emigrated to Australia, where Ruth's husband obtained a position with the

My sister Elsie and her husband Bert Twine taken during their retirement in Sidmouth, Devon. They both died in 1972.

Australian Government Coal Board. They had a daughter Lorelei, and a son John. Sadly the marriage did not last, and they separated about 1970, both still living in Australia.

Herbert and Elsie's third child, Viola, was born in 1928. After an unhappy first marriage, which produced a daughter Judith in 1962, she married Arthur Lincoln, a director of a building firm, and went to live in Yeovil, Somerset, where her next two daughters Celia (b. 1966) and Donna (b. 1968) were born. The couple later moved to Totnes in Devon, where Viola kept a boarding house for students at Dartington College.

Paul, my sister Elsie's youngest child (b. 1930), went to Birmingham School of Art and into the teaching profession, rising to the head of the art department in a school in Kent. He was a talented artist, and in 1957-58 executed seven large mural panels for our works canteen. He also specialised in painting locomotives, and one of these pictures is on permanent exhibition at the Science and Industry Museum, Newhall Street, Birmingham, alongside an actual express engine. Paul married Mary Whitehouse, also an artist, in 1959. They had three children, Rebecca (1961), Robert (1963) and Ruth (1965). He retired from school teaching in 1984 at the age of 54, taking advantage of the early retirement scheme in force. The family then moved to a house alongside a canal, Wharf House, Barton Turn, Barton-under-Needwood, near Burton-on-Trent, where they purchased and maintained a longboat. [Paul died in 2000].

My brother Frank William (1897-1942) was the cleverest of our family. After attending King Edwards School, Five Ways, he went to Birmingham University in 1917 to study metallurgy, gaining an M.Sc. degree in 1921. At that time, few government grants for students were available, and Frank had to earn his fees by driving tram cars from Selly Oak to Birmingham in his spare time. I remember that as a boy he sometimes allowed me to ride with him. I used to sit on the stairs to the upper deck while watching him drive! His thesis for the M.Sc. degree, which was printed in the Journal of the Institute of Metals, Vol. XXVIII, No. 2 1922, was entitled "The Hardness of the Brasses, and some experiments on its measurement by means of a strainless indentation". We still have a printed copy of this thesis; and of a discussion about it at a meeting of the Institute of Metals in 1922, when it was highly praised.

After leaving the University, Frank worked for a time at the Birmingham Battery and Metal Co Ltd, Selly Oak, Birmingham. Feeling dissatisfied with his prospects in England, he succeeded in obtaining a position with the American Smelting and Refining Co, Baltimore, Maryland, and emigrated to the USA in 1923. My father and mother were sorry to see their favourite son go, but realised that he was likely to get ahead much faster in America than in England, where trade was depressed at that time.

Later, Frank moved to St Louis, Missouri, and afterwards to Highland Park, Detroit, where he joined the staff of the Revere Copper and Brass Company. He was married on September 29th 1928 to Helen Crawford, a beautiful American girl. In the previous year, my father had travelled to the USA to see him (taking

Frank Harris, my brother, with his wife Helen Crawford in 1928, the year they married.

me with him) and father went on afterwards to visit his brothers Frank and Alfred in Canada. I remember that we travelled on the RMS Cedric which was scrapped at Inverkeithing in 1932.

Although my brother Frank and his wife Helen had a difficult financial time in the great American depression of 1930-31, his subsequent career with the Revere Company prospered, and shortly before the time of his death he was expected to become a Vice-President of this large concern. Sadly, after visiting us in England in 1937, his health deteriorated. He contracted cancer of the liver in 1942, and died on March 30th that year at the age of 44 a few days before my wife Mary and I were married. His wife Helen courageously sent us a congratulatory telegram on the day he passed away and we did not know about his death until after our wedding.

Frank's loss was a great blow both to his family and ours. His daughters Diane and Frances were only 10 and nearly 2 at the time. He had not been able to build up much financial reserve (apart from insurance policies) and his widow obtained a position as a secretary in the local library, sustaining the family by this full time appointment. I had always looked up to Frank as my clever elder brother, and had been inspired by him to try to succeed in the business career I had undertaken. He was my hero and his father's pride and joy. I was glad in some ways that our father had died some years previously, as Frank's death at an early age would have been a great blow to him. I have in front of me my father's letter to Frank on the attaining of his majority, dated June 21st 1918, written in father's beautiful handwriting.

Frank's widow, Helen, felt his loss tremendously, but courageously brought up her family. Both Diane and Frances later obtained their teaching degrees at the University of Michigan at Ann Arbor. I had felt for them very much, and in 1954 Diane came over to spend 12 months in England, first staying with my wife and me and later having a term at Oxford University. She was followed by her sister Frances, who after touring Europe went on a holiday with us to Norway and Lapland in 1961. Both Diane and Frances met their subsequent husbands at Ann Arbor. Diane married Charles Oldfather from Lincoln, Nebraska. Charles later became a partner in his law firm. After a very busy early few years, he partially retired in 1982, when he and his wife went on a world tour [Charlie died in 1999]. Their son, David, was born in 1958 and daughter Jane in 1960. David studied agriculture at University, and was married in 1984 to Sue Schukert [and secondly Rozanne, by whom he has two daughters]. Jane toured Europe in 1982 [and married a Chicago lawyer, Corey Light, and has two sons].

Frances, Diane's sister, married Jim Baker, a civil engineer, in 1961. They spent five years in Thailand while Jim was working for the large United States concern Booz, Allen and Hamilton. Later he started as a consultant on his own. They had four children, Kirk (1963), Ann (1965), Julie (1969) Jennifer (1972). Kirk has become something of a family historian, transcribing letters between his grandfather Frank and the family back home dating from the 1920s. These are a delight to read, recounting Frank's first impressions of his new life in America. My wife and I stayed with both Diane and Frances for a few days in 1983, after attending the wedding of our son Richard to Judy Rich, in High Falls, N.Y. At that time Diane and Charlie were living in a house in the countryside, at 6719 Old Cheney Road, Lincoln, Nebraska, and Frances at 10204, Garden Way, Potomac (near Washington). Both Diane and Frances gave my wife and me a wonderful time, and we came away feeling what good people Americans are. Both families came to Richard's wedding.

Frank's daughter Frances with me in 1960.

My sister Mabel Elizabeth (b. 1900) remained throughout her life a warm kind hearted lady and an excellent hostess. Educated at the Kings Norton Secondary School, Birmingham from the age of 11 to 16, she then studied morse code and joined the staff of the Post Office as a morse code operator, later joining the Ministry of Pensions, working first at Burton-on-Trent and afterwards in Birmingham. Her final appointment before marriage was as a secretary at the Government Tuberculosis Centre, Broad Street. In 1928 she married Ronald Garman at the Friends Meeting House, Bournville, and lived in Pamela Road, Northfield. Ronald, who had earlier suffered an injury to his leg as a result of war service in the Grenedier Guards which was to be a handicap to him throughout his life, was a skilled electrician with the Midlands Electricity Board. A kindly, rather shy man, he was devoted to his family and was sorely missed by my sister when he died in 1980. They retired to North Wales (where Ronald had been

My sister in law Helen Harris was a widow from 1942 till her death in 1989. Here she is with her two daughters, Diane (right) and Frances (left) in the early '70s.

1979 – My sister Mabel Garman with her husband Ron in the garden of their cottage in north Wales. They both loved gardening.

brought up), and lived in a delightful cottage in the Welsh hills, at Llanfairtalhairn, near Abergele. Mabel had never learned to drive a car, and fortunately before Ronald died they moved to a bungalow in Prestatyn, conveniently placed near shopping areas. They had two children Keith (b. 1930) and Elizabeth (b. 1933). Keith married Ann Larsson in 1958; they adopted two children, Edward (1965) and Eleanor (1968). Keith made his career as a technical officer with the Cast Iron Research Association. His wife Ann [who died in 1990] was a talented artist, and taught for some years at Westhill College, Selly Oak. Keith's sister, Elizabeth qualified as a nurse and worked at the Queen Elizabeth Hospital, Birmingham, before emigrating to New Zealand, where she married Barry Hay-Chapman in 1956. They had four children, Bruce, Jane, Clare and Lisa. [Mabel died in 1993.]

A family group at Ridge End c. 1975. On my left is my father in law, who is sitting next to a friend from Australia (in a yellow dress). Next to her is my mother in law, and on her left is her son Norman Wood, the only member of their family of six who remained unmarried. Beyond our other friend from Australia is our daughter Geraldine.

Our Golden Wedding party held in the Board Room in 1992. Colin (left) and David Harrison can be seen on the right of the picture – they are the sons of my second cousin Trevor Harrison (see family tree).

Chapter 3

MY LIFE STORY

I was born on June 20th 1905, at 29 Beech Road, Bournville, Birmingham. The house was one of the first to be built by the firm of Cadbury Brothers in the model village of Bournville, when my father bought it in 1898. According to the 'Life of George Cadbury' by A. G. Gardiner, the estate was laid out primarily to provide dwellings for the firm's work people, although individuals not connected with the firm were also allowed to buy them which is why my father qualified. Purchasers were expected to deposit 20% of the price, the firm advancing the rest, repayable over 12 years at 2 $^1/_2$% interest, on leases of 99 years. I expect my father took advantage of these generous terms: the price of the three bedroom semi-detached house (with a large garden) was probably about £250.

Although my sister Mabel and I were born in the Beech Road house, my elder sister Elsie and brother Frank were born at 255 Burbury Street, Lozells, Birmingham where my parents lived from their marriage in 1892 (at St George's Church, Edgbaston) until the move to Bournville in 1898.

Our home at Beech Road was most pleasantly situated within a few yards of the entrance to Bournville Park, through which ran the small river Bourn. This small park of 30 acres contained football and cricket pitches, a bowling green and several tennis courts. I haven't much recollection of my childhood days there, but I could hardly have been brought up in a pleasanter and more congen-

My birthplace, 29 Beech Rd, Bournville. Elsie, Frank and baby Mabel (1900).

ial spot. Later, when I was older and lived in Selly Oak, I played a lot of tennis on the hard courts provided.

I was also fortunate in living – to the age of 6 – within a quarter of a mile of my first school. In 1901 George Cadbury had built splendid infants and primary schools in the village, which were far in advance of schools provided at that time by public authorities. They are described in 'The Life of George Cadbury' as furnishing "a model of beauty and simplicity with their noble clock tower, spacious playgrounds, abundant and elaborately planned classrooms, library, laboratories and handicraft shops, the whole providing a model of school architecture and equipment not paralleled at that time by any village community in the country". The photograph I have been able to reproduce will give an idea of the beautiful buildings.

Altogether then, I must have had a most fortunate and happy childhood.

In 1911 my father's younger brother Alfred was living at a rather larger house than ours in Bournville, 96 Oak Tree Lane, Selly Oak. Alfred had decided to emigrate to Canada, and my father sold the Bournville property and bought the house from him. It had a dining room, drawing room, kitchen and scullery, and four bedrooms and a bathroom. When more houses were built in Oak Tree Lane in 1924 the house was renumbered 112. Here I lived from 1911 until moving out to Stoke Prior with my mother in 1939.

After attending the Bournville Infants School (I think from the age of 4 to 7) I went up to the Primary School (the largest of the buildings in the photograph). I remember that the headmaster at that time was a Mr Fielden, of whom I have kindly recollections. Other members of the teaching staff were Mr Horsley (a disciplinarian), Miss Latter and Mr Hemming. Although the standard of teaching at the Bournville Primary School, with its splendid equipment, was no doubt good, my chief memory of my time at the school was of bullying to which I was subjected. As far as I can recollect, I was about the average size for my age, though possibly somewhat thin. However, some of the older boys seemed to think I was fair game, their chief method of torture being to 'run me home'. This consisted of chasing me along the road after school until I was tired out, then pushing me into a hedge or ditch. I remember that my chief concern at the close of school was to dash out quickly to avoid my captors! Nevertheless I probably had a reasonably happy time on the whole. One of my spare time hobbies was to

George Cadbury, founder of Cadbury Bros, and creator of Bournville Village where I was born.

My first school, Bournville Primary School.

run a small club of the boys living near our house, called The Troopers. We met every Saturday afternoon and went on various foraging expeditions to raise money for a club hut. One of my jobs at the age of 10 and 11 in 1916 was to write and edit The Troopers Magazine, of which I still have a copy extant. This caused some of my family to think I should go in for journalism as a career: a short lived idea which never came to fruition.

I cannot remember what scholastic attainments I achieved at the Bournville Primary School, but I must have been about average, because at the age of 11 I passed the entrance examination for admission to the Central Secondary School, in Suffolk Street, Birmingham.

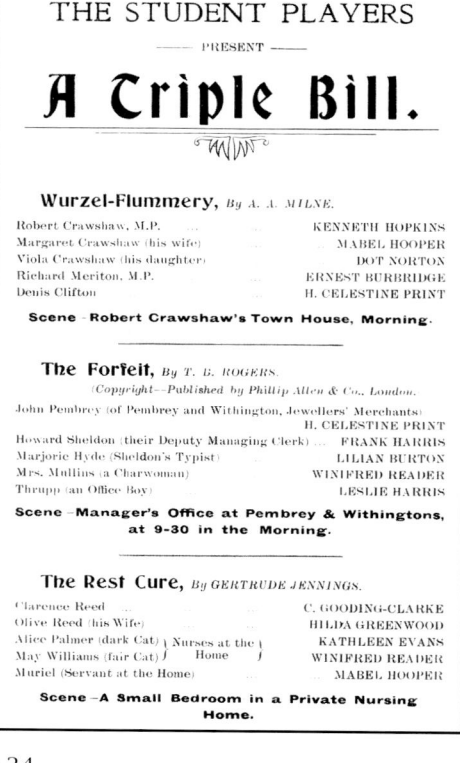

This school would have been about on a level academically with the average grammar school of today, although the cleverest boys at that time went to the King Edward the Sixth Grammar School, then in New Street, Birmingham.

The Central Secondary School which I attended (travelling by tram) was in those days housed in the buildings previously known as the 'Technical School', built about 1880 and demolished in 1968. The Technical School afterwards graduated to Gosta Green, and later formed the foundation of Aston University. I

In 1920 my brother Frank was a member of the 'Student Players' at Birmingham University. Mabel Hooper afterwards became headmistress of Sidcot School, Somerset, where our daughter Geraldine went. My first (and last) appearance on stage!

THE STUDENT PLAYERS
— PRESENT —
A Triple Bill.

Wurzel-Flummery, By A. A. MILNE.

Robert Crawshaw, M.P.	KENNETH HOPKINS
Margaret Crawshaw (his wife)	MABEL HOOPER
Viola Crawshaw (his daughter)	DOT NORTON
Richard Meriton, M.P.	ERNEST BURBRIDGE
Denis Clifton	H. CELESTINE PRINT

Scene—Robert Crawshaw's Town House, Morning.

The Forfeit, By T. B. ROGERS.
(Copyright—Published by Phillip Allen & Co., London.)

John Pembrey (of Pembrey and Withington, Jewellers' Merchants)	H. CELESTINE PRINT
Howard Sheldon (their Deputy Managing Clerk)	FRANK HARRIS
Marjorie Hyde (Sheldon's Typist)	LILIAN BURTON
Mrs. Mullins (a Charwoman)	WINIFRED READER
Thrupp (an Office Boy)	LESLIE HARRIS

Scene—Manager's Office at Pembrey & Withingtons, at 9-30 in the Morning.

The Rest Cure, By GERTRUDE JENNINGS.

Clarence Reed	C. GOODING-CLARKE
Olive Reed (his Wife)	HILDA GREENWOOD
Alice Palmer (dark Cat) ⎫ Nurses at the ⎰	KATHLEEN EVANS
May Williams (fair Cat) ⎭ Home ⎱	WINIFRED READER
Muriel (Servant at the Home)	MABEL HOOPER

Scene—A Small Bedroom in a Private Nursing Home.

have kept a few of my school reports from 1916 to 1921. During the first world war (1914-1918), the mainly temporary teaching staff consisted of elderly men past military age, and a number of ladies. This may account for the fact that my position in form seemed to fluctuate widely between the middle of the 'B' stream to the top (on one occasion) of the 'A' stream. But on the whole I didn't do particularly well, just scraping through the School Certificate when I left in 1921.

1924 – the family's first car, a 10 hp Calthorpe. Self at wheel, sister Mabel and friend Alec Ferneyhough.

The Headmaster in those days was Lionel M. Jones, a Welshman (who once gave me six of the best – I can't remember what for). Other teachers were Mr Foster (Chemistry), M. Guerra (French), Mr Loveridge (History), Mr Humphreys (Physics), Madame Cantrell (German) and Miss Henderson. The latter lady, I remember completely lost control of our class when the armistice was declared on November 11th 1918, all the boys crowding the windows and cheering.

My sister Elsie, as I have already mentioned, was a capable pianist. I was also fond of playing the piano, though I never attained Elsie's standard. I liked the classics, but my chief interest was in the jazz music of the 1920s. I used to play the syncopated piano compositions such as Zez Confrey's 'Kitten on the Keys', and Billy Mayerl's 'The Jazz Master'. I became friendly with a professional pianist named Maurice Udloff, who had his own dance band and played at the local cinema. I used to play duets with him, and on a few occasions took over from him on the piano for periods during his dance engagements, and sometimes relieved him during his cinema performances. Maurice lived with us at our house in Selly Oak for a year or two in the 1930s. I tremendously admired his playing, and wished I could emulate him, but my inefficient left hand was my weakness! He afterwards married Hilda Comley, whose brother was also a professional musician. With their son and daughter, they were evacuated to us in Mill House for some months in 1940. Maurice died in 1982.

The White Star Line
When I left the Central Secondary School in 1921 at the age of 16, jobs were difficult to get. Fortunately, my father had a friend named Mr Coppock, who at that time was manager of the Union Castle Mail Steamship Company's branch office in Birmingham. Mr Coppock was acquainted with a Mr Bull, who came from Southampton and had been given the job of opening a branch office in Birmingham for the White Star Line. Mr Coppock kindly obtained for me an interview at his house with Mr Bull, who agreed to engage me as a junior clerk at the wage of 25/- (£1.25) a week, though looking a bit dubious.

The Olympic was the sister ship of the ill-fated Titanic, and was completed in 1911. She was one of The White Star Line's three principal ships when I joined their Birmingham office in 1921. She was scrapped in 1935. (Facing page) The Cedric was getting a little dated by my time, although when built by Harland & Wolff (who built most of their ships) in 1903 she was one of The White Star Line's 'Big Four'. This was the ship that I sailed on to the USA with my father in 1927 – he returned later, but under company rules I had to return on the same ship.

(Above) The RMS Majestic's maiden voyage for the White Star Line was in 1922, when she was the largest ship in the world. My brother Frank sailed on her when he emigrated to the USA on July 4th 1923, and commented that she had very limited deck space for second class passengers for such a large ship, and that vibration was bad because of her "tremendous speed". (These postcards reproduced courtesy of Robert Wall, whose book Ocean Liner Postcards, is published by Antique Collectors Club).

The White Star Line at that time was the chief company in a vast international shipping combine known as the International Mercantile Marine, originally controlled by Mr Pierpont Morgan in New York. Other companies in the group were the Red Star Line, Dominion Line, Atlantic Transport and Leyland Lines, the Aberdeen Line, and the Shaw, Savill and Albion Line serving New Zealand. So I started business life as a very small cog in an enormous international machine.

In 1922 the White Star Line possessed the largest ship in the world. This was the Majestic of 56,551 tons, which was one of the vessels (formerly Bismarck) originally built in Germany for the Hamburg-American Line. She was taken over by Britain as part of the German reparations after the First World War, together with the Imperator (which became the Cunard Line's Berengaria) and the Vaterland (later the United States Line's Leviathan). Another ship removed from the Germans was the Columbus of 35,000 tons, renamed Homeric. So in the early twenties, the White Star Line was operating three enormous vessels, the Majestic, Olympic of 46,439 tons (built in Belfast in 1911 as a sister ship to the ill-fated Titanic) and Homeric. These ships between them maintained a weekly service from Southampton to New York. In addition, four liners built in Belfast in the 1900s, the Adriatic, Baltic, Cedric and Celtic (all over 20,000 tons), furnished a weekly run from Liverpool to Boston and New York. Then there were weekly Canadian services, monthly Australian and New Zealand schedules, and in addition regular sailings from London and Antwerp to America.

Who would have imagined, when I joined this firm as a humble office boy in 1921, that this whole vast international edifice would come crashing to the financial ground within 10 years?

Perhaps it might be interesting to interrupt my story by telling something of what happened. From 1921 to 1924, most of the ships were fully occupied. Gradually, however, trade declined and by the time the world trade depression came in 1930, the company was involved in large losses. In 1927, Lord Kylsant, the Chairman of the Royal Mail Steam Packet Company, bought the whole of the assets of the White Star Line from International Mercantile Marine for £7 million. In order to raise the money he issued a share prospectus. Trade, however, went from bad to worse, and in 1935 what remained of the White Star Line was taken over by the Cunard Line, shareholders having lost over £11 million, probably £200 million today. In the meantime an accountants investigation into the affairs of the company revealed that the share prospectus issued in 1927 by Lord Kylsant contained a number of false statements. He was then tried and sentenced to 12 months' imprisonment. I remember being told the story of someone who visited Kylsant in prison. Finding him sewing mail bags, he said "Sewing?". "No, reaping!", came the reply. By 1935, therefore, practically nothing remained of the vast international organization I joined in 1921.

To return to my own story. The first offices occupied by the White Star Line in Birmingham were at 63 Temple Row, near the present Bank of England. By 1924 the firm had moved to larger premises at 6 Victoria Square. In that year, I was promoted from office boy to be secretary to the assistant manager of the office, a Mr Seymour-Bell. One of Mr Bell's duties was to organize lectures and slide shows in various parts of the country to obtain publicity for ships of the Line. I remember that he used to take me with him on some of his expeditions in his car, a two-seater 10 h.p. Swift. In his spare time, he was also secretary of the Moseley Rugby Club of Birmingham, and I often had to type letters to other Rugby Clubs arranging match fixtures.

Seymour-Bell had an attractive personality. His qualities were recognized by the Cunard Line when they acquired the White Star Line, and he was later appointed manager of their important New York Office at No. 1 Broadway. He remained a bachelor until his late fifties, when he married the private secretary to President Eisenhower.

When trade declined, the White Star Line tightened up on salaries, and I remember that by the time I was 21 I was only getting £2 per week. I had always had the ambition to start my own business. But what to do?

In company with my next-in-line senior clerk, Jim Boulstridge, we had to deal with firms importing goods from abroad in the company's ships. This gave rise to the disposal of the empty packing cases in which the goods were packed. In conversation one day with the lady manageress of one of the importing firms who had taken an interest in Jim and me, she suggested that we could start a sideline business of buying and selling these empty cases. Her particular firm was importing leather cloth from the Du Pont de Nemours Co of America, which they supplied to the Austin Motor Company for upholstery of cars. These cases in which the cloth arrived were made of planed wood, and were in very good condition. Other firms we dealt with were importing tyres and brass foundry items. So Jim and I started a small business which we called the 'Midland Trading Company' operated from my house, 112 Oak Tree Lane, Selly Oak. We circularised Birmingham manufacturers, advertising the cases we had for sale, and when the orders came in we arranged with a haulage firm to collect and deliver them to the customers. The business, then, was very small, but that was how I put my first foot on the commercial ladder.

By 1926 Jim Boulstridge had tired of the inadequate salaries we were getting at the White Star Line. He wanted to get married, and applied for and obtained a job as assistant to the managing director of J. A. Phillips and Co Ltd of Smethwick, makers of cycle parts such as handlebars, brakes and chain wheels. His commencing salary, I remember, was £3.50 a week, a considerable improvement on the £2.50 he had been getting at the age of 24 at the White Star Line. Later I acted as best man at his wedding to his charming wife Trudy. They are still together in their 80s, though Jim is now (1985) getting rather chairbound.

By a sheer coincidence, the managing director of J. A. Phillips and Co and Jim's boss was Mr Otto Hesmer, who had married a cousin of mine, Miss Ada Deakin. Unfortunately, he died a few years afterwards, leaving his widow with two young daughters, Mary and Margaret. We resumed our acquaintanceship with Margaret (now Mrs Enos) in 1984 when we were staying in South Africa.

Jim Boulstridge, who had a great deal of business acumen, was appointed managing director of his firm when Mr Hesmer died. The firm expanded under his management, and by the 1940s was employing over 5,000 people in Smethwick and Newport, Shropshire. Jim's business ability was highly regarded by many people in the business world. He retired in the 1960s when the parent company, Tube Investments, came under new management.

My Own Business

Jim's departure from the White Star Line left me on my own to carry on our small sideline packing case business. I was only receiving £2 a week at the time from the White Star Line, and felt I could hardly do worse if I left and started on my own. So in March 1928 I gave in my notice and took the plunge. I remember when I handed in my resignation to the manager Mr Bull, he gravely said "I think you're doing something very foolish, Harris. You're with a great international company, and should have a good career with us if you mind your p's and q's". When the White Star Line was taken over by Cunard in 1935 nearly all the staff were made redundant, so I should have lost my job anyway!

By March 1928 when I was 22, I had saved £50 from my wages. The packing case business was expanding, and I managed to rent some dilapidated old premises at the rear of some slum property in Tennant Street, Birmingham, at a cost of 45p a week. The building was about 30 feet long by 15 feet wide, on two floors. I then started bringing the cases from the importers in hired lorries, and having them repaired by an old retired carpenter whom I engaged part time at £1 per week. The photograph gives an idea of the place. I remember that I made my desk out of a piece of plywood which I fixed between two walls, and covered with leathercloth!

Our first premises, back 73 Tennant Street, Birmingham. We were here from 1928 to 1930, paying a rent of 45p per week.

To save money, I cycled every day from my home in Selly Oak, a distance of 4 1/2 miles. From the start, I managed to make a living. My ambition, however, was to be a manufacturer rather than a merchant. What was to be the industry of the future, I thought? Probably aeroplanes! But lacking the technical knowledge, and above all, capital, I felt I had to settle for something more within my means.

From time to time, advertisements appeared in the trade papers by manufacturers on the Continent asking for agents to sell their goods in the United Kingdom. I thought if I could secure an agency of this sort, this might give me a start in the business world which I could develop later by making the goods I was selling. I answered several of these advertisements, some from manufacturers of hollowware, plastic goods, cycles and even furniture. But few of them responded until one day I was offered the agency of a paint brush manufacturer, Unger and Co in Furth, Bavaria. Paint brushes seemed a suitable line to get started in, occupying less warehouse space for their value than larger articles, so armed with a month's credit, I ordered my first trial supplies and set out to sell the goods.

Our second premises were 86/88 Constitution Hill, Birmingham, which we occupied till 1937. Two Victorian houses with warehouse at rear. Rent was £1.50 per week.

Progress, however, was slow. Most of the wholesale buyers of paint brushes were used to selling British goods, and looked askance at the rather inferior German brushes, in spite of an advantage in price. I was glad I had kept the second hand packing case business, which helped to keep me going and save up a little more capital. After about twelve months with the German firm, I made arrangements for better brushes to be made for me by the British firm of C. H. Leng & Sons, Stirchley, Birmingham.

Until that time, the sales of decorating brushes had not been backed by the makers providing any show material or advertising matter. I had the idea of promoting sales by supplying free window showcards and counter selling units. So at the age of 24, I spent some of my hard earned savings on coloured showcards, called the brushes the 'Seal' brand, and had a single sheet sales brochure printed called 'The Paint and Distemper Brush offer of the Century'. This I circularised through the post to ironmongers and wallpaper dealers round the country. The response was quite encouraging, and in a short time I was running out of supplies of brushes. The next step, therefore, was to start manufacturing for myself. For this, I needed larger premises and extra capital. I had saved a little more, and borrowed £500 from my kind father. I remember that father was a little dubious about my prospects of success, and it was very good of him to risk such an amount from his life's savings, since his salary as a local authority offi-

1931 – Our first brushmaking shop, in warehouse back of 86/88 Constitution Hill. The staff consisted of 15 girls and foreman Fred Osborne (on left hand side).

cial at that time was only £600 a year. I am glad to say that I was able to repay the loan with interest by the time my father died in 1935.

By 1930 (at the age of 25) I was bursting with enthusiasm to start my career as a manufacturer. Looking round for larger premises, I noticed an advertisement by the then Great Western Railway for two adjoining Victorian houses in Constitution Hill, Birmingham, with a warehouse at the rear backing on to the railway line. The two houses had six small rooms on three floors – not the most convenient arrangement, but the warehouse at the back had a goods entrance from the road, and the premises were available at a rental of £1.50 per week.

I knew nothing of how to make brushes at that time, so I advertised in Birmingham for a skilled foreman. An old established firm of paint brush manufacturers named Lee & James happened to be reducing staff, and I obtained the services of one of their redundant craftsmen, Fred Osborne. Fred was a skilled man at his trade. He advised me what machinery and equipment to buy, and after obtaining these and making the necessary benches, jigs and fixtures, we started assembling brushes with Fred and twelve local girls in July 1930. I remember the first wages we paid were £3 per week for the foreman, 75p a week for women over 21, and 52p per week for girls of 14 just leaving school. These wages now sound appallingly low, but Fred Osborne advised me that these were the rates being paid by his old firm, and as we had plenty of applications for the small staff we needed, I imagine we paid the usual going rates for that time. An interesting sidelight on these figures is that in 1930 the supervisor received four times as much as the women. Today (1985) our factory foremen are paid only about double the factory operatives.

The machinery and equipment we gathered together only enabled us to assemble and finish the brushes. We had to purchase our handles and ferrules from outside firms. These were bought from Windsor and Newton Ltd of Wealdstone, the old established artist brush makers, which had started a subsidiary making handles and ferrules for the trade.

The year 1930, when we started manufacturing, saw the commencement of a world-wide trade depression. A National Government was formed with Ramsay MacDonald, the former Labour leader, as Prime Minister. Unemployment reached the previously unheard of figure of 3 million. People had very little money to spend, and shop trade declined seriously. Somehow or other, however, our small firm managed to survive. I had not married and was living economically at home with my mother and father. Gradually, the situation improved, and by keeping the overheads low, I managed to make a modest profit. In 1933, we dropped the name Midland Trading Co and registered the business as L. G. Harris & Co Ltd.

112 Oak Tree Lane, where we lived from 1911 to 1939.

I was not satisfied with continuing only the assembly of brushes, and by 1936 I was looking for larger premises in which we could make our handles and ferrules. I was also keen to get into the country and leave the smoky and crowded city of Birmingham.

Stoke Prior
One day I happened to see a notice in the local paper advertising an old flour mill and house for sale in the village of Stoke Prior, near Bromsgrove, 18 miles from Birmingham. I went and looked, and thought that these premises – if only we could afford them – seemed to be ideal for our purpose. The Mill was on four floors, served by a hand operated lift. The Mill House, a Victorian residence with four reception rooms and eight bedrooms, was surrounded by a beautiful

The first page of a letter I wrote in 1933 to my brother Frank in America. At that time, "not far off 30" (actually, I was 28!) I thought that I was "out and out for a bachelor"! Fortunately, this was not to be the case.

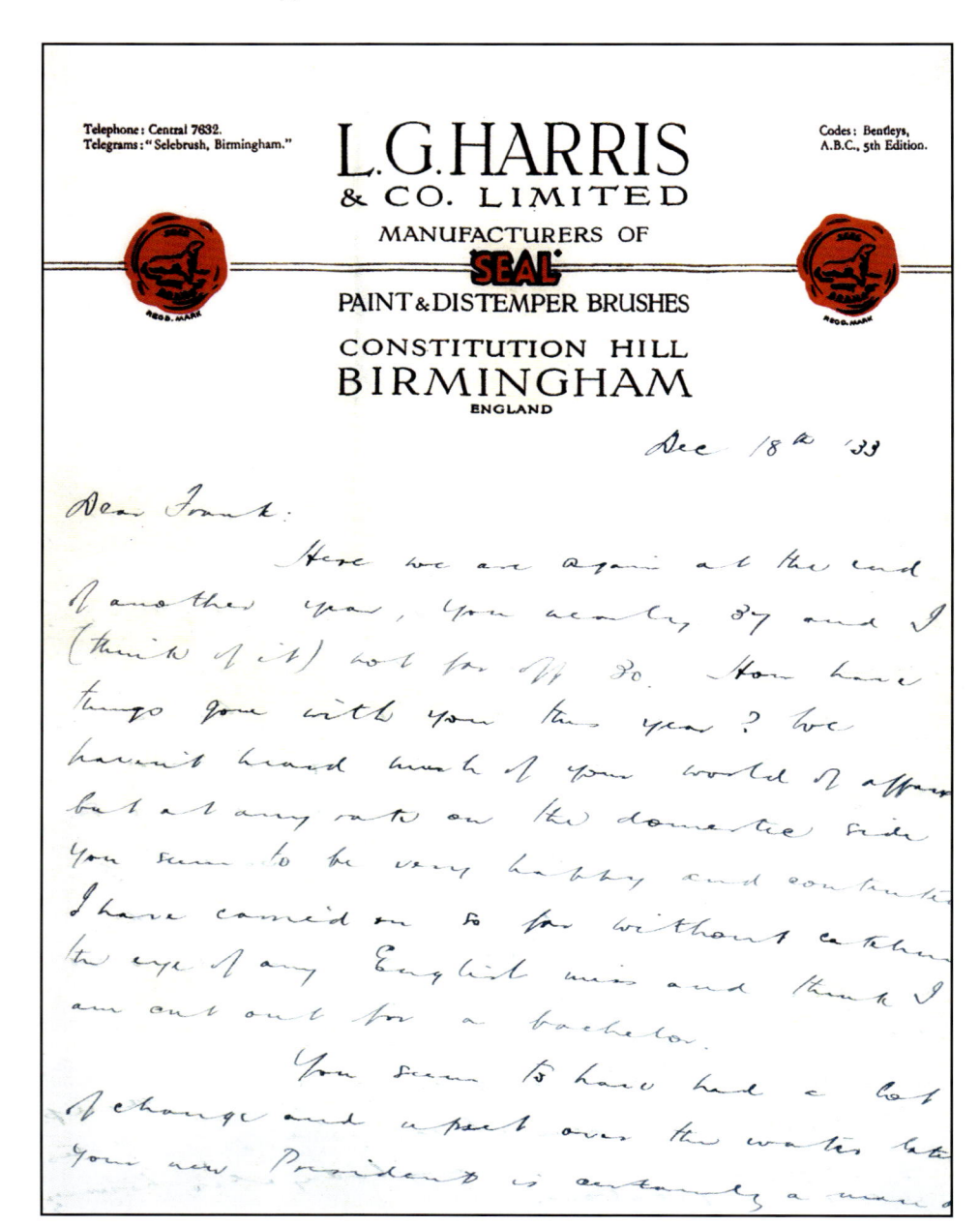

Telephone: Central 7632.
Telegrams: "Selebrush, Birmingham."

Codes: Bentleys,
A.B.C., 5th Edition.

L.G. HARRIS
& CO. LIMITED
MANUFACTURERS OF
SEAL
PAINT & DISTEMPER BRUSHES
CONSTITUTION HILL
BIRMINGHAM
ENGLAND

Dec 18th '33

Dear Frank:

Here we are again at the end of another year. You nearly 37 and I (think of it) not far off 30. How have things gone with you this year? We haven't heard much of you world of affairs but at any rate on the domestic side you seem to be very happy and contented. I have carried on so far without catching the eye of any English miss and think I am out and out for a bachelor.

You seem to have had a lot of change and upset over the water lately. Your new President is certainly a man...

The Mill House, the house behind The Mill, where we lived from 1939 to 1956. Like The Mill, it has now been demolished.

garden, somewhat run down, and flanked by a tennis court. A small river – the Salwarpe – ran through the grounds of 4 ½ acres. A sluice from this had previously driven a water wheel to serve the mill.

    Fired with enthusiasm, I went to see the owners, S. I. King & Sons of Birmingham. I explained that I could not afford the capital to buy the place, but would be glad to rent it. Whether they were attracted by the keenness of the young man confronting them, or whether they were having difficulty finding a purchaser, I shall never know. Probably it was a mixture of both. But they finished up agreeing to a rent of £3.50 per week for the first five years, and £4.50 per week for the second five. In addition to this, they agreed to carry out many alterations to the premises. These involved extra staircases in the mill, new floors in certain parts, and the removal of several partition walls. In the house, I asked for a number of new windows to be fitted, and strip oak floors in two of the rooms. All this work was carried out by their building staff over a period of three months, and we finally left our Constitution Hill premises in February 1937.

    Looking back in my 80s, I must admit I am impressed by the energy and enthusiasm I must have shown during this period. Understandably, only three

Before I took up residence in The Mill House, we used the dining room as our first works canteen, seating 40.

of our former Birmingham employees were willing to travel every day to Stoke Prior. So in addition to supervising the building alterations, I had to engage and train about 40 new local employees. I also had to deal with the transfer of our stock and the installation of our machinery from Birmingham. I still continued to live at Selly Oak with my mother at this period, my father having passed away in 1935, travelling out by train every day from Kings Norton by the express to Bromsgrove station, and walking to the Mill, a distance of three miles. Later I used to catch an earlier but slower train which stopped at Stoke Works station. One of my chief recollections of this period is the pleasure I had in breathing the country air after living in Selly Oak. Birmingham air didn't look dirty, but one immediately noticed the difference in walking from Bromsgrove.

The first works foreman we engaged at Stoke Prior was L. R. Eveson, who had been a supervisor in the paint shop at the Austin Motor Company, Longbridge. His father was a keen socialist, and named his son Leo (after Leo Tolstoy) Ramsay (after Ramsay MacDonald). His brother, who joined us as a mechanic a few years later, was named Omar Khayyam Eveson! Ramsay stayed with us until his retirement in 1972, apart from his war service with the Royal Navy, acting as personnel and welfare manager in his later years. He also capably edited our works magazine 'Shanghai' from when it was started in 1946.

All this expansion strained our small finances to the utmost. I had repaid my father's loan, and was working on a small overdraft at Barclays Bank. I remember that I was able to get six months credit from some of our bristle suppliers. But I still needed more money to finance the growing small business. So I approached Barclays for an increase in my overdraft limit. The local bank manager sent me for an interview with some of the directors in Birmingham. After looking at my last balance sheet, one of them said sternly "What you need young man is a surgical operation, not an overdraft!" Soon afterwards, I moved our account to Lloyds Bank!

My elder sister's husband, Herbert Twine, had always taken an interest in my business efforts, and he very kindly agreed to guarantee my overdraft in the sum of £1,000, an amount probably equivalent to £20,000 today. This involved him risking a high proportion of his life's savings. I had every confidence that I was going to succeed, and I suppose he had some security in the business assets. But I was, and still am, very grateful to him for this timely help, which enabled me to install some handle making machinery and presses to make our ferrules. I was able to release him from his guarantee after a few years had elapsed.

The War
The Nazi regime under Hitler in Germany had given all the people of Western Europe great anxiety. After the Munich agreement in 1938 between Hitler, Mussolini of Italy, Daladier of France and Neville Chamberlain, Hitler became even more aggressive. Britain had given a guarantee to Poland against attack from Germany; so when Hitler invaded Poland the following year, Britain and France declared war on Germany.

Those reading this book who were alive at this time will remember the tremendous upheaval caused in Europe by this calamity. Mr Chamberlain, who was Prime Minister of Britain from 1935 to 1940, was blamed by many people for his policy of appeasing Hitler in the Munich agreement in 1938. But after the mass slaughter of the first World War, which had only finished 20 years previously, surely his first duty was to try to avoid at all costs a second holocaust so

1937 – our first Christmas party, held in The Mill House. My mother is last on the right in the third row from the top, and Mary, later my wife, is third from the left on the left hand sofa.

HARRIS—

the line of Paint and Enamel Brushes you have been waiting for — at the price you want to pay

After several years of trial and experiment, and as the result of intensive specialisation in manufacture, we have introduced a line of Paint and Enamel Brushes for shop sale, of unrivalled quality, at prices hitherto considered impossible.

We ask you to consider the following points, and then compare our prices:

WE GUARANTEE—

1. That **HARRIS** brushes contain no loose bristles whatsoever. This we are able to do through a special process of manufacture adopted by us, and this guarantee is attached to each brush:—

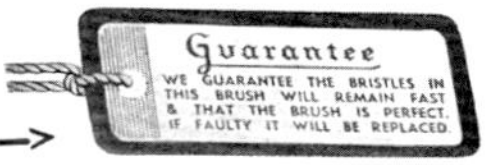

2. That none but the finest quality raw materials obtainable are used in **HARRIS** brushes, and that their quality and finish is the finest possible.

3. By means of our unique and sales-arresting Showboxes, Showstands, Showcards, and free advice leaflets, illustrated in this list, **WE GUARANTEE TO INCREASE YOUR SALES OF BRUSHES BY A MINIMUM OF 25%.** Our experience tells us that this increase will probably be exceeded, but if you do not obtain this increase, or are for any reason not more than satisfied with our goods, **WE WILL UNDERTAKE TO TAKE THEM BACK AT ANY TIME WITHIN 3 MONTHS, AND REFUND ANY MONEY PAID FOR THEM.**

TERMS : Less 5% for cash accompanying order, or 3¾% cash within 3 days of receipt of goods, or 2½% 1 month. Carriage paid over **£2 . 0 . 0.**

24-HOUR DELIVERY SERVICE : All orders guaranteed despatched same day as received.

PAINT & ENAMEL BRUSHES

- Finest pure bristles
- Locked in rubber
- No plug or wedge in centre, solid bristles right through
- "Comfort-shape" polished handles

"**HARRIS STANDARD**" (No. 216)

Width	½"	¾"	1"	1½"	2"	2½"	3"	4"
Thickness of brush (Full of bristles—no wedge)	1/16	3/16	3/16	3/16	3/16	3/16	3/16	3/16
Length of bristle out	1¼	1⅜	1½	2¼	2¼	2¼	2¼	2¼
Price	4/-	5/4d.	6/8d.	12/-	15/4d.	28/-	31/4d.	39/4d. doz.
Retail	6d.	8d.	10d.	1/6d.	1/11d.	3/6d.	3/11d.	4/11d. ea.

Remember! Every **HARRIS** *brush has this guarantee attached against loose bristles*

1938 – aggressive advertising.

1938 – the general office in The Mill. The office staff are (left to right) Mary White, myself, Monica Clarke, Mary Wood and Ian Bradley.

soon afterwards. It has also been said that by gaining an extra 12 months' respite from another war by the 1938 Munich agreement, he enabled Britain to build up her defences so that they were a little stronger when the balloon finally blew up in 1939. This was confirmed by Hitler himself in a statement he made in 1943: "It is the nemesis of this war that it began for Germany too soon on the one hand; somewhat too late on the other hand. From the military point of view, it was to our interest to begin it a year earlier. In 1938 I ought to have seized the initiative instead of letting it be thrust on me in 1939, since it was inevitable in any case. But I couldn't do anything, since the British and French accepted all my demands at Munich" (Hitler, by Joachim Fest, p. 1102). So as one who lived through these tremendous times, I shall always believe that Mr Chamberlain behaved as he should. He was even blamed for not building up Britain's defences earlier, by the very people who had always clamoured in the past for the reduction of armaments. The verdict of the Oxford University Union debate of 1933 was that "In no circumstances would this house be prepared to fight for King and Country".

Another result of Mr Chamberlain's policies was to put beyond doubt that the true cause of the war was German aggression, in contrast to the first world war of 1914-1918, when the issues were not so clear cut. This undoubtedly influenced American opinion towards Britain's support, and encouraged President Roosevelt in 1941 to lease us 50 American destroyers – which Winston Churchill described as "the most unsordid act in history".

1939 – our third factory, The Mill, Stoke Prior, where we were from 1937 till after the war in 1947. It dated from the late 19th century. Members of the staff are (left to right) George Chance, R. Hatton, Monica Clarke, Mary Wood, Ramsay Eveson, Peter Harrison, myself, Molly Dyer, Christine Wood (later my sister in law), George Ridley, Richard Deeley and Omar Eveson. After we left The Mill it remained empty for many years, and was later demolished.

    I must not attempt to write an account of the second world war. For that I must refer my readers to the history books. All I want to do is to touch on some of the highlights as they affected our family. The first part of the war has been called the phoney period, when nothing happened between August 1939 and May 1940, after which Germany launched her attack on the Low Countries.

    Mr Chamberlain – although I have always believed him a great man – was not the Prime Minister to lead the country through a terrible war. So when one of the opposition unfairly quoted Cromwell's speech to the Long Parliament: "You have been here too long for any good you have been doing – in the name of God, go!", he resigned and Winston Churchill took over. We in Britain must thank our lucky stars for Winston Churchill. Had it not been for his courageous stand, we might even today (1985) be living under Nazi domination.

    By July 1940, Britain's position looked desperate. Since May had come successively the collapse of Holland, the German drive to the Channel ports, the capitulation of Belgium, the evacuation of the British army at Dunkirk, the total disintegration of the French and their separate peace with the enemy, and the failure of our attempt to defeat the Germans in Norway. In spite of all this, I think the morale of most British people remained high. It was widely thought that the German invasion of Britain would take place in September 1940, when Hitler's air force staged a mass attack on London and the Channel Ports. Though the RAF was heavily outnumbered, the enemy was beaten off and the immediate threat of invasion receded. This Battle of Britain inspired Churchill's famous phrase: "Never in the field of human conflict was so much owed by so many to so few". Earlier, all he had offered us was "blood, toil, tears and sweat".

In 1940 my age was 35. I had been brought up in Quaker circles, with their belief in pacifism, and I certainly did not believe in wars of conquest and aggression. But I felt that Hitler, with the mania for German domination of other people, and his cruel treatment of the Jews, had to be resisted. Our government in that period was conscripting all eligible men (and later, women) into the armed forces. I was expecting to be called up at any time. I never made any request to be exempted but I was later told that I was to remain in charge of the factory, since we were on a percentage of government work. I then joined the 'Local Defence Volunteers', which the government had formed to help with our defences in the event of invasion. This force later became known as the 'Home Guard'.

Training of the local section of the Local Defence Volunteers took place every week at the Army Drill Hall, which still exists in Recreation Road, Bromsgrove. I remember that our commanding officer was a Captain North, the headmaster of a local school. For some reason, I was allotted a place in the intelligence section. Some of our training consisted of crawling along hedges and ditches, practising hand grenade throwing, and charging with fixed bayonets into sacks, where we were told to twist the blade. I remember feeling revolted at this, and fervently hoped I would never be involved in doing it in action.

1941 – Christmas party in Stoke Prior village hall. Mary Wood, soon to be my wife, in WAAF uniform, front row. Douglas Wride on her left.

The threat of invasion of Britain remained active until June 22nd 1941, when the Germans attacked Russia. This was another example of Hitler's callous disregard of agreements, since he had signed a non-aggression pact with Russia as recently as 1939. In the first few months the Germans advanced quickly, and by November they were within a few miles of Moscow. But their forces were spread out over a wide front, and their advance had out-run their capacity to keep up supplies. In addition, the winter had set in and their armies suffered much hardship in the frozen conditions. The Russians then re-grouped, called up millions of men into their forces and began to roll the Germans back. I have often thought that if Hitler had commenced his attack in April instead of June, the German armies might have been in Moscow before the advent of winter. Perhaps this was another of his strategic mistakes.

The Germans resisted the Russian advance fiercely, but in spite of this they had to gradually retreat. Their nemesis came in January 1943, when they were defeated at Stalingrad. The Russians finally captured Berlin in April 1945, at the same time as the Americans and British, who had attacked from the west after landing in France in June 1944.

Thus ended the cataclysm which had started through one man's senseless ambition, after millions of people had perished and vast amounts of property had been destroyed. I remember Neville Chamberlain's words after the outbreak of war in 1939: "We have to kill one another just to satisfy that accursed madman. I wish he could burn in Hell for as many years as he is costing lives".

However, as Winston Churchill said, "in war, resolution: in defeat, defiance: in victory, magnanimity". The Nuremberg trials were held to punish the German war leaders, but no attempt was made to impose reparations on their country in spite of the immense damage that they had caused.

My own personal part in the war, then, was inglorious. I had made no attempt to evade my contribution, but often felt how grateful I should be for escaping possible death, or physical injury, as so many of my fellow citizens had to suffer.

At the outbreak of war in 1939, I was living with my mother at the family house in Selly Oak, Birmingham. In 1936 we had taken over the Mill House behind the factory in Stoke Prior. It seemed sensible to remove ourselves to this house, since I could avoid the difficult travelling in wartime. (One of the posters issued by the government at that time used to say "Is your journey really necessary?"). We could also avoid the possibility of being bombed out in Birmingham, and spend more time supervising activities at the factory, by living over the shop.

I have already explained that the Mill House contained eight bedrooms and four reception rooms. Shortly after the outbreak of war, the government asked for volunteers to house families evacuated from towns in danger from bomb attacks, such as Birmingham, Coventry, etc. So we were able to make a small contribution by taking in a number of these 'evacuees'. During the whole of the war we had an average of about 12 people in the house. Most of them lived, had their meals and slept in one room. They seemed very grateful to be out of the danger

Living in Stoke Prior during the war, I was away from the bad bombing that Birmingham and other big cities endured. In 1941, bombs fell in Selly Oak not far from where we had lived, and our old house in Oak Tree Lane was damaged and boarded up. But one night in July 1941 there was an air raid on the main Birmingham to Bristol railway line that ran through Stoke Works – there is a junction only a short distance from Mill House. Below is an extract from a letter I wrote to my brother Frank describing the incident.

> But here, of course, we are in a relatively safe area, and though we have a good many "alerts" we have had scarcely any bombing. Curiously enough one did drop, (or rather three bombs dropped) one night on the local Railway Station, just half a mile up the road from this house. It was a rather exciting experience. Round here, of course, we have no protection from low-flying aircraft by barrage balloon or anti-aircraft fire, and the enemy can fly low and bomb much more accurately. It happened one night when we were in the middle of a warning period which had started about 12 midnight. When these warnings sound I am afraid I just stay in bed. But Mother and Auntie and the rest of the household usually get up and congregate in the hall around the staircase, sitting around making cups of tea and generally chatting. We had heard several bombs drop and some of them sounded alarmingly close. Suddenly about 3 a.m. we heard the roar of an aircraft very low, as it seemed, just round the house. A second afterwards there were three terrific thuds and the house shook from side to side. I rushed out of the house as I felt sure the bombs must have fallen only a few yards away, but after a few enquiries I found that the local railway line had been hit about half a mile away.
>
> How our little local raid was dealt with is perhaps interesting as indicative of what happens in hundreds of cases all over the country. It seemed that the aircraft had dive-bombed and hit the main line from Birmingham to Bristol plumb in the middle – an extremely accurate hit made possible, of course, by the ability to dive very low. A large crater had been made extending across the whole width of the track – four sets of lines wide – and about thirty feet deep. About 9 o'clock next morning I went up to have a look at the damage. There were at least 100 men already on the job repairing the line, with several railway officials walking about. By three o'clock the same day the mess had been put right and main line traffic resumed. The whole atmosphere was one of cheerfully and energetically getting on with the job. The poor Stationmaster whose house was just behind the Station was rather shaken as his house had been badly wrecked, and he and his family had had rather a lucky escape. But he had simply accepted the situation and was getting on with his job as though it were all part of the day's work. I offered him accommodation at my house, but he had already had an offer elsewhere. Several of the villagers were homeless for a time but they got fixed up temporarily and the houses have now all been put in order.

areas, but caused us some anxiety by not always being careful to entirely close their curtains at night. Very strict blackout regulations were rightly in force, and if the local police happened to see a chink of light anywhere, the owner of the house would be in trouble. As far as I can remember, the families enjoyed their stay with us. They did not pay any rent, but obtained their own food supplies.

Early in the war my mother's sister, my Aunt Kate (née Deakin) came to live in the house with my mother. She was an elderly lady, then aged 84. Although I did what I could to make her comfortable, I think the many other people living in the house caused her some annoyance. She bitterly complained about her conditions and pleaded with some other relatives of ours living in Solihull to take her into their house and look after her. They duly came and took her away. But after 3 weeks they rang me to say that she was most difficult to get on with, and asked me to find her some other accommodation! We were able to find a house accepting paying guests in Bristol Road, Edgbaston, to which she was transferred. This was rather an unhappy incident in an otherwise reasonably happy house. I think the fact is that some elderly people (not all) get irritable and cantankerous in their old age. Evidently the breach was healed after a time, as I remember going to see her several times at Edgbaston, and later at a house in Gravelly Hill, Birmingham, where she died in 1946.

My mother, who came to live in the Mill House with me in 1939, was then aged 76. She was in good health at that time, and I think enjoyed the country air, though as a sweet and undemanding lady, she was somewhat dominated by her imperious elder sister, my Aunt Kate. Towards her 80th birthday, she became very frail, went to be looked after by my sister in Northfield, and died in 1943.

Engagements and Marriage
Our daughter, Geraldine, says I should say something about my relations with the opposite sex. I had two fairly serious friendships before my marriage in 1942. I started employment as an office boy with White Star Line in 1921. After 5 years' service, employees were granted the privilege of a free passage to and from the USA in one of the Company's ships. So when my father said in 1927 that he wanted to go and visit his brothers in Canada, and his eldest son in America, I was able to go with him. (Under the rules of the Company, I had to stay on board the ship while it was in New York, and return to England with it.) A fellow passenger seated at our dining table was (as it seemed to me) an extremely attractive girl with whom I struck up an immediate friendship. Her name was Dorothy Croft. She was a private nurse who had been trained at the Middlesex Hospital in London, and was going out to America to assist in the birth of her sister's baby in Boston. I had never met a girl like her before, and before the end of the seven day voyage, I had fallen heavily in love. She seemed to reciprocate my feelings to a modest extent, and we agreed to correspond and meet again when she returned to England. We exchanged letters regularly once a week, and in 1928 when she returned, her parents invited me for the weekend to

her home in Kelvedon, Essex, where her father, the Rev Canon Croft, was the local vicar. I enjoyed the weekend, though a little overawed by the social occasions which were different to my rather humbler background at home. I remember that on the Saturday evening, we went to a private dance at the home of the then editor of The Studio, Captain Geoffrey Holme. Dorothy's elder brother, Andrew Croft, was an Arctic explorer who had been educated at Stowe School and Christ Church, Oxford. He was very pleasant to me, but lacking a University education, I felt a little shy. Her sister Christine had married a member of the local aristocracy named Sir Brook (James) Fairbairn.

I came away feeling that I hadn't made a good impression on her family, but nevertheless we continued to correspond, and in the early thirties when she was travelling with her parents in Worcestershire, I took them home to meet my mother, and later to a performance at the Shakespeare Memorial Theatre in Stratford. I slowly got to feel, however, that she didn't want our friendship to blossom out into marriage, and not being one to "waste my sweetness on the desert air" I gradually ceased to write. The one consolation I had was that she was evidently very discriminating, as she didn't get married until 1942 when she was over 40! When her husband, Quentin Riley, died through a car accident in 1979, I wrote a letter of sympathy, and she invited my wife and me to go to stay with her.

By 1934, when the business was doing a little better, I had given up cycling backwards and forwards from home, and used the train to Birmingham from Selly Oak Station every day. I got to know some of my fellow travellers, one of whom, Margaret Trotman, who was studying at the Birmingham College of Art, introduced me to two of her fellow students, Raymond Cowern and Andrew Freeth. Raymond and Andrew later became nationally known artists, both winning the 'Prix de Rome' and afterwards being elected Royal Academicians. Thus started a friendship with two distinguished artists which has lasted all my life. Raymond Cowern afterwards married Margaret. He later became Principal of Brighton College of Art, and afterwards retired to Cumberland. They had two daughters, Anna and Jenny, and a son, Nicholas, my godson.

One of Margaret Trotman's friends was a girl named Hilda Franklin. Margaret introduced me to her one day in the Birmingham Art Gallery. My previous romance was fading, and I remember being attracted by her beautiful face, charming smile, and warm disposition. We struck up an immediate friendship, and began to see each other regularly, becoming engaged to be married in 1935, after having toured Germany together. I then set about establishing a home, and purchased an acre of land in Blackwell Road, Barnt Green, a few miles from Birmingham. I remember that the price was £400 – a lot of money for me in those days. I still own the land, 50 years afterwards! An architect named Knight in Birmingham designed a house for us, and all seemed set for a happy marriage.

But somehow or other, we seemed gradually to become disenchanted with each other. Hilda was passionately interested in art, which subject she taught in one of the Birmingham schools, and I had only a moderate interest in it, although very fond of music. 1936 saw the year in which I transferred the business from Birmingham to Stoke Prior, and I was tremendously busy every day for several months. I was also anxious to improve my financial position, so that we could set up our house. Perhaps the extra strain of all these events made me a rather unsatisfactory lover. But whatever the reason, we slowly drifted apart, and mutually decided to break off our engagement at the end of 1936. So I was again foot loose and fancy free.

Hilda afterwards married a previous girlhood friend named Joseph Cox, who became headmaster of a school in Gloucestershire. She had four children, two boys and two girls, the latter of which were twins. All the children were educated at the Society of Friends School, Sibford, Oxfordshire, of which I later became one of the Governors. This caused Hilda and I to correspond again. Her attractive daughter Josephine was training to be a teacher at the Shenstone Teacher Training College, Bromsgrove, and I helped to obtain some local lodgings for her. After the children had grown up, Hilda helped the family income by resuming her teaching career for several years. Sadly, her husband died in his 60s. She then moved to a house at Newnham on Severn near Stroud, where my wife and I visited her. In her later years, she suffered from angina, and had a cataract operation. She was a competent amateur artist in water colours. At this moment (February 1985) I have a letter from her suggesting that my wife and I go down to see her again. She died soon after we had seen her, in June 1985.

After two feminine friendships which came to an end, I began to think that I was perhaps intended for permanent bachelorhood. A second cousin of mine, Peter Harrison, with whom I had been friendly for several years, joined my firm as sales manager in 1938. He was a few years younger than me. At one time we toyed with the thought of setting up a bachelor home together, but the idea faded out when he was called up for service in the Royal Navy.

In 1936, just before we left Birmingham for Stoke Prior, a girl named Mary Wood had come to help us in the office. Later she agreed to transfer to Stoke Prior, travelling out in the train every day from Kings Norton. She was quiet, good looking and extremely competent. After war broke out in 1939, she stayed

Mary Wood before our marriage, in 1939 aged 19.

1949 – at work in my office. (Below) Andrew, Richard and Geraldine about 1957.

in the Mill House during the week, going to her home in Birmingham at the weekend. Although there was a big difference in our ages – she was 15 years younger than me – we gradually became attracted to each other, and in 1941 I asked her to marry me – one of the best things I ever did. By that time, she had already left our firm and joined the Women's Auxiliary Air Force. At first stationed at Innsworth, Gloucs, she went on a course at St Asaph, South Wales, and with her corporal's stripes returned to Innsworth where we managed to see each other on her days off. We were married on April 11th 1942 at the Society of Friends Meeting House, Cotteridge, Birmingham, and spent a very short honeymoon at the Lygon Arms Hotel, Broadway, and afterwards Minchinhampton. When she was expecting our first child in 1943, she came out of the Air Force to live with me (and several evacuees!) at the Mill House. Our son Andrew was born on January 21st 1944 at a nursing home in Britannia Square, Worcester, and our second son Richard at a hospital in Edgbaston on October 28th 1945. We adopted our daughter Geraldine, through the agency of the Liverpool Child Adoption Society, six weeks after her birth on October 17th 1951.

1979 – Geraldine marries Richard Pinch. The marriage and reception was held in Christ Church, Oxford.

(Right) Three grandchildren – Andrew's sons Dominic (left) and Mark (right), and William (centre) – taken in 1990. (Below) 1985 – Richard with his wife Judy and their son William, born 1984.

1948 – from 1948 to 1962 we held an annual 'Miss Brush Works' competition. The first winner was Joan Walters, a waitress in our canteen. The site of our office block, still awaiting government permission, is behind.

Chapter 4

OUR FIRM AFTER THE WAR

Many people born as I was in the shadow of the great Cadbury chocolate and cocoa works at Bournville, obtained employment in their factory, which in the 1930s employed over 10,000 people. I had the ambition that at some time I might have my own 'factory in the country'. Our move to the Mill at Stoke Prior got us into the country. The Mill, however, was on four floors and inconvenient for manufacture in many ways, and I was still hoping one day to have a purpose built factory, on one floor, surrounded by flower gardens and sports fields – a small edition of the great Cadbury works.

Our New Factory and Offices

Our business had been steadily improving since the move from Birmingham, and in 1939 I was able to buy 32 acres of land (at £130 per acre) in Hanbury Road, Stoke Prior, where I hoped to build my dream factory. The site was an undulating one and had to be levelled before building operations could begin. We asked Mr G C Gadd, the Bromsgrove architect whose father had designed the original Cadbury Bournville complex in 1879, to produce plans for the factory, which was to be 315 feet deep by 250 feet wide, in 9 bays of 35 feet wide, with an office block in front. The whole building was, of course, far beyond our means at that time, but we felt that if we built the small area we could then afford, it should be made to fit in with the final plans.

One of the facilities we had lacked in the Stoke Prior mill was the ability to saw up tree logs into planks, since this required ground floor operations and a crane. So our first half factory bay of 125 feet by 35 feet was designed to house a band mill machine for sawing up the logs, with band saw doctoring equipment and overhead cranage. At the back of the building was a concreted storage yard for logs, surmounted by a 3 ton hand operated crane by Butters of Glasgow. This was later replaced by a 5 ton electrically operated model. So we were now in business able to produce brushes right from the tree to the finished article.

Although the first half factory bay we had built was all we could afford at the time, further building operations were in any case stopped by the outbreak of war in September 1939. During the war we were only allowed to build tem-

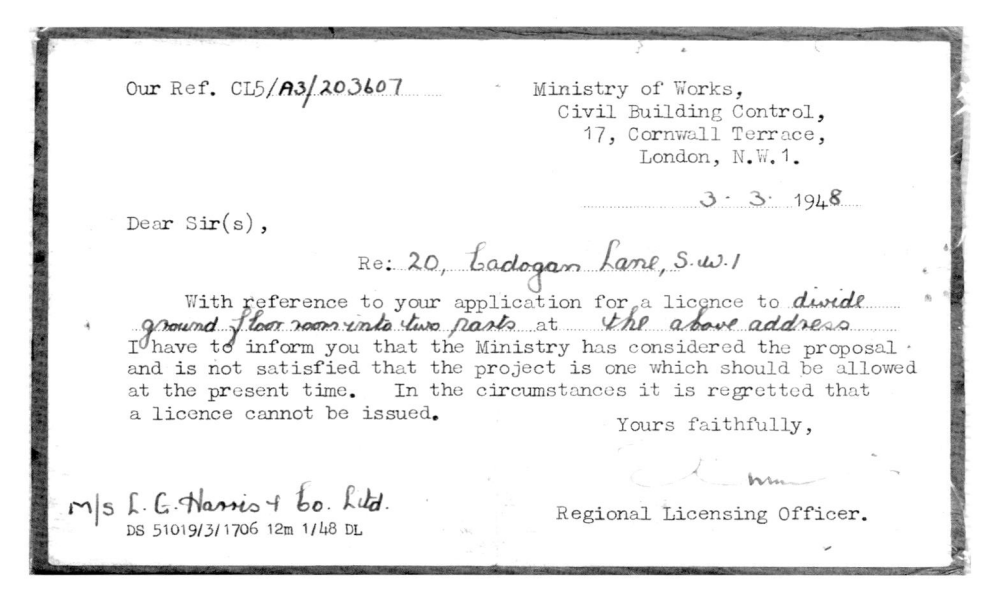

```
Our Ref. CL5/A3/203607          Ministry of Works,
                                Civil Building Control,
                                17, Cornwall Terrace,
                                London, N.W.1.

                                          3 · 3 · 1948
Dear Sir(s),
                Re: 20, Cadogan Lane, S.W.1
    With reference to your application for a licence to divide
ground floor room into two parts at the above address
I have to inform you that the Ministry has considered the proposal
and is not satisfied that the project is one which should be allowed
at the present time.  In the circumstances it is regretted that
a licence cannot be issued.
                                     Yours faithfully,

M/s L. G. Harris + Co. Ltd.
DS 51019/3/1706 12m 1/48 DL          Regional Licensing Officer.
```

1948 – the tightness of the building regulations in the post-war period can be seen from this letter. We wanted to divide a room into two in our London office with a hardboard partition.

porary wooden buildings, so we had to operate for the next 8 years partly at the old Mill and partly at Hanbury Road. For some years after the end of the war factory building operations were strictly controlled by licence. The government's policy was to compel new factories to be built in areas of high unemployment such as South Wales, the North East or Scotland. So when we applied in 1946 for permission to complete the remainder of the factory, this was refused and we were told to go to South Wales. At that time we were employing about 500 local people, including a number of key personnel. The move to another part of the country would have meant making all of them redundant and starting a brand new organization elsewhere. We protested strongly to the government department concerned (then the Board of Trade) but got nowhere. They pointed out that we had moved from Birmingham in 1937, and there was no reason why we should not move again.

In most areas of the Midlands, there was admittedly a labour shortage. But as it happened, the ICI Salt Works, the only other employer in our village of Stoke Prior, had been reducing its labour force, and many local people were glad of the employment which our factory offered. We then solicited the help of our local MP, Mr L Tolley, who arranged for the Board of Trade in London to receive a deputation from some of our work people. This finally did the trick, and we received a licence to build most of the factory we needed – but without any offices, which presumably had to be tucked away in some odd corner. I remember that at the time, we wanted to divide our one room London office into two, by putting a hardboard partition down the middle. Even this was refused, as can be seen from the printed letter illustrated!

In 1947 then, we were given permission to build eight of our nine factory bays, leaving the remaining works bay and the office block in abeyance until the situation became easier. It was not until 1957 that we received a licence to build the remainder. The contract for the latter work was placed with the firm of J & A Brazier Ltd of Bromsgrove, in the sum of £80,000. The area of the additional factory bay was 8,750 square feet, and the office block 13,000 square feet. Work was started in September 1957 and finished in June 1959. The cost of building a similar structure today (1985) would probably be nearer £500,000.

Although we needed every square foot of factory space we could obtain (the stores was particularly cramped) the office block was about 20% larger than we required at the time. The firm was expanding in the 1950s, and we were anxious to avoid the necessity of adding a bit on at a later date. So a room of 50 feet by 26 feet, the extra space we did not need in 1959, was turned into a conference room for the time being, with the intention of being able to use it for additional office space if the need arose later. This room has proved invaluable ever since, and has been extensively used for meetings and Arts Festival lectures.

Ever since 1938, I had operated a profit sharing scheme under which 10% of the profits before tax had been distributed to the employees each Christmas, with the proviso that if the profits of one year fell below those of the previous year, the share out would be increased to a maximum of 15% of the profits, thus providing a sort of bonus equalisation reserve.

The Leslie Harris Employees' Trust

With the completion of the office block, I felt that the time was ripe for the consolidation of the scheme by the gift of 20% of the ordinary shares of the firm

1952 – our male staff in the canteen at Christmas.

1938 – our first attempts at conveyorisation at The Mill. (Above) A brush finishing track. (Below) Brush making track. The brush heads were shaped up in boiling linseed oil at the end of the track, then dipped in rubber solution and vulcanised.

to an Employees Trust, so that in the event of the firm ever being sold, the new owners would be required to distribute a share of the profits to the employees even if the original profit sharing scheme was discontinued. The Trust Deed provided that 80% of the dividend available would be distributed, the remaining 20% being kept as a reserve, to be added to the distributions in subsequent years if the profits fell. The original trustees were myself (the settlor), my son Andrew, Brian Middleton (secretary/director), and Richard Schmidl (production controller). The Trust Deed provided that in the event of the death of any one of the trustees, the remaining trustees would appoint a successor, bearing in mind the settlor's desire that ultimately the trustees should consist of one representative of the directors, one from the supervisory staff, one from the office staff, and one from the operative grades.

It was my intention that the trustees should not be able to sell the shares given to the Leslie Harris Trust and distribute the capital to employees, so a clause was included in the Trust Deed that the shares could not be sold without the consent in writing of the directors of the company for the time being.

The office block was officially opened on July 3rd, 1959, by Mr Edgar Lee, the Chairman of Bromsgrove District Council. I was very touched the following week at being presented by Tom Knight, on behalf of the employees, with an illuminated address, written on vellum in a leather bound volume, containing the following inscription:-

"To L. G. Harris, Esq, on the occasion of the completion of our Hanbury Road factory, June 1959, and as a token of the esteem and affection of all employees of the firm of L. G. Harris & Co Ltd.

"We desire to express our deepest appreciation of your outstanding leadership and example to us over the years.

"We are cognisant of your benevolent disposition, and we wish to permanently record that in our opinion we owe a debt of gratitude to you as our Managing Director for the many acts of kindness and goodwill shown to us all. We instance the Family Allowance Scheme, the Pension Scheme, Profit Sharing, Holidays with pay, the 40 hour week, and the Harris Employees Trust. All these amenities, we know, are now part of our daily life at the Works.

"We conclude by sincerely hoping that you will have a happy, healthy and prosperous life amongst us for many years to come."

After these pleasant recollections, perhaps I should say something about my manufacturing ideas. On my 21st birthday, by brother Frank in America had sent me a copy of 'My Life and Work', the first book written by Henry Ford, the motor manufacturer. As all the world knows, Henry Ford was the first factory manager to employ mass production methods and conveyorised systems. He made only one model of car, and customers could have any colour, "so long as it's black". By this means, he brought the price of his cars down well below his com-

Our new office block, which was completed in 1959. Designed by local architects George and Myfanwy Gadd, it was built by the Bromsgrove building firm of J & A Brazier. Many visitors remark that the building has a 1930s or Art Decco feel about it, with its curved metal windows at the corners, and heavy architectural fittings inside. There is some truth in this, as plans for the offices were certainly drawn up just after the war, even if not before – plans dated 1946 showing the building substantially as built, still exist. (Below) The sales department.

The accounts department in the new office block, and (below) the board room. The offices are well designed and spacious, and furnished to a high standard using Gordon Russell furniture. Even though it is now over 40 years since they were built, very little change has been necessary to accommodate them to the needs of the computer age, and they are still (in 2002) a pleasure to work in.

petitors', at the same time paying his workers high wages. Later I bought his subsequent books, 'Moving Forward' and 'Today and Tomorrow'. I was absolutely fascinated and thrilled by these books, and came to regard them as my business Bibles.

The traditional way to make paint brushes was for each stage of manufacture to be done separately, and the partially made brushes to be put into boxes, then taken out again for the next operation and so on. I would like to have devised a system in which there were no interruptions during manufacture (à la Henry Ford); in other words the bristle would be fed on at the commencement and the finished brushes would come off at the other end of the conveyor. This proved impossible owing to the rubber dipping and subsequent vulcanising process. But I was able to conveyorise the first stage of making the brush heads, and secondly the assembly operations to the finished brush stage. These tracks were first introduced at our works at the Stoke Prior Mill in 1937, as will be seen in the photographs on page 64.

1960 - a visit from our local MP, James Dance (right), PPS to the Secretary of State for the Air. Ramsay Eveson behind me, Leslie Lawrence, foreman of the vulcanising section, in front.

The adaptation of conveyorised methods to the making of wooden handles was somewhat simpler. The sawing of the logs into planks, and subsequent kiln drying has to be done separately. But from the point when the hardwood blanks were fed on to the conveyor track, going past four spindle moulding machines, four sanders, inspection and fixing on to boards for cellulose dipping on one conveyor, it was possible to mechanize the whole process. It is perhaps interesting to recall at this stage that the handle making tracks referred to above required the services of 12 people to produce 1100 dozen handles per day. Today, with hopper fed lathes and hopper fed sanding machines, the same output is being achieved by five people - and even less for plastics (but that is another story).

Machinery Manufacture
During the war of 1939-45, machines for brush manufacturing were unobtainable. We were employing about 20 skilled fitters and tool makers in our maintenance department, so we were able to use their services for producing nearly

Two of the ten machines we made for the brush trade, 1945-1952. (Left) Bristle 'flirting' and cleaning machine. (Below) Handle dipping machine.

all the new machines we required. Formerly, all brush making machinery had been made by independent manufacturers not exclusively connected with the brush trade. By designing our own machines and testing these out in actual production conditions, we were able to iron out the snags before perfecting the finished product. This fired me with the enthusiasm to become a manufacturer of machinery rather than brushes. In 1949 we produced a catalogue of the machines we were making, and advertised them in the trade press. This produced a considerable number of orders, and we were kept busy for about three years coping with the demand. Our catalogue illustrated 10 different machines, all of which were well made, and I think gave satisfaction to the firms that bought them. I was particularly pleased when visiting our friends and competitors the Briton Brush Co Ltd, Wymondham, Norfolk in 1982, to see two of our paint brush machines still working steadily after being made by us in 1951, having given practically no trouble for 30 years. The machines were also supplied to several brush factories abroad, as well, of course, to our own subsidiary factories in South Africa, Ireland, Kenya and Ceylon.

But, as I perhaps should have realised at the outset, manufacturers do not keep on repeating orders for machinery once the capital has been invested, unless required for expansion purposes. So from about 1951 the orders for machines started to fall off. The international brush trade is a comparatively small one, and unless

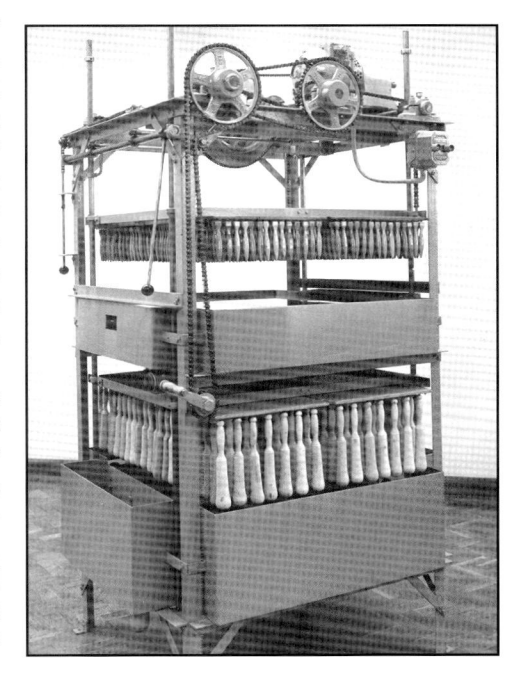

Christmas 1952 – our female staff in the canteen. Myself in the centre with Douglas Wride on my right and Ramsay Eveson on my left. The works nurse, Iris Parker is at the extreme left, and her sister Celia, then my secretary, stands two rows behind her.

we were to embark on making machinery for other uses, I could not see much future for our small manufacturing unit. I was reluctant to come to a decision to close it, as I had enjoyed being involved in the technical problems of machine designing. We still kept our toolroom staff going, and supplied the occasional machine orders which came in, gradually allowing the staff of the department to be reduced by natural wastage to 10 men, its present level.

During the war, brushes, like all consumer articles, were in short supply. We could only obtain extremely limited quantities of Chinese bristle, and had to supplement this by mixing it with horsehair. This made paint brushes of a usable but inferior quality. All our brushes at that time were stamped 'war quality' and when some of our customers found they had a number of them in stock after the war, we had to replace them with the post war products, to keep them happy.

The acute shortage of brushes in the years after the war meant that we had to ration our customers. We were only making at that time three sizes of paint brushes and one distemper brush, in the maximum quantities we could. We were probably fortunate compared with our competitors, since the move into the country before the war had given us ample supplies of labour and manufacturing space. There seemed no end to the demand for our goods. But although we were rationing the customers, we gradually found the demand declining. And when we ceased rationing in 1952, orders plummeted down almost overnight. To cope with the demand, we had built up our labour force to a peak of 600, and suddenly found we had too many people. We were faced that year with our first financial loss (the only one we have made so far in our history). Something,

1950 – a paint brush assembly conveyor in the new factory.

therefore, had to be done. At a meeting of all our employees in the works canteen we explained the position, and asked if they would co-operate by accepting a 10% cut in wages for 2 months, to help the firm financially and avoid the necessity of any redundancies. They co-operated willingly, and we were able to repay the loss of wages afterwards. Had our bankers been willing to bridge the gap, probably even this short term measure would not have been necessary. I was glad to see, in looking at the 1952 Christmas issue of our works magazine, an article appreciating the fact that no redundancies had taken place. We were probably helped in reducing the labour force by natural wastage, as the local firm of Garringtons Ltd were busy producing drop forgings for the motor industry and had been engaging a number of people.

In the 1950s, we commenced releasing our young people under 18 for half a day a week (later increased to one day) for after-school education. Until the Bromsgrove College of Further Education was built, the teachers held the classes in our rest room.

[It is an interesting reflection on changing times that at its peak Garringtons employed well over 3,000 people, mostly on much higher wages than we could offer. But Garrington's fortunes slowly declined, and in 2002 went into receivership.]

Other Activities in the 1950s And 1960s

When we excavated the ground for our factory site in 1946, we took the opportunity of levelling a much larger area on the remainder of the 32 acre site, 250 yards by 250 yards, to provide for possible expansion in the future. In the meantime, as we were employing our maximum of 600 people at that time, the site made an excellent sports ground which we hoped the employees would appreciate. In 1951 we added four hard tennis courts at the north end.

In the 1950s the works was running two football teams, a cricket eleven, and girls' hockey and netball teams. One men's group was even playing bowls on the front lawn. But as our number of employees declined, enthusiasm to join the works teams fell off. The main reason was that other local cricket and football teams in the district could call on a much larger number of players, which our better performers preferred to join.

If we had provided leadership in the form, perhaps, of a sports organizer, this might have encouraged the works teams to continue. But we felt that all the firm should be doing was to provide sports facilities for those that wanted to have them, and that it was certainly no part of any employee's duty to play if he or she didn't want to. So when the enthusiasm for works teams began to flag in the 1960s, we allowed other local teams to use the ground. We now have three full size football pitches and a cricket field on a ground which has been described as one of the best sports fields in Worcestershire. The football pitches are let (on moderate terms) to three local teams, and the cricket field to the Stoke Works Cricket Club. They are fully used throughout the season, and I think are much appreciated. [The decline in interest

(Above) 1948 – works football team, and (below) 1957 – girls hockey team.

in cricket led us to turn all the ground over to football pitches, which are still (2002) well used, mainly by local youth teams.]

As I said earlier, the original object in levelling the large site was to provide for possible expansion in the future. We were somewhat taken aback when we found that the local planning authority in 1960 had designated the area as green belt thus preventing us anyway from using it for manufacturing purposes. But our expansion in recent years has been adjacent to the original factory, so the question does not seem likely to arise. And we feel pleased to have provided extra local sports facilities which are badly needed.

1977 – Andrew shows the Bishop of Worcester, the Rt Rev Robin Woods, round the factory.

The Aerlec Site

During the 1939/45 war a firm known as the Aerlec Co Ltd had acquired a 6 1/2 acre field opposite our works, on which they had built a number of factory buildings. Their business had declined after the war, and in 1954 we purchased the land and buildings for £35,000, borrowing the money on mortgage. We then let the existing buildings to various tenants, and later built an additional office block and warehouse, which was let to Clements and Street Ltd, the exhibition contractors. We already owned 18 1/2 acres adjoining the site which we had planted with trees in our forestry programme, and in 1980 we built a further extension for Clements and Street on part of this land, together with an additional building for Bobby's Confectionery Co Ltd. The capital cost of these further extensions was £170,000. We have now received planning permission to allow us to use a further 9 acres for building extensions, so the excursion into the property field has been a profitable investment for us. [See part 2, chapter 3, for an account of the subsequent development of our commercial property.]

June 20th 1975 – a photograph taken to celebrate my 70th birthday.

The board of directors taken about 1970. This was the original board after I decided to appoint executive directors in 1959, plus Andrew. They are (left to right) Richard ('Dick') Deeley (purchasing), Ramsay Eveson (personnel), Peter Harrison (home sales), myself, Douglas Wride (works director), Andrew (marketing), Henry Reiner (export sales) and Herbert Wynekin (financial director).

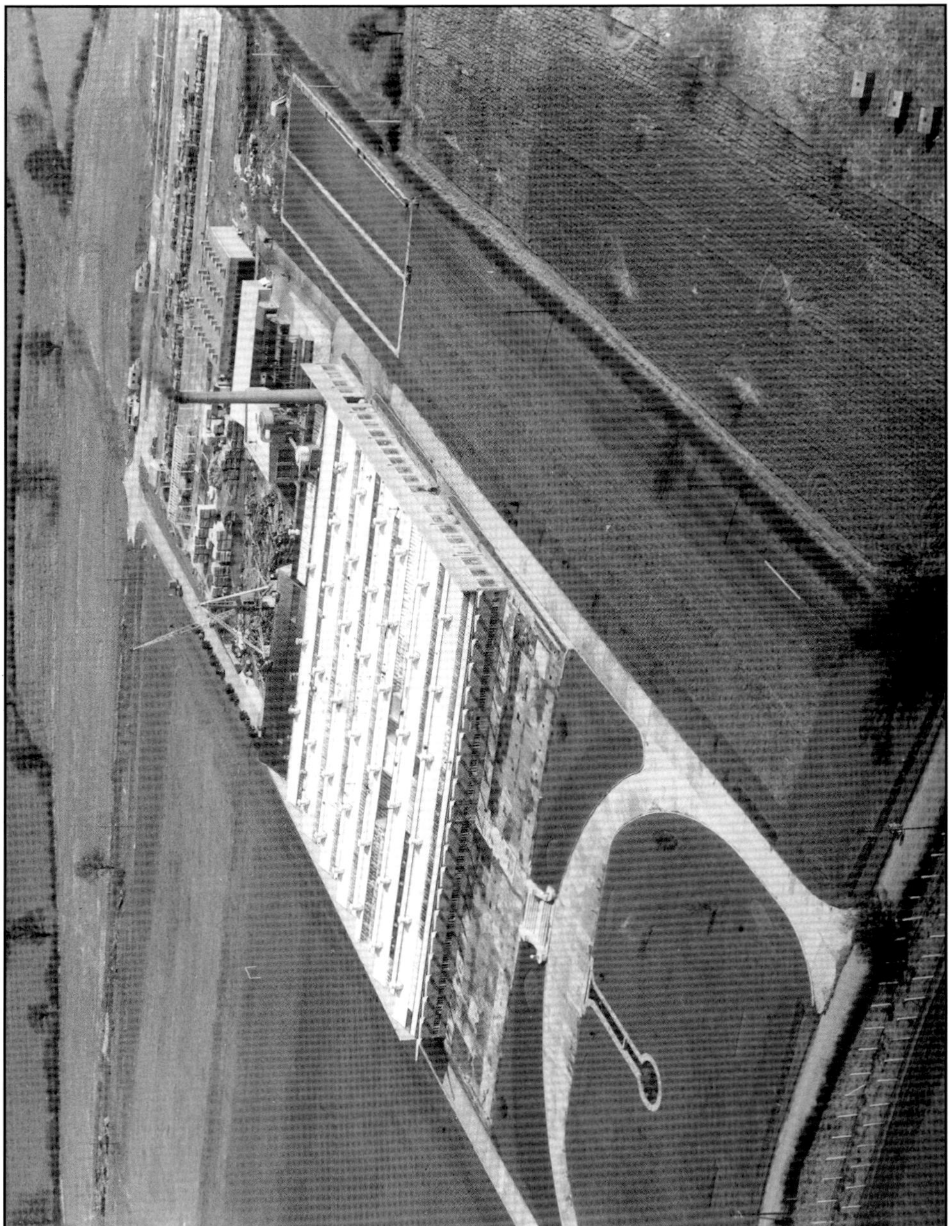

(Facing page) An aerial photo taken around 1950 of our site before the offices were built (1958-9) and the trees were planted all around the factory and playing fields. These were originally levelled for future building, but are now in the green belt! (Left) Taken around 1985 showing the new despatch and warehouse (nearest camera – finished 1974) and the pole storage shed adjacent built a little later. The trees that were planted all over the undeveloped part of the site are beginning to mature. The Birmingham to Gloucester railway runs along the top of the picture, with the Worcester and Birmingham Canal parallel to it. The Aerlec site is just this side of the canal in the top left. (For 2002 photo see p. 268)

THESE SALES-CREATING DISPLAYS FREE OF CHARGE WITH ANY SIZE ORDER

No. 1. Showcard in 3 colours. Strut at back and loop for hanging. Size 18″ × 14″.

No. 2. Display Centre in 3 colours. Size 28″ × 26″. (Only recommended where suitable space available).

No. 10. Showstand, made of polished beech. Label in 3 colours. Size of base only 12″ × 2″.

No. 40. Advice Leaflets supplied free for distribution with brushes. Printed in 3 colours. Includes advice on how to get the best results in using brushes.

the most outstanding Sales Offers in the Brush trade—
HANDSOME STAINED OAK SHOWCASE
FREE OF CHARGE WITH EACH ORDER

THESE ATTRACTIVE COLOURED SHOWBOXES
FREE OF CHARGE WITH EACH ORDER

Note:—For current retail prices of brushes see opposite page.

No. 7. Size 12″ long × 16″ high × 4″ deep.

No. 14 Size 23″ × 11″ × 4″

No. 18 Size of Base 21″ × 10″

FREE WITH ORDER FOR £2.0.10 :

				£	s.	d.
1½ doz.	½″ brushes	@	4/-		7	0
1 ″	1″ ″	@	5/4		5	4
2 ″	1½″ ″	@	6/8		13	4
1 ″	2″ ″	@	12/-		10	0
⅓ ″	3″ ″	@	15/4		5	2
1 Display Showbox (FREE)						
Retail selling value £3.1.2			£2	0	10

FREE WITH ORDER FOR £3.12.4 :

				£	s.	d.
1½ doz.	½″ brushes	@	4/-		6	0
1½ ″	1″ ″	@	5/4		8	0
2 ″	1½″ ″	@	6/8		13	4
1¼ ″	2″ ″	@	12/-		15	0
4/6 ″	2½″ ″	@	15/4		12	10
⅓ ″	2¾″ ″	@	28/-		9	4
⅓ ″	3″ ″	@	31/4		7	10
1 Display Showbox (FREE)						
Retail selling value £5.8.5			£3	12	4

FREE WITH ORDER FOR £7.15.0 :

				£	s.	d.
4 doz.	½″ brushes	@	4/-		16	0
3 ″	1″ ″	@	5/4		16	0
4 ″	1½″ ″	@	6/8	1	6	8
3 ″	2″ ″	@	12/-	1	16	0
1 ″	2½″ ″	@	15/4		10	8
½ ″	2¾″ ″	@	28/-		14	0
½ ″	3″ ″	@	31/4		15	8
1 Stained Oak Showcase (FREE)						
Retail selling value £11.12.6			£7	15	0

Compact . Neat . Sales Creating
Strongly made with labels printed in 6 colours. Sloping fronts for greater display value.

Above quantities can be varied if necessary provided order totals £7.15.0. Made in polished Canary wood stained light oak. Label printed in 6 colours. Rack at back for Invoice Books, etc.

WE GUARANTEE THESE DISPLAYS WILL INCREASE YOUR BRUSH SALES BY AT LEAST 25%

Chapter 5

SALES ORGANIZATION

I have related elsewhere that I acquired my ambition to be a mass production manufacturer from reading the books of Henry Ford. I have often wondered from where I also got my enthusiasm for aggressive selling and advertising methods. But undoubtedly any modest success we have achieved has largely been due to our use of the latter.

Show Material
In 1930 no brush manufacturer, as far as I can remember, provided any show material, much less indulged in press advertising. Brushes were just packed in brown cardboard boxes, and the selling was left to the retailer. It is, of course, true that the do-it-yourself movement did not achieve its great expansion until the 1960s, when professional help got so expensive. But even in 1930, some brushes for the ordinary householder were being sold, and we were the first brush manufacturers to provide free show material and dispensers to assist sales. Our first effort in 1932 (illustrated opposite) was a showcard, featuring an attractive girl, printed in colour on stiff board, holding one sample of each of the five sizes of brush we were making, affixed to the card by elastic. Originally we used the trade name 'Seal', which we changed in 1935 to 'Harris'. Later, we provided polished wooden boxes for the counter, holding a quantity of each size, in which the retailer could keep his stock. These were made from plywood stained light oak, about 2' 6" long, with the advertising transfer on the lids, on which were printed the retail selling prices opposite each size. Retailers have always preferred to have the retail prices clearly marked, both for the use of the public and of themselves. We continued this practice consistently until the 1970s, when owing to the frequent changes due to inflation the marked price rapidly became out of date.

As the years went on, the wooden stock boxes were replaced by taller and narrower showcases occupying less counter space, including free advice leaflets for the use of the public. The elasticated showcards gave way to an improved type holding the brushes through magnets at the back, so that the articles could be taken off and replaced. For the small retailers, who only wanted a limited stock, we provided attractive coloured and partitioned cardboard counter boxes.

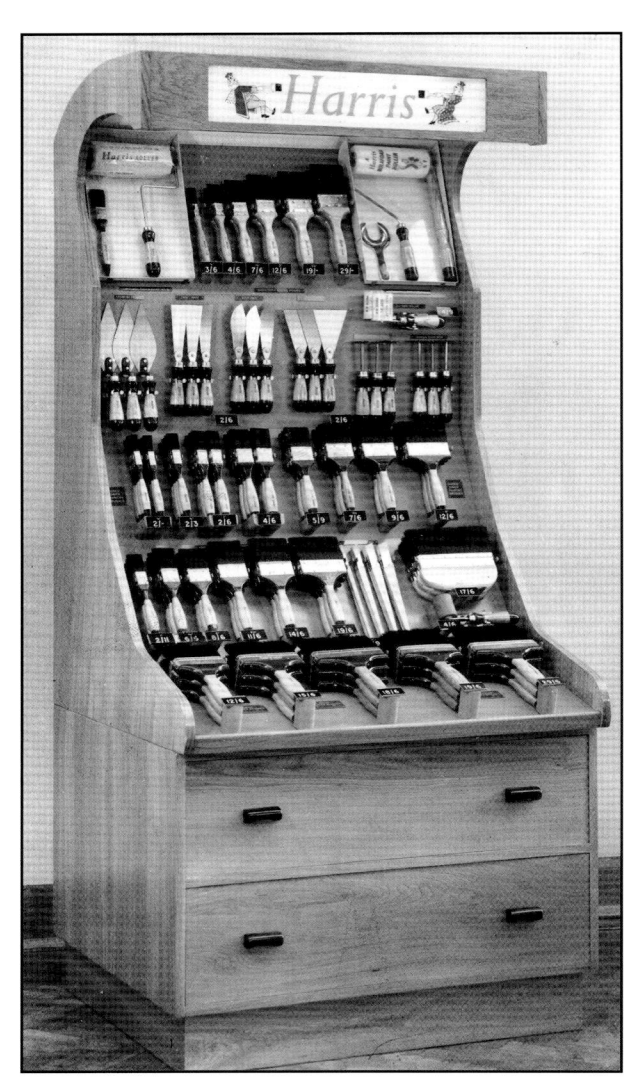

All these sales promotion items were well received, and enabled us to get our name established ahead of most competitors, who were slow to copy us, probably considering the expense not worthwhile. The illustrations on these pages show something of the development of these sales aids over the years.

After the war, we were asked by some customers to provide a complete sales cabinet, containing a comprehensive range of all the items we made, rather than have them shown in several different places. So in 1955 we launched our first show case of this type (the 'P3'), containing a comprehensive supply of three ranges of paint brushes, painters tools, distemper brushes and paint rollers, with two drawers underneath for stock. Attractively made in light oak by Messrs Pollard & Co, the well known London shopfitters, they were much more expensive than any of our previous showcases, and for the first time we asked customers to pay half the cost. Surprisingly, this was not greatly objected to, and several thousand of these were distributed over the next ten years, some of which are still in use in the 1980s. We did receive a few complaints that the open display of the goods in these cabinets led to pilfering, so in 1957 we launched a

1955 – our first, and very popular, combined showcase, the P3. These were despatched to customers all over the country using our own transport.

glass enclosed counter (see picture) for the larger shops. These, however, were not a success. The main reason was their cost (£200) of which the customer paid £100 – probably equal to £700 in the 1980s – and the length (6ft 6ins) which only the larger shops could accommodate. About 40 of these counters were distributed, after which they were withdrawn. A misconceived marketing idea which flopped!

In response to the complaints about pilfering, we provided perspex strips across the brushes in the P3 cabinets, so that the content could only be extracted with difficulty. This idea was well received at the outset, but subsequently, with the increasing popularity of self service, the practice was dropped. To placate the customer, for some years we offered to replace items pilfered. Surprisingly, this was very little taken advantage of.

Until the 1960s, practically all the retail trade in paint and hardware and sundries was carried on by separately owned individual shops, of which we had about 18,000 on our books in

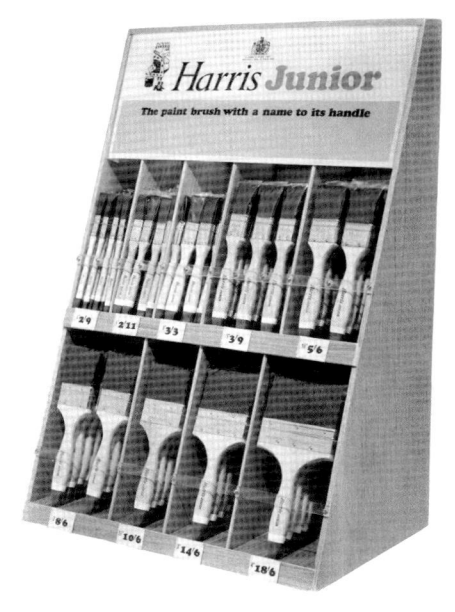

The 'Junior' range was our best-selling brush for many years. Later it was called the 'No. 203', and then the 'Classic'. (Above) This smart wooden showcase with anti-pilferage strips dates from about 1970, and (below) this popular magnetic metal showcard dates from a little earlier (as can be seen from the prices!). (Below left) this cardboard counter box dates from 1951.

Page 81

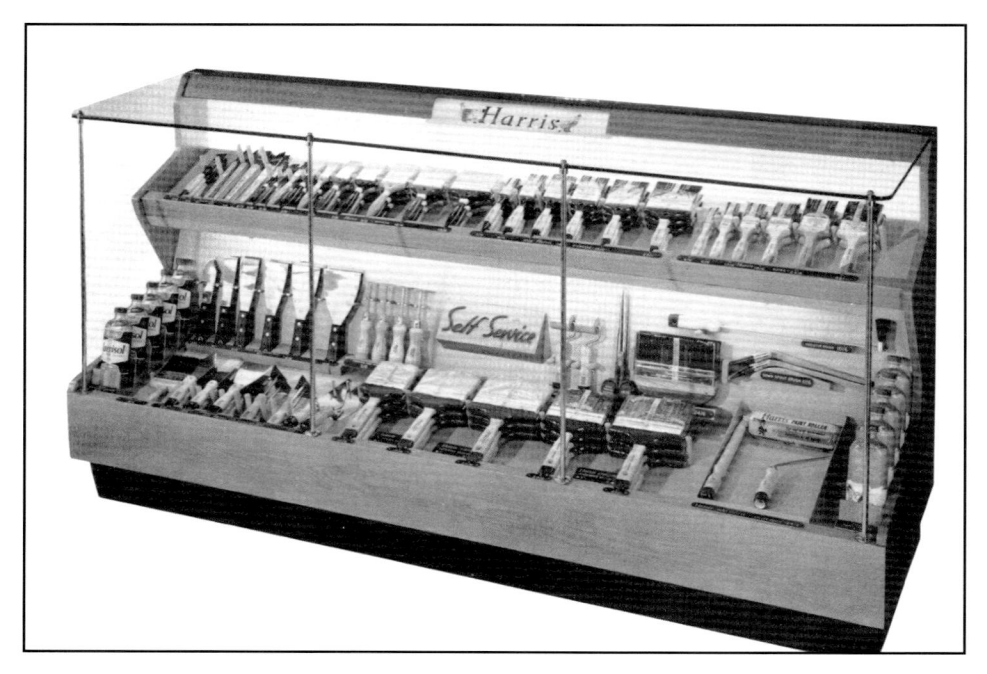

1958 – an attempt at providing self-service counters. Although attractively made and finished, these were too big and expensive for the average shop at that time.

1965. A few chains of retail shops were being established but these were only comparatively small, and the really big comprehensive D.I.Y. stores of 20,000 to 40,000 square feet only started to come into being in the 1970s. The competition of these big chain concerns, and their superior buying power, gradually forced the small man out of business, and by 1980 our retail customers had been halved to under 8,000. By 1985 about 25% of our total retail turnover was being taken by only four of these big groups [2002 – 66%!]. Although their splendid big stores undoubtedly provided an excellent choice of every conceivable item which the D.I.Y. man could want, the tremendous purchasing power of the firms' buyers enabled them to insist on larger discounts, which we had to give, reducing our profit margin in some cases to little more than a contribution to overheads. However, this was a fact of life which had to be faced. We had always been keen on exports, and felt that this was an avenue on which we should concentrate strongly. Our overseas factories had always been reasonably successful, and I personally felt that we should be opening more. But this was another story.

The big chain stores did not require any of the specialised individual show material items we supplied, as they preferred to use their own display units. They did, however, insist on our providing header cards attached to our brushes and tools, printed with the bar code so that the items could be passed over their computer stock control systems. By the 1980s, therefore, we have largely dropped the window showcards, and provide instead counter dispensers for the smaller shops we still have on our books, with bigger merchandisers for the larger establishments, illustrated on these pages. Some of our multiple customers require every single item we produce to be mounted on a small display card, and this method of self-service selling is becoming increasingly important.

Our Sales Force

When we started selling our brushes in 1931, we were not in a financial position to pay salaries to sales representatives. So we advertised for salesmen carrying other lines, to sell our goods on commission. This arrangement, however, soon proved unsatisfactory, and by 1935 we were employing six full time representatives, who were paid 12.5% commission on sales, plus a contribution to expenses of £2 per week (later increased to £5) on condition that they carried our lines exclusively. These amounts sound ridiculously small today, but with petrol at 6p per gallon in those days, £2 was probably equivalent to £40 in 1985. I remember that Mr J. M. Burlinson covered north London and the northern home counties; A. G. Bear - south London, Surrey and Sussex; F. J. Morgan - South Wales; H. J. Cattermole the West Country; and J. W. Poole, the Midlands. During the war years, such goods as we could spare from our production for the home trade,

Wire dispensers like these were the most popular type of display from the '60s onward. Both date from about 1970, and were available free with a 'qualifying order'. The rotary stand needed much more space than the smaller one.

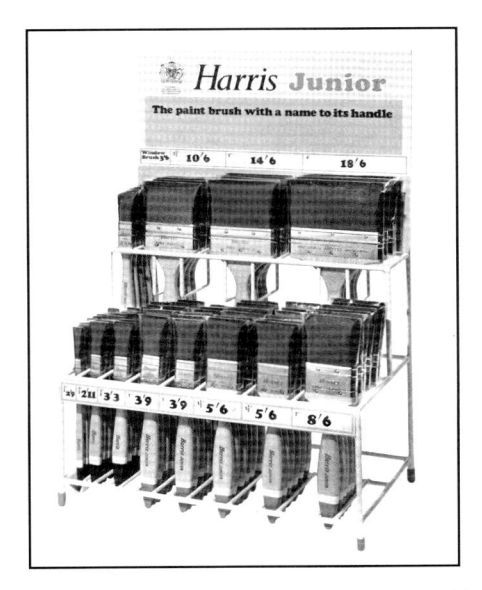

(Above) These showcards were popular with 'cash & carry' wholesale customers for resale to small retailers. (Right) A small rotary dispenser. When prices were rising rapidly in the '70s we stopped marking retail prices, as every time prices changed we had to supply replacement price strips.

very much increased the earnings of these gentlemen.

From 1947 to 1951 (during which time the arrears of the wartime demand was still being overtaken) salesmen's duties were not so much concerned with selling, as letting customers have whatever could be spared. But after we discontinued rationing orders in 1952, selling again became more important, and we rapidly increased our retail sales force until by 1960 we had 36 full time representatives, supervised by nine divisional sales managers. Remuneration was gradually improved by increasing the salary element and reducing the commission rates, with a car and expenses provided by the firm. We also initiated a minimum weekly draw so that the men could be sure of receiving a certain amount, even if the commission they had earned did not cover the payment. The debit balance arrears from this scheme were deducted when the men's earnings afterwards increased.

Even with these improvements, however, our turnover in sales representatives was considerable, averaging some 20% a year. It was not until the 1970s, by which time the salaries had gradually increased to around 70% of total earnings, that it became very unusual for a representative to leave us. Our divisional sales managers occasionally complained that with the great reduction of the incentive element, we had reduced the ambitious man's ability to earn more by harder work. One of the factors in this connection, however, is that once the big

This merchandiser was designed in the 1970s, and was available in 4 foot (the '900', shown above) and 6 foot versions. Unlike the earlier P3 the layout was flexible, as the hanging bars and strips could be positioned to suit the customer's requirements. They were very popular for many years among both shops and supermarkets, indeed at one time every Tesco branch had one.

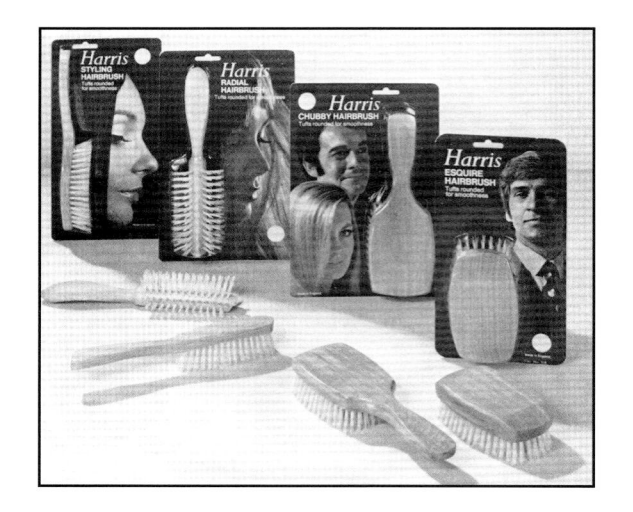

Attempts to sell toilet brushes were not successful. We had to call on different outlets, and we found it difficult to make inroads with a limited range against well-established manufacturers. Since then, we have concentrated on expansion within the decorating products sector.

modern chain stores have agreed to stock our lines, there is little an individual representative can do to improve the situation. Conversely, when sometimes the head office buyers decide to off-list our goods (as has happened!) causing a representative's sales to drop, it can hardly be said to be his fault. We now have a regular annual review of representatives salaries, so that we can consider the particular circumstances of each salesman on his area, and award increases where we think they are justified. One of the main considerations is that we want our staff to feel they have steady and secure employment with us, with payment for sickness periods, and reasonably generous pension schemes to look forward to. This seems to be appreciated, and I think we have now gathered together a loyal and hard working sales staff.

Going back to the 1960s, then, our trade with the retailers was covered by an active team of some 36 representatives, a sales force far bigger than any of our competitors. At that time our sales, according to the government figures, amounted to about 15% of the country's total production. How could we increase this share?

I had always been impressed with the successful financial results of the firm of Kleeneze Ltd, of Bristol. This company of brush manufacturers had been established in the 1920s by a Mr Crook, who had copied the sales organization of the Fuller Brush Co of America, ("I'm your friendly Fuller Brush man") by establishing a team of salesmen selling direct to the householder. The earnings of the Kleeneze salesmen were by commission only (averaging about 33%). As they booked orders (usually from housewives), they obtained the goods from the factory each week, got the householder to pay on delivery, and remitted the money to the factory before they could obtain any more supplies. So the parent company was not involved in giving any credit, or of any responsibility for supporting the salesman if he encountered a bad patch. The firm was very profitable, and the founder Mr Crook (who later became Lord Mayor of Bristol) died a millionaire. They employed as many as 1,600 salesmen in the 1950s, but as more normal employment became readily available it became difficult to persuade men to undertake this type of work. By 1970, their sales force selling direct to householders had dwindled to a very small number, and the firm had instead developed a more normal sales pattern, by selling direct to industry.

I never intended to copy the house to house method of selling for two reasons. In my opinion, it was humiliating for men to have to depend for their living on the sympathy of housewives, and in any case I wanted to build up an organization which would be worth working for, and provide secure and stable employment. I was, however, very impressed by the financial results of Kleeneze Ltd, which were far in excess of any other brush manufacturer in the

The Scottish Regional Conference in 1952 – manager W. Kettles seated on extreme right.

Sales conferences were held in each sales region once per year. These were attended by myself, the sales director (Peter Harrison), and the regional manager. Around 12 sales representatives were employed in each of our nine regions, and up to the 1970s each region had an office and secretary. Each sales territory had a retail rep. and a trade rep. and each side had their separate conference during the day. Peter and myself used to enjoy travelling round the country to the different venues, and we used some of our favourite hotels, such as The Bull at Gerrards Cross, for many years in succession. (Above) The East Midlands regional conference in 1956 (manager Jack Grant, extreme right) and (below) the North Midlands conference in 1958 (manager Albert Ellis on my right).

Page 88

country. It therefore seemed to us that we might develop a separate sales force apart from the retail trade, selling direct to users such as builders and decorators, factories and public authorities. So in the 1950s, we started to engage a number of salesmen in this field, who were provided with cars and given much the same conditions of employment as our retail representatives.

Small vans were supplied to our industrial representatives to enable them to carry stock and offer immediate delivery to the customer. In practice much paperwork was involved and orders were usually small, and they were later withdrawn.

Selling our goods direct to users, however, was much more difficult than the retail side of our business. We had built up the latter over a period of 30 years since 1930, and had some advantage over our competitors by the more attractive sales aids we were supplying, backed up by press advertising since 1948. The sales turnover of our trade representatives was usually much smaller than on the retail side, so that we had to ask relatively higher prices to cover the weekly salaries and expenses although we could still supply brushes at cheaper prices than the user usually had to pay. Another factor in this situation was that we were primarily known as manufacturers of do-it-yourself brushes, as distinct from the professional side. Although we made a range of top quality brushes, some builders and decorators required a lot of convincing that our brushes were as good as Hamiltons, whose name and reputation stood high in the decorating field. The fact that our brushes were prominent in Woolworths did not help.

However, by persistence, we gradually managed to build up an industrial selling side, which has stood us in good stead by making us a little less dependent on the large retail chain store buyers, many of whom want own brand products. Our reputation was enhanced by the granting to us in 1961 of the Royal Warrant as manufacturers and suppliers of painting and decorating brushes to H. M. The Queen. Firms receiving this distinction have to supply Her Majesty for three continuous years before the application is considered. We started supplying our goods to the Sandringham Estate in 1957. Later, this was followed by orders for Windsor Castle and the Queen Mother's Castle of Mey in Scotland. We have not yet supplied brushes direct to Buckingham Palace, which is maintained by the Office of Works. Nevertheless, we were glad to receive the award, which we still hold in 1985.

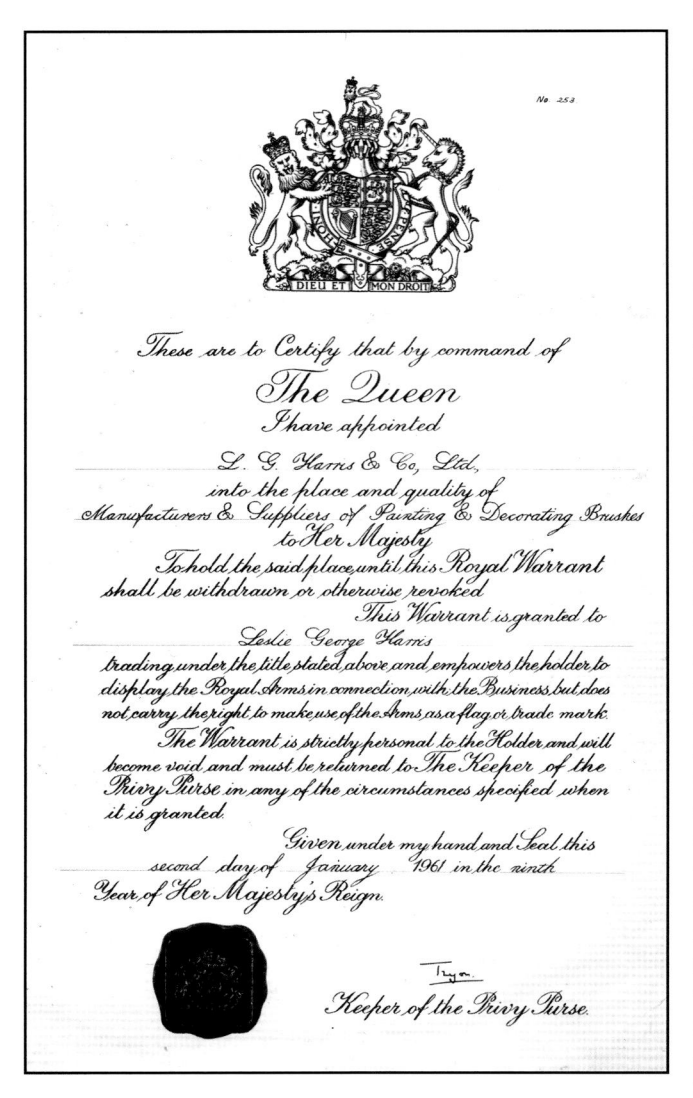

These are to Certify that by command of
The Queen
I have appointed
L. G. Harris & Co, Ltd,
into the place and quality of
Manufacturers & Suppliers of Painting & Decorating Brushes
to Her Majesty
To hold the said place until this Royal Warrant shall be withdrawn or otherwise revoked
This Warrant is granted to
Leslie George Harris
trading under the title stated above, and empowers the holder to display the Royal Arms in connection with the Business, but does not carry the right to make use of the Arms as a flag or trade mark.
The Warrant is strictly personal to the Holder and will become void and must be returned to The Keeper of the Privy Purse in any of the circumstances specified when it is granted.
Given under my hand and Seal this second day of January 1961 in the ninth Year of Her Majesty's Reign.
Keeper of the Privy Purse.

In the 1960s, when we still had some 18,000 retail and about 5,000 industrial customers, we increased our total number of full time representatives to over 100. This was very large for our size of firm, and I think in retrospect we expanded too quickly. Another development which proved ultimately unsuccessful was to provide our industrial representatives with small vans carrying stock (illustrated), so that they could supply orders immediately on the spot. The idea was that supplying direct from the vans would cut out packing and carriage charges, and enable the representatives to sell the user small quantities if required. But usually customers were not waiting for immediate delivery of brushes, and the scheme caused many complications by the checking of stock and its replacement every two weeks. It was therefore discontinued after a few years.

With the increasing cost of salaries, which have gone up more than inflation, and the cost of generous pension provisions based on final salaries at retirement, also the increase in cost of modern cars, we have gradually (1985) reduced our total sales representative staff, by natural wastage, to 60, with six divisional sales managers. This is still considerably more than our chief competitors Moseley Stone Ltd, and the Briton Brush Co, who each have a much smaller total. Whether the superior service afforded by our men's regular calls (every two weeks on the large D.I.Y. stores and about every six weeks on others) is sufficiently appreciated by our customers, is open to question. An increasing number of our multiple shop retailers are installing bar code computer mechanisms, so that sales of every individual line, and stock levels, are recorded at head office, rendering calls by sales representatives largely superfluous. If we were to reduce our sales force to that of our competitors, we could appreciably lower our prices. It looks in 1985 as if this is the trend we shall follow in future.

Advertising

Our first press advertising was commenced in 1947. In our search for a good advertising agent I had been impressed by the work of C. R. Casson Ltd of London. They had been responsible for the publicity for Murphy Radio, which some older readers will remember. These advertisements were characterised by a candid 'under emphasised' approach which seemed to me to carry more conviction than the usual blatant appeals. Another of their clients in the 1930s had been the makers of Jowett cars. These were advertised as "good, solid, and reliable", without any claims to particular superiority. One advertisement, I remember, carried the phrase "we were trying to think of a phrase to boost our cars, and thought of calling them 'a symphony in steel', until someone asked us what a symphony in steel was, and we had to reply that we didn't know!" Rightly or wrongly, this type of approach appealed to me, and C. R. Casson Ltd have remained our advertising agents ever since, although now absorbed into a larger firm. [In more recent years our advertising, now much reduced in scale, has been handled by Admen of Burton on Trent.]

Their first campaign for us was based on a humorous theme, featuring Dukes and Duchesses using our brushes, the idea being to connect us with the "Harristocracy". Cassons coined the phrase "the paint brush with a name to its handle", which has remained perhaps our main trade mark ever since. My favourite advertisement was the one showing a lady in hunting habit being offered a fox's brush, and haughtily refusing it demanding "a brush with a name to its handle"!

1972 – we celebrate the 25th anniversary of our association with C R Casson. Graham Barnes, our account executive is on my left.

In 1948-51, we took a quarter page every fortnight in The Radio Times (which at that time had a circulation of 8,000,000) in addition to regular ads in the national press. Although one can never exactly evaluate the effect of advertising, it is significant that we had to keep rationing our customers supplies right until 1952. I have the feeling that constant repetition of the catch phrase "the paint brush with a name to its handle" remained in people's minds.

After the success of the first few years, C. R. Casson Ltd pressed us to supply them with some more concrete reasons why people should buy our brushes. We had always tried to make sure that our bristles would remain fast, loose hairs being a cause of irritation to people who had to pick them out of their paintwork. So we began to feature the phrase "the bristles won't come out" in advertisements. This claim was quite justified in general terms. Unfortunately, bristle being a natural product, sometimes a hair or two might break off, and a few brushes might occasionally get through without adequate cleaning in our 'flirting' machines. We only rarely had complaints from the public, but since it was impossible to guarantee that not a single hair would come loose, we dropped this claim after a few years. [But in 1990 we launched a brush using synthetic filaments which was guaranteed against loss: the 'No-Loss' range, which

(This page and next) Early post-war advertising. The Harristocrat theme was very popular, and was the mainstay of our campaigns for some time. The phrase 'The Paint Brush with a Name to its Handle' caught on nationally.

proved a very successful first in the industry.]

In the 1970s and 80s, our advertising has become rather more general and diverse, with perhaps no particular central theme. So I think we have lost the original "schwerpunkt" appeal of the early years. The fact remains that according to the government figures which are published every quarter, our share of the country's total production of paint brushes has increased from about 12%-15% in the 1960s, to an average of 20% in recent years, in spite of greater competition. A modest increase, but still an increase! However, there still remains another 80% to go at... [By 2002 we believe our share of the UK market is nearer 50%.]

Chapter 6

OVERSEAS FACTORIES

South Africa
Our first export trade started in 1937 with South Africa, selling through a commission agent, Godfrey W Volkwyn of Johannesburg. Later, we expanded our overseas trade to a total of over 40 countries. But South Africa remained our chief market until 1949, when the South African government suddenly imposed quota restrictions which very much reduced our trade with that country.

In 1934, I had become friendly with Walter Stapp, the assistant professional at Harborne Golf Club, Birmingham. During the 1939-45 war, Walter served with the RAF. After the war, he told me that he didn't want to return to professional golf, and asked if I could find him a job with our firm. I thought he would make a good sales representative, and appointed him to a vacancy which we had in the Lancashire area. He did very well, and when our South African trade seemed likely to be stopped, I asked him if he would like to go out there with a view to starting a factory in the country for us. He readily agreed, and travelled out with his family in 1948, by the very restricted air services in those days. His first action was to open a small warehouse

(Left) Myself with Walter Stapp, managing director, outside the first South African factory in Darling St, Port Elizabeth. (Facing page) This is the letter I wrote offering Walter a post in South Africa. It makes interesting reading today.

2nd January 1948

Dear Walter

While on a recent visit to South Africa, I formed the conclusion that although we are doing a fair trade with that country at the present time, there would be very good possibilities for our brushes if we founded our own organisation in that country.

I am now writing to ask if you would like to consider an offer of the appointment as our permanent resident sales representative in South Africa.

The appointment would be conditional on your residence in Johannesburg, and the commencing salary would be £18 per week, plus full expenses, and the Firm would pay the whole of the cost of the removal of yourself and family from this country. We would also be prepared to help you with the cost of a new house in South Africa.

The appointment would be a permanent one, and I would rather you not consider it unless you feel a definite desire to go to South Africa, as it would be very unfortunate if, for any reason, you wanted to come back after a few months, after we had made all transfer arrangements, and paid for your removal.

The job would consist, in the first instance, mainly of travelling and booking orders, and it is also our intention to establish a distribution depot in Johannesburg, so that small lots could be supplied from stock. The supervision of this depot would also come under your jurisdiction, and it would possibly be necessary later to appoint one or two additional assistant travellers. The salary mentioned is of course, a commencing one, and remuneration would steadily increase as results accrued.

I feel sure you realise the necessity for stimulating this country's export trade, and I can tell you, from my own recent experience, that the standard of living in South Africa is substantially above that obtaining here. I understand the cost of living averages approximate more than in this country, as, although some things are dearer, there is no Purchase Tax. I feel sure you would find it a very pleasant country to live in, but of course, as to whether you would be home sick for the home country is a matter entirely for you to decide. Certainly that country, I think, has a greater future in front of it than we have here.

I shall be glad if you will give this matter your careful consideration, and let me know as soon as possible whether you would like to accept our offer.

With all good wishes,

in Johannesburg, to which we shipped our products, leaving him to distribute them locally.

Many orders were placed by South African importers in 1948, in advance of the 1949 quota restrictions, and in that year we increased our shipments to that country to the value of £21,400 – probably equivalent to £200,000 in 1985. In 1949, we established L. G. Harris & Co. (South Africa Pty) Ltd, and purchased a factory in Darling Street, Port Elizabeth, to which the machines (most of which had been made by us in Stoke Prior) were shipped in 1950. Our maintenance foreman, Peter Bloomfield, went out to supervise the installations, and Gladys Wood, forewoman of our women's brushmaking section, trained the local South African operatives. We also sent out Geoffrey Fulton, who intended to settle in South Africa, and who had been getting experience in our factory for some eighteen months, so that he could supervise the operation and maintenance of the machinery. More capital was needed to purchase the factory, and Mr Cecil Freer of Port Elizabeth, who had become friendly with Walter, took up a quantity of preference shares.

With the reduction of imports, and energetic management by Walter Stapp, the factory made good progress, and showed a profit from the first year, in contrast to many overseas ventures, which often make losses over the initial period. Our first factory, which included 6 $^1/_2$ acres of land, was sold in 1968, producing a surplus of some £40,000, a satisfactory transaction which helped to finance the building of a new factory in the Grahamstown Road Industrial Estate, Port Elizabeth, in 1969. Although the South African firm made consistent profits, these remained fairly modest for the first twenty five years, but in the 1980s they increased to an average of £70,000 to £80,000 per annum, on a sales turnover of between £500,000 and £600,000. The manufacture of household brushes and brooms was added to their production in the 1960s, in which period Walter's sons Michael and Peter came into the firm. My wife and I visited them in

(Below) South African factory staff in 1966. Michael Stapp on his father's left, Piet Kemp seated far left.

1969 – the second South African factory in Grahamstown Road Industrial Estate, Port Elizabeth.

December 1984, and came away feeling that the factory was in good hands and set fair for a prosperous future. We presented Walter with an inscribed silver plaque in appreciation of his 36 years of good management, and remain firm friends of Walter and his wife Vera, whom we have now known for over 50 years. [The shares in the company were in Mrs Harris's name, and the British company only had a small stake. In 1995 Peter and Michael purchased the company in a management buy-out. Their father died in 1997, their mother in 2001.]

Ireland

Before the 1939-45 war, we were exporting regularly to Southern Ireland. Our Agent in Dublin in those days was a Mr Boland. In 1954, however, the Irish government imposed a ban on the importation of decorating brushes, and our trade came to a full stop. So in 1955, we bought a small factory in Kill Avenue, Dun Laoghaire just south of Dublin. The premises, which cost £10,000 and had formerly been used as a slipper factory, stood on $1/2$ acre of land, and were on a long lease. We installed the paint and distemper brush assembly machinery, and appointed as managing director Geoffrey Wilson who had previously been a sales representative for us in the Lancashire area, with Dermot Nelson of Dublin as works foreman. It was not intended that the factory would make its own handles and ferrules, as the size of the Irish market did not justify it, so these components were imported from our main factory in England. We supplied the working capital from Stoke Prior, and borrowed £10,000 from the Friends Provident Life Office on a 10 year repayment, to finance the purchase of the factory.

As could be expected, the first year's trading resulted in a loss amounting to £4,875. This was followed by reducing losses of £1,651 in 1957, £1,346 in 1958, and £ 1,324 in 1959. In 1960, the first profit of £2,355 was recorded and from then on the profits steadily increased to £12,416 in 1974, on a sales turnover of £76,000. The Irish market, with a population of 3,500,000, remained small, but both Geoffrey Wilson and Dermot Nelson, with their small staff of eight girls and two sales representatives, managed the business very economically. Unfortunately, Geoffrey Wilson's health gradually deteriorated, culminating in his death in 1977. He had been a very loyal member of our staff, and his services were greatly appreciated.

The factory's sales until then had been of a very limited range of goods, as they did not have the machinery to make all the lines we were manufacturing in Stoke Prior. With the entry of Ireland into the European Economic Community, the import restrictions were removed. So when we received an attractive offer in 1980 to purchase the factory for £105,000, we decided to sell and operate the business as an importing agency, enabling it to market the much larger variety of goods we were making in England. Frank McKeon, who had been our leading sales representative, was appointed managing director, with Mr Nelson in the despatch and stores, and Mr Lowry as the other representative. We then took a lease of some warehouse premises at No. 1, Glasthule Road, Glasthule, Co Dublin, and stocked it up with a full range of our Stoke Prior products.

Unfortunately, things did not work out as we hoped. The small Irish economy left wide open to imports from the EEC countries, suffered drastically, and the Irish punt, which had previously been on par with sterling, was soon worth only 75% of the English £1. So as we had to be paid in sterling for our exports, the two other remaining Irish brush factories were now able to compete with us, with their lower wages and favourable exchange rate. In 1981, our Irish firm made a loss of £18,307. This has been followed by steadily reducing losses (1984 £8,171) but it does not seem likely in 1985 that we shall do much more than break even on our Irish operations.

Geoffrey Wilson (centre) was appointed manager of our new Irish factory in 1955, and remained in this position until he retired and died in 1977.

We still have a good connection with Ireland, and I think our goods have an excellent reputation there. We do much better in Northern Ireland than in Eire, the reason probably being that Ulster is part of the United Kingdom, which has been able to withstand the competition of the EEC countries better than the small Irish econ-

A corner of our Kenya factory canteen, with seating for 60 people. (Below) With Geraldine, Danny Davies (managing director) and R. Shibutse (foreman) during a visit to Kenya in 1969. Danny was helped by his wife Elsie in the company management.

omy. We have now been approached by a firm, Evode Ltd, who operate a similar Irish subsidiary warehouse, to take our goods and our representatives under their wing and combine our efforts in Eire with theirs. We have not made a final decision in this matter, but the suggestion may possibly be a way of improving the financial results. Having supplied the Irish market for 50 years since 1933, we don't want to gracefully retire if it can be avoided! [In 1991 we closed our operation and transferred our distribution to an independent Dublin company RS Sales, and Ireland has remained our largest export market.]

Kenya

We started exporting to East Africa in 1938. Our agent in Nairobi was then a Mr Black (covering Kenya, Uganda and Tanganyika), whom I visited in 1947. I remember that at that time very restrictive arrangements – to our shame – were in

1966 – our Kenya factory in Liverpool Road not far from the centre of Nairobi just completed. A further two factory bays were added later at the rear.

force against the native people, who were not allowed in most hotels or clubs. This may have been partly responsible for the agitation and violence carried on by the so-called Mau-Mau in their campaign for freedom from UK rule, which was finally granted by Britain in 1963.

After doing very well for us in the early 1950s, Mr Black retired from business, and we appointed in his place a Mr Thanawalla, who was already representing other British manufacturers. Mr Thanawalla further increased our trade with the colony. But after independence in 1963, Kenya ran into balance of payment problems, and imports began to be restricted. So we were now facing the same difficulties as we had encountered in South Africa and Ireland. The factories we had started in those two countries were doing well, and this encouraged us to try to retain our trade in Kenya by starting our own manufacturing enterprise there.

We could have reduced the capital outlay by renting some premises in one of the back streets known as 'go downs'. But we felt we wanted to carry on the tradition which we had started in Stoke Prior, by building a small Kenya factory which both the workers and ourselves could be proud of. In 1964 we negotiated with the Land Development Department of the government (still run at that time by British civil servants) to purchase the lease of a block of land in Liverpool Road, Nairobi, and engaged a local firm of architects to design a factory for us. We then obtained a loan of £10,000 from the Development Finance Corporation

Handle making in our Kenya factory. There are good supplies of suitable local hardwoods.

of Kenya to make a contribution to the capital cost, and placed a contract with a local firm to build the factory, which was ready for occupation in 1967. We were particularly anxious to provide good working conditions, and paid special attention to the canteen and toilet facilities.

The first managing director we appointed, W. D. 'Danny' Davies, had previously been sales manager of our London division. We purchased a pleasant house in Hatheru Road, Nairobi, for the use of his wife and self for £7,500 (1966) (sold 1985 for £45,000) and sent several members of our Stoke Prior staff to install the machines and train the local workers. All went reasonably well, and after the first year's loss of £14,100 in 1968, the factory broke even in 1969 and made its first profit of £2,780 in 1970. Over the next four years to 1974, profits averaged about £10,000 per annum. A small loss of £3,100 was incurred in 1975, when the remaining two bays of the factory were built.

Elsie Davies, wife of the managing director, was unfortunately attacked by a robber while at the factory that year. She did not suffer much injury, but the shock caused her and her husband to wish to retire early, which they did in 1976. Their place was taken by Mr W. E. Matthew, who had previously been our divisional sales manager in Scotland, and had just carried out a successful two years managing our Ceylon factory. At that time, Kenya was experiencing a boom due to higher prices for tea and coffee, and the firm's profits increased to £24,853 in 1976 and £35,620 in 1977. Although Mr Matthew had improved the situation during his time in charge, he felt he wished to return to England in 1977.

Mr Davies then said that his wife had recovered, and that he would like to have another go at managing the Kenya firm. He was then aged 65, and said he only wanted to do two years, but as he had previously managed the factory successfully, we felt we would like to give him the opportunity. He certainly did well in 1978 and 1979 to increase the profits to an average of £51,000 per year.

Our policy up to that time had been to promote members of our existing staff to managerial appointments. The manager of our bristle factory at Stoke Prior, W. C. 'Bill' Caleb, had asked several times if he could be given the chance of managing our Kenya factory. Then aged 63, he had given our firm excellent service ever since he joined it in 1948. Looking back, I think we made a mistake in offering him the appointment. Although he ran the Kenya factory quite successfully during the two years 1980-1981, the fact that he was the third managing director in 10 years was somewhat unsettling for the staff. He was due to retire in December 1981, and we received an application for his position from Marshall Steel, who had been works manager for a competitive brush factory in Nairobi, which was closing down. Mr Steel was in his 40s, and said that both he and his wife wanted to live permanently in Kenya until his retirement. In view of this, and of his previous experience in the brush trade, we accepted his application, and he took over from Bill Caleb in November 1981.

Unfortunately, Kenya ran into a period of exchange difficulties during 1982 and 1983, and import licences for raw materials were very much restricted, so that for a time our factory had no bristle to work on. The country's troubles culminated in an attempted coup, trying to take over the government, in August 1983. Much violence and damage was caused, and although the authorities managed to get the situation under control, trade suffered very much, and our factory sustained a loss of £6,000 in the first year of Marshall Steel's management, following profits of £38,000 and £19,000 under Bill Caleb. Mr Steel's second year produced a loss of £22,262. During this time, he had said once or twice that he could see no satisfactory future for our factory, so Brian Middleton and I went out in 1983 to discuss the situation with him. He said that some financial interests in Kenya had approached him with a view to buying our firm. We did not feel we wanted to give up so easily, after the factory had had such a successful record in the 1970s. Mr Steel then said that in view of the violence caused by the coup, and the unsatisfactory prospects (in his opinion) for the firm, he and his wife wished to return to England and give up his appointment as soon as possible. I think the truth was that although a pleasant man in himself, Steel was not used to taking executive responsibility, and when faced with difficulties, preferred to opt out to somebody else.

Never say die! What were we to do next? We wanted to take time over selecting the next man to manage the factory. So as the situation was rapidly going from bad to worse, we asked Danny Davies if he would like to go out for a third time for 12 months, to try to pull things round while we selected a new managing director. This he readily agreed to do, and took our firm on again in November 1983. He soon managed to improve the situation, and by the spring of 1984, things were looking much more hopeful.

This time we felt that the new managing director we appointed must be perhaps not more than 35 or 40 years of age, must have had some managerial experience, and must have the intention (provided he was successful) of staying in Kenya at least 10 years. No member of our Stoke Prior staff seemed to fulfil these qualifications, so we engaged the services of a firm of management selection advisors to advertise the post. Over 100 applications were received, and from the short list of six candidates we selected Michael Finch-Newey. He had for a long time been on the staff of I.C.I. Paints Division, and for the previous seven years had been in Indonesia as marketing manager for their factory there. He took over from Danny Davies in November 1984 after a preliminary visit to the Kenya factory in September, from which he came back full of enthusiasm. By May 1985 (the time of writing) he has already made a good improvement in the sales, and the outlook looks promising.

We are following our Stoke Prior practice, of operating a profit-sharing scheme for the Kenya workers. Although there has been no distribution in the last two years, I think the staff have appreciated the scheme. We certainly want to do our best for them. I am sorry to have had to recount so many details about our Kenya factory history, which has been through a number of vicissitudes since 1981. I am glad to say that since the beginning of 1985, the factory is again operating in the black. [Mike Finch-Newey's management was not successful, and in 1988 there was a cash crisis. We then sold the company to local Asian interests at a considerable financial loss.]

Ceylon (now Sri Lanka)
Both before the 1939-45 war, and in the 1950s and early 1960s, our exports to Ceylon were flourishing. We had been fortunate in having an excellent agent in Mr W. D. Carolis Snr. of Colombo, whose son, Godwin Carolis, took over the agency when his father died. By 1960, we were supplying 95% of the paint brushes imported into Ceylon.

1970 – our factory in Meegoda, near Colombo. This was built on land we bought from Godwin Carolis our former agent and investor in our Ceylon company.

For several years after 1948, when the country received its independence from Britain, Ceylon obtained high prices for its principal exports of tea, copra (dried kernels of coconut), rubber and precious stones. But as post-war trade conditions became more competitive, prices gradually declined, and by 1966 Ceylon was facing serious balance of payments problems. Imports were severely restricted, and Mr Carolis suggested that we might consider opening a manufacturing plant in the country.

(Above) 1969 – Geraldine lighting a ceremonial lamp to open the Ceylon factory. Gerry Summerfield and his son David on the extreme left, Mrs Carolis behind Geraldine, Oscar Perera (office manager) in centre, Noeline Thomas (managing director's secretary) on my left, and Mrs Summerfield at far right. (Below) A staff picture taken in 1979. Michael Dias, by then managing director, is seated in the centre, Oscar Perera on his right, and Nihal de Silva, factory manager and later a director, on his left. [2002 – the following are still employed: Chandra Jayawrdena (seated, far left); first row standing: Mrs Karunawathie (3rd from left), Beryl Moses (centre) Pushpa Ranjanie (on Beryl's left), W A Karunawathie (on her left), S Kularathne (far right); second row standing 3rd from left K D Gunasinghe; back row D Premathilakaratne (4th from right) and Sammy Rajapakse on the far right.

Another photograph of the Sri Lanka factory opening in 1969. (Left to right) Godwin Carolis, our previous agent and partner in the new business with us, Albert Smith (electrician from Stoke Prior), David, Emily and Gerry Summerfield, myself, Mrs Carolis, Geraldine, and Christopher Carolis, son of Godwin and Christobel.

Encouraged by the success of our other overseas ventures, Henry Reiner (then our export manager) and I went out to discuss the proposal in 1968. Mr Carolis said that the Ceylon government was keen to stimulate local production, and that as and when manufacturing plants were set up, imports of any item being produced in the country would be banned. We were reluctant to lose our existing trade with Ceylon, and decided to set up a factory. Under the then existing Ceylon government's laws, we were not allowed to own 100% of the ordinary shares, so Mr Carolis took up one-third, leaving us with the remaining two-thirds. This law was later amended so that any future firm starting would have to have Ceylonese majority shareholding.

Mr Carolis owned 2 acres of land opposite his country residence at Meegoda, 17 miles from Colombo. This was rather more land than we required, but the price was reasonable. So we then purchased it to provide for future expansion, and engaged a firm of Indian architects in Colombo to design the factory for us. The building contract was later placed in the sum of £56,000, and we obtained assistance towards the cost of this and the machinery by borrowing the sum of £36,000 from the Development Corporation of Ceylon. We then sent out a team of our people to install the machinery, with Douglas Wride (works director) in charge, assisted by Peter Bloomfield and David Hutchison (installation), Albert Smith (electrician) and Pat Clarke to train the women operatives. After some building delays the factory was officially opened by my daughter Geraldine, who lit a ceremonial lamp to mark the occasion, on November 16th 1969.

In accordance with our policy at that time, we invited applications from our existing staff for the position of managing director. One of our senior sales representatives, Gerry Summerfield, had been stationed in Ceylon for some years during the war. He had given the firm good service since he commenced with us in 1951, and in view of his previous experience in the country we decided to offer him the appointment. After three months training at Stoke Prior, he went out with his wife and son in March 1969. Mr Carolis had offered to allow him to live in his country bungalow opposite the factory, which seemed a very convenient arrangement. The first year's financial results, after production of brushes was commenced in 1970, came out at a loss of £13,124. This was followed by reduced losses of £7,630 in 1971 and £2,293 in 1972.

We were hoping that Mr Summerfield would want to stay as managing director for several years. In 1972, however, he said that the climate was not suiting his wife and young son, and he returned to England at his own request to take up his work with us again as a sales representative. We were still keen on appointing members of our staff whom we had known for several years, and offered a two-year contract to W. E. Matthew, who had previously been our divisional sales manager in Scotland. After the spade work which had been done in the previous period, he was able to improve the situation, and the firm's profits increased to an average of £12,000 during his two years 1972-1974.

Although in many British companies operating overseas factories, it is quite usual to offer two year contracts to expatriate managers, we felt that constant changes of management such as we had had in Kenya were undesirable. The Ceylon government had in any case passed a law that overseas owned factories

Godwin and Christobel Carolis pictured on a visit to the UK. We have much appreciated our association with the Carolis family, which now stretches back over four generations. Godwin's father was our agent till his death shortly after the war, and Godwin was able to build up our sales considerably in the post-war period. His son-in-law Michael Dias is the present managing director of our factory there, and his brother-in-law Christopher is a director. [Michael's son Sujan is also now working in the business – 2002].

must be managed by Ceylonese nationals. So we then appointed as managing director, Michael Dias, Mr Carolis's son-in-law, who had had previous managerial experience in the tea planting industry. He came over to Stoke Prior for a period of training, and took up his duties in August 1974. In his first year, the financial results suffered, but by 1977 he had regained the previous level of profits, which have steadily increased to £14,000 in 1983 and 1984. These figures are, of course, calculated at the current rate of exchange of 36 rupees to the £1, as against the rate of 14.3 before devaluation in 1977, so the profits in rupees have increased very much more than the sterling figures indicate.

After a period of some hesitation, Michael Dias is now (1985) embarking on the production of household brushes and brooms as well as decorating brushes, for which we are sending him the machinery. In order to foster reciprocal trade, for several years the Ceylon factory has been making large quantities of our cheaper hand made brushes, and exporting them to us in the UK. At the present time, the factory is employing about 40 workers. The quality of the work produced is excellent. The standard of wages paid to Ceylonese factory operatives is, of course, extremely low compared with the British rate – some £4 to £5 per week for women and somewhat more for men. We have instructed Mr Dias to pay them at least 10% more than the going rate locally, and we have, of course, operated our usual profit-sharing scheme ever since the factory was started. We get very willing and loyal co-operation from the factory workers, and would like to see their standard of living steadily rising. We have not yet started a pension scheme for them, but hope to do so in the near future.

We have long and pleasant relations with Godwin Carolis and his wife Christobel, and their family, including of course, Michael Dias. So barring possible economic difficulties, we think our Ceylon factory (now Sri Lanka) has a bright future. [In 2001 Michael's son Sujan, sales director of the company, tried to get backing for a management buy out, which we would have agreed to if sufficient funds were available, but economic problems after the general election at the end of 2001 meant that his backers decided not to go ahead at the time.]

Portugal
We had never exported more than a few shipments of our brushes to Portugal. In 1959, the firm of Rufino Alves Ribeiro & Filhos of Vergada, near Oporto, got in touch with us to ask if we would enter into an agreement for them to make our brushes under licence on a royalty basis. In 1960 we shipped the plant and machinery, most of which was made in our own works, to make everything except the handles which they were to make from plastic (which we didn't like at the time!). They have an efficient tool room for making plastic injection moulding tools, and we have reciprocated by placing orders with them for some tools for our machines, which have proved satisfactory.

Unfortunately for them, the model brush factory which they established in Angola in the 1960s was taken over by the Communist regime when the Portuguese government was overthrown, and they lost the whole of the capital

1978 – Andrew and Douglas Wride pay a visit to Oporto in Portugal, where the Ribeiro family had a factory that made our paint brushes under licence. Their factory produced corks, and had expanded into household and tooth brushes, and then wanted to make paint brushes. Vasco Ribeiro (left) and his cousin Luis trained at Stoke Prior in 1960. Luis's wife Maria and daughter Betty on his right.

which they had invested. This was a sad blow for them, compensated a little by a request from the communist manager who took over, to go back and show him how to service some of the machines, which they did at his expense!

We have formed firm friendships with both Luis and Vasco Ribeiro, two of their younger directors. The firm is still making Harris branded brushes, and we have had pleasant relationships with our Portuguese friends over the 25 years since 1960. [Unfortunately the Portuguese company got into financial difficulties and ended their relationship with us in 1990. We were then able to export goods from Stoke Prior again.]

Turkey
Since 1938 we had always had a good trade with Turkey. Our agent in those days

was a Mr Behare. But the same difficulties happened in Turkey as had occurred in our other overseas markets – the imposition of restrictions in 1954 to reduce imports, after which our trade dropped to very small levels. In 1963 we were approached by the principal paint makers in the country, Messrs Durmus Yasar Ve Ogullari of Izmir, asking whether they could come to an agreement to make our brushes in Turkey. After preliminary discussions, we agreed to supply them with a complete plant to make our paint brushes, including handles and ferrules, and train their workers, in return for an agreement through which they were to make our brushes under licence at a percentage royalty on the sales turnover. Messrs Yasar built a new factory for the manufacture of our brushes, and we shipped all the equipment to them in 1965.

Izmir 1965 – I visit the Dyo paint factory to make final arrangements for them to make our brushes under licence. On my left are the two brothers Yasar, sons of the founder of this large Turkish industrial conglomerate, and on my right is Mr Peterson of the Sadolin paint company of Denmark, with whom they already had a similar arrangement. (Below) Andrew visited the factory in 1979, and was pictured with Mr Gokalp, who was manager of the paint brush factory at that time.

We have had pleasant relationships with Messrs Yasar ever since, and supply them regularly with bristle and various other items. Unfortunately in 1977 and 1978 Turkey ran into an acute shortage of foreign exchange, and in those years we supplied goods valued at over £100,000 for which we have not yet been paid (1985). We have received payment for our subsequent transactions, and have been assured that the old debt will ultimately be settled. [Although this old debt was paid, our commercial relations with Turkey have dwindled, although the original royalty agreement is still in force].

West Germany

In 1972-74 we were supplying a firm named Meiser of Germany with our painters tools. Afterwards, they found a cheaper source of supply, and discontinued buying from us. In 1983 we came into touch with a Mr John Stone, who was representing the Harrison curtain rail firm in West Germany. He was intending to give up his connection with Harrison's, and thought there should be good prospects for the sales of our tools in the country. So we set up L. G. Harris & Co. (G.M.B.H.), rented a warehouse in Hockheim, near Frankfurt, and appointed Mr Stone sales manager on a trial basis. Up to 1985, sales have been disappointing, but Mr Stone says he hopes to open more large chain store accounts, and is hopeful of a major increase in sales. We do not intend to lose money indefinitely on this venture, so its future at the moment is uncertain, but I thought I should include a reference to it before this book goes to press. [Our venture in Germany with John Stone did not last very long. But soon afterwards we started supplying a distributor, Lenhartz, under their own label, and this business still continues.]

Singapore

After our relatively successful ventures overseas, I was keen on looking for another market where we could set up a factory. The ex-British territories of Malaysia and Singapore seemed a good place to look, even though our sales there had never been very great. Money seemed to be available to support suitable projects, although one potential investor whom Andrew and I met quickly withdrew his support when he learned that bristle is from pigs – he was a strict Muslim! Andrew went out to Singapore and Malaysia twice in the 1970s, but concluded that the strength of cheap Chinese brushes in the market would make it difficult for us to gain a large market share.

In the 1970s, our business in Singapore had been handled by a Chinese gentleman, Alfred Ong. Although his sales were not large, he felt that there were good prospects in the paint roller market, but advised us against setting up in Malaysia, whose population was indolent compared to the hard working Chinese in Singapore! In 1983 we decided to start a small assembly factory in the city, mainly for paint rollers. We rented a small flatted factory and registered Harris Brushes (Far East) Ltd in 1984. A friend of Mr Ong's, Henry Seah, invested 25% of the capital, but early results were disappointing. Our first manager did not last long, and his replacement, Lawrence Goh, was appointed by Brian Middleton in March 1985. But success has been hard to achieve, and the future of this small venture at the moment seems in some doubt. [In 1994 Lawrence Goh submitted his resignation, and we decided to take that opportunity to close the company, and supply our customers there direct from Stoke Prior.]

1992 – Andrew with the manager of our small Singapore factory Lawrence Goh, and his assistant Madelaine. It was located in a flatted factory near the overseas trade centre.

1968 – alder (alnus glutinosa) trees 20 years after planting in Ockeridge Wood. These trees were planted in a damp valley, very suitable for alder. Trees in the foreground have a breast height diameter of 12 inches (30 cms), 50 feet (15 metres) high. Exceptional growth, yielding rather soft timber. As many of our woodlands had rather heavy, damp soil, we planted a lot of alder trees – despite quick growth they have a tendency to develop new growth from the base, so are not ideal as a timber tree, although they would have coppiced well.

Chapter 7

FORESTRY

I must now go back to 1946. I felt that if I could emulate Henry Ford, I might be just as successful in the brush trade as he had been making motor cars. (A theory only partly true, as I found to my cost in later years.) One of Ford's beliefs was in "reaching back to the sources". This involved him in vertical integration by producing his steel right from the iron ore, logging timber from his own forests (much wood was used in cars in those days), establishing his own rubber plantations in Brazil for the tyres, and even buying a local railroad to improve his transport.

The handles of the humble brush had for centuries been made of wood. So I conceived the idea of planting hardwood trees to provide our own timber requirements. We only needed trees of comparatively small dimensions, since most of our handles were small. The timbers we used were mainly sycamore, ash and alder. All of these are what is known as coppicing species, in other words, when felled after having been grown to timber size, they grow again from the root, avoiding the necessity of replanting for the next generation. The three hardwood trees referred to usually achieve a diameter of nine to ten inches, the size we required, in about 50 years. So my idea was to acquire and plant 50 acres a year, achieving a forest of 2,500 acres over 50 years, which would then, after being felled, grow again by themselves for future use. The fact that I would be over 90 by the time this arrived, was beside the point – the next generation would get the benefit, and our brush factory by this time would be getting its timber almost for nothing.

We started in 1947 by acquiring and planting up a 33 acre wood known as Cobblers Coppice, near Upton Warren not far from our factory. This was followed by Ockeridge Wood, near Holt Fleet (157 acres) planted over the three years 1948-49-50, and then by Monk Wood, Sinton Green (153 acres) planted 1951-52-53. All the woods we purchased had been felled during the second world war. In the intervening years before we took over, the undergrowth and brambles had grown up to a considerable height. This was before the days of mechanical scrub clearing machines, and all the scrub and undergrowth had to be cleared by hand before planting, an expensive operation in labour, partly com-

Our forestry nursery about 1952. The seeds are first sown in the 'Dunemann' beds and transferred to the transplant lines (on right) after one year's growth, to develop the root system before planting out in the woods.

pensated for by the low purchase price of the land, which in those days only averaged about £15 per acre.

For the record, I will list the succeeding woods which we bought and planted up in the following years. After Ockeridge and Monk Wood, Shortwood near Redditch (175 acres, planted 1955-56 and later), Stoke Prior (60 acres, planted 1956-57), West Grove near Alcester (84 acres, planted 1956-57), Temple Grafton near Alcester (65 acres, planted 1958-60), Roundhill, Stock Green, (92 acres, planted 1960), Binton near Temple Grafton (76 acres, planted 1961), Trench Wood near Himbleton (104 acres, planted 1962-63), Goosehill, Hanbury (135 acres, planted 1964-65), Butlers Hill near Redditch (97 acres, planted 1966-69), Atch Lench near Evesham (135 acres, planted 1969-70), Brockhill near Redditch (72 acres, planted 1971-72), Wellesbourne near Stratford upon Avon (170 acres, planted 1971-74), Ellbatch Wood, Great Witley (115 acres, planted 1976-77), Kings Wood, Great Witley (22 acres, planted 1977), and Uffmoor, Romsley (212 acres, planted 1977-9). These woods together with other small areas, made up a total of 1,946 acres acquired and planted by 1984, an average of 53 acres per year. Until these plantations produced timber large enough for our own requirements, we had, of course, to purchase our timber from other woodland owners, mainly from the Cotswolds.

In the 1950s, the use of plastics for the manufacture of brush handles was practically unknown. But as the years went on, with the advent of new types of plastic and more sophisticated injection moulding machines, plastic paint brush handles began to appear. The early types had a 'soapy' feel, and had a poor reception by the trade. But they gradually improved, and by the 1970s, after being lacquered, only an experienced person could tell them from wood. Many users of paint brushes had the habit of soaking them in water after use, which caused wooden handles to swell and afterwards shrink, a point in favour of plastics. But the main advantage was that with plastics, much less labour was involved. Although wood was cheaper as a basic raw material, it had first to be sawn from the log into boards, then kiln dried to 10%-12% moisture content, sawn into lengths, cross cut, machined, sanded, and finally dipped in lacquer. There is also a high wastage factor of probably 25%-30%. Plastic handles can be produced by the latest types of injection moulding machines at a fraction of the cost in labour compared with wood. All that is necessary is to keep the machines loaded with the moulding powder and the handles are automatically discharged, not even needing inspection.

As I have related above, in the early years of plastic handles they were regarded as 'cheap', and wooden handles were preferred, particularly by the tradesman. But faced with increasing competition, and with the steadily rising cost of labour, which multiplied five times between 1965 and 1982, we had to start using plastics for some of our handles in the early 1970s. The final cost of a brush (or tool) fitted with wooden handles is about 7%-10% more than one with a plastic handle. We are now (1985) using plastics for about half our production. A few customers still prefer wood. It remains to be seen whether the public at large will be willing to pay the little extra involved for the natural product. Wooden handles still seem to be widely used in America, surprisingly enough.

All these developments caused us to look again at our forestry planting programme. By 1984 we had acquired and planted up nearly 2,000 acres of woodlands. Our forestry team had been gradually reduced to eight men, from fifteen in 1947. This expense had only been partly offset by small returns, such as shooting rents and slowly increasing amounts of small timber. We had, nevertheless, built up a capital asset of considerable value. In addition to this, we had invested about £400,000 in plastic injection moulding machines and tools, by borrowing from the bank.

It seemed to us that in future years we should probably be using a reduced quantity of wood, and more of plastics. Our woodlands in 1985 had a capital value of approximately £1,500,000. It looked, therefore, somewhat foolish to be borrowing from the bank at the present high rates of interest, and at the same time sitting on a capital asset which had only a long term future. So in that year we decided reluctantly to start selling our woodlands. The first woods we offered for sale were those in Warwickshire (387 acres). For the time being, we still kept our forestry team of eight men engaged in pruning, cleaning and thinning our other plantations.

In 1981, we entered all our hardwood plantations in the Royal Agricultural Society of England's competition for woodlands and plantations. We were pleased to receive a Judges Special Award (and a goblet), presented by Lord

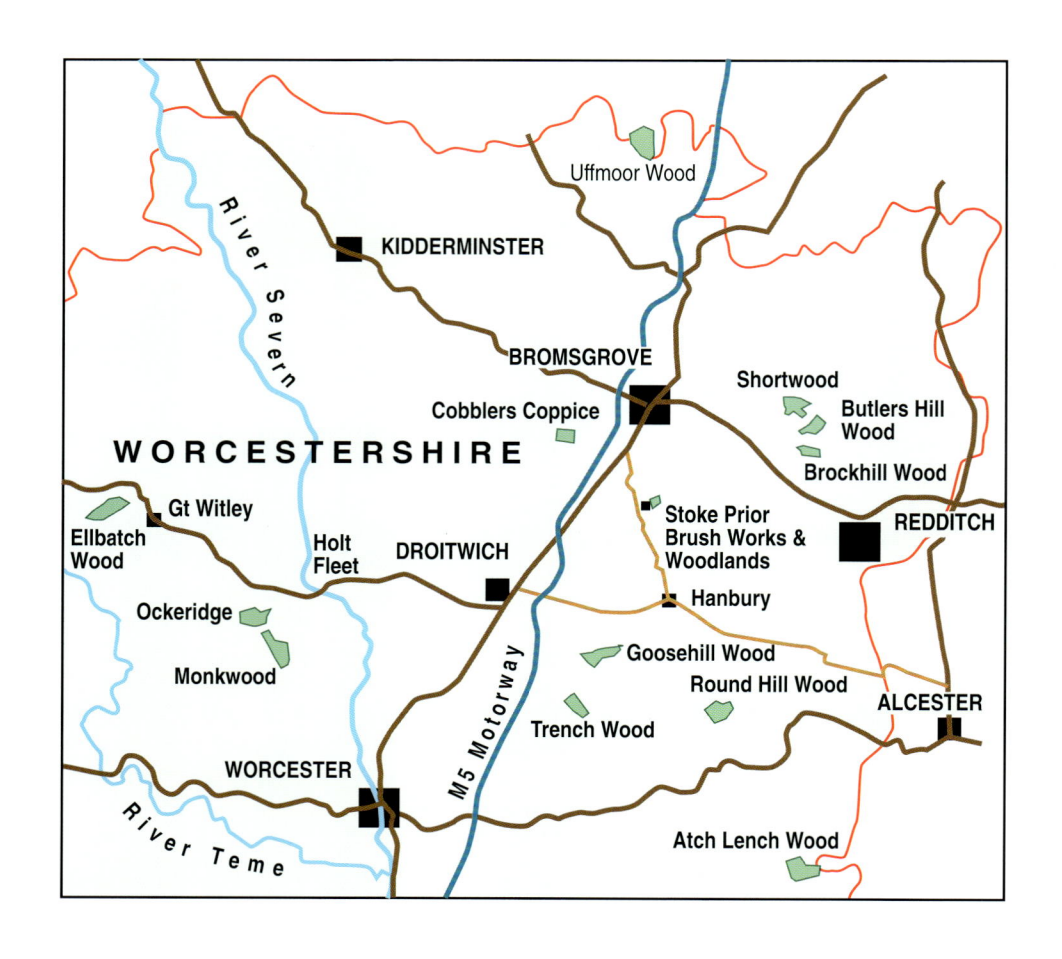

This map of north east Worcestershire shows the woodlands we owned in the county. The map on the facing page shows those in west Warwickshire. Selected roads only shown.

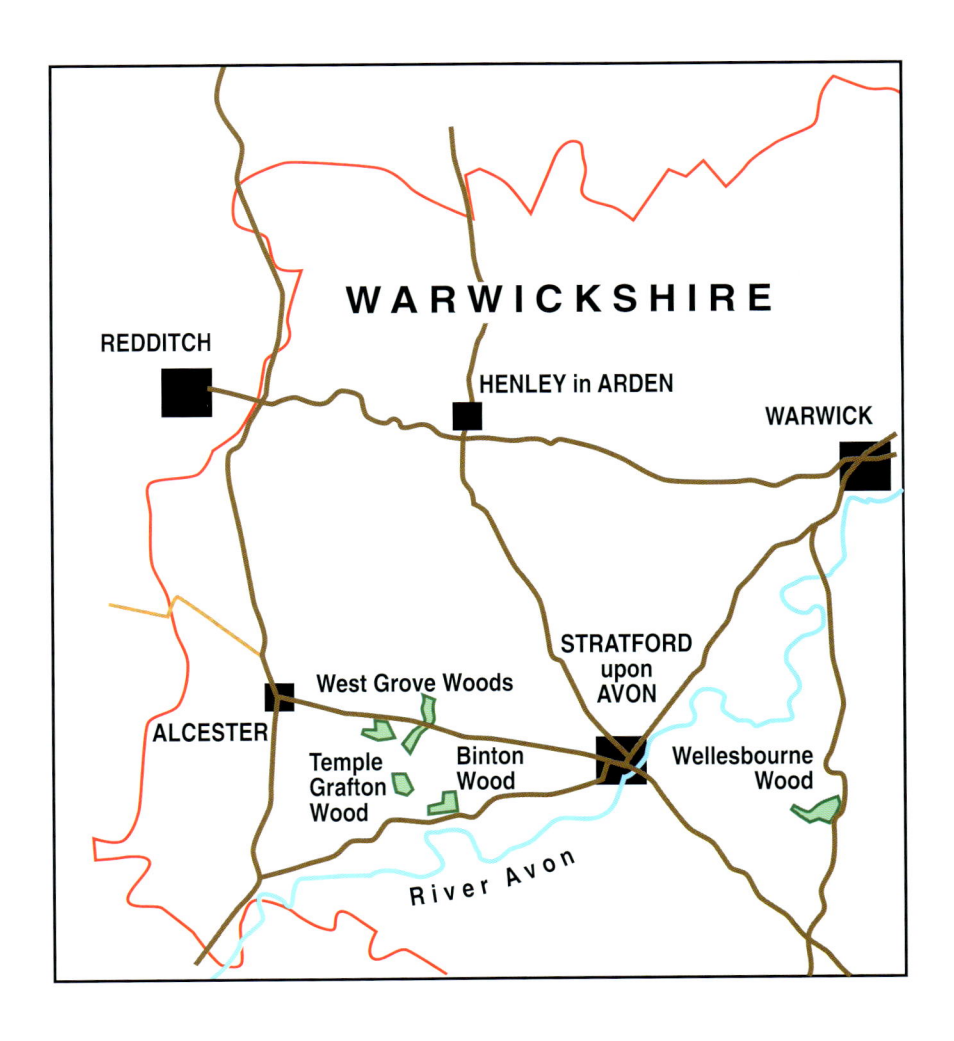

WARWICKSHIRE

- REDDITCH
- HENLEY in ARDEN
- WARWICK
- West Grove Woods
- ALCESTER
- STRATFORD upon AVON
- Temple Grafton Wood
- Binton Wood
- Wellesbourne Wood
- River Avon

(Above) 1968 – Japanese larch (latrix leptolepsis) 20 years after planting in Ockeridge Wood, Sinton Green, near Holt Fleet. (Right) Sycamore (acer pseudoplatinus) in Short Wood, Tutnall and Cobley, 20 years after planting. The tree in the foreground has grown exceptionally well. Sycamore usually attains a diameter of 4 inches (10 cms) at breast height at this age, 30 – 35 feet (10 metres) tall. Edgar Jones, forestry manager, is in the picture.

Clinton, of the Forestry Commission. The certificate reads:

"These woodlands cover 784 hectares and, though still immature, are being managed to a very high standard both in sylvicultural and commercial respects. The whole venture is highly specialised and grown to provide suitable materials for brush making. Most of the production is absorbed direct by their own factory. The standard of plantations, roading, fences and gates is excellent, despite great difficulties with very heavy surface clay in many areas. Combined with the highly efficient production and handling the woodlands do, we feel, deserve recognition by a special award. Here is an exceptionally fine example of industrial and sylvicultural integration unique in the United Kingdom."

The previous year the same Society awarded a Silver Medal for the management of Rough Hill Woods near Alcester.

Looking back, although our original intention of providing our own raw materials had been frustrated by events, our whole forestry enterprise had enabled us to build up a capital resource at a relatively small net outlay, since the cost of clearing, planting and weeding had all been allowed for taxation purposes, only the value of the land having to be capitalized. Most other forestry planting in the previous 40 years had been of conifer trees. We had planted hardwoods almost exclusively. It may be that their relative scarcity in the 21st century will enhance their value, as well as beautifying the countryside.

Planting a tree is one of the very few human actions which can really be called altruistic.

"A person plants a tree for his children, his grandchildren, or even for their children, but not for himself" (from a book on tree planting).

(Below) After felling our timber lorry brings the logs, cut to a standard length of 7 feet 4 inches (2.2 metres) back to our saw mill.

(Left) with Edgar Jones, forestry manager, when we received our award in 1981. (Below) hardwood poles extracted from our plantations as thinnings having the bark stripped off in three places by a machine. This helps the poles to dry out naturally without deterioration of the timber.

1980 - after bark stripping, the poles are stacked for drying in an open sided building. After a few months the moisture content is reduced to 12%-15%, and they are ready for turning into broom stocks. (Below) Sawn hardwood boards stacked in our timber shed awaiting kiln drying. This takes about 14 days in steam heated kilns, and the moisture content is reduced to 10%-12%. This timber is not from our own woods, but from timber contractors working mainly in the Cotswolds.

On our site on a mountain top near Trawsfyndd, central Wales, where British pig hair was taken directly from slaughter houses, and spread for an initial weathering, prior to preparation at Stoke Prior.

Chapter 8

BRISTLE – OUR NEXT VERTICAL INTEGRATION PROJECT

Since we first started manufacturing paint brushes in 1930, I had always been concerned at our reliance on one country, China, for our bristle supplies. In the 1930s, a small quantity of bristle came from Russia; this source dried up after 1939. Some Indian bristle was imported, but this is too stiff for making good quality paint brushes. So in practice, the Chinese had the monopoly.

Bristle, as the reader will know, is defined as the hair of the hog, pig or boar. In the early part of the 20th century, a small bristle dressing industry had grown up in France and Germany using domestically produced pig hair. This was nearly all yellow in colour, and somewhat softer than the Chinese black variety. It was used fairly widely by French and German brush manufacturers, but never gained much acceptance in Britain, being higher in price than Chinese.

Brush manufacturers in the United States had always used Chinese bristle until the 1950s, when America cut off relations with China. This gave a great opportunity to the German and French bristle dressers, who profited considerably by exporting their bristle to the States until 1970, when President Nixon again opened the door for trade with China.

A Chinese pig. Note the long bristle on the spine.

In Britain we continued to import Chinese bristle throughout this period. But in 1960, the Chinese government suddenly increased their prices overnight by about 80%. Presumably they were aware of their virtual monopoly position and saw no reason why they should not take advantage of it. This caused us to wonder whether we might emulate the German and French by starting our own bristle factory using British pig hair. The idea appealed to me tremendously, as I was always fascinated by the possibility of producing our own raw material. We were growing our own timber. If we could produce our own bristle as well, we might be the leaders in the paint brush industry. I remembered a saying I had seen quoted in one of my Quaker books. "Stick to your business, young man. Stick to your brewery, and you will be the greatest brewer in London. Be brewer and banker, and manufacturer and merchant, and you will

(Above) 1971 – a bristle washing and drying machine, adapted from machines in the wool industry by Petrie and McNaught Ltd. The raw bristle was brought in from our Welsh mountain depot after being weathered. The first machine regulated the rate of feed, the second washed the bristle and squeezed it between rubber rollers, which was followed by a conveyor drying oven. (Below) our own home made bristle washing machine. Overhead beaters thrashed the bristle round in warm water.

1962 – early methods of straightening bristle. The hair was bound on perforated aluminium tubes, boiled for four hours and dried. This age old method copied from European dressers was superseded by machines pressing the bristle onto stainless steel belts.

soon be in the 'Gazette'" [the London Gazette publishes official announcements, including bankruptcies].

The British government at that time was very concerned about the country's deteriorating balance of payments, and was encouraging the increase of exports and reduction of imports. Our bill for imported bristle was averaging £250,000 a year. So I thought that by producing our own bristles we could not only reduce our dependence on China, but also make a small contribution to reducing the country's import bill. (This was before the days of North Sea oil, when the balance of payments problem seemed to solve itself.)

No bristle dressing factory had ever been started in Britain before. We knew Mr Moss, the manager of Avoncroft Cattle Breeders, the artificial insemination centre, and asked his advice. He said that the longest pig hair could be obtained from what was known as the 'heavy hog' of 250lbs, of which 8,000 per week were being slaughtered at the Walls sausage factory in North Acton, London. So we went down to see them. After the hogs were slaughtered, they were passed through a long revolving drum, fitted inside with short knives. The pig carcasses rotated along the length of this drum, and the knives scraped off the hair, which was deposited on the floor underneath. They had apparently practically no market for the hair, except for a small quantity sold as agricultural fertiliser. So they agreed to have it bagged up as produced, provided we would collect it weekly. The price we agreed to pay them was £3 per ton.

Having secured a source of supply, our next job was to install a pilot plant to see if we could produce satisfactory bristle from Walls' raw material. The hair

1973 – seven 'dragging' machines, sorting out the hair into various lengths from 2 inches to 3 3/4 inches in 1/4 inch steps by conveying it past rubber rollers set at an angle to the conveyor. After this the hair had to be 'turned', so that all the 'flag' ends (the fine end of the hair used for painting), pointed the same way. (Below) The final process. A battery of bristle 'dressing' or mixing machines of our own manufacture. These mix different qualities together to produce a uniform end product.

Although most of the hair we used in our bristle processing plant was light coloured, paint brushes traditionally have black bristle in this country, derived from the colour of Chinese pigs. So we dyed most of our production black in this dyeing plant. This did little to improve the quality of the hair, but unfortunately the natural colour of European hair is a rather dirty yellow, and not very attractive.

as recovered from the carcass contains pieces of skin adhering to it, and smells strongly of urine (one of our chief problems). It is also mixed up with numerous toe nails from the carcasses. So the initial process is to wash it. We built our first fairly crude washing tanks (1962) in brick, with mechanically propelled beaters overhead, which thrashed the material through the water (see illustration). These tanks worked satisfactorily, though on a small scale.

All pig hair as removed from the animal is curly. So the next process after washing it and removing the skin and impurities, is to straighten it. The traditional way of doing this on the Continent was to wind and bind the hair with string on to perforated aluminium tubes. These were subsequently boiled and afterwards dried in an oven, leaving the hair reasonably straight (see illustration).

Our bristle at this stage was now clean and straight, but contained a great deal of hair shorter than 2 inches (50mm), the minimum length we normally use. The short bristle less than 2 inches was then extracted by passing the hair through rotating drums perforated with holes of 1¾ inches diameter, the short

China has always been the principal source of supply of pig hair for the British brush industry. As the common Chinese pig has black hair, in Britain brushes are traditionally made with black bristle. But in Europe and Russia bristle was prepared from pigs with white or yellowish hair, which is why brushes in Europe are often made this colour. Another country which produces bristle is India, where pigs often have a mixture of white and black, or 'grey' hair. The three colours are shown above. In South America pigs have a reddish hair, although this hair is not used in Europe. (Below) Synthetic filaments have been available since the 1940s – their development started in the USA, as trade with China was banned in 1948. Their use in Europe was for many years restricted by their high price compared with bristle, but as Chinese pig production gets more intensive, with the animals therefore being slaughtered earlier and with less hair, and synthetic filaments become cheaper, this situation is due to change, and some predict the end of natural bristle altogether in the future.

bristles falling through underneath. These machines, which we made in our own works, were not perfect, as they allowed some long bristles to fall through the holes. They were later superseded by more efficient Italian machines which extracted the long bristle by passing past rubber rollers. The hair we then produced at that stage contained much less unusable short bristle, leaving about 30% of the original bristle of a length of 2 inches and up.

Three further processes followed. Firstly, we had to grade the bristle into different lengths in $1/4$ inch steps from 2 inches up to $3 1/4$ inches (82mm) (very little British bristle was over this length). This operation was done in 'dragging' machines by passing the hair past a series of rubber rollers, which extracted the longest bristle first, followed by the shorter lengths. Of the material produced, about 50% would be 2 inches long, 25% $2 1/4$ inches, 12% $2 1/2$ inches, 7% $2 3/4$ inches, 4% 3 inches and possibly 2% $3 1/4$ inches.

All hair has a root end, through which it is attached to the skin, and a flag end, the fine end which is used to paint with. So all our bristle had now to be turned, leaving the flags all one way and roots the other.

Bristle normally tapers from the root to the flag. So the next (ingenious) machines passed the bristle underneath rapidly oscillating belts, which had the effect of pushing the root ends to the outside and leaving the flags in the centre. As the material went through the machines it was then folded together, leaving all the flags one way and the roots another.

The colour of British bristle is practically all yellow. We frequently had to mix it with Chinese black bristle, so the final process was to dye it black. This we did in the usual type of textile dyeing machines.

I hope I have not wearied the reader by relating all these technical processes. But I thought I would like to set them down for the record.

As the years went on, we gradually improved our methods. The washing tanks were superseded by large concrete tanks which we built ourselves, discharging the washed bristle continuously on to a conveyor belt. The winding of the bristle on to perforated rods gave way to four large German machines which pressed the hair on to stainless steel belts and discharged it completely straightened. The short extracting process was much improved by passing the hair past rubber rollers instead of through revolving drums.

After we found in 1962 that we were producing our bristle about 20% cheaper than the new Chinese prices, we gradually expanded our raw bristle supplies, until we were collecting from about 20 slaughter houses all over the country, using a fleet of four lorries. But with the expansion, trouble awaited us. The smell produced by the initial pilot plant was comparatively little. When our raw bristle intake grew to about 50 tons a week, the odour produced became very obnoxious, and we began to receive complaints from local residents. We installed so-called smell removing machines, but they made little difference. So we felt we should have to start thinking again.

By 1966, our bristle processing plant was making quite a satisfactory profit. It seemed a pity to have to close it down because of the smell nuisance. We had been washing the material immediately on receipt at our works, which created the smell. If the bristle is left out in the open to weather, the smell gradually goes out of it. We tried spreading it about 6 inches thick in the hardcore rides in some of our woods, but were immediately assailed by neighbouring farmers telling us to stop it. So, not being willing to give up, we looked around for some isolated area where the smell would not be likely to offend any local people. We asked the help of the Forestry Commission in Wales. They had no woods of their own which they could offer, but said they knew of a mountain top 1,500 feet high, near Trawsfynydd, Merionethshire, which had been covered with tarmac during the war for use as an army depot, which might be suitable. The area involved was 15 acres, four of which were covered in tarmac – ideal for our purpose of spreading the bristle for weathering. We were able to negotiate with the farmer owner (who wasn't using it) and bought the area for £750. We afterwards increased the area of tarmac to 7 acres at a considerable expense, and planted the remainder of the land with spruce trees in 1969.

As we collected the bristle from the slaughterhouses, we took it straight to our Welsh mountain top. After it was spread out to a depth of about 6 inches it had to be turned over once a week to prevent the hair underneath going rotten, for which we engaged a local man. We also erected a wooden building on the mountain to house the necessary tractor, and provided a small room at the end with heater and toilet. After the bristle had weathered on the mountain for about eight weeks, the smell had disappeared. We then sent other lorries to collect it and bring it back to Stoke Prior. We commenced operations on this site in July 1967. It was a lonely spot, and our two attendants lived there – sadly, one died when returning from Dolgellau on foot in a snowstorm one night.

The extra cost involved in taking the bristle to Wales, spreading it out and then fetching it back, reduced our profit margin. We were, however, still able to produce the bristle cheaper than Chinese prices.

When we started our bristle production in 1961, we were not sure whether the venture would be a permanent success. So we housed the plant in temporary asbestos buildings on a site at the rear of our main factory. In spite of the setback through the smell problem, it still looked in 1968 as if the production of our own bristle from British raw material had a good future. We were not happy

Our new factory for the bristle processing department under construction in 1969.

with the temporary buildings in which our employees were working, and decided to build a new purpose-built factory to enable us to expand our production and provide first class working conditions. The size of the new building, which was opened in 1970, was 250 feet wide by 200 feet deep, with adequate toilet facilities and a canteen. We then equipped it with a great deal of additional machinery, much of it made by a clever manufacturer in Venice, Italy, Mr Paggin. We also purchased a new large British machine 60 feet long, for continuously washing and drying the raw bristle, adapted from similar machines used in the wool industry, and two separate dyeing plants. Altogether a total of 28 new machines were installed in the new factory, at a cost of £260,000. This investment, plus the cost of the building itself (£130,000) represented a considerable act of faith in the future. We were then employing 70 people in the department, and our daily production of finished bristle rose to about 500 lbs per day, of a value of approximately £220,000 per annum. The cost of the basic raw material was very small, almost the total expense being transport, labour, electric power and interest on the capital invested.

We had been told that some of the Irish bacon factories were using heavy hogs which grew longer hair. We needed to get the maximum amount of raw material we could obtain, to justify our enlarged plant. The Northern Ireland government at that time were anxious to create new jobs, and were giving grants to assist the establishment of new factories. So we went over to investigate. The government officials suggested we should take over a disused factory on the coast at Ardglass, Co. Down, for washing and drying the bristles. They were also willing to allow us to spread them after collection on a disused airfield at Bishopscourt, four miles from Ardglass. This seemed ideal for our purpose. We then arranged for a local builder to construct the concrete washing tanks, and placed an order for the necessary bristle drying machines. The local manager we appointed, Brian Fitzsimmons, hired three lorries and twelve local people, and started collecting the bristles from ten bacon factories, both in Northern and Southern Ireland. All went reasonably well, and the factory was soon shipping us over about eight tons of dried bristles a week. The cost was a little more than our English figures, mainly on account of the transport of the finished product.

The whole enterprise was a venture of faith. I thought it was justified on four counts: we were providing employment, we were making our factory self sufficient in raw material, we were producing wealth out of something formerly wasted, and making a small contribution to the country's balance of payments.

Further trouble, however, still lay round the corner! Pigs (even in China) grow more hair in the shorter lengths than in the longer. The economic value of our bristle production depended on our getting a reasonable percentage of the longer lengths. The value of bristle in the 1960s was approximately £2 per lb for 2 inches, £2.40 for 2 $1/4$ inches, £2.80 for 2 $1/2$ inches, and so on up to £4 per lb for 3 $3/4$ inches. When we first started collecting British hair, our finished production consisted of approximately 50% of 2 inch length, with the remainder longer. As the years went on, British (and Irish) bristle gradually became shorter. The reason for this was that more and more pigs were being reared intensively rather than in the open air, and slaughtered very young, conditions not conducive to growing a good coat of hair! Although our production methods had become more efficient, the value of the bristle produced, therefore, declined.

In the late 1960s (before America again allowed the import of Chinese bristle) the German and French bristle dressing factories were prosperous. German and Dutch raw bristle at that time was appreciably longer than the British hair we were collecting. We felt we must run our bristle factory on an economic basis. If we could import German and Dutch raw material, already washed and dried, this would cut out the cost of collecting our British raw material, transporting it to Wales, weathering it and bringing it back to Stoke Prior. The cost of dried German raw bristles at that time, although considerably more than our hair from British bacon factories, made it more economical (with its greater length) for us to use. Another point in its favour was that the English slaughter houses insisted on our collecting their bristle throughout the summer as well as in the winter. Summer produced bristle is so short as to be not worth processing. All we could do was to sell it at a low price for curled hair. We were only required, however, to buy German and French hair produced in the winter.

We were very reluctant to discontinue using British bristle. But it was obvious that the use of European hair would result in our bristle factory being more financially successful. Our brush trade competitors have always relied on importing the fully finished Chinese bristle. We would still, we told ourselves, be making a useful contribution by providing employment and reducing the country's import bill, even to a smaller extent. So in 1976, we reluctantly told our British bacon factories that we were having to discontinue collecting their bristle and closed down our Irish factory. We then commenced importing already washed and dried raw German and Dutch bristles.

A further slight improvement in the position occurred when America resumed trading relations with China. This reduced German exports of bristle to the States, causing a slight reduction in the price of their raw bristles. Unfortunately this was soon offset from our point of view by the decline in value of the British £.

The cost of Chinese bristle (by which we valued our production) for some reason remained practically the same during the whole of the 1970s. But our factory wages steadily increased with inflation. In 1978, they were four times their level in 1965. So although we had increased our efficiency, from 1977 we started to lose money on our bristle factory. The final blow, however, came when the length of German and Dutch bristle, like the British, began to get shorter. The battery habit had spread to Europe!

Oh dear! All the effort and expense we had put in over 20 years to make ourselves self sufficient, seemed to be doomed to failure. So in 1980, we ceased to buy any more Continental bristle and decided to close the department down, absorbing the personnel in our other departments.

This was a sad blow, the worst real failure I had experienced in my business career. In retrospect, had the venture been a sensible thing to embark on? Could we have foreseen the steady decline in the length of the bristle, and the multiplication of our wage costs by four times over twelve years, when Chinese bristle remained stable in price?

One consolation we had – and that a negative one – was that practically all the German and French bristle dressing factories had to close down for the same reason as ourselves. What had been a thriving industry has now (1985) almost disappeared – all we know still to exist are two small factories, one in Germany and one in Italy.

In view of the demise of the industry in Europe, there was little chance of our selling the plant and machinery. We have still kept it intact in case Chinese bristles go up again in price. They have in fact increased by about 25% during 1984 – and one wonders whether the Chinese were waiting for the collapse of the European industry before resuming their monopoly position. Our own wages, however, have gone up with inflation by about 30% between 1980 and 1985. So unless Chinese prices go up even more substantially, prospects for a resumption of our bristle production look fairly small.

Oh well! We tried...

[As a footnote, Chinese bristle prices actually started to decline about the time the above was written. This was caused by decentralisation in China – whereas previously all exports had to be channelled through Beijing, later the provinces were allowed to export directly. This introduced competition, and bristle prices dropped to very low levels in the early '90s, making it hardly worthwhile for the Chinese to ship it, let alone for European factories to be competitive. After all, the raw material is an abundant waste product, and the processing almost entirely done by hand in rural factories where wages for the female operatives are very low. And there is always the threat of competition from synthetic materials, where prices are also tending to decline. As I write this in 2002, it looks as if the end of Chinese bristle production may not be far away, particularly as the Chinese themselves have recently started to produce good quality synthetic filaments at much lower prices than was demanded by the old-established US manufacturers of this material.]

Our range of 'Classic' painters tools as illustrated in our 1986 catalogue.

Chapter 9

PAINTERS TOOLS, HOUSEHOLD BRUSHES AND OUR NEW FACTORY (1974)

In the 1930s we had been buying a line of cheap painters' tools made for us by a firm in Sheffield. These were afterwards made by us from 1956. The blades of the first types were made from pre-hardened steel strip. They were not hollow ground or polished, and were fastened to the handles by a heart-shaped steel tang and riveted on to the blades, which were then forced through a ferrule, into the wooden handle. This method relied on the timber being thoroughly bone dry. If it were not, the tang of the blades might come loose, and it was then possible to pull the blade right out of the handle. In addition, the absence of hollow grinding in the centre of the blades caused the point of pressure to be at the narrowest part of the blade nearest the handles. The blades would therefore sometimes bend and stay bent, having to be re-straightened. This was the unsatisfactory method of making amateur type scrapers and putty knives in those days. Since they were retailed in the 1930s at 6d (2 $^1/_2$p) each perhaps the public couldn't expect more.

In 1958, we brought back some U.S. made tools from an American trip. The blades of these were hollow ground, causing the point of pressure to be in the centre rather that at the hilt. They were also highly polished, and riveted to the plastic handles. This fired us with the ambition to make our tools in a similar way. In 1960 we imported four 'Nicholson' American grinding machines to do the hollow grinding, and purchased three Clairpol Sheffield-made machines for polishing the blades.

The Nicholson grinders, the type used by American tool manufacturers, were somewhat slow in operation, grinding only one blade at a time, and were later replaced by two British Lumsden grinders. These were based on an angled grinding head, lowered down by micrometer adjustment on to a rotating circle of 40 or 50 magnetically held blades. This was far more efficient than the American

After blanking the blades using soft steel strip, they have to be hardened. This is done using a salt bath process, during which the blades are raised to a temperature of over 800°C, then rapidly cooled. George Lucas is the plant attendant, Ramsay Eveson looks on. (Right) This Lumsden grinding machine hollow grinds the tool blades. The grinding head is slightly tilted, and is gradually lowered onto the rotating jig of blades.

method – an encouraging instance of British engineering superiority. In the case of the British blade polishing machines, however, we had later to change over to German methods. In the Clairpol polishing machines, the blades had to be held in jigs, which were offered to the machines and first located in the glazing rolls to remove the grinding marks, then taken out and inserted into the polishing rolls. This was a dirty, noisy and labour intensive method, but we

Four Siepmann blade polishing machines. The blades pass by conveyor past the polishing rolls, which have successively finer grit, the last of which produces the 'mirror' finish, for which our tools are well known.

believe is still used in some of the Sheffield cutlery factories.

We used these polishing methods until 1973, when we heard that the German cutlery industry in Solingen had perfected an improved system for blade polishing. We then went over to the Siepmann factory to look at their machines. These were based on a conveyorised principle, passing the blades past four separate machines, the first two rolls removing the grinding marks (called 'glazing'), the third polishing the blades, and the fourth giving a final buffing. In 1975, we ordered three of these machines (later increased to four), together with I.C.I. degreasing equipment, a total investment of £60,000.

Household Brushes

Following our policy of extending our range of products, in 1962 we commenced to make a range of household brushes, by the 'drill and fill' method. This technology was not totally new to us as we had already used it to make paperhanging brushes. The first household brushes to be made were shoe and clothes brushes, followed a few years later by brooms.

This was entering into a field in which competition was keen, and growth slow or non-existent, but we felt the products could be sold by our existing salesforce, to customers already on our books. One small advantage was that in the case of shoe and clothes brushes, we were able to use $1\ ^1/_2$ inch bristle, which was too short for anything else, and was being produced in our bristle factory surplus to our requirements. The shoe brushes were specially designed with an

1975 – our household brush production track. Brooms, deck scrubbing brushes and suede brushes are being produced by machines alongside the track, for inspection and packing at the end.

angled tuft at the end, and were well received at home and abroad, including for some reason in Kenya, where hundreds of thousands were sold through the Bata organization.

I have explained elsewhere that we also produced in this department a range of hair brushes and tooth brushes (pictured on page 86). These, however, were not a success, as selling them involved calling mainly on chemists, who were not covered by our existing sales representatives. We did set on two men on an experimental basis to call on chemists, but our range was not sufficient to make this profitable. We had also hoped that they might have met with some demand in the export field, but this also proved disappointing, and we discontinued these lines in 1975.

In the manufacture of brooms, we were able to use the hardwood poles extracted from our woods in the first thinning stage. Unfortunately, a number of the poles contained unacceptable knots, and these had to be used in our wood-burning boiler. But it was a way of using up thinnings which would otherwise have had only firewood value, and as the years went on, and we came to the second thinning stage, the quality of the poles improved.

New Despatch and Warehouse

When we first started making household brushes, we installed the machinery in our existing factory. Our despatch department and stores were also housed in the original building. But as we added extra lines to our production, the congestion became acute. We therefore decided to design a new building at the rear of our existing works. Finished in 1974, it was 400 feet long by 120 feet wide. About two thirds of it was occupied by the new despatch department, and the remainder partly by a new household brush department, and an extension of our wood turning section.

The new despatch department was fitted out with a total of 2,232 steel bins, and was operated by electric fork trucks on the pallet system. The packing stations were connected by roller conveyors, and as the goods were packed they were automatically transferred to the despatch loading deck. Flooring was of terrazzo tiles, and the working conditions were a great improvement. Entirely designed by Andrew, the new department worked most efficiently from the start, and it was a great feather in Andrew's cap. It was partly financed by a loan of £200,000 from the Eagle Star Insurance Company.

New Handle Production Line

At this stage, I should like to say something about a new automatic system for producing wooden painters' tool handles, which we ordered from the Hempel wood turning machinery firm of Germany for the new building. Costing £40,000, it comprised three lathes with automatic transfer mechanisms to end-shaping machines and drilling machines. We had always had respect for German engineers, but this installation gave constant trouble, and was never a production proposition from the start. The German firm sent their engineers over on three occasions, but their efforts failed to make any improvements, and we finally scrapped this system after three years, retaining the lathes, which we still use for the production of small handles.

We then commissioned Mr G. Whitworth, a specialist woodworking engineer from Oswestry, who had been recommended by W. A. Fell Ltd of Windermere, to design a new automatic system for making these tool handles. His invention included an 'under and over' planing machine, from which the handles were automatically transferred to an end-shaping machine (both of which he made), and from then on to two large Rye shaping machines, and finally two sanding machines. The entire production of 1,500 dozen per day was manned by only two men, a tremendous improvement on our old method, which required eight operatives to produce only 1,200 dozen. We felt proud that a British engineer had so far surpassed the Germans, and at a lower expense. We later added three Fell (British) lathes to expand our handle production. These again were much more efficient than the German Hempel lathes. We hear so much about German superiority, that I am very pleased to be able to recount our experience in the woodturning industry.

Chapter 10

JOINT CONSULTATION and THE INDUSTRIAL PARTICIPATION SOCIETY

Up until 1946, while our number of employees remained small, we had not any official method of communicating with the workers, other than talking on the shop floor to Sally. In that year, however, we started a Joint Consultative Committee comprising ten representatives elected from the factory operatives, and ten nominated by the management. At first, the idea was a great success. The Committee met once per month, with tea and sandwiches provided by the firm, and we encouraged the workers to bring forward any ideas they might have, both for improving working conditions, and any suggestions for production methods. We were anxious to make sure that the Committee was not just a talk shop, and made great efforts to accept any suggestions put forward. But gradually over the next few years, interest in the Committee declined, and by 1951 it was difficult to persuade enough workers to allow their names to go forward as representatives.

Other Joint Consultative Committees in many firms have remained successful, and I have often wondered why it was that ours failed. I can't think it was because the management took no notice of the workers' suggestions. I like to imagine that it may have been because working conditions had by then improved, and that there didn't seem much to talk about! But whatever the reason, the Committee was obviously becoming a dead letter, and something new seemed to be needed.

In 1954 we happened to hear of a new system of worker involvement called Free Discussion Groups which had been introduced at the factory of a friend of mine, Robert Best of Best & Lloyd Ltd, Birmingham, a firm which had been established about 50 years previously by his father. Specialist manufacturers of architectural lighting fittings and metalwork, they had employed about 500 in the 1920s, but by the 1950s their workforce had dropped to about 70. Robert Best thought that the shrinkage of his family's concern was probably due to the firm's previous autocratic methods, and he was anxious to introduce a completely democratic management philosophy. He had recently read a book entitled 'Free Expression in Industry' by a man named James Gillespie. Gillespie had been a supervisor in a Scottish steel works. He had become revolted by the bowler hat type of management, and had been allowed to introduce a completely new system under which the workers were divided into groups of about 24 men. They were given two hours off per month in the firm's time, each group electing its own chairman and secretary, and were encouraged to discuss anything and everything that occurred to them pertaining to the firm, its working conditions, its management and its methods. No members of the management were present. The minutes of the meetings were drawn up by the secretary, and subsequently presented to the works manager, no names of the people making contributions being mentioned. James Gillespie claimed that this system was greatly superior to the traditional works council, since the workers could let off steam without being inhibited by the presence of the management. His book had inspired Robert Best to introduce Free Group Discussion into his own small firm. Robert was so keen to let the workers have their say that he called his group council the Management Board and allowed them control over the firm's whole management policy, including pricing, new products, and capital expenditure.

So in 1956 we started a Free Group Discussion system of consultation in our own works. James Gillespie came down to help us to get it started. At that time, we were employing about 500 workers in the factory. They were divided into 20 groups of 24 people each, each group approximating to its local manufacturing section. The personnel manager gave each group an explanatory talk, suggesting that they should meet at 3 p.m. each month, on a date to be laid down by the personnel department, so that not too many people would have to leave their work at the same time. Tea and biscuits were provided by the firm, and a room in the office block designated for the meetings. The minutes of each group meeting were to be written by the group secretary, and handed to the personnel

1948 – our first factory Joint Consultative Committee in session. The chairman at that time was Vic Ford (centre), works carpenter.

department for inclusion in the monthly typewritten Group Newsletter. No names of individuals were, of course, to be mentioned in the minutes.

At first, like our experience with the previous Joint Consultative Committee, the meetings were a great success from the point of view of free expression. Up to that time we had imagined that we had a reasonably happy ship, but the first few months showed that a lot of previously hidden resentments about various matters had been simmering under the surface. To try and maintain the initial enthusiasm for the holding of the meetings, we hastened to accept and act on practically every complaint and suggestion. Some of the factory foremen occasionally grumbled about the loss of $1 \frac{1}{2}$ hours of production time, and when some members of the groups complained about the attitude of their supervisor, this presented us with a tricky problem, since we did not want to undermine the authority of the foremen. We usually tried to resolve the matter by a quiet talk to the supervisor concerned, which gave rise after a few months to the group minutes being known as the Bellyachers Bulletin!

I think, on the whole, the introduction of the Free Discussion Groups helped to improve the relationship between the firm and its workers. But to our disappointment after a few years, some of the groups started to fail to meet each month, and when they did meet, not all the members attended. We found it difficult to stimulate enthusiasm, since we wanted to preserve the entirely voluntary aspect of the meetings. It was just possible that the decline in interest was due to there being too little to talk about, as had been the case with the previous Joint Consultative Committee. Although the system continued for many years, in the end it also failed for lack of interest.

We are still anxious (1985) to keep every employee informed of how the firm is progressing, and we now hold regular briefing meetings in the conference room, at which members of various sections in the factory are asked to attend. These are held every few months, addressed by the managing director, who gives a talk about any new developments or new products, and the state of trade, at which the employees are invited to ask questions. We have also for many years held monthly foreman-management meetings on the same lines, which are always well attended. The works magazine 'Shanghai' is also published periodically, and combines articles about the company, its employees and its products with others of a more general local interest. [Shanghai still continues in 2002]. I suppose the moral of our efforts is that communication is one of the more difficult areas of management to get right, and that to keep up interest regular changes have to be made.

Trade Unions
During our first 45 years from 1928, we had never been asked to sign an agreement with a Trades Union. In 1973, we were approached by a member of our maintenance staff, David Lewis, asking if we would agree to the establishment of a branch of the Transport and General Workers Union in the factory. We have never had any objection to Trades Unions – in fact we think they are necessary

even if sometimes wielding too much power; but I must admit I was disappointed to hear that our workers felt they had to combine in a Union in order to get fair treatment from our firm; I liked to think they had always had it anyway. However, we did not raise any objection, and after a visit from Mr Chesshire, the local T&G organizer, we signed an agreement recognising the Union and agreeing to give such of our workers as joined it $1\ 1/2$ hours off per month in the firm's time to hold their meetings. We also signed a similar agreement with the ASTMS, representing supervisory and office employees. We have never known exactly how many of our employees became members, though we have heard that the early figure was about 60%. At first, their meetings held in the canteen were well attended, but as the years went on, the numbers gradually declined. We still have no knowledge of the exact number in the Union, but with the decline in our works employees from 500 in 1968 to 300 in 1985, we think the present numbers must be relatively small, and like our other experiences, there is now probably little to talk about.

It is possible that the relative failure of our Free Discussion Group meetings caused the feeling that a Union of some sort should be started. In 1982 when the then Union Secretary resigned, one of our tool room staff, George Cooper, took the job on. I was interested when he said to me after 12 months as Secretary "I've resigned – there's no need for a Union here". We have never made any of our workers in the factory redundant, preferring to rely on natural wastage to reduce our numbers, and we hope this has given our staff a sense of security. [For an account of a later Union dispute, see Pt. 2, Chapter 3. At the end of 2002, union membership had fallen to under one quarter of the workforce.]

Industrial Co-partnership Association (later Industrial Participation Association)

I think it was about 1937 when I first read about the profit-sharing schemes operated by various enlightened firms. The earliest and most famous had been in existence in the textile firm of J. T. & T. Taylor Ltd, of Batley, Yorkshire, since the 1880s. Mr Taylor had many times expounded in public speeches the value of his firm's scheme, which he said had been the main reason for their commercial success. In the 1930s they were employing 1,500 people, and had never had a strike in 40 years. Another successful scheme was in force in the Quaker firm of Kalamazoo Ltd, Birmingham, where the so-called Kalamazoo Workers Alliance, which had been given a portion of the firm's equity by the founding owners, gradually increased their holding until by 1980 they possessed over 50% of the company's shares.

When I started out on my business career, my main ambition was to be a successful manufacturer. I certainly incidentally hoped to obtain a good standard of living for myself. But I was not mainly motivated by the idea of acquiring large personal wealth. I wanted to share my commercial success with those who worked with me. I remember being influenced by a remark by the President of the vast American firm of Sears Roebuck & Co of Chicago, who said "Our first concern in running this firm is the interests of the employees. The second is the customers. The third is the stockholders. And I believe that works out best for the stockholders."

So in 1938, when our firm was still located at the Stoke Prior Mill, and when we were employing about 50 people, we started our profit sharing scheme. This provided that 10% of the profits before taxation were to be distributed to the employees each December, in addition to their wages. Since profits often fluctuate up and down, a clause was added that if the profits of one year fell below those of the previous year, the amount distributed would be the same as the previous year, subject to an overriding maximum of 15% of the current profits. The effect of this was that following a bumper year, after which results declined, the share-out in subsequent years frequently averaged 12%-13% of the profits, providing a sort of bonus equalisation reserve. The distribution was in proportion to salaries, and those with longer service received more than those with less service. So some got substantially more than others. This was about the same formula as the Kalamazoo scheme, in contrast to that of our neighbours the Nu-Way Heating firm of Droitwich (founded by Henry Usborne), where the amount available for distribution was divided equally between all employees, a newly-appointed office boy receiving the same as the managing director. I never agreed with this, as I considered the share-out should be in proportion to the responsibilities of the individual.

Firms operating profit sharing schemes are sometimes asked whether the share-out, dependent on profits, provides any incentive for the employees to work harder. We had not started our scheme with any intention in mind other than a small act of social justice. It was not very likely that any individual employee – perhaps someone operating a machine – could have much influence on the firm's profits, which are mainly affected by matters outside their control, such as a trade depression, the launching of an unsuccessful new product, the loss of a major customer, failure to follow aggressive marketing policies and so on, and we had never adopted piece-work. So all we could hope for with our small profit sharing scheme was to promote general goodwill and contribute towards a happy ship. It has been a matter of regret to me that our share-outs have never been large, averaging perhaps between one and three weeks wages at Christmas. Distributions by more profitable and larger companies such as the British American Tobacco Co, and Kalamazoo, have given employees two or three times more than ours. Nevertheless, many companies have no profit-sharing schemes at all, and I think our workers have appreciated their regular payments, which perhaps they have come to look upon just as the Christmas bonus, without relating it very much to profits. We have only failed to pay out any share-out in one year, 1951, when we made a loss.

In 1884 a number of firms believing strongly in the value of profit sharing schemes, among them J. T. & T. Taylor Ltd, and Rowntree & Co of York, set up the Industrial Co-Partnership Association with the idea of persuading other firms to adopt similar schemes. Our firm joined the Association in 1948. The organization held annual Conferences, alternately at Girton College, Cambridge, and St Hugh's College, Oxford, which I started attending in the 1950s. The Conferences usually included addresses by prominent industrialists, and trade union leaders. They were held from Friday evenings to Sunday, with an average attendance of about 100 representatives from various member firms.

I found the personal contacts formed through these conferences valuable and stimulating. In 1962 I was invited to address the conference (at Girton College) on the subject of 'What can a management do to ensure that its successors will continue to develop the co-partnership practices it has introduced?' I was able to say that in 1958 I had given 20% of the firm's ordinary shares to an Employees Trust, so that they would be able to share in the profits in perpetuity. The Chairman of the Association at that time was the Rt. Hon. Sir Geoffrey Shakespeare, a director of the Abbey National Building Society and other firms. One of nature's gentlemen, he had been a member of Mr Churchill's government during the war. I had not done much public speaking until then, and was a little nervous at addressing a high-powered group of business executives. Sir Geoffrey was most kind in giving me encouragement and advice, and invited me to join the Executive Committee of the Association, on which I served until 1970. The distinguished president of the Association in those days was the Viscount Amory, another avuncular character who radiated friendliness and goodwill. He had been Chancellor of the Exchequer from 1958-60, and remained a bachelor. I was also very fond of Ward Daw, the salaried director of the Association, a lovable friend who unfortunately was killed, with his wife, in a car accident a few years later. I still cherish a letter of appreciation which he wrote to me after a speech I made in St Hugh's College, Oxford, in 1967.

One of the members of the executive committee in my time, was Nigel Vinson. He had started a successful firm called Plastic Coatings Ltd, which he later sold to the British American Tobacco Co. for a large sum. Afterwards he became chairman of the Association, and pressed for a change of its name to the Industrial Participation Association, as he felt its scope should be widened. This was done in 1972. Later, Nigel Vinson served on a number of government committees, and became chairman of the Development Commission. He was created a peer in 1984.

The annual Conferences of the Association are still being held in the 1980s, usually now at Churchill College, Cambridge, regularly attended by two members of our staff, George Chance and Paul Chandler. In 1984 they attended the centenary banquet of the Association, held in the Mansion House, London.

Looking back over the years, I am glad that our firm has participated in profit sharing for 47 years since 1938. I can only hope that my successors will manage to increase our prosperity, so that bigger dividends can be distributed.

Management Research Groups

In 1926 Mr Seebohm Rowntree, the Quaker industrialist and psychologist who had been responsible for the setting up of the Oxford conferences of employers, managers and foremen in the early 1920s, founded the Management Research Groups, a sort of junior edition of the British Institute of Management. Small groups of directors and managers of companies in this organization meet once a month during the winter, either in a local hotel or university, to discuss various aspects of management. The meetings are usually addressed by a speaker (often one of the members) specialising in his particular subject, which is followed by a discussion, and afterwards, dinner. The idea behind MRG was that the personal contacts involved, and the small number attending (usually about 20) provided a more intimate atmosphere, and led to a more fruitful discussion, than attendance at the larger meetings held by the BIM.

As far as I can remember, we were invited to join the Midland area of the Management Research Groups in 1947 by Miss Beryl Foyle, a director of Boxfoldia Ltd, the carton manufacturers of Selly Oak. At that time, the director of MRG in London was Col. Radcliffe, a brother of the well-known jurist Viscount Radcliffe. Although having had no experience in industry, he had a very attractive personality, and the ability to make every member feel welcome.

Interest in the Groups increased rapidly in the 1950s, and branches were established in London, Birmingham, Manchester, Glasgow, Norwich and Bristol. The members were encouraged to prepare papers of their own for discussion. I have preserved a copy of the notes of a meeting held in April 1954, when I gave a talk on the relative merits of concentrating production on one, or very few products, on the Henry Ford principle, as against wide diversification. In other words, which of these two management policies was the best to follow for firms which wanted to progress.

This subject, I think, was a challenging and interesting one, but both my paper on this occasion, and the subsequent discussion, didn't seem to lead to any definite conclusions. I listed the advantages of diversification as (a) less dependence on one narrow range of products, (b) ability to obtain higher rates of profits on certain lines (such as the de-luxe versions of basic motor cars), and (c) the constant consideration of new lines probably leading to new fields for sales. The disadvantages were that advertising campaigns failed to achieve the ideal of maximum concentration on one particular product, and in factory organization, small batch production led to inefficient methods and higher costs. Another difficulty was on the sales side. Representatives can only sell a certain amount, and the wider the range, the less the concentration on particular products.

I was able to point to the success of Mars Ltd, of Slough (founded by Mr Forrest Mars of America), who started in the UK in 1930 a factory based on a single confectionery product only – the Mars Bar. They had later added a few other lines, but were still highly specialised and very profitable. Another successful firm specialising in one product only was Chappie Ltd of Melton Mowbray. On the other hand, widely diversified firms such as the Dunlop Rubber Co Ltd, and Imperial Chemical Industries, were equally successful. [Perhaps these unfortunate examples tend to support the argument against diversification!]

The discussion which followed my paper came to the conclusion that both policies could succeed equally, depending on the quality of the management concerned. Perhaps this could have been said to have been fairly obvious from the start! But I think the contacts made in these meetings were very useful, and we have kept up our membership of MRG which has now been absorbed into the larger British Institute of Management, while retaining its separate identity.

An interesting sidelight on the question of 'Diversification or Concentration?' occurred in the history of our firm a few years later. Seeking to expand our range, so as not to be so dependent on the painting and decorating side of our business, we designed and launched a range of hair brushes, tooth brushes and shaving brushes. I think the items were quite well made – the hair brushes had polished wooden backs, which gave them a quality aspect as against the plastic brushes on the market – but selling them was difficult, for reasons already explained. A few orders were obtained, but the idea in general was a failure. The existing toilet brush manufacturers such as Addis Ltd were too strongly entrenched in the chemist trade for a small competitive range such as ours to get a foothold on the market, and the additional time spent by our sales representatives took away their concentration on our main business. With hindsight, we should have foreseen the difficulties. The lesson we learnt was that any new products we produced should be saleable in our existing trade outlets such as hardware shops, and not require a separate sales force to put them on the market, a policy which we have followed ever since.

Thinking this matter over after writing this, I am bound to admit that the very firm we failed to compete with in this connection – Addis Ltd – who had over the whole of their long history sold to the toilet trade, did successfully invade the hardware field, with their plastic articles, such as bowls, buckets, washing up brushes and household brushes, in the 1960s. Why did they succeed in invading our market while we had failed to get into theirs? The reason was that they had (a) the capital to engage a completely new sales force, and (b) the ability to manufacture a completely new and comprehensive range of products which had a sufficiently wide scope to justify the engagement of about 30 full time representatives. Their firm had been in existence since the 18th century, and has remained consistently profitable until the 1980s. [It may be commented that when Addis entered the household plasticware field, it was a relatively new market that they themselves helped to create, but, as observed elsewhere, they were not so successful when they entered the paint brush market.]

In 1958, I was invited to become chairman of the Midland area of MRG, which I did for two years. After Col. Radcliffe died in 1960, he was succeeded as Director by Brig. Mainprise-King, another ex-army man whom I came to like very much. He expanded the idea of persuading member firms to invite Group members to visit their factories, when discussions could be held on the spot. I remember particularly useful visits to General Foods of Banbury, Mars Ltd, Kalamazoo, and Boxfoldia. In November 1976 we hosted a visit from member firms.

The mural panel for April painted by Raymond (sometimes known as Dick) Cowern for our canteen. This was one of the paintings that was damaged by a fire in 1956, which is why the colours appear faded.

Chapter 11

MURAL PANELS IN THE FACTORY

The works canteen in our new factory, which was opened in 1948, was used for many social occasions, such as public meetings and dances, in addition to functioning as a dining hall. In 1949 we commissioned Raymond Cowern RA, a distinguished artist and an old friend of mine, to produce twelve mural panels in colour to adorn its walls, one for every month of the year. The whole twelve were installed by 1954. The largest one for December, 'The Adoration of the Angels', was 15 feet wide by 10 feet deep. The others, ranged round the walls, were each 6 feet by 5 feet, representing scenes relating to the various months.

Much to our regret, six of these panels were destroyed by a fire after a dance in the canteen in July 1956. Raymond Cowern was then the Principal of Brighton College of Art, and could not give much time to their replacement, so this had to wait until his retirement in 1970. In the meantime my nephew Paul Twine, an art teacher in Crayford, Kent, produced excellent panels for the months of June to November, temporarily replacing those lost.

Raymond Cowern recommenced work on the missing panels when he retired. These new panels, however, took a long time, as I think he was anxious to produce some of his best work. By 1985 we have only had three replacement panels from him, one of children on a roundabout in a summer fair, one of a pigeon loft and one of boats in Whitehaven harbour. Two of these have been exhibited in the Royal Academy Summer Exhibitions. They are supreme works of art, and have been widely praised.

Another distinguished artist, H. Andrew Freeth RA, has provided us with a woodland scene 17 feet by 5 feet for our entrance hall, and for the office block a painted montage panel showing some of our workers performing various manufacturing operations in the factory. Another artist friend of mine was Eric Malthouse (b. 1914), whom I met, like Raymond Cowern and Andrew Freeth, at the Birmingham College of Art when they were students. We commissioned Eric, who lectured at Cardiff Art College, to paint six abstract panels for our bristle factory canteen.

"Man does not live by bread alone", and I think these excursions of ours into the art world have added colour to the factory scene.

Raymond Cowern RA with 'Pigeons'. This was exhibited in a Royal Academy summer exhibition in 1984. Mr Cowern won the 'Priz de Rome' when at Birmingham School of Art, and was later principal of the Brighton School of Art. (Below) The large panel showing a nativity scene representing December which was hung at the end of the canteen. This was one of those saved from the fire, which started after a Saturday night dance, and burnt out the other end of the canteen.

Page 150

The mural panel 'Roundabout' for July painted by Raymond Cowern for our canteen. This was one of the canvases he painted after his retirement in the 1980s to replace those destroyed in the fire.

'Harbour' (August) is another replacement canvas painted by Raymond Cowern for our canteen. It was exhibited at the 1983 summer exhibition of the Royal Academy. Raymond retired to the Cumbrian coast, and this is a local scene.

Raymond Cowern did not complete his cycle of mural canvases before his death in 1986, and the final three were painted by his artist daughter Jenny in 1990-92 – this one represents September. They form a perfect ensemble with the earlier work.

Many of our Arts Festivals featured modern design, and this picture shows a dining table and chairs by the Broadway firm of Gordon Russell with attractive modern place settings.

Chapter 12

THE STOKE PRIOR BRUSH WORKS ARTS FESTIVALS
(Contributed by Mr George Chance, Festival Director)

Our Arts Festivals grew out of a conversation between the writer and Leslie Harris which took place in our conference room early in 1960. At that time it was our practice to present lunch hour film shows to any of our employees who cared to attend, with the writer arranging the programmes and projecting the films. I suggested that we might use our conference room to present occasional record recitals on a Sunday evening and borrow a few paintings to add atmosphere, the intention being to invite employees and local people to these evenings, thereby making a small contribution to the cultural life of the village. Our conference room was newly built and could be used either for concerts (it had a very good sound reproduction system) or as a cinema, and could seat up to 120 people in comfort. Mr Harris, however, had a more imaginative proposal which was that we present a week of lectures, music, poetry readings and films in addition to paintings, and also to make use of the corridor walls, the board room and one or two offices. The more one looked at the proposal the more attractive it became. We would be making the arts – in particular, music and painting – locally available, not only to our employees, but to the surrounding population also, and the fact that this would be taking place within our factory made the occasion unique, as it remains so today. And so the die was cast. The second week of October was chosen as a suitable time, the writer was made Festival

Director with a budget to match the expense likely to be incurred. But where to start? We had no experience of running a Festival and neither had we any contact with the arts world. Our obvious course was to approach the Arts Council and ask for their help. In 1960 there were no regional arts associations, the Council being represented by a Regional Director – in our case, Ronald Pickvance.

1960 – our first Arts Festival. George Chance (festival director), myself, my wife and Tom Bromley (pianist).

We invited him to visit us, and when he did so our idea of a Festival in the factory was put to him but the response, to say the least, was cool. There was a suspicion that the Festival would be used for commercial gain, and the Arts Council could not become involved if that was the case. How times have changed! However, Mr Pickvance was persuaded that this was not the case, and he agreed to help us present our first Festival. He would contact galleries and individual artists with a view to selecting paintings to form a small exhibition of contemporary work. The onus of arranging the evening events was our responsibility, but with the Arts Council's blessing upon our efforts, a degree of respectability was assured.

One of the first people we approached was the late Sir Gordon Russell, who lived not far away, and whose company had recently furnished our office block. Without hesitation he agreed to deliver an illustrated lecture and, for good measure, put us in touch with the Craftsmen Potters Association of Great Britain, upon whose council Sir Gordon sat. This resulted in the Association lending us work by leading British potters. With Sir Gordon's name on our programme we felt more confident in approaching other distinguished persons, and so wrote to Dr Mary Woodall, the Director of Birmingham City Museum and Art Gallery who,

1961 – Andrew and my wife greet Vanessa Redgrave, who gave a poetry recital with Max Adrian (below). Both were appearing in the Royal Shakespeare Theatre at the time.

like Sir Gordon, readily agreed to give a lecture. Both speakers generously gave their services free. Two evenings of art films were arranged, the Bromsgrove String Orchestra was booked, as was Tom Bromley, a professional pianist, while a local amateur drama group agreed to present an evening of music, poetry and drama.

In trying to arrange a poetry reading we soon discovered that Sunday was virtually the only day one could engage professional actors and further, in the period we are writing about, there were not the co-operatives of actors which exist today which can offer poetry readings on diverse subjects. These co-operatives embrace actors who may be working in different theatres, but who are linked together, thus enabling readings to be given, drawing from a pool, and with bookings being handled through one member of the group. All members of the group would be conversant with the programmes on offer thus ensuring that should an actor have to drop out, another could easily take his place. However, it was not like that in 1960, when engagements had to be made with individual actors and which meant one was restricted to a solo performance or one given by two or more artistes appearing in the same production.

Actors appearing in a touring play were out of the question, but those working in a repertory season were the best to contact, and a few miles from our factory stood one of the greatest repertory theatres in the country – the Royal Shakespeare Theatre. It was to members of this theatre that our letters were addressed, and we were fortunate in persuading Elizabeth Sellers and Max Adrian, who were both appearing in Troilus and Cressida, to give the first poetry reading. Volunteers from employees formed the front of house staff, posters, programmes and leaflets were printed, and press advertising space booked. Six weeks before the Festival began on 8th October, the posters and leaflets were sent out to various bodies such as libraries, Women's Institutes, schools and colleges, whilst two weeks later our first newspaper advertisements appeared. It might be of interest, at this point, to record the content of the visual side of the Festival together with admission charges on the evening events. Admission was, and remained, free to the exhibitions. On display were 31 paintings by leading contemporary artists including works by John Bratby, Josef Herman, Patrick Heron, Rodrigo Moynihan, John Piper and Ruskin Spear. Twenty four pieces of pottery by Geoffrey Whiting, Michael Casson, Ray Finch, Tessa Fuchs, Lavender Groves and others were exhibited. Thirty six paintings by local amateur artists were also shown. Admission charges to the evening events ranged from 1/6d to 3/6d (7.5p – 17.5p), with free admission where the lecturers had waived their fees, and the exhibitions were open from 2 p.m to 10 p.m. every day.

George Chance with school children in the office corridor

Attendance at this first Festival encouraged us to present a further event in 1961 but on a more adventurous scale, and, taking into account that poetry readings could only be given on a Sunday, it was decided to lengthen the Festival to include the second Sunday, thus making a total of nine days.

An important step forward was taken during this Festival in that we were able to exhibit work from a public collection, the Birmingham City Art Gallery, in the form of fifty one 18th century watercolours. For this we had to thank Dr Woodall who, when approached by the writer for the loan of these, agreed to recommend to her committee that this be done, and the committee approved. This was important to us for work from a public collection was normally only loaned to recognized galleries, and for it to come to us was a mark of approval which would stand us in good stead.

1961 also brought us into contact with Henry Moore (again through Dr Woodall) who kindly lent one of his pieces to be exhibited in a small group of sculptures we were including in the Festival. We also tentatively explored overseas sources and succeeded in obtaining glass, fabrics, ceramics and tableware from Sweden and Finland which we formed into a small design exhibition. The Festival was growing in stature for we now had the blessing of the Arts Council, a major public gallery and that of the country's most eminent sculptor. Not only was it growing in stature, it was also growing in size, for the number of exhibits had increased nearly three-fold from 90 in 1960 to 256 in 1961. In the summer the writer saw Vanessa Redgrave at the Royal Shakespeare Theatre as Katherine in The Taming of the Shrew, a performance which brought her great acclaim from

1963 – Sir Mortimer Wheeler with George Chance. Sir Mortimer gave a lecture entitled 'Digging up the Past'. Entrance charges to the evening events was increased to 3/6d (17.5p) in 1963!

One of the old master paintings in the 1963 festival.

both critics and public alike. A letter was dashed off to Miss Redgrave asking if she would appear in our Festival together with Max Adrian who was also appearing there. By this time we had learnt that actors will very rarely commit themselves to accepting an engagement such as we were offering more than six weeks ahead, and even then they reserved the right to opt out should a more professional engagement arise, such as a film or television play. Fortunately, over the years this right has only been exercised on two or three occasions, but the writer only felt on safe ground when the actor actually walked through our doors! Mr Adrian accepted, but getting Miss Redgrave to do the same took a great many telephone calls to the theatre, rehearsal rooms, both at Stratford and London, and to her home. Eventually, contact was made and agreement was reached which resulted in a poetry reading which attracted a full house. Other speakers included Michael Kustow (now commissioning editor for the Arts, Channel 4), Ronald Pickvance, Maurice Richardson (then television critic for The Observer), Gordon Hales (film director), as well as art films and the Avoncroft Drama Group. Admission was 2/6d to all events. In addition to the watercolours, sculpture and the design display, there was a large selection of prints from the Arts Council and the St George's Gallery, Fiehl reproductions and amateur paintings, with many of the exhibits being offered for sale.

Attendance at the 1961 Festival had increased over the previous year with visitors from further afield, and colleges and schools began to send parties. In preparing for our 1962 Festival the writer wrote, late in 1961, to the Chinese Embassy in London, to ask if they would approach the appropriate department in Peking to ask if we could borrow paintings by some of their leading artists. There had been no exhibition of Chinese paintings in this country since before the Second World War, and our request was very much a long shot. However, we

1963 – Peggy Ashcroft and John Barton, both from the Royal Shakespeare Theatre, give a poetry reading.

were asked to call at the embassy to discuss the matter in greater detail, when we emphasised our long trading links with China (pig bristles) and the fact that the paintings would be on show in a factory. Several such meetings followed, the outcome of these being that the Chinese agreed to send us a selection of paintings. Subsequently fifty one paintings arrived, causing quite a stir in the arts world, and which attracted a great deal of interest from all quarters. Peter Swann, Keeper of the Department of Eastern Arts at the Ashmolean Museum, Oxford, who made a special journey to Stoke Prior wrote: "There is no doubt that the firm has achieved a major artistic scoop. They have secured, direct from China, 51 paintings by modern Chinese artists, the like of which have never been seen in this country. It has been a matter of speculation what the standards of art in communist China are. To see this collection of landscapes, bird and flower paintings and figural compositions is enough to show that modern China is entering a new period of artistic achievement. I found it most exciting."

Artist Nancy Kuo gave a lecture and demonstration of 'Chinese Painting' as part of our third Chinese Festival in 1965. (Below) A painting from our 1965 exhibition of Chinese Paintings and Handcrafts.

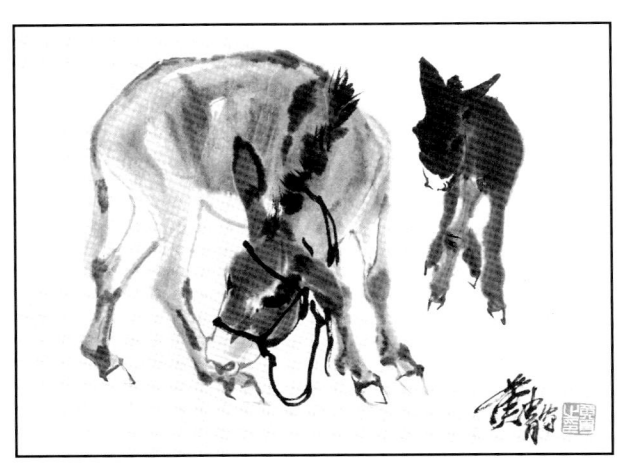

Details of this exhibition were televised by Monitor (BBC-TV National Network), Midlands Montage (ATV Regional), and Scan (BBC-TV Regional), whilst broadcasts were made by Midlands Miscellany (BBC Regional) and the Overseas Service of the BBC. The exhibition was reviewed in The Times, The Birmingham Post, The Sunday Times and The Guardian as well as most local papers, and it was visited by Nancy Thomas of Monitor, Dr Ch'en of the BBC Overseas Service, Michael Barratt also of the BBC, and the Chinese Attaché with a party from his embassy.

The secondary exhibition (although in fact it was planned as the primary but it got overshadowed by the Chinese paintings) contained a selection of old master paintings on loan from seven stately homes – Madresfield Court, Stoneleigh Abbey, Hartlebury Castle, Eastnor Castle, Hanbury Hall, Shrawley Wood House, Ombersley Court and Hagley Hall. Negotiations had been going on for some months to bring this exhibition together, but the time and effort expended was certainly worthwhile, for it marked another step forward in the quality of our Festival. Seventy paintings were on view including works by Van Dyck, Tintoretto, Rubens, Gainsborough, Lely, Reynolds and Cranach, as well as suits of armour. In a manner of speaking the content of this exhibition was just as remarkable as that of the Chinese, for here were extremely valuable works of art being displayed, not in a gallery, but on the corridor walls of our office block, and the generosity of their owners in lending them to us should not be overlooked. Their co-operation was exceptional for it was only rarely that a request for a painting was refused. The third exhibition in the

Sunday evening poetry readings soon became well-established regulars, and in 1965 Janet Suzman and Eric Porter gave one. (Below) Mrs Mary Whitehouse achieved a certain notoriety in the 1960s with her opposition to some of the less salubrious TV programmes. Her 'National Viewers and Listeners Association' at one time represented over 1m people. In the 1969 Festival she had a debate with the dramatist David Rudkin on 'In the Public Good?', and one can imagine that they didn't see eye to eye on some things!

Festival was devoted to Indian crafts coupled with paintings by three contemporary Indian painters – Avinash Chandra, F. N. Souza and A. D. Thomas. Amateur artists were also on display (although we were beginning to look at this section afresh for as the standard of the exhibitions rose, so amateur paintings were beginning to look out of place) bringing the total number of exhibits to over 300.

Because of the high value of the old master paintings, round-the-clock security had to be provided, and, of course, a higher insurance premium was demanded. Most of the collections and returns of the paintings was carried out by our own transport, with a specialised carrier being used when requested.

Yonty Solomon (piano), Richard Pasco, William Squire, George Rylands and Peggy Ashcroft from the Apollo Society gave an entertainment 'Liberty: Equality: Fraternity' in 1968. (Below) Prof. Nicholas Pevsner (right) gave a lecture in 1967 on 'Truth and History in Victorian Architecture'. Pevsner was famous for his series of books on English county architecture. The chairman was Freddie Charles (left), a Worcester architect who specialised in restoring old buildings, and who assisted Pevsner in writing the book on 'The Buildings of Worcestershire'.

In arranging the evening events, for the first time we included a concert by a leading string quartet – The Netherlands String Quartet – whilst other events included lectures by Lord Queensberry, Sir Hugh Casson, Gilbert Spencer R.A. and David Kossoff. Marius Goring gave a poetry reading. Screenings of the film 'Cinderella' with the Bolshoi Ballet were attended by over 600 people, whilst it was estimated that overall 6,000 people came to the Festival. It was clear that we were now firmly established in the public's mind and that we had built up a following which was reflected in our ever growing mailing list. But the success of the Festival raised a question which the writer noted at the time: "It would seem that our problem is to try and maintain a very high standard set by this Festival. There is a reasonable chance that a further exhibition of old masters coupled with Chinese paintings could be presented, but it is doubtful

RST Actors Helen Mirren and Ian Richardson (with guitarist Martin Best) gave a poetry and prose recital entitled 'Courtship' in 1967.

The distinguished actress Dame Edith Evans gave a Sunday evening entertainment 'Reading for Pleasure' in 1969. Our driver could not find her London home, so, rather than let us down, she came all the way by taxi!

1968 – The Earl of Euston (centre), chairman of the Society for the Protection of Ancient Buildings, gave a lecture on 'Great English Houses'. In the picture he is talking with Mr Matley Moore of Greyfriars, Worcester. The Chairman was Admiral Sir Derek Holland-Martin (left).

whether it could be repeated again. Not only is there a diminishing pool of old masters to draw upon, but the public would soon tire of such repetition."

However, the 1963 Festival did present another such combination under the title 'Paintings from Country Houses' and 'Paintings and Handicrafts from Peking'. The former drew from collections of nine houses namely: Cirencester Park, Berkeley Castle, Spetchley Park, Burghley House, Castle Howard, Kedlestone Hall, Ombersley Court, Althorp and Charlecote. Fifty six paintings were on view containing work by Bassano, Van Dyck, Battoni, Lely, Kneller, Lorraine, Poussin, Wright of Derby, Pannini and others. The Chinese exhibition consisted of 192 items which comprised original and reproduction paintings, ivory, jade and wood engravings, lacquer ware and pottery.

Early in 1963 the writer came across an article in a medical journal describing how painting pictures could help patients express themselves to their doctor when they could not adequately do so in words. This form of therapy was mainly used for those people suffering from nervous illnesses and usually when lysergic acid (LSD-25) was being administered in their treatment. We knew that the superintendent of Powick Hospital for Mental and Nervous Diseases was using this drug, which uncovered the deeply-seated feelings of inadequacy, aggression and sexuality which express themselves in various forms of neurotic illness, and so approached him with a view to enlisting his help in presenting a small exhibition of such paintings. It so happened that a previous patient of his, an artist who had been receiving treatment, recorded her progress from start to finish through a portfolio of remarkable paintings. The superintendent kindly agreed to lend these, and also wrote the introduction to the exhibition together with an analysis of each painting. We called it 'The Healing Art' and presented

Two Royal portraits from our 1966 Festival. (Left) the Queen Mother by Sir Gerald Kelly, and (below) HM Queen Elizabeth II by Edward Halliday.

1974 – a group of china, glass silverware and fabrics in our modern design exhibition.

it as a small contribution towards making people aware of the need for a greater understanding towards medical illness. Lectures, music and poetry readings were given by Dr Michael Sullivan, John Braine, Sir William Emrys Williams, Sir Mortimer Wheeler, Sylvia Syms, The Allegri String Quartet, Diana Rigg and Paul Hardwick. Art films, always popular, were also shown. It was during this Festival that we had to move an evening event from the conference room into the canteen, the occasion being the lecture by Sir Mortimer Wheeler which attracted around 250 people.

    The 1964 Festival saw us continuing to widen the range of exhibitions when we presented no less than six exhibitions from five countries: Germany, Switzerland, the USSR (two), Austria and the UK. The German Arts Council sent an important exhibition of German Expressionist Prints which included work by Barlach, Beckmann, Dix, Kandinsky, Klee, Kokoschka and Nolde. From Switzerland paintings by Teodoro Stravinsky (his debut in this country) the son of Igor Stravinsky, and from Austria paintings by contemporary artists all connected with the Academy of Fine Arts in Vienna. Two exhibitions from Russia: firstly, 'Shakespeare In The USSR' a unique exhibition of over 200 illustrations for books, magazines, theatre programmes and costume design celebrating the poet's quater centenary lent by the Ministry of Culture in Moscow. This exhibition was specially assembled for our Festival and was returned to Moscow when it closed. Secondly, 'Aspects Of Contemporary Soviet Art' contained work by leading Soviet painters and was lent to us by The Grosvenor Gallery in London. Barbara Hepworth's monumental sculpture 'Square Forms with Circle', her newest creation, was lent to us by Dame Barbara, whilst paintings by Kit Barker, William Gear, Alan Davie, Jone Levee, Donald Hamilton Fraser and Karel Appel completed the UK section.

Of the evening events, two related directly to 'Aspects of Contemporary Soviet Art' and 'German Expressionist Prints'. A lecture on the former was given by Eric Estorick, who had kindly lent us the paintings, whilst we screened three films describing the work of Kathe Kollwitz, Ernst Barlach and Wassily Kardinsky, some of whose work was included in the latter exhibition. Other lectures on widely differing subjects were given by Professor Robert Hoggart and Sir Anthony Blunt (as he was then). The London String Quartet gave a recital following on the decision taken in 1962 to present quartets of repute. For the poetry readings we were honoured in being able to present Dame Peggy Ashcroft, together with John Barton (both of whom were to return in subsequent Festivals) and Max Adrian, on his third visit, partnered by Janet Suzman, of whom we observed at the time "Miss Suzman it would appear has a great future ahead of her, and it is hoped to engage her for our 1965 Festival" which we did when she was partnered by Eric Porter.

November 1981 – I am presented with an award by the Duchess of Gloucester from the Association for Business Sponsorship of the Arts. The citation reads "The Stoke Prior Arts Festival, organized by L. G. Harris & Co. Ltd, has made a great contribution to the cultural life of Bromsgrove since 1960". Although I was proud to receive this award, credit should go to George Chance who did most of the organization.

In endeavouring to write a history of our Festival one is faced with the difficulty as to what should be left out, but for the writer each Festival was special and meriting a full account but this would certainly bore the reader. However, at the risk of doing this perhaps the writer might be allowed to recall the Festival which gave him the greatest pleasure.

It was our 1966 Festival in which we celebrated 900 years of the monarchy, an event which appeared to have been ignored by other bodies. The idea was to present an exhibition in which each monarch, from William I to the present

Queen, would be represented by a portrait, and where one of these was not available, then by a seal or document, medal or a coin. Most of the evening lectures would have a royal theme as would the music, poetry readings and films.

Research into the project began early in 1964 for the task which lay ahead was formidable in that we had to gather together exhibits relating to 42 monarchs, and it was essential that planning was done well ahead. We know that both the Royal Academy in London and the Walker Art Gallery in Liverpool had mounted similar exhibitions in 1953 on the occasion of the coronation, and so we wrote asking if they had catalogues still available. Fortunately they had, and so we were able to use these as a valuable source of information as to the whereabouts of exhibits. It need hardly be said that both the London and Liverpool exhibitions were on a national scale, and the chances of borrowing any work from these seemed remote. We wrote to almost all of the exhibitors and were delighted with their response, which far exceeded our greatest hopes, when the following agreed to lend us portraits: The Earl of Bradford (Richard III, Anne Boleyn, Charles II, Catherine of Braganza and George II); Sir Gerald Kelly (George VI and Queen Elizabeth); Lady Birley (George VI); Dulwich College (William I, William II, Henry II, Richard I, John, Edward I, Henry VI, Henry VII, Henry VIII and Edward VI); Edward Halliday (Elizabeth II and Prince Philip); and The National Trust (Henrietta Maria). With such support the task of

Our last Arts Festival was in 1984, but it proved as lively as its predecessors. It included an exhibition of portraits by the doyen of theatrical photographers, Angus McBean, including this one of Lawrence Olivier as Othello, taken in 1966.

obtaining further exhibits was made very much easier, although a great amount of time had still to be spent on tracking these down. This entailed a period of time at the National Portrait Gallery, visits to possible lenders and much correspondence. It was during this period that we learnt of a portrait by Annigoni of Prince Philip which hung in the Fishmongers Hall in London; our request to borrow this painting was turned down, and so we wrote to Mr Annigoni to ask if he had any preparatory sketches he could lend. He replied that he had not but he knew that the Queen Mother did have one of these. Taking the plunge we wrote to Her Majesty asking if we could borrow the drawing, and to our great delight she graciously agreed to our request. Gradually the exhibition was built up until, with the co-operation of owners such as Earl Mountbatten, the Duke of Richmond and Gordon, Lord Brownlow, Earl Bathurst, Earl Beauchamp and the Deans of Gloucester, Hereford and Worcester Cathedrals (from the latter came King John's will), we were able to present 84 exhibits. We also commissioned an illustrated history of the Royal Arms with a text by Rodney Dennys, Rouge Croix Pursuivant of Arms. During the evenings the Royal Shakespeare Company gave a performance of The Hollow Crown, Hugh Trevor-Roper lectured on The Stuarts, Maurice Ashley on Cromwell and Sir Philip Magnus on The Edwardians. David Munrow and his Consort gave a concert entitled Music of Kings and Queens. Together with twenty two paintings from The National Trust forming the secondary exhibition, the 1966 Festival reached an extremely high standard and attracted a great deal of attention.

Henry Moore sculptures featured in a number of Festivals. This one is in plaster and called 'Internal and External forms', which we showed in 1961.

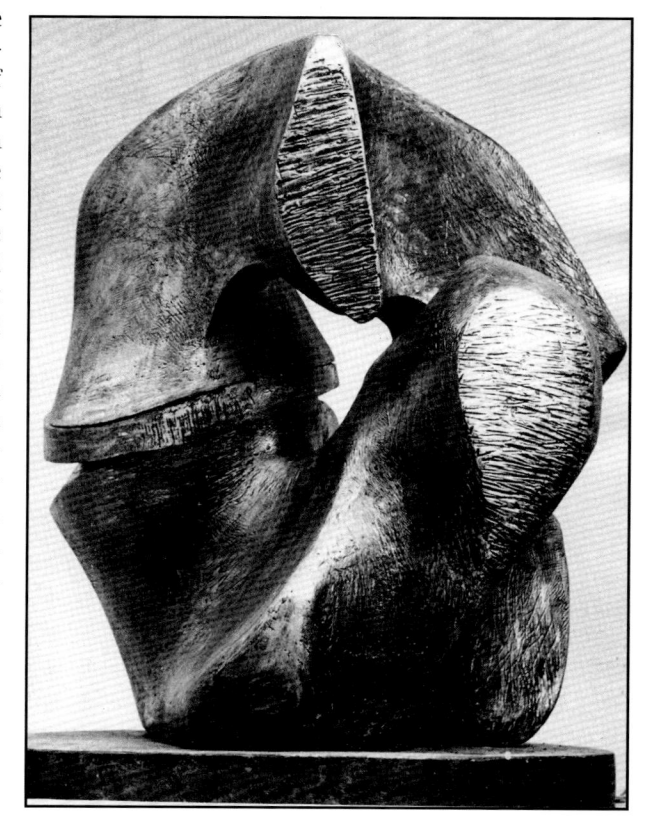

This Festival was the last in which we could exhibit old masters, for times were changing. Stately homes were beginning more and more to

One of our festivals was visited by a rally of Rolls Royce cars, which attracted a lot of attention.

open to the public, insurance premiums were rising, more security was demanded, and owners were also less inclined to lend their pictures because it had been discovered that the pigment could be loosened as a result of the vibrations which occurred during transit.

We turned then into the field of contemporary design, and presented our first exhibition in 1967, when we put on display well-designed products which had been recommended by Design Centres in twelve countries. We also mounted an exhibition of furnishings and fittings from the newly launched liner QE2. Thanks to Sir Paul, later Lord Reilly, the Director of the Council of Industrial Design, and to Sir Gordon Russell, a former Director of the Council, we were able to elicit the help of the Design Centre in staging this exhibition, as indeed they had done whenever asked.

After the 1972 Festival it was decided that future Festivals would be held only on even years, the reason being that it was becoming more and more time-consuming in arranging exhibitions, and also in trying to maintain the high standard the public was used to. Since then we have mounted four major design and craft exhibitions; presented contemporary paintings from China; costume, jewellery, crafts and paintings from Mongolia; photographic exhibitions; holograms; and furniture.

It can be seen that over the years our Festival has grown from being a small affair to becoming one of the West Midlands major arts events, and all without public subsidy. Our success was recognized in 1981 when we received an ABSA/Daily Telegraph Award in recognition of our sponsorship of the Arts, a sponsorship which has brought to a small country village distinguished musicians, actors and academics as well as exhibitions. We hope that of the many thousands of visitors who have made the journey to Stoke Prior, some will remember our efforts with kindness. [1984 was the last Arts Festival – George Chance retired in 1988.]

Section II

PERSONAL INTERESTS

August 29th 1985 – opening of Harris House, Olton, the eighth Margery Fry Trust Home for Homeless ex-prisoners. Mrs Betty Morgan (house committee chairman), Graham Stych (warden) and myself, the Trust President.

Chapter 13

PRISONS – AND REHABILITATION HOSTELS

"The mood and temper of the public with regard to the treatment of crime and criminals is one of the most unfailing tests of the civilisation of any country. A calm, dispassionate recognition of the rights of the accused, and even of the convicted criminal against the State – a constant heart-searching by all charged with the duty of punishment – a desire and eagerness to rehabilitate in the world of industry those who have paid their due in the hard coinage of punishment: tireless efforts towards the discovery of curative and regenerative processes: unfailing faith that there is a treasure, if you can only find it, in the heart of every man. These are the symbols, which, in the treatment of crime and criminal, mark and measure the stored-up strength of a nation, and are sign and proof of the living virtue in it."

(Winston Churchill, when Home Secretary, 1910)

The Society of Friends (of which I became a member in 1947) has always taken an interest in penal reform. A Quaker named John Howard was responsible for the passing of the first General Prisons Act of 1791, calling for the building of cellular prisons, the first one built under this act being in Millbank in London, opened in 1812 with 300 cells. Later, in the 1830s, the Quaker Elizabeth Fry visited prisons up and down the country and persuaded the government of Sir Robert Peel to build many more institutions between 1840 and 1850, including Pentonville, Wormwood Scrubbs, Strangeways (Manchester), Barlinnie (Glasgow), Armley (Leeds), and Birmingham (opened in 1848). So when our local Society of Friends formed a Penal Affairs Group in the 1950s I became a member of it. The Secretary of the group was a Friend named Leonard Broomfield. He was very concerned at that time with the lack of work for the inmates of Birmingham

Prison. In those days, they were only working for 21 hours a week, due mainly to shortage of orders. So far from being rehabilitated, they were being trained in habits of idleness. So we conceived the idea of making a contribution to the situation (with the consent of the authorities) by installing a plant for waste bristle reclamation in Birmingham Prison. I cannot do better than quote an article from our works magazine Shanghai on the subject which appeared in June 1958:

"One of the increasing difficulties of the Prison Commissioners for several years has been to find enough work to keep prisoners occupied inside prisons. The consumption of mail bags is apparently falling off, whilst the introduction of machinery to sew them instead of former hand methods, has very much increased output. The Commissioners have been able to obtain various other forms of work, such as coir mat making, breaking of disused Post Office cables, etc, but nowhere near enough work is obtainable to keep enclosed prisoners fully occupied.

"When Mr L. G. Harris attended a meeting some eighteen months ago, at which an appeal was made to industrialists to help in providing work in prisons, it occurred to him that the reclamation of waste bristle might form a useful occupation for prisoners. It should be explained here – for the benefit of the uninitiated – that we use at these works between forty and fifty tons of bristle per annum, and in the course of our bristle dressing and manufacturing processes, a certain amount of waste occurs. It is perfectly usable again, provided all the individual hairs are turned the right way round, with all the flagged ends in one direction and the roots in another, also if the bristle is graded according to size, viz, 2 inches, $2\,1/4$ inches, etc.

"Between 1951 and 1952, we installed a complete processing plant for reclamation of waste bristle at these works, including several machines of our own manufacture, and some from Germany. The plant was in use for nearly two years during the time when the brush trade was somewhat slacker than it is today, and we employed up to fifty of our workers on this process during that period. Fortunately for this firm, our trade has steadily increased over the years since that time, and we have not for several years had enough spare employees to put on this work of reclaiming waste bristle. In consequence, our stock of waste bristle has been accumulating, and we now have several tons of this valuable imported raw material.

"Early in 1957, we proposed to the Prison Commissioners that we would be prepared to loan them our complete plant for this purpose, in order to test the feasibility of putting prisoners on this work of reclaiming bristle inside prisons. The Commissioners were a little dubious about the proposition at first, as they had no experience whatever of this class of work, but we offered to do all the installation of the plant and send one of our supervisors to train their own supervisor and prisoners for a period of three months, and after some delay (not unusual in government departments) they stated they would like to give this work a trial.

"A complete workshop, size 90 feet by 34 feet, was therefore cleared out by the Commissioners at Winson Green Prison, Birmingham, and our machines and equipment (some eighteen in number) were installed in a carefully prepared layout which had been worked out by our technical manager, Mr Wride, in collaboration with Mr Eric Smith (bristle foreman). The machines were all freshly painted in a light green colour, and white lines and squares were painted on the floor of the workshop, thus creating an atmosphere of orderliness and normal factory practice. Production commenced on these machines in Birmingham Prison at the beginning of May, and after several teething troubles the plant is now functioning very satisfactorily, some fifty five prisoners being engaged on it. The prison authorities actually put eighty men on the machines at one time, but we had to ask them to limit the number to fifty five as they were overcrowding the machines.

"We are paying the Prison Commissioners prices for this bristle which are economic and fair, and about what we would have to pay if we purchased the material outside or reclaimed it by our own labour. When the prisoners are on mail bags, mat making etc, their average earnings for the Commissioners are between 1s and 1s 6d per hour, but they are earning about 1s 9d per hour on our bristle processing, so that the Commissioners are making a very satisfactory return on the men's work. The prisoners themselves, of course, only receive very small wages, a minimum of 1s 7d a week, with a maximum of 6s or 7s. Even these rates are double what they received until last year. The Commissioners are

1958 – the prison workshop, Winson Green Prison, with machines installed by us for bristle reclamation. Fifty five prisoners were employed on this work. The proceeds went to the prison authorities – the men were paid no more than 7/- (35p) per week.

studying whether better rates of pay can be granted to men in prison so that they can have a few pounds to carry them over when they are discharged. But it may take a long time to get public support for this.

"The average cost of maintaining a man in prison is between £6 and £7 per week [now (1985) £240 per week] so that if enough work could be obtained of the nature we have provided, and prisoners could be made to work full time, their keep could nearly be provided for by industrial work. One of the unsatisfactory features of the present set-up is that prisoners are only working an average of twenty one hours per week, due both to a shortage of sufficient work and also lack of sufficient disciplinary staff. We are trying to persuade the Prison Commissioners to work our plant at Birmingham Prison at least forty hours per week, which will be both to the financial advantage of the authorities, and in the interests of the men themselves.

"Unfortunately, in the case of the particular processes we have installed at Birmingham Prison, there is of course only a limited supply of waste bristle available, and it would not be possible to extend this work to every prison in the country, on this account. Nevertheless, fairly considerable expansion should be possible with waste bristle from other manufacturers. (Note. When our own supplies of waste ran short, we did obtain supplies from other brush makers).

"The Commissioners have already expressed appreciation of our cooperation by installing this plant, and we are hoping that the success of the venture will encourage them to install similar equipment in a number of their prisons. The photograph was taken in the prison workshop whilst work was in progress. The prisoners faces have been obliterated for obvious reasons."

Leonard Broomfield, the secretary of our small Society of Friends Penal Affairs Group, was devotedly interested in the welfare of prisoners, and after the installation of this machinery, he encouraged me to become an official prison visitor at Birmingham Prison in 1957. The object of prison visitors (who were first allowed by the Home Office in 1926) was to give the prisoners some contact with the outside world, and to show, particularly to men not receiving any outside visitors, that at least someone was interested in them, in the hope that the friendships formed might lead to a favourable influence after their discharge. Winson Green Prison in 1957 held about 800 prisoners in 350 cells, so that many men were sharing three to a cell. Any inmate who wished to have an outside prison visitor approached the prison chaplain, who would put him on the list. Usually there were not enough prison visitors to see all the men applying. Each visitor would be given a list of six names of men whom it was hoped he would be able to see regularly. I remember that one of the first men on my list, Patrick Tear, was serving 3 $^{1}/_{2}$ years for driving repeatedly without a licence. Another, Arthur Salisbury, was a painter and decorator who had been going round collecting deposits from householders on promises to paint their houses, and failing to turn up. I was able to give both men employment with our firm after their discharge, Tear as a sales representative and Salisbury in the factory.

Douglas Wride, our works director, who, like me, was a prison visitor, had taken an interest in these men, and did what he could to help them. This influence spread to Ramsay Eveson, our personnel director, who went to great lengths to put them on their feet.

An interesting experience I had was in connection with a prisoner I visited named Thomas James. His sentence of five years was the fifth he had received for sexual assaults on young boys. I had heard that the medical profession was able to prescribe treatment for the suppression of this sort of trouble, and I asked James whether he had ever asked his doctors for advice. He said that when he asked the Birmingham prison doctor if he could have some treatment, he received the reply "This is your treatment, my lad – five years inside". Apparently James had already decided to appeal against his last sentence. I felt strongly that repeated imprisonment was not going to cure him, and decided to ask Dr O'Riley, who had supported James on his last trial, if he would come with me to the Appeal Court in London, to plead on his behalf and put forward the case for a medical cure. We both appeared before the Lord Chief Justice, who was impressed by the evidence, and decided to put James on probation with a requirement to undergo treatment for twelve months. I then took him back to his home in West Bromwich and kept in touch with him for about two years, during which time he did not get into any further trouble. The case was reported in The Times, as shown in the extract on the following page. [This makes an interesting contrast with the hysteria surrounding this subject today.]

Altogether, I continued prison visiting for nine years until 1966, going into the prison every fortnight, and was able to give several of the men employment – though most of them were 'rolling stones' and left after a few months. The only instance in which our firm was defrauded by one of these men was by an individual we appointed (probably unwisely) as a salesman, who went round collecting accounts and disappeared.

Looking back, do prison visitors serve any useful purpose? It must be admitted that most of the men receiving visitors resort to crime again after their discharge. But it may be that a few of them are encouraged to live a more useful life. Several of the prison visitors (not myself) used to meet the men on coming out of prison, and help them to get re-established. I knew two visitors who even took the men into their own homes to live with them. One wife, I remember, rebelled against this after a few weeks! Although some of the wives of the prisoners were remarkably loyal, and continued to stand by their husbands even after two or three sentences, many of the marriages had broken up – and the husbands had nowhere to go after their discharge. They then frequently got in touch with their former associates and started their criminal activities again.

One arrangement started by Leonard Broomfield was the holding of Quaker Meetings in the prison on Sunday mornings for any prisoners who wished to attend. Usually only two or three men came, but I felt the Meetings served a use-

COURT OF CRIMINAL APPEAL

TAKING A RISK

REGINA v JAMES
Before the LORD CHIEF JUSTICE, MR JUSTICE MARSHALL *and* MR JUSTICE WIDGERY

The Court allowed this appeal by Thomas James, aged 50, lorry driver, of Princes Street, West Bromwich, against a sentence of five years' imprisonment imposed on him on September 10, 1964, at Walsall Quarter Sessions (Recorder: J C B W Leonard, Esq.), after he had pleaded Guilty to indecent assault on a 15 years old boy between 9.55 p.m. and 12.30 a.m. on August 3 and 4, 1964. The Court today made a probation order for three years, with a condition of treatment, and, no probation officer being in Court, made a prison visitor responsible for escorting James and handing him over to the probation officer.

Mr Nicholas Budgen appeared for James; the Crown did not appear and was not represented.

JUDGMENT

The Lord Chief Justice, giving the judgment of the Court, said that it was a bad case, and might well have been charged as attempted buggery. His Lordship would like to say at once – leave to appeal against sentence having been granted by a differently constituted Court, on January 18, 1965 – that the object of granting leave to appeal was to double the sentence, and to give James 10 years, the reason being that since 1942, he had been guilty of five offences of indecent assault on boys and had been to prison for periods ranging from two months to five years – having received two sentences of five years in 1953 and 1957, the boys concerned being aged 9 and 12 respectively.

Clearly it was a very serious case and, notwithstanding the evidence of Dr James Joseph O'Riley, director of the Midlands Centre of Forensic Psychiatry, at All Saints Hospital, Birmingham, the Recorder thought – and this Court sympathized with him – that he really could not take the substantial risk of making an order under section 4 of the Criminal Justice Act, 1948, putting James on probation with a term of residence in a hospital for treatment. Dr O'Riley having very fairly said that there was only a 75 per cent chance of treatment damping down James's sexual urges, and that that was so only if treatment were continued, and the he (Dr O'Riley) could not watch over him for ever.

This Court had been very impressed with the evidence of Mr Leslie George Harris, a prison visitor for some eight years, who had visited James every fortnight since his conviction. Mr Harris certainly had the impression, and had conveyed it to this Court, that James really did desire treatment, was anxious to have it, and to keep it up, which was the most important thing of all. In all the period of 22 years since 1942, James apparently had never had any treatment, and had not desired it. Whether that was so or not, he apparently desired it now. Certainly, imprisonment for another period of five years would do him no good whatsoever.

The Court felt that, since two people had actively interested themselves in James, there really was a chance. Not only had Dr O'Riley come to give evidence again in this Court, but also Mr Harris had come. On the whole the Court had been persuaded to take a risk, although realizing that it was a grave risk and involved accepting Mr Harris's view of the case.

The most that the Court could do by way of supervision was to make a probation order for three years and to make it a term that, for 12 months, James receive in-patient treatment under Dr O'Riley at his hospital. At the end of the 12 months it was entirely up to James to continue the treatment, the Court could not compel him to do so, but would make it a term of the probation order that, when residential treatment had finished he should report once a month to Dr O'Riley. This would be explained to the probation officer – who would, no doubt, see that James reported to Dr O'Riley – and the Court was quite satisfied that Dr O'Riley, so far as was within his powers, would keep an eye on James and see that he went on with the treatment.

His Lordship (to James) – I think that you have to thank Dr O'Riley and, particularly, Mr Harris for the course we are taking – a course for which we shall be blamed if anything goes wrong.

The appellant – Nothing will go wrong.

The Times' account of my appearance in speaking for Thomas James in the Court of Appeal in 1965.

ful purpose. They are still being carried on (1985) by the present Quaker prison chaplain.

The Margery Fry Memorial Trust

It was about 1959 when some of us in the Quaker group heard of a hostel for homeless discharged ex-prisoners which had been opened in 1954 in Highbury, North London, by Mervyn Turner, the son of a Methodist Minister. Turner had been a prison visitor at Pentonville, and had come to the same conclusion as us – that if homeless men could be befriended on discharge, they might be helped to live lives more useful to the community. So we went down to see the hostel, came away impressed by the atmosphere, and felt inspired to start a similar hostel in Birmingham. It so happened that Dame Margery Fry (1874-1958) (at one time Principal of Somerville College, Oxford), who had been keenly interested in penal reform the whole of her life, had left a small sum of money which she hoped might be used to help men coming out of prison. This money had come into the hands of a friend of Dame Margery, Florence McNeille, who was known to some of us. So with her, we formed a small committee, raised a further £7,000, and with the money purchased two adjoining Victorian houses, 42 and 44 Forest Road, Moseley, Birmingham, called Newell House, with accommodation for 17 men. We then registered the Margery Fry Memorial Trust as a charitable trust, persuaded a well-known Quaker magistrate, Edwin Ransome, to become chairman, appointed the first warden and wife, and received the first homeless ex-prisoners in April 1961.

Inevitably, a number of teething troubles were experienced in the first year, e.g. some men unsuitable for family life were accepted in the early months, and some stayed too short a time to benefit from life in the home. Nevertheless, things gradually settled down, and in the first three years till 1964 we were encouraged by the fact that no resident had committed a crime while staying in the house. We received much support and encouragement from the probation service and the police, though the Home Office did not provide any financial help until 1966, when we started to receive a modest subsidy of £100 per bed per annum, following a visit to Newell House by Sir Frank Soskice, then Home Secretary. Until then, the cost had to be met from our voluntary subscription list. The Home Office gradually increased its financial support, and since p 1978 they have met nearly the whole of the annual deficit.

Sadly, our first chairman, Edwin Ransome, died in 1962. The Committee then asked me to succeed him as chairman. By 1966 we had opened three further hostels: McNeille House, Selly Park (named after our first secretary); Middleborough House, Coventry; and Dormer House, Olton (with self-catering facilities). These were followed in subsequent years by Avon House, Leamington (for young offenders); Cope House, Nuneaton; Field View House, Bromsgrove (for specially inadequate men); and Harris House, Olton, with individual small flats. In some cases, we encountered much local opposition before we were allowed to open the hostels. But after the homes had been open for some time, the resent-

THE MARGERY FRY MEMORIAL FUND
Homes for ex-Prisoners

The second Margery Fry home for homeless prisoners in Uplands Rd, Selly Oak, opened in 1964. The house had accommodation for 18 men. It had previously been the home of the grandfather of the writer Godfrey Winn, whose brother was Lord Justice Winn.

ment usually died away, and we received support from the local residents, which was referred to in a speech by the Bishop of Exeter in the House of Lords about the happenings at McNeille House. Similar difficulties occurred with the opening of Field View House, Bromsgrove, where public protest meetings were held, but local people were later reconciled.

As our President, Alderman Eric Mole, was an ex-Lord Mayor of Birmingham, we were allowed to use the main council chamber in Birmingham Council House for our annual general meetings. Over the years, we managed to persuade a number of distinguished people to be the principal speakers at these gatherings. These included Lord Gardiner (Lord Chancellor), Roy Jenkins (Home Secretary and later Chancellor of the Exchequer), Lady Reading, Shirley Williams (Minister of Education), Lord Donaldson (Chairman of Nacro), Lord Hunt, Duncan Fairn (Head of the Prison Service), Lord Stonham (Home Secretary), and Lord Longford. All the speakers seemed to be in favour of what we were trying to do. After the meetings, I used to entertain the members of the executive committee to dinner at the Grand Hotel, Birmingham. Sometimes, the principal speakers used to come as well.

Looking back, I am amazed how many of the staff at our firm helped the Trust in a voluntary capacity. These included Douglas Wride, our works director, who became hon. secretary to the Trust after the death of Mrs McNeille, Henry Reiner, export manager, who was chairman of the Newell House committee, Denzil Smith (sales representative), Chairman of McNeille House, George Chance (Personnel Director) who followed me as Chairman of Field View House, and Andrew, who was the first secretary to the Field View House committee. I expect the reader will imagine that I put some pressure on these members of our staff, but nothing could be further from the truth. I can only assume that they felt that what the Trust was doing was worthwhile, and wanted to help in a voluntary capacity. Both Douglas Wride and Denzil Smith later became magistrates.

Field View House, Stoke Prior. This Margery Fry house was intended for about 20 men who had been in and out of prison for many years, and who had become to some extent institutionalised, and incapable of looking after themselves – some even committed offences to be put back in prison. Margery Fry built a new workshop in the grounds of the house, in which the men did light work under close supervision for up to 6 months to get them back into the habits of industry before taking on outside employment. The brushworks provided much of the work in the early days.

    By 1972 I felt I should hand over to someone else as chairman, and we were proud when George Jonas, a well-known Birmingham solicitor and former city councillor, agreed to take over. Our president Eric Mole later retired, and I was kicked upstairs as President of the Trust, where I have remained until now. In the first six years since the Trust was founded in 1961, Mrs McNeille had acted as hon. secretary. She had done a wonderful job, but as the work expanded we felt we had to appoint a paid staff, and Stanley Williams, who until then had been secretary of the old Discharged Prisoners Aid Society, took over as general secretary. The DPAS was then wound up, and its assets taken over by the Margery Fry Fund. Stanley Williams gave devoted service to the Trust until 1985, being succeeded by Frank Bailey. Mrs McNeille died in 1973 after a lifetime of service.

    Newell House, the discharged prisoners hostel which we opened in 1961, was only the second one of its type in the country. Its fame spread, and many vol-

PRISONERS AT WORK

From Mr L G Harris

Sir,—Since 1956 no fewer than four separate committees have been formed, all with the intention of increasing the hours of work in our closed prisons. The net result, however, has been a steady decline.

Surely, the fact that over half our present prison population of 33,500 is being kept in idleness is an outstanding criticism of the way we run our affairs. Not only is the labour of these men being wasted, but so far from being rehabilitated, they are actually being trained in habits of idleness.

On a recent visit to China I was allowed to go round Peking Prison. This establishment houses 1,700 men and 100 women, all of whom work a 48 hour week, half the production being hosiery, and the other half plastic footwear of all types. The inmates are paid about 1/6th of the wages they would have in civilian life, compared with about 1/40th in our prisons. I was freely allowed to take photographs inside the prison, and was most impressed with the general standard of industrial efficiency, in particular the new tool-making department, a fine lofty building with the latest type of new machine tools, which would do credit to a first-class British engineering works.

In Sweden – to quote only one more example – all prisoners work a 40 hour week, mostly on outside projects. The position is the same in many other countries. It is probably true to say that the present working week in British closed prisons is the lowest in the world.

Our prison authorities are admittedly hampered by shortage of staff and buildings. Lord Stonham was quoted yesterday as saying that "we cannot afford to get rid of our Victorian prisons". Some of these are situated in the centres of our cities on extremely valuable sites – the prisons at Reading, Gloucester and Shrewsbury are three typical examples. Would it not be possible to sell some of these sites for re-development at the present high market rates ruling, and build fresh prisons at selected spots in the country where land is far cheaper? Some years ago the trustees of King Edward's Grammar School in New Street, Birmingham, sold their site for over £1m, and were able to build a magnificent new school in the suburbs with the money.

Our habit of keeping prisoners in idleness has gone on far too long. It is time the whole matter was considered at Cabinet level and drastic action taken.

Yours faithfully
L G Harris, Chairman, The Margery Fry Memorial Fund, Birmingham and West Midlands Area
Ridge End, Hanbury, Worcestershire
Sept 7

1967 – letter to The Times which aroused the interest of the Lord Chancellor, Lord Gardiner.

untary societies opened similar homes. Later, the official Probation Service became interested, and by 1985 over 300 hostels, some run by voluntary bodies and some by the Home Office, existed in various parts of the country. So the original idea started by Mervyn Turner in 1954 had set an example which was widely copied.

Winson Green Prison, Birmingham, had been built in 1847. Having very little provision for physical exercise, and practically no industrial training facilities, it was hopelessly out of date by modern standards. One of its chief drawbacks is the lack of proper toilet facilities for the inmates, who are locked in their cells from 8 p.m. to 7 a.m. with three chamber pots between three men. The Prison Commissioners had built two or three modern closed prisons since 1945, and had converted a number of ex-army camps into open prisons for first offenders. But the majority of the fortress-like institutions built in the 1840s still existed. Shortage of money was given as the official reason for the inadequate building programme.

Many of the Victorian prisons occupied positions in the centres of cities, and the thought occurred to me that if some of these valuable sites were sold, the high prices realised might go a long way towards building new prisons in the country. I wrote to The Times

Report on prison building

NEW GAOL FROM OLD SITE SALE

Home Office study Birmingham plan

BY OUR HOME DEPARTMENT CORRESPONDENT

A plan to raise money for building new prisons is being "actively considered" by the Home Office. As a first stage it is suggested that Winson Green prison in Birmingham should be pulled down and proceeds from the sale of the site should go towards a new prison outside the city.

The plan has been put forward by Mr L G Harris, chairman of the Margery Fry Memorial Fund, which runs homes for former prisoners in Birmingham. Conservative and Labour leaders on the City Council have agreed in principle to the idea. Lord Gardiner, the Lord Chancellor, wrote to Mr Harris supporting it.

Winson Green prison would be demolished and the 10 acre site used by Birmingham for housing. It is estimated that the sale of the site to the corporation would yield about £200,000.

Land badly needed

Previously schemes of this kind have run up against the difficulty that if the Prison Department vacate a prison the site reverts to the local authority. The scheme can go through only if the council waives its rights and, although there is not yet any firm commitment in Birmingham, the signs are hopeful.

If there was no prospect of financial compensation the Home Office would be unlikely to give up their rights to the property and might eventually rebuild on the same site. Thus Birmingham would lose a site badly needed for housing.

From the Home Office point of view an injection of £200,000 into a new building project would be more than welcome. Winson Green was built in the middle of the last century and, like most Victorian prisons, has many design defects.

Local councillors at Birmingham might well feel that a new prison would give prisoners an opportunity for more constructive work, and prison officials would probably welcome the better security. In 1964 Charles Wilson the train robber escaped from Winson Green.

Mr Harris said yesterday the principle of the Birmingham plan could be applied to other prisons which occupied central sites. Among these were Reading, Leicester, Shrewsbury and Gloucester.

Mountbatten blessing

Other prisons occupying valuable sites could be found in the south possibly including one or two in London, and the movement of prisons housing men serving long sentences outside large population centres also has the blessing of Lord Mountbatten of Burma.

In his report on prison security Lord Mountbatten said that some nineteenth-century prisons would have to be replaced and "there may be advantages in some towns in disposing of the existing sites of old prisons and building a replacement on the outskirts". He gave a warning that sites would not be easy to find and that in some cases legislation would be needed.

A parliamentary statement on the Mountbatten report is expected to be made soon by the Home Secretary. He is likely to announce that about two-thirds of the Mountbatten recommendations are being put into effect, and that the Government will agree to provide the money to carry out the improvements.

I got some hope from this article in The Times that something positive might be done to improve some of our oldest prisons, but very little happened, the problem being the relentless rise in prisoner numbers which has continued up to the present.

1972 – outside Buckingham Palace with Geraldine and Mary, after receiving my award of the MBE – this was partly for my work with Margery Fry.

about it, and received a favourable reply from Lord Gardiner, the Lord Chancellor. The Times then published a short article (illustrated). Although I followed the matter up with the Home Office, nothing was done, but the government did approve a much expanded budget for new prison building in the next two years.

In 1973 I was invited by Lord Donaldson, the Chairman of NACRO, (National Association for the Care and Rehabilitation of Offenders) to take over the chairmanship of the Midlands region of the Association. The object of this job was to co-ordinate the various activities being held in the region in aid of ex-prisoners. A local paid Secretary was appointed (Mr E. Porter), and representatives of the various independent groups were asked to attend regional meetings, which were held in the Margery Fry Home, McNeille House, Birmingham. Possibly I was an unsuitable person to chair the co-ordination of these activities, and I did not think very highly of the efforts of the paid secretary. But the various groups continued to act very much on their own, and after two years I came to the conclusion that very little was being achieved. I then asked Lord Donaldson to close the regional arrangements down, which he did. I was sorry not to have made a success of this, as I very much admired Lord Donaldson, but I felt the job was too amorphous and vague.

My interest in our prison system, then, has lasted half my lifetime. It has been largely stimulated by my association with the Society of Friends. Whether all the various so-called progressive moves, such as the vast increase in the staff of the Probation Service (trebled since 1970), the suspended sentences, the introduction of community service orders, and the 300 hostels for discharged prisoners, have done any good, is difficult to say. The fact remains that our prison population has steadily increased until in 1985 it reached an all time high of 48,000, as against an average in the 1930s of 18,000 [over 70,000 in 2002]. Would it have been even higher if the above measures had not been introduced? Some consolation may perhaps be drawn from the fact that our number of men in prison is low in proportion to the number of men in the United States, where an average of over 500,000 men are incarcerated out of a population four times our number. However, according to a 1985 report by NACRO, the United Kingdom has a larger number of people per 100,000 of the population in jail than any other European country, twice as many as France and four times as many as Portugal. One of my theories is that the decline in religious observance since the 19th century has something to do with the problem.

One of the rules of the Home Office is that the object of prison is to train the men to live a good and useful life after discharge. I am afraid that all the people I have met in the criminal justice field would say that nothing more than keeping them out of harm's way is achieved by our present system. I can only hope that by the time this book is read (I trust) in 2085, we shall have radically reformed our methods of dealing with people offending against the law.

Chapter 14

FEDERAL UNION

"Those whose indication is to bow their heads, to seek patiently and faithfully for compromise, are not always wrong. On the contrary, in the majority of instances they may be right, not only morally but from a practical standpoint. How many wars have been averted by patient and persistent goodwill! Religion and virtue alike lend their sanctions to meekness and humility, not only between men but between nations... The Sermon on the Mount is the last word in Christian ethics. Everyone respects the Quakers."
(Winston Churchill, The Gathering Storm, Vol. I, pp. 250 - 251).

At the time of writing (1985) I cannot remember any period of my life more fraught with worry than the six years before the second world war, 1933-1939. Hitler, who had taken over as Chancellor of Germany in 1933, had denounced the Versailles Treaty of 1919 and had marched into Austria in 1935, and seized power in Czechoslovakia in 1938. He then announced that Poland was to be his next target. People all over Europe were wondering what was going to happen next. Were we going to have to face another holocaust so soon after the mass slaughter of the first world war of 1914-1918? These fears gave rise to the Munich appeasement agreement of 1938, in which the governments of Britain and France gave way to Hitler's demands. But appeasement came to an end when the Germans attacked Poland, and our grim foreboding of a second world war came true in August 1939.

In 1938, I had been fascinated to read a book entitled Union Now, by an American, Clarence Streit, advocating what seemed a breath-taking idea at the time - nothing less than the formation of a political federation of all the Western democracies - the USA, Canada, Great Britain, France and Scandinavia. The proposal seemed to hold enormous possibilities for peace, since it was very unlikely to imagine any country or combination of countries daring to take up arms against such an immensely powerful union. And the tariff-free area envisaged held unlimited opportunities for an increase in trade.

The proposal attracted widespread international support, but in 1938, when the book was published, Hitler was getting more and more aggressive, and Britain and France were more concerned with increasing their defence forces than engaging in sweeping new political ideas – even assuming that the USA would have agreed to join in.

Nevertheless, some form of political federation or union seemed to me to be the only alternative to the intense nationalism propagated by Hitler. At about that time, another new idea was put forward by three young men, Derek Rawnsley, Patrick Ransome and Charles Kimber – the formation of a United States of Europe. Rawnsley was the son of Canon Rawnsley, one of the three founders of the National Trust in 1895. Having been at Oxford together, and knowing several well known people, they decided to form a political pressure group called Federal Union to advocate their ideas. Some of their early supporters, I remember, were Dr C. E. M. Joad, Barbara Wootton the economist (later Baroness Wootton), W. B. Curry the Headmaster of Dartington Hall School, who later wrote a book entitled The Case for Federal Union, Lord Beveridge, and Sir George Catlin, father of Mrs Shirley Williams.

When a branch of Federal Union was formed in Birmingham in 1939, I enthusiastically joined and for a time acted as secretary. The Birmingham group was supported by the Rev Leyton Richards, the Minister of Carrs Lane Church, and by John S. Hoyland, a well known Quaker who was Principal of Woodbrooke College, Birmingham. Both these men were first class public speakers and addressed many Federal Union public meetings in the Midlands. They taught me a lot and I had a great admiration for both of them. Later, John Hoyland wrote a book called Federate or

1949 – The Birmingham Post supports Henry Usborne's and my efforts to publicise the Crusade for World Government.

Perish (quoting Mr Attlee's phrase), which I helped to get published. About 20 of us in the local group used to meet for lunch every week in a restaurant in New Street, Birmingham, to discuss propaganda ideas for the movement. Afterwards, having spoken at a number of public meetings, I became a member of the London executive committee of Federal Union, and attended the first international conference in Luxembourg in 1946.

But however enthusiastically Federal Union ideas were received by the public, nothing seemed to be getting achieved politically. We came to realize that the only people who could actually do anything were the powers that be in the form of the Prime Minister and Foreign Secretary. It was interesting that Winston Churchill had advocated union with France in 1940. And the French Premier Aristide Briand had proposed a United States of Europe back in 1928. Mr Churchill also pressed for a federation in his Fulton, Missouri, speech after the war. Ernest Bevin, the Foreign Secretary, had said "We need a new study for the purpose of creating a World Assembly elected directly from the people of the world. I am willing to sit with anybody,

Henry Usborne, with whom I shared my life-long interest in Federal Union, although I didn't share his belief in pacifism. He was a Labour MP from 1945–59, when he lost his seat in the Tory landslide, although he often objected to having to vote for the party line when he didn't agree with it. He founded and ran the Nu-Way Heating Co. in Droitwich, which was later sold to the Wolseley Group. Photo taken in 1992 at our Golden Wedding party. He died in 1996 aged 87.

of any party, of any nation, to try to devise a franchise or a constitution for a World Government". So our political leaders gave lip service to the idea – but failed to take any practical steps to bring it about.

I was therefore excited when our Birmingham member Henry Usborne (then an MP) got together in 1946 with a number of distinguished people to form a Crusade for World Government. His Committee then published a Plan in Outline to describe how this could come about. He was appealing for £1,000,000 to further the idea, and I sent him his first donation of £1,000. Later in America he was invited by Prof Albert Einstein and the Association of American Atomic Scientists to fly over at their expense and explain the idea to them. At a meeting which they set up in Chicago, Mrs Blaine, a wealthy American lady, offered a million dollars to persuade Americans to join the Crusade. In India and Japan, too, the enthusiasm was astonishing.

A 'Peoples World Constituent Assembly' to further the idea was held in Geneva in 1950, attended by over 500 people, and various public meetings continued to be held in the UK, supported by publicity efforts. But little actual progress was made. As an educational programme, the Crusade was probably successful, but politically it made no impression whatever. To quote Henry Usborne's words "We nevertheless learnt a lot from it. For instance, we now know that in certain circumstances it is possible to generate public enthusiasm for the idea of making peace by federation. We also know far more about the difficulties involved in the process."

Some progress was made when the Common Market was formed – not (to our shame) due to any initiative on the part of the British people. The UK was in any case kept out of the Community for several years at the instance of General de Gaulle of France, only being admitted in 1972, although a referendum (the first of its kind) was conducted by the Labour government later in 1975 to confirm our membership. Although many people hoped that the EEC would eventually develop into a United States of Europe, nationalistic fervour soon began to rear its head again, and some member countries (particularly France and Italy) later imposed various restrictions which reduced the flow of trade in the community. The establishment of the European Parliament in Strasbourg in 1978 seemed to be a step forward, though at the present time its very limited powers can be overruled by the Council of Ministers in Brussels. And the Common Agricultural Policy, designed to enable Europe to become self-sufficient in food production, has achieved this object only at the expense of producing vast agricultural surpluses through the large subsidies given to farmers. This has also had the effect of reducing the ability of many overseas countries which used to export food to Europe to buy our own manufactures through their shortage of foreign exchange. So it has been a two-edged weapon. Nevertheless, in spite of these difficulties and disappointments, the existence of the European Economic Community surely represents a vast improvement over the chaotic state of Europe in the 1930s. Although many people nowadays fear the power of Russia, it is difficult to imagine war breaking out again between the EEC member countries. And provided nationalism, which I believe to be fundamentally harmful, can be kept in check, perhaps one day the European Parliament will have sufficient power to bring permanent peace to Europe.

My friend Henry Usborne, whom I very much admired, remained an MP for 14 years from 1945 to 1959. Although his Crusade for World Government had not achieved any political results, he had the initiative while in the House of Commons in 1946 to persuade 160 of his fellow MPs to join a Parliamentary Group for World Government, which started out with high hopes. Henry, then, had actually done something for the furtherance of world peace, while most of us just sit on the sidelines and watch the world go by.

Nevertheless – perhaps influenced by his early disappointments – Henry Usborne took a pessimistic view of the developments in Europe. He felt that the nationalistic feelings of the member countries would never allow them to merge their sovereignties in a political union. After the lapse of some years, he began to feel that a solution to world problems would be for the nations of the Middle World – those other than America, Russia and China – to band together in a neutral minimal federation. The great powers, he felt, would remain separate, and the existence of a neutral federation of the smaller powers would have a restraining influence. He wrote a well written book outlining his proposals entitled Prescription for Peace, which we published privately in 1985. The federal constitution he outlined envisaged that the federal government would have absolutely minimal powers, all the member countries having the right to govern their own local affairs according to their own wishes.

Although I did not share Henry's pessimism about Europe, and felt that it would probably be difficult to get his Minifed established, I was glad he had not given up in despair, and was still trying to further the federal cause. I was able to give him some help in connection with the book, and attended some meetings in the House of Commons with him, to persuade some MPs to sponsor the book, which the Parliament Group for World Government agreed to do. A number of members of the House of Lords also supported his proposals, and the Rt Hon Peter Archer MP (Solicitor General in the Labour government of 1974-1979) wrote a preface to the book strongly commending the ideas outlined. In 1985 it remains to be seen what effect the book will have, and we are anxiously awaiting the reviews in the national press.

The establishment of world peace, then, seems to me to be the outstanding issue confronting mankind today. I sometimes wonder what a man from Mars would think if he looked in at our world and saw the way we murder each other. He would probably think that we were worse than a lot of stupid, irrational children. The right of nations to be both judge and jury in their own cause must surely be stopped. I fervently hope that by the time this book is read in 2085, mankind will have come to its senses.

"It is probable that no plan we propose will be adopted. Perhaps another dreadful conflict is to be sustained. But if to please the people, we offer what we ourselves disapprove, how can we afterwards defend our work? Let us raise a standard to which the wise and honest can repair. The event is in the hands of God."
George Washington addressing the Philadelphia Convention, 1787

"The unleashed power of the atom has changed everything save our method of thinking, and we thus drift towards unparalleled catastrophe."
Albert Einstein, 1946

"Every gun that is made, every warship launched, every rocket fired, signifies in the final sense a theft from those that hunger and are not fed, those who are cold and not clothed.

"The cost of one modern heavy bomber is this – a modern brick school for 30 cities. It is two electric power plants, each serving a town of 60,000 population.

"This is not a way of life in any true sense. Under the cloud of threatening war, it is humanity hanging from a cross of iron."
President Eisenhower

[I regret that this is one area of my father's activities with which I could not agree. I do not believe that binding nations together in artificial federations is a recipe for peace, indeed quite the opposite, as many events post WW2 have shown. Furthermore I do not believe that having to adopt all the EU rules and regulations is in this country's interests, especially economically. If all the nations of Europe could speak with one strong voice on foreign policy, this might be a force for good in the world, but the divisions between EU governments have never been so obvious as they are when I write this in January 2003. The deep-seated French anti-Americanism, mirrored in Germany as well, is in stark contrast to Tony Blair's support for Pr. Bush over Iraq. EU foreign ministers cannot even agree on how to treat Pr. Mugabe of Zimbabwe. Divisions like this do not augur well for the so-called European army. So I have also been politically active in this field, being secretary of the local branch of the UK Independence Party, which opposes our continued membership of the EU!]

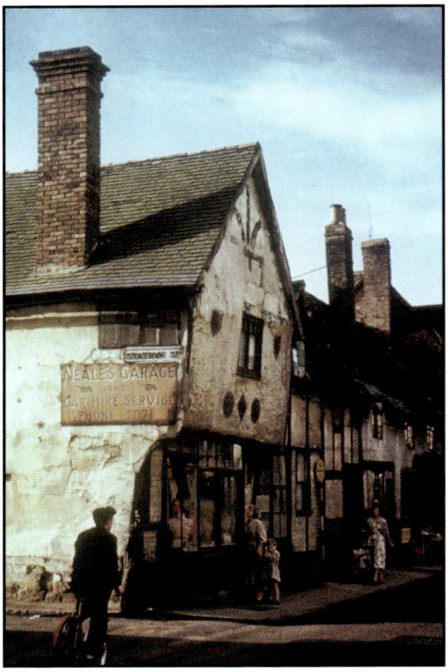
STATION
NEALE'S GARAGE

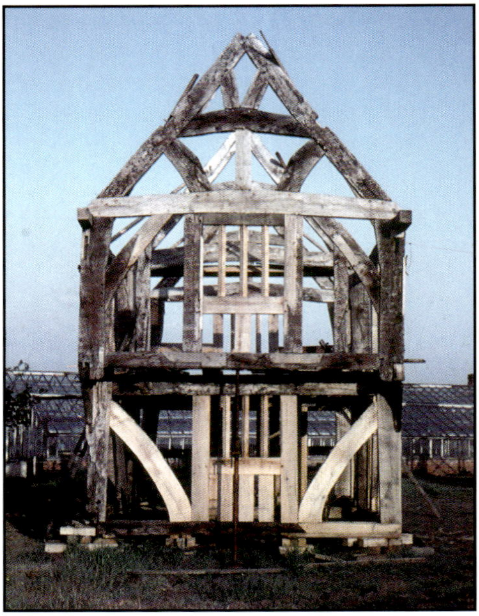

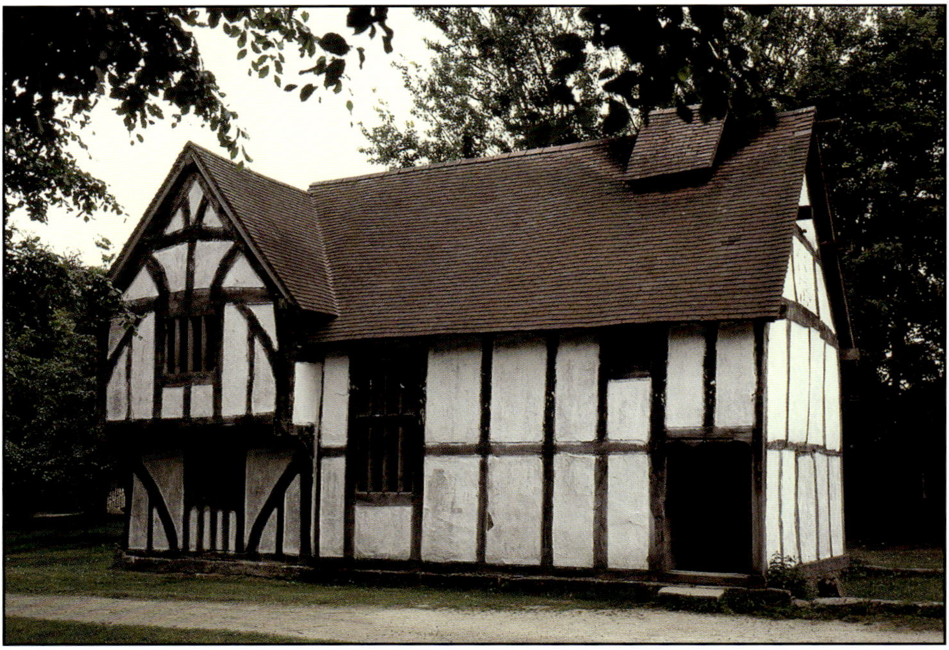

(Opposite page) The Bromsgrove House was the first building to be re-erected at Avoncroft. The pictures show it as it was in Worcester Rd, Bromsgrove; during rebuilding in 1966; and as it was in 2002. It can be seen that the front of the cross wing had to have a great deal of timber replaced, and our firm helped supply the new oak required, and by loaning our carpenter, but the principal carpenter was Gunold Greiner who was recruited specially for the project.

Chapter 15

AVONCROFT MUSEUM OF BUILDINGS

In 1961 a 15th century merchant's house in High Street, Bromsgrove, was threatened with demolition. Its intended disappearance caused great local concern, as it was the last example of a house of the period in Bromsgrove. A public meeting was held in the Parish Hall, at which the architect Freddie Charles, adviser on timber framed buildings to the Worcestershire County Council, appealed for financial support for its reconstruction in the district. The meeting was chaired by Christopher Cadbury, the chairman of the Worcestershire Nature Conservation Trust, and several offers of financial help were forthcoming. Arising out of this meeting, the Fircroft Trust allocated an acre of land adjoining the Avoncroft College, Stoke Heath, on which the medieval house was reconstructed between 1965 and 1967. The rebuilding took a long time because a number of the timbers of the framing had been damaged, and had to be carefully repaired.

The original intention had been merely to save the Bromsgrove House from destruction. But in view of the considerable public interest aroused, the group of people concerned with the re-building conceived the idea of creating a museum in which other important historical buildings might be preserved. The Fircroft Trust agreed to lease a further 10 acres of land adjoining Avoncroft College, and the Avoncroft Folk Village Association (later renamed the Avoncroft Museum of Buildings), a company limited by guarantee, was set up. Sir Hugh Casson agreed to be its first President, and I was asked to be the chairman of the management committee, which I did until handing over to Lord Sandys in 1979. The Committee appointed Michael Thomas MA as the first Museum Director. The first hon. secretary was Alfred Gregg, who was then warden of Avoncroft College. He was followed by my son Andrew. These arrangements, then, saw the start of the first museum of buildings in England. It is interesting that at about

The Bromsgrove House was opened in 1967 with a ceremony with some of the participants dressed in medieval costume. Geraldine third from right, Annie Harris second from left. (Below) Sir Gordon Russell (second from left) officiated at the opening, and Alfred Gregg, the first hon. museum secretary, is on my left. Miss Foster of the Avoncroft Arts Society in the centre.

the same time, the Stoke Prior Factory Arts Festivals were commenced, also creating a precedent. So the initiative shown by these two efforts, in a small way, created local history.

The next major project at the museum after the Bromsgrove House was to dismantle and re-erect at Avoncroft a magnificent 14th century roof from the Guesten Hall. Built in the 1320s for the reception of guests at Worcester Cathedral, the Guesten Hall had been dismantled in 1860, and the roof used in the construction of the new Holy Trinity Church elsewhere in Worcester. In 1960 this Church, in turn, was awaiting demolition, and the roof was threatened a second time.

The Guesten Hall roof was said to be the finest of its kind in existence. The timbers, which were in very good condition, were taken apart, and the 14th century trusses were re-assembled at Avoncroft. The idea was then conceived of using the roof again in the construction of a small concert hall in the museum seating 200, of which the town of Bromsgrove was much in need. Plans were prepared and a brochure produced to launch of an appeal for £250,000. Unfortunately, trade and industry were going through a difficult time in the early 1970s and the response was very disappointing, only about £25,000 being raised.

The opening of the 16th century 'String of Horses' building from Shrewsbury. Left to right: Roy Beard (project architect), Malcolm Booth of Associated Architects (site architects and responsible for the Guesten Hall), Alfred Wood (committee member and head of planning for the West Midlands County Council), Michael Thomas (museum director) and myself.

These pictures show the Cholstrey Barn being dismantled and being rebuilt at Avoncroft. Richard acted as manager to this project, which was completed in 1975. We were able to help with the dismantling of the barn with our timber lorry and crane (left). The barn, which was from a farm just west of Leominster and dates from around 1600, had an oak frame with cruck trusses made of black poplar, and was fairly easily taken apart once all the oak pegs holding the mortice and tenon joints together had been taken out. A feature of the reconstruction was the use of new oak rafters, made by splitting young oak trees into two, and squaring them off. The picture on the facing page shows the barn and Temple Broughton granary in 2002.

It was perhaps rather an over-ambitious effort to be started in the early days of the museum when its reputation had not yet been established. The restored roof trusses were then re-erected as a temporary exhibit on the Museum's site, and have been viewed by the public regularly ever since. It is still hoped (1985) that the proposed hall, which would add very much to the amenities of Bromsgrove, will one day be built. [The New Guesten Hall is now complete and used for a variety of activities.]

However, undeterred by this early disappointment, the management committee pressed on with the preservation and re-erection of several historical buildings which were offered to them. Over the next few years, an average of one old building a year was reconstructed at Avoncroft. These included an 18th century granary, a thatched barn from Cholstrey in Herefordshire, a cockpit theatre from Shrewsbury, a Victorian nail-making shop (an ancient Bromsgrove industry), an ice-house from Weston Park, Shropshire, and an 18th century windmill from Danzey Green, Warwickshire. The windmill, which took two years to reconstruct, produces stone-ground flour which is sold to visitors to the museum. My son Richard was architect to the granary and barn projects.

The largest building to be rescued at Avoncroft was a 16th century Inn known as the String of Horses, which was demolished due to road widening in Shrewsbury. This took a total of three years to be reconstructed, at a cost of some £80,000. It comprises a Long Room (named after the Museum supporter Mary Long) used for exhibitions and conferences, a shop on the ground floor, the

These pictures show the granary from Temple Broughton Farm, Hanbury, which was re-erected at Avoncroft in 1972, a project managed by Richard. As can be seen, it was in a very dilapidated state, and would soon have collapsed without our intervention. A feature of the building (which dates from around 1800) was the round brick columns that supported the granary, and these were strapped rigid and placed in position at the Museum in one piece. The timber framed granary, kept well clear of the ground to keep the grain dry and vermin free, was built of elm, a common local tree before Dutch elm disease struck in the '70s. We were able to help provide the sawn replacement timber from the many dead local trees. The project was completed in 1972 when I opened the building with Godfrey Baseley, creator of The Archers (see facing page).

museum offices and library, and toilet and storage accommodation. Recent further additions to the Museum have been a covered area to exhibit parts of buildings, 18th century cottages, stables and wagon sheds, a 100 year old dovecote, and a reconstructed prefab house erected after the war. An amenity provided in 1975 was a picnic site and car park of some 3 acres, which has been widely used by the public. This was paid for partly by the Countryside Commission and partly by the Fircroft Trust.

Public interest in the Museum has steadily grown, attendances increasing from 20,000 in the 1960s to 50,000 in 1984. Unfortunately, the reconstruction of the various buildings has been a constant drain on its financial resources. In spite of help from various charitable trusts and the Victoria and Albert Museum (which contributed 50% towards certain projects), by 1984 the Museum was indebted to the Bank in the sum of £70,000. Attempts are being made (1985) to reduce this by a £1 for £1 appeal to which local charitable trusts have contributed the first £35,000.

Since the inception of the museum in 1961, its example has been followed by the inauguration of

The Guesten Hall roof was used in the nineteenth century as part of Holy Trinity Church, Shrub Hill, Worcester. This church became redundant, and the roof was taken off, the timbers repaired, and the whole roof was initially re-erected at ground level (facing page). When the timbers had been used as the church roof, the span was about 6 feet less than over the original Guesten Hall, and in the restoration the span was restored, making it about 35 feet. The repairs to the timbers can be clearly seen in the picture.

several other similar museums in various parts of the country, some funded entirely by public authorities. Practically all the museums of buildings on the Continent of Europe are financed from public funds. It has been a matter of disappointment to the management committee of Avoncroft that local public authorities in the district have made practically no contribution to the expenses of the museum, in spite of the fact that it undoubtedly provides a considerable tourist attraction.

Nevertheless, somehow or other a total of over £500,000 has been raised over the last 20 years for the re-erection of 20 historical buildings at the museum since it opened. This gives the Management Committee, with its present chairman, Stephen Gibbs CBE, and its director, Michael Thomas MA, a feeling that something useful has been done in preserving this heritage from the past, and a determination to continue in spite of the present difficulties. I also take pride from the fact that Richard gained much of his early experience working on Avoncroft projects, which led to him being research director [since 2001, director] of the Weald and Downland Museum in Sussex.

The New Guesten Hall as finally built is shown on the previous page. The interior (above) is now used for a variety of functions, including Bromsgrove Festival concerts, when an audience of 200 can be seated. An inscription in a window (right) records the dedication of the stained glass windows to the late chairman. These pictures were taken in 2002.

THE EIGHT SMALL WINDOWS ALONG THE WEST WALL OF THE HALL ARE IN MEMORY OF LESLIE G HARRIS, A GENEROUS BENEFACTOR AND THE MUSEUM'S FIRST CHAIRMAN, WHO DIED IN MARCH 1995.

DESIGNED AND MADE BY ALEXANDER BELESCHENKO, THEY REPRESENT A 'MEDIEVAL SKY' DRAWN FROM LOOKING AT MEDIEVAL ILLUMINATIONS AND THEIR COLOURING.

THIS MEMORIAL, UNVEILED ON TUESDAY, 25TH JUNE 1996, WAS GENEROUSLY DONATED BY FAMILY, FRIENDS AND BUSINESS COLLEAGUES OF LESLIE HARRIS.

The windmill from Danzey Green in Warwickshire. The mill's reconstruction was done by the Museum with much help from a local windmill enthusiast, Michael Field. The mill's sails are new, and it is worked periodically, and grinds flour that is sold in the museum's shop.

Chapter 16

EDUCATIONAL AND RELIGIOUS INTERESTS

Fircroft College

In 1966, I was invited to join the governing body of Fircroft College, Selly Oak, Birmingham. The college had been established by George Cadbury junior, a son of the earlier George Cadbury who, with his brother Richard, had founded the firm of Cadbury Bros in Birmingham in 1855. The factory was transferred to Bournville in 1879, and became the centre of the nationally famous garden village. George Cadbury senior was known as one who loved his fellow men, and served them with ceaseless devotion. His photograph, with one of the Bournville schools he built, is reproduced earlier in this book.

His son George Cadbury junior had been concerned about the lack of provision for the education of working men, and in 1909 he acquired a large house in Oak Tree Lane, Bournville, in which Fircroft was founded as a residential college. The first Warden (or Principal) was the self-educated teacher Tom Bryan, who held the post until 1917. The education was intended to be generally broadening, in such subjects as economics, history, English, art and drama. It was hoped that as well as their studies, the men would learn something more important – the art of living together with thirty or forty others. The college gradually expanded over the years, though the student numbers were depleted in the two world wars. Leslie Stephens, a friend of mine, was Principal from 1946-1957. George Cadbury junior died in 1954. In 1957 his son Christopher, who took over as chairman of the governors, transferred the college to Primrose Hill, Selly Oak, the beautiful mansion in which he was born. In 1966 a new residential building and library was built in the grounds, financed by a grant from the Department of Education and Science, and the student numbers increased to 50. The Principal at that time was Philip Hopkins, who later wrote a widely acclaimed book

'Workers Education – an International Perspective'.

Shortly after I joined the governing body, Mr Hopkins retired. The new Principal appointed was Anthony Corfield. He ran the college successfully until 1974, when trouble arose between him and the tutors and students. The main cause of the dispute, according to the latter, was the Principal's failure to consult the staff fully about the curriculum, and the absence of an academic board. The students even went so far as to say that they should decide the syllabus, not the Principal. Widespread disruption ensued. The tutors and students refused to obey the instructions of the Principal, the founder's portrait was thrown in the fishpond, and the Bursar's office ransacked. The four tutors were then suspended, the students sent home, and the college closed. This was a most tragic incident in the otherwise tranquil history of the college for over 60 years. As the only industrialist on the governing body, I would like to have been brought in to try to pour oil over the troubled waters, but the governors only met three times a year, and the trouble was raging before we had a chance to stop it.

As the college was being supported financially by the Department of Education and Science, the government appointed a committee to enquire into the causes of the dispute. All the governors, including myself, and the tutors and students, gave evidence to the committee, which was chaired by a leading barrister, Andrew Leggatt QC. Their report, of which I have a copy in my archives, criticised both sides equally. It described the Principal as a "weak man, infirm of purpose". The Governors were "elderly, reasonable, well intentioned and ineffectual". The tutors were said to have been politically motivated (two of them were members of the communist party) and to have shown outstanding disloyalty to the Principal. The committee recommended that both the Principal and the four tutors should be dismissed, and the college reopened after an interval of 12 months. It was later confirmed to our astonishment that Harry Newton, the tutors' leader in the dispute, was at the time an employee of the government security agency MI5, though I never understood what this had to do with the upheaval. Two of the tutors later appealed to the Industrial Tribunal, alleging wrongful dismissal, but their complaint was not upheld.

My own feeling was that although the main trouble was caused by the tutors' disagreement with the Principal, the latter had turned out to be the wrong man for the job. He had been a Trade Union official in his previous career, and had had no previous experience of long term residential colleges. The former fact led to an approach to the governors by the Trades Union Congress asking if they could take over and run the college. This was seriously considered, but the request was declined as the Trustees did not want the place to become a Trade Union institution .

In Selly Oak, Birmingham, there existed a total of nine small colleges of various types. These had formed themselves into a Federation, of which Fircroft had become a member in 1957. The Council of the Federation had been worried about the situation in Fircroft, a college they felt had long served a useful social purpose. They were anxious to secure its future, and after discussions with the

Fircroft Trustees, appointed a new board of governors under which the college reopened in 1979, with Brian Wicker as Principal.

This has proved a most satisfactory arrangement. The Fircroft Trustees, under their new name The Croft Trust, have leased the college rent free, and have given substantial grants for bursaries for overseas students, also for extra amenities in the buildings. The Department of Education and Science is still funding the remainder of the cost of running the college. They have guaranteed that this will continue until 1988, after which the future will be reviewed. However the Chairman, Christopher Cadbury, is now 75, and all the rest of the trustees (except Roger Cadbury, Christopher's son) are getting on in years. So the future of the Croft Trust, which owns the college, and has substantial investments, will have to be considered. One suggestion is that it might hand over its assets to the Federation of Selly Oak Colleges, a permanent body which could ensure the future of Fircroft.

I have been glad to have been associated with the college for nearly 20 years. It has brought me in touch with other aspects of the educational world of which I should otherwise have had no experience.

Sibford School, Sibford Ferris, Oxon
This school, which is a co-educational establishment started by the Society of Friends in 1842, is situated in a beautiful position in the Cotswold hills, a few miles distant from Banbury. I was appointed to the Board of Governors in 1965, and served for 10 years. This was another interesting experience which I have much valued. I imagine I was asked to serve because of my business knowledge. The school was expanded several times during my period as governor, mainly funded by generous donations from old scholars and various Quaker Trusts. Fees have had to be raised very considerably due to inflationary increases in expenses. Fortunately there exist various bursary funds which have lightened the burden on some parents. The school now accommodates some 200 boys and 130 girls, with about 40 day pupils.

Not all was sweetness and light during my 10 years. The school on the whole has been a happy place, though various disagreements have broken out from time to time between two of the three headmasters I have known and the staff. These have never reached serious proportions, and I imagine they are probably inevitable in what is really a closed community. The governors have always tried to smooth them over, usually successfully. My conclusions at the end of my time at Sibford were that a tremendous lot depends on the nature and character of the Headmaster appointed. The governors have before them usually a reasonably wide selection of applications, but can only do their best to choose the man who seems to them to be the most likely candidate. Having appointed him, the character and progress of the school is very much in his hands. All the governors can do is to give him as much support and encouragement as possible. One of the improvements which could be made at Sibford is to invite various members of the teaching staff to attend Governors meetings as well as the Headmaster and

Bursar. This was not done in my day.

But I am very glad that Sibford, with the other seven schools all run by the Society of Friends, still exists in its beautiful countryside to give, I believe, happy lives to the boys and girls who stay there.

Birmingham University

I was very surprised and honoured in 1972 to be appointed a life member of the Court of Governors of Birmingham University. I never found out why I should have been invited, unless it was something to do with the various branches of voluntary work with which I have been connected. In case there is any misunderstanding, the actual management of the University is carried out by its Executive Council. The Court of Governors is really an honorary body, which meets only once a year. Nevertheless, I always attend these meetings, and have appreciated being appointed.

Society of Friends

As a boy, I was brought up in the circle of the Society of Friends in Bournville. My father and mother were not actual members of the Society, although father was a keen member of the local Fircroft Adult School, which met on Sunday mornings. So I was sent to the Bournville Quaker Sunday School, and for a time acted as secretary to a section of it – the YPA, or Young People's Association. I later went with my brother Frank to the Fircroft Junior Adult School, which met in some converted lofts in Bournville Lane. But after Frank left for America in 1923, and I became 18, I gradually lost interest in local religious affairs, although occasionally attending the Sunday morning Friends Meeting in Bournville Meeting House.

It was not until 1932, when I was 27, that I started regularly going to the Sunday Friends Meeting at Cotteridge, near Kings Norton. There I came under the influence of a well known Quaker, John S. Hoyland. A son of John William Hoyland, at one time Principal of Kingsmead College, Selly Oak, he was a brother of Geoffrey Hoyland, for some years Headmaster of the Downs Preparatory School, Colwall, where we sent our two sons Andrew and Richard. John was a strong, vital Christian of a type rare both in his day and ours. In Cotteridge Meeting he was sometimes referred to as "on back-slapping terms with God"! He was a splendid public speaker, and I used to attend meetings with him when he was speaking in support of international federation, in which he strongly believed.

Another member of Cotteridge Meeting who influenced me very much was Horace Alexander, at one time Principal of Woodbrooke College. He had spent much time in India, and was a personal friend of Mahatma Gandhi. A gentle learned and erudite man, he was said to have done much to persuade Gandhi to carry out his policy of non-violence.

In 1943, I was encouraged to apply for full membership of the Society, having been previously only an attender. I was visited by two elderly Friends (one of whom, I remember, was Harrison Barrow, of an old established Birmingham Quaker family), to try to ascertain whether my views and background made me suitable for acceptance. To my surprise, they saw no particular difficulty about my agnostic views, but when I explained that I was a member of the Home Guard (this was during the second world war) they felt that this was not in line with

The old Quaker meeting house in Cotteridge, south Birmingham. This was built in 1901 and, being not far from Bournville, was patronised by various members of the Cadbury and other well known Quaker families. It is similar in style to the larger meeting house in Bournville. The old building was demolished in 1964 to allow the site to be redeveloped, incorporating a new meeting house on part of the site. I attended meetings here from 1937 till 1965 when I changed to the newly built meeting house in Barnt Green, illustrated on the facing page. (Drawing reproduced by kind permission of David Barlow.)

Quaker pacifist principles, and my application was declined by the subsequent Monthly Meeting. It was not until 1947, when the war was over, that I was accepted into membership.

Although I am only a sort of half-baked Quaker in the sense that I am an agnostic with regard to such things as the miracles, the virgin birth and the resurrection – sometimes called the mumbo-jumbo by humanists – I feel that if everyone could follow the basic principles of Christianity, the world would be a happier place. Constant attendance at the Society of Friends does at least serve to remind me to try to follow these tenets frequently. Since the 1930s, I have regularly attended Sunday morning Meetings of the Society, first at Cotteridge and since 1965 at the new Meeting House built at Barnt Green, where I served as Clerk (or secretary) of the Meeting for seven years.

I have greatly valued my membership of the Society, and feel that it has had a good influence on my attitude to life. As I said in the account of my prison experiences, I believe that the present decline in religious observance is partly responsible for the increase in crime and anti-social behaviour.

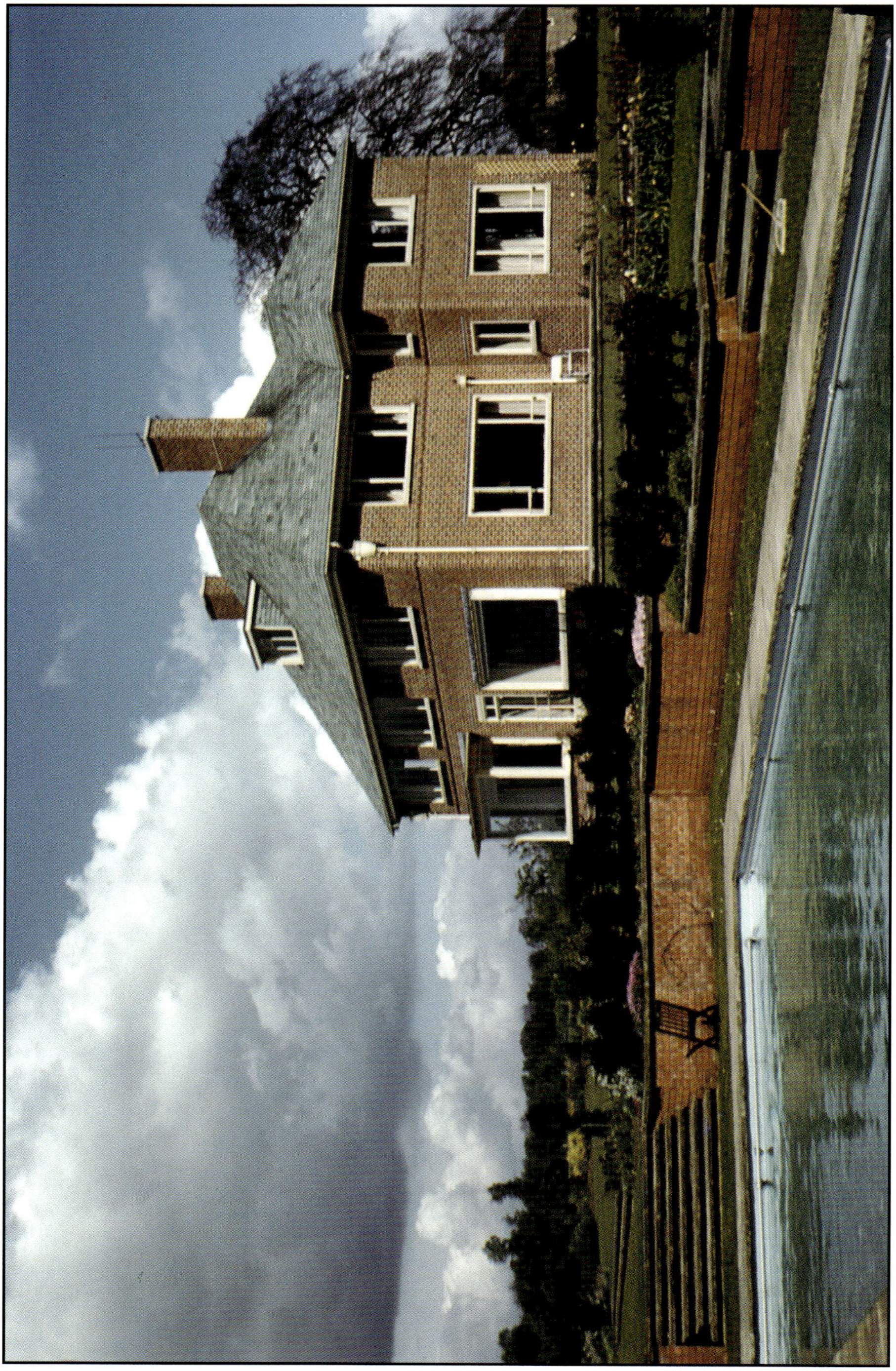

Chapter 17

HOUSE BUILDING AND HOBBIES

Ridge End
In the 1950s I became friendly with Mrs Hill, a charming, aristocratic and intelligent old lady who lived at The Mount, Hanbury. Mrs Hill (née Auda Letitia Vernon), the daughter of Sir Harry Vernon (1834-1920), was the widow of a Col. Hill, whom she married in 1926 when she was 64. Her brother, Sir George Vernon, died in 1940. Mrs Hill had no children, and when she died in 1957 aged 95, she was the last of the Vernon line, although Sir George's widow (from whom he had been estranged, and who had born him no children) continued to live at Hanbury Hall till she died in 1962. The Vernons had lived at Hanbury Hall (now owned by the National Trust) since it was built in 1701, and had bought The Mount house in 1818 for various members of their family. It had a most beautiful view over the surrounding Worcestershire countryside.

My wife and I had never intended to stay permanently at the Mill House behind the factory at Stoke Prior, and when Mrs Hill said she was thinking of selling her house, we asked if we might buy it. She replied that she was intending to dispose of it to some distant relatives of her family. We felt so enamoured of the view from her house that we then negotiated with the Church to buy a one acre field next to her property, which had an equally attractive aspect. We asked Mr G. C. Gadd, the Bromsgrove architect, to design a house for us on this site. When his plans were finished in 1954, we placed a contract for the building with Mr W. R. Mansell of Bromsgrove. After the work had commenced, Mrs Hill said she had changed her mind, and offered The Mount to us! It was, of course, too late at that stage to cancel our arrangements. But as The Mount property included a cottage at the entrance to our drive, also a one acre paddock next to the garden, we bought the house from her with the intention of retaining the cottage and paddock. We later sold The Mount house to Mr Chandler, the father of our present neighbour Roy Chandler.

After 16 years in the old Mill House at Stoke Prior, we were much looking forward to a new modern establishment, which was to be the house of our dreams. Ridge End was designed with six bedrooms (one for each of our three children, one for our au pair girl, and one guest room), with a lounge, study, dining room, kitchen, pantry, and basement for the central heating boiler. The top floor was made into a large attic in which I installed a Bassett Lowke model railway with a layout about 50 feet long. I spent a lot of time laying out the track and running the railway, and found it a fascinating hobby. The (false) rumour later went round that I used to stand in the attic operating the trains with a station master's cap on. One of the electric locomotives was a beautiful Bassett Lowke scale model of a Great Western engine Hartlebury Castle with tender about 16" long. When our boys, unfortunately, later lost interest in the railway, I gave this locomotive model to the then Bishop of Worcester, whose home was Hartlebury Castle. It is still on view in one of the rooms in the Castle.

Building of the house was commenced in September 1954, and finished in June 1956. The contract price was £17,000, quite a respectable figure for those days. I took a ciné film of the various stages of the building, which we still have in 1985. When the house was completed, our architect Mr Gadd very kindly gave us a bronze toposcope (made by the Bromsgrove Guild) delineating all the surrounding points of interest within a radius of 50 miles from the house. The one acre site was, of course, just a ploughed field when we took it over. We were keen to surround the house with a beautiful garden, and engaged Percy Cane, a

'Ridge End', the house we built in Hanbury, Worcestershire, which was completed in 1956.

Looking across our garden to the south west. The Malvern Hills are usually visible, and on a clear day we can see the Black Mountains, 45 miles away. (Below) The garden, designed by Percy Cane, featured extensive use of York stone, and long herbaceous borders. There is a rotating summerhouse, sited to take full advantage of the views. There was also a large kitchen garden. We modified the design a little over the years, and always had to battle against the strong prevailing winds, to which the garden was fully exposed.

I chose the site of Ridge End for its marvellous views to the south and west. This picture shows Hanbury Church, situated on the top of a prominent hill (supposed to have been an Iron Age Hill Fort), taken from the garden. The garden terminates with a 'ha-ha', so as not to interrupt the views with a fence. (Below) When the children were young the pool was very popular with them and their friends in summer. Now I am in my 80s, I still enjoy a swim every morning (summer only!).

Ridge End in the winter. The pool had to be emptied to guard against ice damage. (Below) Mary was always a keen gardener, and my role was restricted to mowing – quite a big task, even with a large mower.

well known landscape architect, to design and lay out the gardens for us. He commenced the work when the house was being built, and finished it in 1957. My wife and I have occasionally disagreed about the appropriateness of some of the plants he recommended, but there is no doubt that the finished result is a delight to the eye. Ridge End is known by many local people as 'the house with the beautiful garden'. The layout included a formal rose garden and fish pond, and we later added an open air swimming pool 50 feet by 20 feet.

Mr Cane, a delightful old bachelor who lived to be 92, had been responsible for the design of many famous gardens, including Dartington Hall, Falkland

Palace and the Imperial Palace at Addis Ababa. Later he wrote a book 'The Creative Art of Garden Design' published by Country Life in 1967, in which he included a photograph of our Ridge End garden. He also designed the small Memorial Garden in Hanbury village, with which we were connected in 1958.

The cottage at the start of our drive, which we acquired with our purchase of The Mount, has a sizeable vegetable garden and two greenhouses, in which we grow most of our requirements. In the 1960s, it was lived in by our gardener, but since 1970 it has been occupied by Mrs Gwen Parish, who helps my wife with the housework. Gwen has become almost a member of our family, and we have been most fortunate in having her help over so many years. Our present (part time) gardener is a capable young man named Colin Aldridge. My wife supervises the maintenance of the garden, and all I do is the weekly lawn mowing!

The architect for our new house in Hanbury was Cyril Gadd (1898-1959), shown above with his wife Myfanwy (seated left), who worked in partnership with her husband, and a friend. Cyril also designed our office block, which was built by J & A Brazier and opened in 1959. Cyril's practise was based in Bromsgrove, but his father George had been an architect to Cadbury Bros in Bournville. Cyril and Myfanwy's daughter Jean worked for a time as our canteen manageress, and her husband John Smith in our toolroom.

Golf

I started trying to play golf in 1928, when I was 23. In 1931 I joined the Harborne Golf Club, Tennal Road, Harborne, Birmingham and in 1947 transferred my membership to the Blackwell Golf Club, Barnt Green. By 1985, I was the Club's oldest living golfing member, and probably one of the feeblest! I have always been an indifferent golfer, never attaining a handicap lower than 18, though I did win two small tankards in the monthly medals in the 1930s. In recent years, I have been playing about once a month with three friends, Henry Usborne, Frank Davies, and Philip Southall, all of whom are better players than I, alternately at Blackwell and at Broadway. I often slip up to Blackwell when I have a spare hour or two, sometimes playing on my own. Although I have always been disappointed at my poor showing at the game, I still enjoy it, since it doesn't rely only on brute strength, but also on concentration, which even an old man like myself ought to be able to use!

Walking

I have always tried to supplement my golf with at least one hour's walking every day. Since my retirement, if I haven't time to go to one of our woods, I regularly traverse my local circuit walking round the Hanbury lanes, which takes me just an hour and 10 minutes. But I find rambles through our forestry plantations, looking at the growth of the trees we have planted, more interesting than walking along country roads, and I do this whenever I have the time. I shall certainly miss our woods as and when they are sold – but perhaps the new owners will give me permission to wander through them.

Music

As I have previously related, I used to play the piano a lot in my young days, mainly syncopated dance music, with some of the lighter classical pieces. In my later years, when I am reading, I get much pleasure from the gramophone, principally chamber music, with some concertos and piano records. I have heard that the latest Compact Discs give better reproduction than even the best records, and I am thinking of trying these.

Theatres

I started attending the old Birmingham Repertory Theatre in about 1929. This little theatre was built in 1913, in Station Street, Birmingham with funds provided by Sir Barry Jackson, a wealthy independent gentleman who was anxious to improve the standard of presentation of drama in Birmingham. The plays presented were mainly by classical dramatists such as Shaw, Shakespeare, Ibsen, Galsworthy, Strindberg and Drinkwater. Some actors and actresses who later became world-famous – Lawrence Olivier, Peggy Ashcroft and Cedric Hardwicke – served their apprenticeship at the Birmingham Rep. It had a specially intimate atmosphere which I have never found repeated in any other theatre since, and I attended practically every play presented at Station Street until 1940.

I also enjoyed in the 1930s the Shakespeare plays at the Shakespeare Memorial Theatre, built at Stratford-upon-Avon in 1932. In those days the plays were presented mainly in the traditional way, with realistic scenery and contemporary costumes. I have seen all the principal plays probably six or eight times over the years, and know most of the plots almost backwards. I find the style of productions of the 1980s, with a mere back-cloth for scenery, and the actors often in modern dress, rather incongruous, but the Stratford theatre is nowadays still very well attended.

Photography

In 1954, I started taking 16mm colour ciné films of the family doings, our travels, and at work. I have now accumulated twenty four 800 feet reels over the years until 1985. So far, the colours in all the films (Kodachrome), including the oldest ones, have kept remarkably well, and I am hoping they will form an interesting family record for future generations.

Cars

I have always had a lot of pleasure from driving good cars. My first one (following the family 10 h.p. Calthorpe in 1923) was a second-hand Austin '12-Six' two-seater in 1934. In 1937, I bought my first new car, a 10 h.p. Rover saloon no. DOB 933. I remember it cost £250, and was capable of 70 mph, a great thrill. After that, I had three more Rovers over the next 14 years, another 10 h.p. in 1940, a '16' in 1948, and a '90' in 1951. My next love was the Alvis, of which I had four, finishing up with the T.C.100 in 1967. This was a beautifully designed car, and I was very sorry when the firm ceased manufacture in 1969. I ought to have kept the last one, which would have become a vintage car in course of time.

As a lover of good cars, I felt that I should never have really motored until I had had a Rolls-Royce. So my next car was a Bentley (the same as Rolls-Royce, but it sounded a bit more modest). I was, however, disappointed with this. I waited a year for delivery, and I remember the cost was £8,500. I only kept it about four months, during which time I had a variety of troubles with it, including a failure of the heating system, the fusing of the lights, and a pronounced roll when the car was going round corners. I also felt self-conscious when driving such an expensive car, so I sold it, for about the same price as I paid for it. Since then, I have stuck to Jaguars, a very good car which is value for money.

Travel

Unfortunately, space does not permit a detailed account of the many interesting and varied trips I have made abroad, both on business and on holiday. Ever since I worked in a shipping office I have tried to travel as much as circumstances permitted, and I managed to make my first trans-Atlantic trip on the Cedric in 1927. I have always enjoyed travelling in the USA and Canada and seeing my relations there, and in 1960 I took our two boys across Canada by train to Vancouver and Victoria, and returned from San Francisco as far as Denver also by train. Our association with Africa has allowed me to travel there several times, usually by air, but my wife and I have also enjoyed sailing on the Union Castle line ships from Southampton to Cape Town, sadly no longer possible. In Africa I have seen the racial discrimination present in such countries as Kenya and Rhodesia before independence, as well as in South Africa where apartheid still rules. I hope such a lovely country will find a way to settle the political problems that continue to blight it. I have seen other African countries become independent and prosper, but it is depressing that so many of them seem to fallen into the hands of undemocratic governments and dictators, and in some cases are less prosperous now than they were when colonies. This is one of the great sadnesses of the present century. In the 1970s I had a very interesting trip to Russia and China, where I was able to observe at first hand the very different life styles enjoyed by people living in communist countries. This did nothing to dent my faith in the benefits of capitalism! In 1969 I made an extensive tour of India, much of it by train. In Delhi I visited a brush factory, and was appalled at the primitive hand methods used by workers, mainly sitting on the floor. But numerous government restrictions scuppered my idea of starting our own factory there.

I have also been with Mary to Australia and New Zealand where we met our relatives – Mary has two brothers and a sister who emigrated to Australia, and I have a niece living in New Zealand. Finally we have enjoyed some marvellous holidays in the West Indies, where there is so much of interest to explore.

I took my ciné camera with me on the many overseas trips I made, both for pleasure and for business. This picture was taken in the Addo elephant park, near Port Elizabeth, South Africa, when I was filming the animals as they came for their late afternoon feed and drink. This visit was made during a voyage around the African continent made with the whole family in 1958 on the Kenya Castle, a Union Castle ship.

EPILOGUE

I make no apology to the reader for having written so much about myself: I set out to do it and now it is done.

As I said in the preface, I have written this book mainly to record the facts – and the illustrations – pertaining to my generation, for the people who come after us, perhaps in 100 years time. If it also has some little interest for my family in the 20th century, so much the better.

One of my relatives remarked after reading the draft of this book "It reads to me rather like the confessions of a money-grabbing capitalist". I will admit that I believe in free enterprise, which I am convinced works in the end in the interest of the consumer. One has only to look at the material standards of living in the Communist countries, and compare them with those of the West – USA, Germany, France, Switzerland, Britain, Scandinavia – to say nothing of Japan – to realise that capitalism may not be entirely ethical, but it does work.

And is it, after all, so unethical? How should we in Britain, as we would in Russia, like to be told that we could not travel abroad or emigrate without official permission? And criticism of our government has been an inherent right of the British people for centuries, but in Russia and the central European countries it would be suppressed and we might be clapped into jail.

The basic theory of Communism – to each according to his need, from each according to his ability – has always seemed to me to be the nearest approach to basic Christianity that we know. But somehow or other in the present state of human nature, this theory doesn't seem to function. I write this book just after the completion of a prolonged coal strike, and on the eve of a rail strike. Both these institutions are owned by the people of this country. Nevertheless, hundreds of thousands of their men are willing to put their fellow citizens to loss and inconvenience, in spite of the fact that they have all been guaranteed their jobs, whatever the circumstances. The Communists would say "Don't put profits in the hands of private capitalists". But the miners and railway workers are working for their fellow countrymen, who have had to support the losses of their organizations for years. The miners even went so far as to try and persuade the power workers to cut off the electricity supplies, fortunately without results.

I suppose the answer must be that most of us in Britain are mainly concerned in the interests of 'No. 1', and not with the generality of mankind at large. Are our human motives likely to change, I wonder?

I believe, as I said, that the competition stimulated by private enterprise brings out the initiative and inventiveness of individuals and companies, which works to the benefit of the community. We, in our small firm, regret the demise of many small shopkeepers in the face of competition from the self-service supermarkets. But the advent of the latter has definitely meant lower prices for the consumer. The present state of the motor-car industry, exposed to world wide competition, has kept the price of cars lower than would otherwise have been the case. And the record of industrial relationships in the private enterprise concerns, although sometimes disturbed in the larger firms, has been on the whole appreciably better than that in the nationalised industries.

Having said so much in favour of private enterprise, may I confess that I am a socialist in my belief in the welfare state. I feel that our support for our less privileged citizens, particularly for the unemployed, should if possible be increased. It may be that this would encourage some to take advantage of the system – there are always black sheep in every fold. But when I see people in poor circumstances, I often think "there but for the grace of God". Even in the case of prisoners I used to meet who offended against the law – one of whom I remember, had a criminal for a father and a prostitute for a mother – I wonder how I should have got on with a similar birthright. Another aspect of the welfare state which gives me pleasure is the state pension scheme. We have (I hope) a reasonably generous pension scheme (started in 1951) in our own firm, which provides, when added to the State scheme, for a pension of 1/60th of final salary for every year of service, with half the pension for the widow or widower when the beneficiary dies. I always try to see employees of ours who are about to retire. They invariably say something like this: "I shall be quite alright, thank you, with the firm's and government pension". They are therefore looking forward to a comfortable and secure old age, which gives me a lot of satisfaction.

Through the establishment of our small firm, I have admittedly been able to give our family a good standard of living and our children a good education. I have given away to our Employees Trust, our Charitable Funds and our family, practically all the shares of which I once had 100%. Had I sold the firm when I owned it, I could have been an extremely wealthy man. Perhaps that might have enabled me to distribute more to charity than I can now do. But I am grateful for having spent an interesting life, for the opportunity of (I hope) maintaining pleasant industrial relations in a community of a few hundred people, and for the good health with which I have been vouchsafed.

My connection with the Society of Friends constantly reminds me of my frequent failure to carry out the advice of Stephen Grellet:

> "I expect to pass through this world but once: any good thing therefore, that I can do, or any kindness that I can show to any fellow creature, let me do it now; let me not defer or neglect it, for I shall not pass this way again."

If we could all remember these words, the world might be a happier place.

Hanbury, Worcs 1985

PART 2
by Andrew D. Harris

Chapter 1

MY FATHER'S LAST YEARS

My father only printed a small number of copies of his Mixed Memoirs, and they soon became quite scarce. His circle of acquaintances was quite large, and even today, when people hear he wrote his life story, they often ask for a copy. In 2000 I decided to publish a second edition, and, as it is now over 15 years since it was written, it seems logical that anyone interested enough to read the original story might want to know what has happened since. I have therefore written this postscript mainly covering the subsequent history of our company and filling in some gaps in his text, but I have not attempted to write my own life story.

In 1984, at the age of 79, my father said he was going to retire, and did in fact stay away from the office for a few weeks writing his book. But the family house 'Ridge End' was not far from the factory, and once he had completed his initial task, he soon started popping into work to see how things were going. This had the potential for being a very unsatisfactory state of affairs, but in fact he allowed me and the other directors to do more or less as we wished, although obviously there was a little friction from time to time. As we were not very profitable at that time much of his energy was devoted to trying to reduce expenses, and sometimes if he thought that something should not be purchased, but which we knew could not be avoided, we had to indulge in a certain amount of subterfuge to make sure he didn't know that his wishes had been circumvented!

Unfortunately, no one can avoid the decline of one's powers with advancing age, and as the period during the remaining 10 years of his life were difficult ones for the company as we struggled to adapt to a radically changing market place with the growth of the DIY supermarkets, he felt very frustrated at his inability to influence the course of the business for the better. He no longer had the mental powers to see what needed to be done, nor the strength of argument to convince his colleagues that a particular course of action needed to be followed. This was made worse by increasing deafness, which had started when he was in his 50s. In particular, he was very worried when we actually lost money for two consecutive years in the early '90s, and it is very sad that he died in March 1995 just at the very moment the fortunes of the company turned, and at the beginning of our most successful period ever.

1992 – my father and mother with my wife and my mother's brother Geoff and his wife Sheila, over on a visit from Australia.

    I suppose it is inevitable that people like him should find it difficult to distance themselves from their life's work just because of old age, but if there is a moral to this story it is that one should always arrange life to be within the compass of one's own influence, and one must accept that over the age of 70 one's powers will inevitably decline, and that not accepting this is a recipe for unhappiness. Many people retain remarkable powers into a ripe old age, but these powers change, and one is more able to make a significant contribution to life by, for example, writing and advising, than by being actively involved in a large scale organisation. My father had many interests in the prime of his life, as the reader will have observed, and it is sad that he gave these up one by one in later life, only retaining the one he was least able to influence.

    He had always enjoyed good health, helped by a good life style and the avoidance of indulgence all his life. He drank very little, and only dallied with cigarettes when young, and was a fanatical walker and swimmer. In his prime, he used to walk every morning from Ridge End to the office (1 $1/2$ miles), then at 6.00 p.m. leave work to walk back home by a longer route that took an hour. Dinner was arranged promptly for 7.00 p.m., and later he would set off again for an evening walk. And these walks were not strolls - he would set a vigorous pace, and keep it up throughout. When away anywhere the pattern would be repeated. Swimming, similarly, was not so much a pleasure as exercise. We had a pool both at Mill House and in our new house at Ridge End, and he would swim a number of lengths every morning in the summer, even though the pools were unheated. In the winter he would have a cold bath instead – the sound of his morning bath running is one of my enduring memories from childhood. He also would always sleep with the bedroom windows wide open. He must have picked up these habits as a young man when such ideas were in vogue – I have read that Lord Lever, for example, slept outside, and always began the day with a cold bath.

So it is hardly surprising that his health remained good throughout his 70s, and it was not until he was in his 80s that he received a serious set-back when he was diagnosed as having diabetes. This came about when he decided to go by train to London to see the company's stand at a DIY exhibition. However, he became unwell on the way there, and went into the café at Euston station to recover on arrival. There he was noticed looking rather sorry for himself by a policeman, and he was admitted to University College Hospital nearby, where diabetes was diagnosed. Thereafter his health started to deteriorate, and my mother dedicated herself to looking after him. In spring 1994 he suffered a serious but 'quiet' heart attack. He finally slipped quietly away on 24th March 1995, just short of his 90th birthday.

So much of my father – what of his business? Reference has already been made to the growth of supermarkets, and this has, of course, fundamentally affected our business. Perhaps I could therefore begin the next section with a discussion of the DIY supermarket business, as its development has had such a big impact on our own development.

Chapter 2

SUPERMARKETS AND DIY

Asda were the first major supermarket to introduce a hardware section in the early 1970s, and they were followed by Tesco. But the last 25 years have been dominated by the growth of the specialist DIY supermarket chains, and in the 1980s the grocery supermarkets eventually pulled out of offering directly competing products, and this is still the case at the present time. There have been many attempts over the years to establish in this country large modern variety stores – the term hypermarket was at one time popular for this concept. In the 1970s Woolworths opened some 'Woolco' stores – much larger versions of their High Street stores in out-of-town locations, based on the American plan. About the same time the French hypermarket group Carrefour announced their intention of opening some very large stores here. But in both cases the concept never really took off. One of the main problems was finding suitable sites for large new out-of-town stores due to our restrictive planning laws. The well-known grocery supermarkets were already very well established, and for new groups to form a large national chain proved difficult in a realistic time scale. Woolco eventually disappeared, and Carrefour became absorbed in the Fine Fare, later the Asda, chain.

The situation did not change much during the 1990s, when the grocery supermarkets by and large avoided anything sold by their DIY cousins, even though some, particularly Tesco and Asda, have re-established themselves in some other non-food sectors. In 2000 there was a major development when the American chain Walmart bought Asda in their drive to internationalise. They had earlier entered the German market, but had encountered problems there because, as someone remarked, the Walmart philosophy is basically against the law in Germany. Walmart has been outstandingly successful in the USA, where in a fairly short space of time they have established a chain of stores in almost every town from coast to coast selling a very wide range of goods including food (although not fresh food in many of their stores), clothing, housewares and hardware, electrical goods and home entertainment and sportswear and equipment. Their philosophy is based on discounted prices, long opening hours and excellent customer service. I suppose one could argue that the growth of Walmart had

Lorries from two of our major customers await loading, prior to delivering to their central warehouses.

parallels in the growth of Woolworths in this country before the war. But, as I have explained above, the variety store concept has not really caught on in the UK in more recent times, and it will be very interesting to see how successful Walmart are here. At the time of writing the only plans they have announced are to extend some of the Asda stores, and use the extra space to turn the stores into more of a Walmart type outlet. One new Asda Walmart has already been opened near Bristol selling a much wider range of goods, but I would imagine that their ambitions go beyond just a name change and the introduction of extra goods in stores where there is room. But they face many problems – government guidelines are against new out-of-town shopping complexes (which I believe is wrong – I don't think it is up the government to tell us where to shop), so they will find it very difficult to find sites for large new stores. And many of the sectors in which they operate such as DIY, electrical goods and white goods, and clothing, are already served by very well-established British retailers, who are not readily going to allow a newcomer to eat into their market share. Some of these sectors, such as clothing, have remained mainly High Street based, and I suspect that, if nothing else, Walmart will push these retailers to open more out-of-town stores, although, as I have said, this is easier said than done.

As the retailing scene has changed over the last 30 years, so has our customer base. When I joined the business in the 1960s Woolworths were by far our biggest customer, taking about 10% of our turnover. They had nearly 1,000 stores, all stocking a range of paint brushes and paint, and they achieved a large market share with these products – for example, I believe their own-brand 'Household' paint had the highest sales of any brand of paint at that time. Their dominance was only really challenged when some of the new chains of grocery supermarkets started to sell non-food items in the early '70s. As noted above, Asda were the first, and took on some well known brands such as ours and discounted them – I can still remember the sign in the first Asda I visited reading '33% off all Harris goods'. Bearing in mind that they only received a 47.5% discount from us, they must have operated on much lower margins than today's DIY supermarkets, who think nothing of doubling their buying price then adding a bit more for luck, before adding VAT. Asda were very successful in this new venture and soon became one of our largest customers. They were still largely northern based, but were followed by the bigger chain of Tesco stores, who at one time stocked paint and decorating tools in every one of their stores, and became, in their turn, our largest customer – by this time, Woolworths were in decline.

This was the position in about 1980, since when the growth of the specialist DIY supermarkets has eclipsed the grocery supermarkets. As our business has been increasingly dependent on these stores, I shall say a little about each one in turn.

B&Q
B&Q started with a store in Southampton run by Richard Block and his brother in law David Quayle in 1969, and from the start the concept was to stock a wide range of DIY goods at discounted prices in large stores. This idea soon caught

The large B&Q Warehouse store near Halesowen

2001 – Stuart Hobbs, Chris Willmott and Gary Jordan. Chris is the decorating sundries buyer at B&Q, and in 2001 we negotiated a major product review with them based on 'shelf ready' packaging, which can be seen in the picture. Some of the new items were 'B&Q' branded, other items used our brand. This review confirmed Harris as the largest supplier to B&Q in our field.

on, and B&Q branches appeared all over the country, often in such unlikely premises as converted cinemas in the early days. They stocked our goods from the very first (our local representative Dennis Maloney heard about the new store, and went to find David Quayle before it opened), and I am pleased to say they still do. Mr Block soon disappeared from the scene, but his partner David Quayle remained with the company till after it was sold to Kingfisher, the group put together to try and rescue the ailing Woolworths chain. A big jump in size was achieved when B&Q purchased the Dodge City chain (with whom we were not doing business), and at the time of writing they have around 400 stores. In the early days suppliers delivered direct to each B&Q store, and this entailed our representatives calling every fortnight and 'merchandising' the stock (tidying up and counting it, then making out a replenishment order). But in 1990 they opened their big new central warehouse, and from then on our goods were sent in bulk to this warehouse, and our reps were no longer required to call in the stores. Central distribution was a trend amongst all retailers at that time, and it was this that eventually caused us to make substantial reductions in our selling force, which I shall come to later. I shall make a few general remarks about central distribution below.

 B&Q's recent growth has been achieved not so much by opening new stores as by concentrating on their 'Warehouse' stores. This concept goes back to 1990 when the first 'Depot' store was opened. This was unashamedly based on the US Home Depot stores, and involved much larger stores placing more emphasis on building materials and the tradesman, and stocking a wider range of goods. The name was later changed to Warehouse, and there are now over 50 Warehouse stores accounting for nearly half B&Q's turnover.

 For almost twenty years now B&Q have been one of our largest customers, usually second behind Wickes, and we have always enjoyed good relations with them. Perhaps we have been lucky with the buyers we have dealt with, but on the whole we have found them to be more fair and reasonable than some of their competitors, and always ready to discuss a problem or new idea. Their success as a business shows that 'brute force' by the buying staff is not a necessary concomitant to success. In the 1980s we dealt with Jeff Moss who worked with us in introducing a range of 'own brand' brushes and tools, and he was succeeded by John Frost, who was widely respected in the trade. More recently we have enjoyed working with Phil Duddridge and his successor Chris Willmott, under whom B&Q became our largest customer for the first time in 2000. I think it is true that B&Q have always had a policy of not giving all their business to one supplier, which is why they were not our largest customer before, but we have found that if you give a good and consistent service your share of their business will tend to increase.

One way that B&Q have got tougher in the last few years is with their 'Cost Price Reduction' (CPR) programme. As I understand it, this came out of a review by consultants in 2000, who reported to B&Q the fact that the best way of increasing their market share and profits would be to put pressure on their suppliers – quite why they needed to employ consultants to tell them this, I don't know! This gave rise to the CPR programme that was put to our sales people at a meeting in 2000, and which meant that all suppliers had to demonstrate that they had reduced their prices by 5% every year (to make sure that the B&Q buyer followed the correct text, a consultant sat in on the first meeting). One could obviously say that CPR gave B&Q a rather crude but effective weapon, but, bearing in mind that product ranges have a habit of changing every year or two, comparisons of one year with the next are not always as straightforward as they might be. It might even be open to a supplier who was clever with figures to manipulate them in such a way that the advantages they gave to B&Q seemed bigger than they really were. Not that we would ever dream of indulging in anything like that! These annual CPR meetings are now a feature of life with B&Q.

At the end of 1998 B&Q took a large minority stake in the large French DIY chain Castorama, as part of their drive to internationalise and increase the size of their business, a policy pushed strongly by Jim Hodkinson, their chief executive for much of the 1990s. He seemed to be a believer in 'size for size's sake', and was very disappointed when the proposed merger with Asda came to nothing after Walmart stole the bride. Personally, I think there is much more to growing a business than simply buying more companies, and British retailers' success in venturing abroad has been very mixed. M&S have invested heavily overseas without any notable success (this venture was ultimately closed), Wickes were never successful in integrating their European stores (which were eventually sold), and Texas and Tesco found it difficult to repeat their British successes in ventures abroad. In 2002 it was announced that Kingfisher, under new management and having already sold off Woolworths, would do the same to Comet and their other electrical retailers, and concentrate on DIY. They said they wanted to purchase the remaining shares in Castorama, as it was admitted that so far the relationship had not given either side a great financial advantage (contrary to what was said at the time of the original merger). Now Castorama is a wholly owned subsidiary of B&Q, I hope will be able to use our favourable position as a leading supplier to B&Q to at least gain an interview in Lille, Castorama's head quarters.

Environmentalism

Before leaving our relationship with B&Q I would like to say a little about environmentalism, which is a subject close to B&Q's heart. B&Q's commitment to having a positive environmental policy goes back to the 1980s, when their chairman was Jim Hodkinson, who worked closely with their environmental manager, Dr Alan Knight, later called their 'sustainability' director. I remember going to a B&Q conference in December 1991 at which their environmental policy was outlined – Jim was obviously driving it, and said they spent at least 30 minutes of every board meeting (weekly) on this topic. Jim has long since moved on, but Dr Knight is still a powerful force in the Kingfisher Group, and B&Q still have a large department dealing with environmental matters. Their policy is now implemented through the Quest programme, which covers all matters even remotely connected with the environment, which all their suppliers are supposed to adhere to. The avoidance of timber (which comes into many DIY products) from forests that are not properly managed has always been one of the main points of their policies, but they now also cover such matters as employment policies in overseas suppliers' factories, disposal of waste, use of solvents, the use of 'environmentally friendly' packaging, recycling, and many more. Not only are we supposed to adhere to all these policies ourselves, but we are supposed to vet our suppliers to see that they do as well, and our suppliers must vet theirs, and so on down a very long line.

Most other major DIY supermarkets also implemented similar policies, including the insistence that all timber products should be approved by the 'Forestry Stewardship Council' (FSC), but our impression is that some of these have subsequently lost their enthusiasm somewhat, and that sometimes the temptation to buy a cheap product (usually from a third world supplier) overrides the strict implementation of their policies.

Although no doubt B&Q had commercial considerations in mind as well as being purely altruistic, I think their commitment to environmentalism was genuine and stemmed from the highest motives. But environmentalism has become extremely fashionable in recent times, and has, I think, been taken far further than is justified by pure science. Many environmental arguments, which are often high-sounding, are often repeated without really being analysed, and I think that many of these matters are much more complicated than many people realise. Indeed I think the unthinking acceptance of environmental mantras is rather reminiscent of religion – you are expected to <u>believe</u> certain things even if they are not totally rational, and, it seems to me, the worship of the God Earth, is replacing the worship of the Christian God.

If one wanted to be completely cynical, one could say that life is short, whatever we do now is unlikely to have much of an effect on the planet for more than a few hundred years at most, and, as this is a mere tick in the 10 billion year plus life of the earth, why worry? No-one can foretell the future, and if one thing is certain, it is that all the dire projections now made of what might happen unless we dramatically change our way of life will prove incorrect. Some people even imply that life itself is threatened by man's activities; but this ignores the fact that life is an extremely powerful and enduring force, that it has survived and multiplied through changing environments for millions of years, and survived a number of catastrophes, such as meteor impacts, ice ages and changing sea levels without any long term damage. Of course the balance of species is always changing, and man is no doubt having a major influence on that as well, but so what? Any gardener will tell you that it is almost impossible to eradicate garden weeds; I think the same applies to life in general – as long as conditions make life possible, it will flourish in one form or another.

Perhaps I could illustrate my doubts about environmentalism by discussing greenhouse gas emissions, and the Kyoto protocol. All economic activity depends on energy, and most energy comes from burning fossil fuels in one form or another. Indeed the industrial revolution, which is the source of all our wealth, could not have happened had not ways been found to exploit coal, and later oil, in various industrial processes such as the production of iron and other essential metals, and the generation of electricity. The only way to reduce greenhouse gas emissions is to reduce the burning of fossil fuels, but in my opinion this is bound to reduce economic activity in the long run, unless ways can be found to produce energy in other ways than burning fossil fuels. A reduction in economic activity will inevitably lead to a reduction in standards of living, and it is fear of this that has lead the US and Australia to refuse to ratify Kyoto. They feel that it is one thing to pay lip service to an idea; it is altogether another to explain to voters why their standard of living has got to decline.

Environmentalists, of course, have got an answer to this. Firstly, they want to see an increase in the use of so-called renewable sources of energy which, with a few exceptions, do not produce greenhouse gases. But I feel that the current fashion for these, which in the UK means mainly wind turbines, is very much over-done. The big advantage with fossil fuels is that they pack a great deal of energy into a very small space, which makes them ideal for transport applications in particular, whereas renewables are much less 'dense', and require a lot of input to generate any worthwhile power. In UK terms, this means covering very large areas of land (or sea) with turbines. This also raises issues such as new national grid lines taking the power from where it is generated in such places as the north of Scotland to where it is used further south in England. Then there is the very important point that wind, even in the outer Hebrides, does not blow all the time, and there are significant periods when it is either too weak or too strong for the turbines to operate. What will happen to our electricity supplies then?

The other point emphasised by environmentalists is that there is considerable scope for energy conservation, so that we can achieve the same output using less power. This may be true, but even if considerable advances in this field are achieved, in practice I think that conservation in this sense is a delusion. Yes of course we can all buy our new super efficient washing machines or cars, and save money on fuel. But what will we do with the money saved? Spend it on more goods and services will be the usual answer. But goods and services consume energy, so although we may well feel better off because we have bought a fuel efficient car and had an extra holiday with the money saved, our overall energy consumption is no lower. In other words, we spend all our incomes on activities that consume energy, and unless we are prepared to see our incomes drop, overall energy consumption will go on climbing.

A final point about fossil fuels is that, whatever else you argue, they are obviously finite, and ultimately we will have to find alternatives. So if we slow down their use now, will this not mean that they will be available for use for a longer period? In other words, in the long run we will burn most of the fossil fuels that the earth holds, and whether we burn them quickly and run out quickly, or burn them more slowly for longer, would not seem to matter much to the planet, which will still be supporting life for billions of years after the last drop of oil has long since gone.

Personally, I think the answer to these problems is to depend on nuclear energy for the lion's share of our future energy needs. Other than chemical energy stored in fossil fuels, atomic energy stored in various isotopes is the only other form of energy that can be released in large quantities from a small mass. Nuclear power stations all over the world have provided base-load electricity reliably and safely for nearly 50 years – as much as 70% in the case of France, but unfortunately nuclear power has become a dirty word for environmentalists, who, perversely I feel, prefer to see our most attractive scenery covered in windmills! So environmentalism is not always very logical.

I have obviously strayed a long way from B&Q's environmental policy in saying all this, but I would like just to illustrate the point that these matters are much more complicated than they may appear superficially, and the obvious answer to a problem may not turn out to be the best one on proper analysis.

Wickes

As noted above, Wickes were for many years our largest customer, not because they were the largest chain of stores, but because we have always been their sole supplier of brushes. Up till about 1990 their paint rollers were supplied by Beechwood, but when they suddenly closed we were able to step quickly into the breech, and since then have been their sole supplier of these items too.

Wickes in the UK was originally an offshoot of the eponymous American firm, but when their parent went out of business they floated as an independent company, together with some Wickes stores in Germany, Holland and Belgium.

The Wickes store in Redditch. Wickes are now part of the Focus Group, but still trade separately. We have been their sole supplier for many years.

In the '80s and early '90s Wickes had a tremendous growth record, and our turnover grew with them. Their policy of having a few large suppliers obviously helped us, and we even started to supply other sundry items such as masking tape that they could not conveniently obtain from their other suppliers. Wickes always had a policy of supplying 'own brand' goods, and in the late 1980s they decided to make this policy 100%, and change the remaining items that carried a manufacturer's brand. This included our goods, although for a period they had a policy of having both the manufacturer's brand and their own name on goods, as they believed that by this means they might get the best of both worlds. Later dual branding was dropped, and all goods were branded Wickes.

The next major change initiated by Wickes concerned distribution. Up to this time we had supplied all their branches direct, but when they came to follow the 'central distribution' fashion, they did it differently from their competitors. In those days Wickes was run by Dick Clark, whom I respected very much for his open, honest and analytical approach. Most DIY chains hold, or have held, suppliers' conferences, but these were usually slickly run PR exercises, trumpeting the success of Texas/B&Q/Homebase, berating suppliers for not supplying everything on time, and trying to sell suppliers an advertising package, which was a thinly designed way to get us to pay for their advertising budget. Wickes was different. The day was spent analysing their success or otherwise in different product categories, and when Dick Clark felt that they could have done better he was not afraid to say so – this, of course, was often the supplier's fault, but not always, and I remember him once asking Peter Dale, their buying supremo who was also on stage, what he was doing about a particular matter. When Peter gave a less than satisfactory answer, Dick said "I wish you'd get on and do it, then!" Always different, Wickes spurned TV or press advertising, and again I remember Dick analysing thoughtfully the reasons why they did this, and admitting they could be wrong – much more convincing than the usual flashing lights and dancing girls.

So when they decided to update their distribution methods, they found a novel solution. But I always thought they would run into problems when they opened their 'Break-Bulk' centre (BBC). Under-estimating the difficulty and cost of warehouse management and order picking has been a consistent fault of all the supermarkets. The idea was that they would order every week from us the goods required by their stores, and we would supply them in bulk, then they would break them down on the floor of the BBC and send them straight on to the stores. No stocking of goods, just a quick re-packing that would shorten the supply chain. Needless to say, the idea of re-packing around 100 orders on the warehouse floor was much more difficult than they had anticipated – even at that time we were supplying them with well over 50 lines. So only a short time after the BBC opened we got a telephone call saying that as from a date in only about two weeks' time we would have to make up the store orders at Stoke Prior, and supply them in this form for the BBC centre to send on to the stores. This obviously considerably increased our costs, and this raised a problem that was never really resolved – when we asked the buyer to give us back some of the discount that they had negotiated for supply to the BBC, we were referred back to the manager of BBC. The same happened in 1990 when the Gulf War increased fuel prices (only temporarily, as it turned out), and we were subjected to a surcharge as Wickes were now paying for transport to the BBC. I can imagine what reply we would have got if we had been paying the transport, and asked for a surcharge! Having to negotiate with two different people made life much more complicated, and I recall it was not until early 1993 that Steve Collinge, at that time our Wickes national account manager, managed to sort these problems out.

It was also at about that time that we first became aware of Wickes' rather unconventional accounting methods, that would later land some of their directors in court. Like most major accounts, Wickes would re-negotiate their terms of business every year, trying to get us to recognise their increasing turnover in bigger discounts and other benefits. The first time that I became aware that something was rather unusual at Wickes was one year in the early '90s when, approaching Xmas (the end of their financial year) we negotiated the trading terms for the following year. This included an extra level of discount if their purchases from us reached a certain level, which they predicted they would. When all this was finalised, they had an extra request – that we write a letter "for their auditors" summarising the deal we had just quite properly concluded. When we read their draft, there were two peculiarities. Firstly, instead of being given as a % of their purchases from us, the discount was shown as a fixed sum. Secondly, they called this sum a "1992 marketing allowance", even though it was being negotiated in December 1992 in respect of 1993, for example.

I was mainly concerned by the first anomaly (what they called the arrangement was up to them), as I wanted it made clear that the rebate or discount would depend on the purchases they actually achieved, and was not a fixed sum come what may. When I pointed this out to them, they first said: "don't worry – we guarantee to meet those purchase figures," then also agreed to write us a "side letter" confirming the arrangement. But they still wanted us to write the letter "for their auditors". Once the side letter had been received, we did not unduly concern ourselves about the other letter. We were pleased that the negotiations had been satisfactorily concluded, and that it looked as if our trading relationship would continue for the time being. Nevertheless, we were conscious that we had signed something that wasn't strictly true.

It was only somewhat later, after recounting this matter to others including some other suppliers, that we came to realise that Wickes had probably used this letter to get the 1993 rebate included in their 1992 profits. What they had actually told their auditors, of course, we never knew, neither did we hear who was aware of what was going on within Wickes other than the fairly junior people we were dealing with. This incident was the only occasion in which I personally was aware of something not quite right at Wickes, although their various and increasingly complicated negotiations with us for discounts, rebates, "preferred supplier agreements", "booklet allowances", "break-bulk discounts", and a few other things made life so complicated that at one stage we were fairly sure that their buying team had lost track of what had been agreed. In all these matters they always preferred to talk about fixed sums of money rather than the % that we had usually agreed, but we got used to Wickes' approach, and we certainly did not think that the allowances agreed may have been used to boost profits in a period before that in which they actually applied, although it now seems that this was the case.

The situation was complicated in 1993 in that we were informed by Wickes that they had received a very competitive quotation from Mosley Stone, one of our competitors, and what were we going to do about it? They made it clear that they would prefer to continue to deal with us, but that we would have to meet Mosley Stone's prices, which was fair enough, particularly since it was probably true that at that time they were not receiving prices from us that fully reflected the tremendous growth that their business had made in the last few years.

I won't try now and recount, blow for blow, the negotiations we had with them at the end of 1993, but it centred mainly on the 'slug of money' that they claimed Mosley Stone had offered to get in. We felt it was impossible for us to match this, and we announced to our employees at one stage that we had lost the Wickes account. But Wickes seemed not to want to change suppliers if they could help it, and in January 1994 talks were still continuing. Eventually we did come to a new agreement and kept the business, but only by offering an extra 28% discount over our present prices. To make matters much more complicated, they did not want us to reduce our prices as charged on our invoices, but to give them a fixed rebate of £105,000 per quarter. This was finally agreed on 13th January 1994, and I must say that, although we had to swallow very hard at the time, I think it turned out to be the right decision. Of course we were never sure how far what we were being told about our competitors' offers was correct, but on the whole I am inclined to think that it was. Although this extra rebate had an initial bad affect on our finances and contributed to the loss we made in 1993/94, it set us up for continuing supply to Wickes, who were and remained our largest customer for several more years.

It seemed to be generally known that Wickes were mis-timing their suppliers' rebates in their company accounts, and we continued to feel uneasy about it. If their directors knew that the accounts they were publishing were wrong, this would be a serious criminal offence. As Wickes in any case were never financially very strong, we decided to try and seek credit insurance to cover our largest customers (it would not be possible to cover just one customer), which we effected in 1994. Even our insurance brokers said that "everyone knows" about the rebate payments.

It was nevertheless a shock to hear on the news in June 1996 that the directors of Wickes had issued a statement "following the discovery yesterday of serious accounting problems relating to the timing of recognition of profit from supplier contributions". Apparently, one of their employees in Europe had blown the gaff. The rest, as they say is history. A large sum of money was taken out of their latest published profits, the shares collapsed, and the chairman, Henry Sweetbaum, and several directors resigned. But it was another 6 months before it was announced that the police were investigating the matter. In April 1997 two officers from the Metropolitan Police came to visit us and take statements from those involved, and in April 1998 we had a further visit. Subsequently in 1999 Henry Sweetbaum, Trefor Llewellyn, Geoffrey Battersby, Terence Carson and Leslie Rosenthal were charged with false accounting, and the trial lasted for most of 2002. I had never met any of these gentlemen except the last named, who was much involved with us in the renegotiations of 1993/4, although Henry Sweetbaum had been chairman for a number of years and had kept a high profile throughout. I remember one year when Wickes' profits (misstated, as it turned out) had grown well and the press cottoned on to the large bonus that Sweetbaum received. As he emerged from the AGM a reporter asked him whether he expected to receive such a big bonus next year. "I very much hope so," he replied jauntily!

I would just make two comments. Whichever way you look at the case, it is extraordinary. It is either extraordinary that the directors did not know what was happening, when apparently everyone else did, and if they did know then they surely must have known that they were doing something very wrong, and that it was bound to come out in the end. Secondly, these fraud trials seem to take longer and longer to come to court, which means that it is very difficult for the true facts to emerge. Gary Jordan, Stuart Hobbs, Geoffrey Braithwaite and I were called to give evidence in the trial in early 2002, and we were talking about events that were a minimum of six years old, and up to ten. Although in the event our time in the witness box was relatively short, and we were questioned on only a few matters of detail, we found it very difficult to remember details of some of those events which happened so long ago. The accused admitted that a fraud had taken place, but eventually the jury believed their assertion that they were not aware of it. However, Les Rosenthal is to stand trial again separately.

Despite Wickes' problems since the scandal unfolded, it was only in 1999 that their growth has faltered. After the old guard resigned, Bill Grimsey ran the company, and as well as being a hard negotiator, he seems to have been an effective manager. In 2000, when Wickes were bought by Focus Do It All, Bill moved on to run another troubled retailer, Iceland. Wickes' problems in 1999 were caused when they opened their new "intermediate" warehouse which replaced their break bulk centre. This was a new fully-fledged warehouse into which we would send goods in bulk, and from which they would send goods to the stores. The main difference between this and those operated by the other big DIY supermarkets is that we would supply our goods into it on a 'consignment' basis. This means that the goods would remain our property until they were despatched to their stores, at which point they would raise a 'self-billing note' on which they would pay us. They told us, of course, that the new system would lead to several financial advantages to us, and asked for an appropriate rebate, which we felt obliged to agree to. In fact, several of these advantages have proved somewhat illusory, the main one being in practice that we haven't had to pack the store orders individually any more.

My father was always against any arrangement that involved consignment stock, and he was quite right. There is inevitably some shrinkage of stock which is out of our control – is this our responsibility or theirs? Wickes, of course, assured us that they would make up any shortages, but how this will work remains to be seen. As it is our stock, it is essential that we know what it is so that we can produce our accounts, and again Wickes assured us that we will have access to it at all times. But in practice we have to rely on them to give us the stock count figures, and it will be very difficult to check any queries. Perhaps we should not have agreed to participate in the scheme in the first place, but they would no doubt have tried to find a supplier of our goods who would, and in general in these situations we find it is best to keep a 'low profile', and await the unfolding of events, which will usually put unsatisfactory situations right in any case. Wickes admitted at the end of 1999 that the operation of the new warehouse was causing them problems, mainly due to the fact that it was taking them longer to pack store orders than they anticipated (we could have told them that before they started) leading to out of stocks in the stores.

In 2000 Wickes became part of the rapidly expanding Focus Do It All group, which was backed by Duke Street Capital using money of US origin. FDIA have used the group's much increased size to demand extra discounts from their suppliers, and also they have carefully compared buying prices for the same goods bought by Wickes and FDIA, using any anomalies to extract more discounts from suppliers. Both these strategies resulted in our having to make significant concessions on margin, which was a major factor in the much reduced profits we earned in 2000/01.

Central Distribution
Having discussed Wickes' attempts to introduce central warehousing in different forms, it might be appropriate to make some more general remarks on this subject. In my time in business we have seen all our major customers go over to central distribution, which has not always been a happy experience. Woolworths did it in the '70s, followed by Tesco, then in the late '80s and early '90s by all the DIY supermarkets – the odd one out, not for the first time, being Wickes who only went fully over to this concept in 1999, as I have described above. The reasons for going over to central distribution were varied, but there were usually two main factors: they believed that it was inefficient to have suppliers' lorries arriving throughout the day in every store – delays in unloading often occurred, and a mountain of paperwork was generated for head office to process. Secondly, it was believed that the warehousing and order picking operation could be conducted more efficiently by the new central warehouses, and the extra costs involved would be more than offset by the extra discounts obtained from manufacturers in respect of their costs savings.

Although in theory some of these arguments might be correct, in practice we have experienced problems working with nearly all central warehouses over the years. Perhaps the main one concerns demand forecasting – in the days when our reps took an order in each store every fortnight or so, there was rarely a problem with out of stocks as people on the spot can usually judge fairly accurately what goods will be required to last until the next delivery. But central warehouses come equipped with sophisticated computer systems, that can, so we are told, even build factors such as popular TV programmes into their forecasts. Unfortunately, these computer forecasts have proved much more fallible than human beings', and there has always been a tendency for feast and famine. For example, if a new line proves popular, the computer will generate ever bigger and bigger orders, often to the extent that when sales settle down the warehouse is grossly overstocked, and orders eventually dry up as the computer catches up with itself. As a result, we have found that orders from central warehouses tend to be rather erratic. This is important, as we are always told that we must supply every order in full and on time (there is usually only a few days between receiving the order and despatching it), and if demand varies wildly from week to week it is very hard for us to meet these requirements.

Focus Do It All and 'own brand'
We have supplied Do It All since its inception. In their early days it was run by Barry Lingaard, and his philosophy was to stick to manufacturers' brands, rather than indulge in the own-brand policy being adopted by some other DIY supermarkets, and, of course, the grocery supermarkets. Perhaps it might be appro-

priate at this stage to say something about own-brand and our attitude to it.

Up to about the time my father wrote his book, the question of own brand had not really arisen except in the case of some export customers. In markets where our brand name isn't known such as Germany, we were happy to brand our goods with the name of the distributor, but in the UK with our strong brand we didn't feel the need to put private brands on our goods, especially as in most cases volumes would not have been large. Obviously, manufacturers prefer to use their own brand as it makes it more difficult for the customer to change supplier, promotes the manufacturer's brand, and generally leaves him in a stronger position than by supplying under a private label. But I have always recognised that own brand in the grocery business is very strong, and I believe that in the likes of Sainsbury and Tesco over half the goods they sell are own branded. If it has succeeded in that field, why not in DIY? This is a very big question, of course, and the success of own brand relates to a number of factors, including the size and image of the retailer. The big four grocery supermarkets in the UK are very strong and have a good image, therefore own brand works well.

The DIY supermarkets, on the other hand, have had rather a mixed success in this field, and most of them have had rather vacillating policies. Do It All, once Barry Lingaard had gone, went rather strongly to own brand, and Homebase in the early days had similar policies. B&Q had a certain amount of own brand, although they have tended to go away from it of late, whereas Wickes, as noted above, are 100% own brand. I think the reason the DIY supermarkets have had rather mixed policies is the lack of management of their own-brands. In DIY, as in most other things, everything is always changing: products, packaging, graphics, quality levels and so on. To keep pace with these changes, manufacturers must always be adapting their product offerings. But with own brand the supplier will tend to leave this to the retailer. If

A Homebase store in Worcester. Homebase was sold by their parent company Sainsburys in 2001 to a venture capital house, Schroder Ventures, who, less than two years later, sold it to GUS. In trying to improve their profitability, Homebase have launched 'Project Niagara', which aims to source as many goods as possible from the Far East.

the retailer doesn't give management time to its own brand offerings, then they will fall out of date. On more than one occasion we have had customers come to us and say that the products we supply under their own brand are looking a little dated, and can we come up with some suggestions, using the Harris brand?

Other than Wickes, we have supplied own brand products to B&Q, Do It All and Homebase, but at the present time the trend seems to be away from own brand, at least as far as manufacturers with a strong brand are concerned. But in the longer term I do not believe it will go away. As consumers become more sophisticated and educated they will realise that better value is often found amongst retailers' own brands – it is certainly true that the less sophisticated the market, the more powerful is the manufacturer's brand. Of course, the retailers' name must also be respected and trusted, and here the DIY supermarkets are not so powerful as the grocery supermarkets, which have a much longer history behind them. But this will change, and I think that in the longer term own brands will tend to get more powerful in Britain.

When Barry Lingaard left DIA, there was a feeling within W H Smith, their owners, that his policies had not been too successful, and several changes were made, including removing the concessions from the periphery of the stores, and a major switch to own brand. This did not affect our product offerings unduly, and we continued to be major suppliers to them when the merger with Payless was announced in 1990. We had not done any business with Payless, and fortunately we were chosen as suppliers to the new enlarged chain after months of deliberation in 1991. Subsequently DIA had rather mixed success, and sold some of its stores in a programme to improve margins. Control of the group eventually returned to Boots, who had owned Payless, and it was well known that they wanted to sell it. Finally in 1999 the privately owned Focus group, which we had been supplying for some years, announced that it had acquired DIA from Boots, and it is was then known as Focus Do It All. Later FDIA phased out the Do It All name altogether to concentrate on the Focus brand. In 2000 FDIA announced a hostile take over bid for Wickes, and, after initial failure to gain the necessary number of shares, the bid eventually succeeded.

U-Build and Retailers' margins
In passing, it might be interesting to mention U-Build. This company was formed in 1994 by ex-managers of Wickes, including Peter Dale and Dick Clarke. They were going to take over some stores from DIA in the London area, and hit the market hard with low prices. This is not as fantastic as it may sound, as margins on many goods sold by the leading DIY supermarkets are high. Looking back, when we first supplied Woolworths after the war they accepted our normal retail margin of $33^1/_3\%$ discount from retail prices (plus $2^1/_2\%$ cash settlement). When I joined the business in the mid-60s this had increased to $33^1/_3 + 20\%$, equivalent to 47.5%. Later we increased our standard discount to large customers to 50%, which meant that they had a 100% mark-up. By the mid '70s retail price maintenance had disappeared, and by the '80s the power of our largest customers

meant that we began to give larger and larger discounts, not to mention such extra allowances as annual rebates, advertising contributions, &c. By the later '90s the situation was such that mark-ups were nearer 200% on some products, with VAT on top. Some of our range, particularly roller sets, are price sensitive and have much lower mark-ups, and, of course, many other products, such as paint, have much keener margins. Nevertheless I think it is true that retailers' gross margins these days are higher than they were in the past. Why? Perhaps it is partly because profit-conscious companies have found they can achieve quite high margins on non-price-sensitive products like ours, without unduly affecting sales, but I think it is also because the cost of operating a retail DIY superstore is relatively higher than it was in the Woolworths' days. Even after the consolidations of the '90s, there are still around 1,000 DIY supermarkets in Britain, and it could strongly be argued that this number could be lower.

Whatever the reason, the market is open to cut-price competition, and this is what U-Build intended to inject. When they opened in early 1995 they created quite a stir, and the established players quickly realised that there was a threat to their margins – small at the time, but likely to grow. They decided that the U-Build threat should be 'nipped in the bud', and by a combination of actions U-Build was quickly put out of business. Suppliers to U-Build (including ourselves) were given veiled threats, and stores local to the new U-Build ones cut prices vigorously. The result was that U-Build went bust only a few months after it opened. I think this is rather a sad reflection on the trade, and that some of the things that happened during that period could have done with some investigation.

Texas, Homebase and Great Mills
We dealt with Texas from its inception, and in the mid-'80s they were one of our biggest customers. I think it was in 1985 that we heard through one of our reps that some Mosley Stone goods had appeared locally in place of ours, and we immediately tried to find out why from the buyer. He said that they had received a very good offer from Mosley Stone, and they were conducting a trial in a number of stores to see which goods sold the best. Geoff Fox, Glyn Lowe (recently appointed as national accounts manager) and I went to Texas head office to find out more, and we were told that we must put in our very best offer for the period of the trial. We always expected that there was more to the appearance of Mosley Stone goods than we knew about, but we duly examined all our prices and discounts to make them as keen as we could, and awaited the results. Later in the year we were again summoned to head office, and told by a junior (the buyer being too busy to see us) that the result of the trial was that Mosley Stone's goods were a better proposition for them, and that ours would be discontinued.

This was a major blow to us, and we fought on to get the decision reversed. I put together a detailed report showing why we believed that their decision was wrong financially, and eventually in the autumn I got an appointment with their buying director. He listened politely to what I had to say, but appeared to know little about it, and I strongly got the impression that had we been more aggressive in the earlier stages of the trial we could have kept the business. But now it was too late, with the result that our turnover went down in 1984/5 compared with the previous year.

Homebase was started by Sainsburys together with a Belgian retailer in about 1980, and they did not stock our goods early on. We made a few attempts to get in, of course, but we found the buying team rather less 'genteel' than one might have imagined from a group connected with the well-respected Sainsburys, and we got nowhere until the 1990s. In 1992 we started supplying special offers on rather unfavourable terms, but a couple of years later, after Stuart Hobbs had formed a more positive relationship with their buyer, we managed to get our 'No-Loss' brushes into their group. This was a major plus for us, and it heralded a very fruitful relationship. In 1997 they agreed to take our new 'Sure Grip' paint brushes, and in 1999 our paint roller range and other items. This coincided with a period when, for some reason, they had become unhappy with their major supplier, Stanley (ex-Mosley Stone). Earlier in the decade they had bought Texas from their owner, Ladbrooks, so we now had the pleasure of being back in the group we had lost 10 years earlier. This substantial increase in business from the Homebase group has been a major factor in propelling our turnover to £25m and beyond.

Homebase's parent, Sainsburys, had been having their own troubles, slipping down the league of grocery supermarkets, and, after protracted negotiations, it was announced in 2001 that the Homebase stores had been sold to a venture capital group, Schroders, although as part of the deal a number of their biggest stores and sites had been sold to B&Q, who will use them to strengthen their Warehouse stores. Then finally in late 2002 Homebase was purchased by Great Universal Stores at a substantial premium to the price achieved by Sainsbury less than two years before. This may not be unconnected with the fact that in 2001 Homebase launched 'Project Niagara', whose aim was to source as many goods as possible in the Far East. In November 2001 I had to give a presentation in Hong Kong with Gary Jordan and Stuart Hobbs to a number of senior Homebase executives, demonstrating why our company was well placed to supply goods originating in China as well as from our own manufacture. This trend has been mirrored in B&Q and Focus, and was the main reason for us believing that it was essential both to strengthen our overseas sourcing function, and to establish our own factory in China, which is described later.

Great Mills was the minnow of the DIY supermarket groups, with branches concentrated in the south west. We used to supply them but in 1996 we lost out to Hamilton Acorn, with whom we were told Great Mills had signed a "long term supplier agreement". Our prices seemed hardly to come into the calculation. However, in 2001 it was announced that FDIA had purchased Great Mills from RMC, their parent, and they were integrated into the main FDIA shops, now rebranded 'Focus'. FDIA went out to tender for the supply of the newly enlarged group and in 2002 we became a supplier to this whole group.

Chapter 3

L. G. HARRIS & CO. LTD 1985 – 2002

The foregoing discussion of the major DIY supermarkets is intended to set the scene for a summary of our varying fortunes during the last 17 years. Despite the loss of Texas and Asda in the '80s, our turnover did increase during the decade, although probably only in line with inflation. In the financial year 1989/90 it reached the £10m mark for the first time, but the recession of the early '90s left its toll, and over the next two years our sales declined to about £9.5m. During the '80s we had always made a profit, but the margin was generally below 5% on sales. This was clearly an inadequate amount to enable us to invest properly in the new plant and machinery we required, but we were saved by one factor – woodland sales, which have already been referred to in the first part of this book. These added to our trading profits throughout the '80s, and gave us the extra cash we needed to keep up a reasonable investment programme. Woodland sales had dried up by 1990, and our results in the early '90s were disappointing, with a losses in 1993/94 and 94/95.

By 1993 we felt that something urgent needed to be done to boost sales, which had still not returned to the level of 1990, and we actively went looking for new business. At that time there was a lot of interest in cheap three and five brush sets, sold on special offer in the supermarkets, and we quoted both B&Q and Do It All for them at a keen price. In early 1994 we received orders to supply both these chains with large quantities. To meet these orders we had to boost production quickly, and we arranged shift working in our brush making departments. It soon became obvious that we were trying to do too much too quickly, and the extra hours worked did not produce proportionate extra production. A further problem was that this coincided with a time when bristle supplies from China were becoming erratic, both in terms of quantity and quality. Chinese bristle prices had been going down for some time, and, as it later turned out, the Chinese began to think that it was hardly economic to ship the shortest sizes, where prices were lowest, and what bristle they did ship was of the poorest quality.

These factors meant that production costs of these brush packs were higher than we had predicted, and I think this was a major factor in the poor financial results that we posted for the financial year ending 30 June 1994, despite an increase in sales. When our poor results became clear, we decided that more drastic action was needed to get our results back on track. Encouraged by our financial director Geoffrey Braithwaite and our bankers, we had already considered appointing management consultants in early 1994, but it was not until the end of that year that we finally took the step. We chose Consulting Principles, a Midlands based firm who would advise on modern manufacturing methods, "world class manufacturing". They started work in March 1995, and aimed to reduce our response time, making goods more or less on demand, and thus considerably reducing our high stock levels. They wanted to re-organise our manufacturing areas into 'cells' or teams (I dislike the former word), each led by a team leader, who would replace our more traditional supervisors or foremen.

By the late summer results were already becoming visible. The main changes were in the brush manufacturing department which had previously been 'vertically' organised, with separate brush making and brush assembly departments. It was now re-organised into three teams, each of which did all the operations and so made the entire brush. We later added a fourth team as production needs increased. Each team had a leader, and, when the re-organisation had finally been completed, we appointed a manager, Keith Westwood, over the whole department as well. In other departments the re-organisation was not so drastic, but the team concept was applied throughout.

The idea of teams was that they are small and responsive. They should have daily meetings with their leader to discuss the day's work, and be briefed more generally about the firm's progress at regular intervals. All members of the team should be as broadly skilled as possible, able to undertake all the jobs within that cell.

One of the immediate problems with this concept concerned team leaders. It was recommended that they receive a relatively small bonus over that of the other members, which gave them a considerably smaller wage than that enjoyed by the supervisors, who were on a relatively high wage. We never fully resolved this problem, but it will disappear in time. Some of the older supervisors took either voluntary redundancy or early retirement, and some were appointed managers. One thing we have not done is to reduce anyone's wages. In a few special cases where employees have requested a lower level of responsibility we have lowered both their status and wages, but I have long since found out that reducing wages is not usually an acceptable answer to problems such as this.

Another major change was in the production planning process. Previously we had planned production up to about three months ahead, so that we could first obtain the necessary raw materials (especially bristle), then manufacture the components, before finally making the finished article. As we used a batch production system, and had a policy of ensuring that we were in stock of all items all the time, we tended to have large stocks. Batch quantities were usually about 6 months' sales, and, taken with a buffer of a month or so in our warehouse, this meant that at any one time we might have about four months' sales of our goods in stock. This tied up a considerable amount of capital, and was commented on regularly by our auditors, but I could not see how we could make any major changes. Consulting Principles had the rather extreme notion that future production should not be planned at all: under the Kan-Ban system you should wait until the Kan-Ban, or stock of goods, is nearly empty, before making any more. They suggested that this principle should apply to our finished goods warehouse, but I never saw how this could be made to work in practice. However, we did undertake a radical reassessment of our production planning system, and, with the help of the new team structure with their shorter change-over times, planned to reduce batch sizes significantly. This would reduce the overall level of stocks, and, as we would be planning production with a much shorter lead time, would mean we could react more quickly to changing market conditions.

How effective were these actions? Certainly, judging by our much improved results from 1995 onwards, very effective. Of course there were other factors that came into the equation, but the consultancy certainly played its part. On the broadest level, it made it clear to all our employees that changes had to be made, and that resistance to change would not be welcomed. I must say that our company staff had always been more ready than that in many other companies to encompass change – as so often it was the smallest items that caused the most argument. The dispute over the tea break in 1995, which I shall describe below, is one such example. But we never had any problems making the changes the consultants recommended. As I have already said, no-one lost out financially as a result, which was a big factor, and on the whole everyone recognised that adaptability and multi-skilling were essential. We did make a few small changes in our labour contract, but the only one which caused any difficulty concerned the afternoon tea break.

As soon as we knew that our results for the year to 30 June 1994 would be poor, we had to decide what action we should take. The appointment of consultants has already been discussed, but it was essential to keep our labour costs down – these represent by far our largest cost. At that time 1st August was the date when any new wage deal would start, and we decided that we couldn't afford a general wage increase in August 1995. I also thought that it represented a good opportunity to do away with something I regarded as somewhat anachronistic – the afternoon tea break.

The Tea Break Dispute
In the days when we worked a 40 hour week, we had a 10 minute break in mid-morning, and another in mid-afternoon. We also had vending machines, and we took a fairly relaxed attitude to employees going to help themselves to a drink when they wanted to. But our hours were now only $37^1/_2$ per week, and the afternoon work period was from 13.00 to 16.30. I therefore felt that to have a 10 minute break from 15.00 to 15.10, only 50 minutes before work in any case stopped, was not necessary, and we therefore announced that it would be abolished, thus adding 50 minutes to our working week. I should make clear that, unlike the lunch break, the two 10 minute breaks were in paid time, so we did

not really think we were doing anything unreasonable.

But we had reckoned without the British worker! As usual, we announced these decisions to the work force at large, and to the TGWU and MSF representatives – the unions then represented about half the work force. The wage freeze was accepted almost without comment, but the loss of the tea break drew immediate opposition, and the two unions registered a 'failure to agree'. Further discussions were held through the autumn, during which we followed proper procedure and maintained the status quo, but we did not want to climb down, even though the issue was not one of make or break importance. I felt that our hours were already somewhat below the average for our type of industry, and there was no really genuine reason to maintain the afternoon break.

Eventually the unions balloted their members on whether they wished to take action short of a strike on the matter. When the result was announced in January, both ballots revealed a clear majority in favour of action. I was very disappointed at the time, although the total of those voting in favour was only 61, which is a pretty small number out of a workforce over 250. By this time, the dispute had engendered a certain amount of bad feeling. The unions were conscious that they only represented about half the work force, and wanted to increase this. They therefore conducted a recruitment campaign, and put about the idea that anyone not joining was letting down his or her colleagues. At the same time, we let it be known that we did not approve of the action the union was taking, and tried to discourage people from joining. Because of all this, a number of people did join the union for the first time, and a few resigned.

As a result of the ballot an overtime ban was announced. We took legal advice, wondering whether an employee could be dismissed for breaking his or her contract of employment by refusing to work overtime. The position was fairly complicated, but fortunately it never got to that stage, although we did tell employees that they would be breaking their contract of employment at their own risk. We were particularly disappointed with some members of office staff who were in the MSF – their hours of work (35 per week) were even lower than those in the factory, but a few still thought the afternoon break should be sacrosanct. The two unions had formed a joint committee, and in one of our meetings one of the committee, Keith Bint, came up with a compromise. "If," he suggested, "we agreed to do away with the afternoon break, would you accept an increase in time of the morning break to 15 minutes? The 10 minutes currently allowed is very short for the increasing numbers who want to have breakfast at this point, and as a consequence it often stretches to 15 minutes anyway."

I immediately saw that this was a sensible suggestion, even if it did involve us in giving a little ground, and will always be grateful to Keith for coming up with this compromise. I discussed the idea with my colleagues, and we agreed to accept the compromise as a way of ending what could become a damaging dispute. There was only one "but" as far as we were concerned – we did not think the offices should have the extra 5 minutes on the morning break. Their hours only started at 08.45, and I did not see that they needed a long breakfast break only 75 minutes after starting in the same way as the factory did. Even to have one paid-for break for office staff was rather unusual, as we found from doing some research. So we said that the offices would only have the single 10 minute break.

Keith Bint was not, of course, putting forward something that had already been accepted by the union members, and the next stage was to get their acceptance. But we had stern resistance from certain members of the office staff who did not want to accept losing the afternoon break, but we dug our heels in as we felt that we were on strong ground. I felt then, as I still do, that there is a strong case for making office hours the same as in the factory rather than make a further reduction in them. It is true that office staff are supposed to work a certain amount of unpaid overtime if the need arises, which isn't the case in the factory, but in reality this rarely happens for most of them.

The crunch of the dispute came on Friday 27th January when a meeting was held with the joint union committee and the two full time union officials, Ivor Braggins (TGWU) and Ken Morris (MSF). I had met them both on a number of occasions before, and got on quite well with Ken Morris, but not always with Ivor Braggins, who could be rather unnecessarily abrasive. That day was no exception, and I was soon having cross words with him. But things calmed down, and it was agreed that I would address the whole membership of the unions, putting the company point of view. This would be followed by separate meetings of the membership of the two unions. Mr Braggins agreed not to recommend rejection of our proposals (what he actually said, I never knew). We then retired for lunch, nervously awaiting the result. Quite soon Ken Morris came down to say that his members had accepted the deal. He said that some of them took some persuading, but they had now asked for an assurance that no-one would be victimised. This, of course, we gave. Finally Ivor Braggins appeared to say that his members had also accepted and that the dispute was therefore over.

I think that everyone, management and unions, were glad that this argument over something that was really rather trivial had been resolved. Only later did I learn of one twist of fate that may have swung the T&G behind us. David Lewis was their chief shop steward, and the only person about whom you might say that he was an old-fashioned union person, and perhaps not averse to keeping the dispute going for its own sake. When the T&G had their private meeting to consider our offer, David had to leave before it was finished because he had to attend to his elderly mother who lived a short distance away, and who was disabled. It has therefore been suggested that old Mrs Lewis played a big part in getting the dispute settled!

Our Sales Structure
In the earlier part of the book, my father described the large sales force he built up, which, at its peak in the '60s, consisted of over 100 sales representatives organised in nine regions, each with a manager who had an office and secretary. In the early '70s the regional offices were dispensed with, and in the '80s

the number of reps and managers started to come down, so that by 1990 we had five regional sales managers looking after 55 representatives.

At the beginning of that year we decided on a major re-organisation due to two factors. Firstly the 'B' or trade sales force had never been consistently successful, and did not look like becoming so. In theory, the idea of selling direct to the user is a sensible one, but in practice we always had a majority of men who failed to reach a satisfactory level of sales. I think the problem was mainly that in this type of business it was difficult to reach the person who made buying decisions, and even when orders were obtained, they were often small. Whereas it is usually easy to find a retailer in his shop running his business, and ready to talk to our rep, an industrial buyer will not see a rep without an appointment, and the purchase of paint brushes is usually well down his list of priorities. Builders and decorators can be just as difficult to contact – they are often out on the job in the day time, and some of our more successful reps got business by approaching them in the evening. Our most successful trade reps had established one or two good big customers, but this was more easily said than done.

The other new factor was the beginning of the switch to central distribution by our supermarket customers. Up till March 1990 we had to call on all B&Q stores every two weeks, and merchandise them and make out an order, which kept some of our reps very busy indeed. But at that date store visits were stopped, and B&Q switched to bulk orders for their new warehouse. The same had happened, or was likely to happen, to our other supermarkets customers. So

Our sales force with some head office staff pictured at the annual conference at the Miskin Manor Hotel near Cardiff in July 1998. Our most successful salesmen during the 1990s were Mark Ankers (second from left, seated) and Mike Capper (fifth from left, seated), who have shared nearly all the honours.

it was clear that we would no longer need the 30 or so retail reps we then had.

So we decided to merge the two sales forces, and reduce the overall number significantly. In July 1990 we formed 44 new sales territories organised under five regional sales managers. Each rep had control over all their accounts, including the user ones. But it soon became clear that even this reduced number was more than could be supported, partly because the user side of the business declined considerably under the new regime, helped by the national recession in the building trade that took hold at that time. So as the opportunity presented itself we further reduced numbers, including the reduction of the regions to four on the retirement of John Churchill as manager of the west country region in 1993.

When Gary Jordan took over as sales director in 1995 we still had well over 20 reps and four managers, but Gary believed that the numbers could be reduced even further without losing sales. The supermarkets by this time had all gone over to central warehousing, and the independent retail business had continued to shrink due to the ever greater power of the supermarkets. So in 1996 we cut the numbers to 17, and did away with the regional managers altogether. Gary took over day to day management of the new-look sales force, and a new remuneration structure was worked out, with a greater emphasis on incentives. I am pleased to say that this structure has remained in place ever since although numbers are now down to 15.

Thus between 1990 and 1996 we had lost 43 reps and regional managers, with obviously a great saving of money, and in particular the changes brought about by Gary Jordan were a significant factor in our improved results in the later '90s. Nearly all this reduction was brought about by natural wastage and early retirement. Faced with the need to reduce numbers, we offered an incentive to reps approaching retirement age to retire early. Under our scheme rules, anyone retiring before normal retirement age was paid a pension based on his or her service at their retirement date, reduced by a factor determined by the scheme actuary to account for their increased life expectancy compared with someone at normal retirement age. To make early retirement more attractive, we offered to make no actuarial reduction in the pension of any rep retiring early. This proved quite attractive to anyone in their late 50s or early 60s, and several took advantage of it. Under our pension scheme, normal retirement age was 65 for men and 60 for women (the scheme rules were changed to equalise these at 65 in 1995), but as long ago as the late '70s I felt that reps should retire at 60 rather than 65, so all reps engaged since 1978 were employed under new rules with a retirement age of 60. But in 1990 many reps were still in the older scheme, and I think did not welcome the idea of driving round in a car all day searching for business when in their 60s, although we have, of course, had representatives who have continued to be successful till the age of 65.

There were also a few reps whose sales were so bad that we were finally forced to terminate their employment, and some others who left of their own accord for various reasons or who were forced to retire early through ill-health, so that in the end I think there was only one rep and one manager whom we had to make compulsorily redundant.

It would not be right to discuss our sales organisation without referring to the national accounts team. Our first national accounts executive based at Stoke Prior was Glyn Lowe, and when he was promoted to the position of sales director we had to find a replacement. At this stage we increased the staff to two, John Love being one of the early appointments, and later still to three, then four. We took the view that national accounts were so important that it would be impossible not to give them too much attention, and as it was becoming clear that the team was beginning to open new accounts and increase the business with existing ones, we thought it sensible to devote as much resource as we could. For a period John Love, who joined us in 1990, was leader of our national accounts team, but in 2001 we decided to appoint him as a full time director in charge of overseas sourcing. At about the same time we appointed Stuart Hobbs, who had joined us in 1992 and had been our most successful national accounts executive, to the board as national accounts director. Stuart has been particularly successful in establishing a good personal relationship with his opposite numbers in B&Q, Homebase and Wickes, and has been an excellent ambassador for the company.

A final note: I have referred a number of times to salesmen, and this might be taken to mean that I am rather sexist about sales staff. Far from it – it is a cause of regret to me that we have only ever had three female representatives. One was not very successful and left, and the next was a member of our office staff, and decided to return to her previous job. The last was Lorna Hobbs, wife of Stuart, who has had previous experience in our field, and I hope it is 'third time lucky'! I believe that women can make just as good, perhaps even better, representatives than men, and I hope we will have more in the future. Higher up on the sales side we have had two very successful ladies: Christine Davis (export – see below) and Ruth Cattell, who was a national accounts executive from 1996 to 2000.

Our Pension Scheme
It was very fortunate that we had a strong pension fund in the 1990s, as it enabled us to offer attractive early retirement terms to employees whose services were no longer required. My father started the scheme with great foresight 50 years ago, and it was certainly unusual in those days to have a scheme that embraced all grades of employees. In the early '60s the fund was invested with Scottish Widows in their new managed fund, and therefore benefited from the stock market boom that we have had almost continuously from 1974 to 2000. In the '80s our company contribution was around £200,000 per year, a large sum in those days, but by the early '90s it became clear that the scheme was somewhat over-funded, and the company contribution was cut back. The actuarial valuation made in April 1997 showed the position was even more over-funded, and as this was not permitted by the Inland Revenue, we had to take steps to reduce the

surplus. Other than a major increase in benefits, which I was against as it would be a permanent burden on future generations, the only way was to have a complete halt in all contributions to the scheme, both by employees and the company, which started in January 1998 and is still continuing. This has obviously been a positive factor in improving our profitability.

Our scheme is a traditional final salary one, with the pension calculated at 1/60 of pensionable salary for every year of service. To calculate final salary a deduction of £63 per week is currently made from actual earnings. This deduction has got a bad reputation in some quarters, as it is thought somehow immoral not to give a 'full' pension. But the reason for the deduction is quite logical. The original aim of the scheme was for someone to retire on two thirds final salary after a forty year working life. This was to include the state pension, and originally the deductible was one and a half times state pension. A quick calculation will show that after forty years the total pension will therefore be exactly the two thirds intended.

Obviously if there was no deductible there would be a higher pension, but it is all a question of money, as contributions are also based on pensionable salary. Sometime later we did reduce the deductible to once times the state pension, putting up both the cost and benefits of the scheme, and as part of our efforts to reduce the surplus we then made the deductible £60 per week, a small reduction on what it was. My aim in this change was for it ultimately to 'wither on the vine', as its real value will get smaller and smaller if it is not increased in relation to wages. On the other hand, if the fund becomes not so well funded, it will be open to the trustees to make an increase in it. In 2002 it was increased to £63, a reaction partly to the continued slump on the stock market.

Pensions have always been a hot political potato, and rules and regulations have come and gone (mainly the former) with monotonous regularity in the last 40 years. We have had the graduated pension, then SERPS, and now the stakeholders pension. Regulation has got progressively tighter, particularly since the Maxwell scandal. I was once told that the first regulations concerning these schemes covered two side of paper. Now they are the equivalent of two Bibles! I think this latter is an example of over-reaction to a one-off situation, and I feel in the long run these new rules will have the opposite result to that intended. The running of a final salary company pension scheme is now beset with official control, making it a less and less attractive proposition for companies to run them, and I should imagine that very few new ones are being set up. The alternative is, of course, the defined contribution, or money purchase scheme, where each employee has his or her own investment fund contributed to by both the employee and the employer, so there are no trustees running a pooled fund. Such an idea has much to recommend it, and, I predict, will in time be the only type of company-run scheme. Indeed had our own fund not been so over-funded we might have seriously thought of changing ourselves. But the major snag with money purchase schemes is that the level of contributions generally being made into them, even by large reputable companies, is often nothing like sufficient to ensure an adequate pension. Unfortunately, this will only become clear when the schemes have been running for 30 years or so, and long serving employees start to retire. The total % of salary being contributed is often no more than 10%, and although it is impossible to say accurately what the long term funding rate will need to be, in the past it has been nearer double this figure to give a two thirds pension. At least as far as we are concerned, it looks as if our employees should retire with a reasonably good level of pension in relation to their service with us.

In 2002 there has been a lot written about pension schemes, as the severe down-turn in the stock market and prolonged low interest rates have meant that returns on savings have been very poor. Defined contribution schemes are not looking very healthy, and companies with defined benefit schemes, such as ours, are fearful that they might need to put substantial extra funds into their schemes if promises are to be met. In a sense, I suppose, these schemes are actually a fraud – no employer can guarantee that in 20, 30 or even 40 years time there will be sufficient money in the fund to meet the scheme's obligations. If there isn't, then it is up the employer to top it up, but who can guarantee the employer will have the cash, or even still be in existence? If the scheme is small in relation to the size of the employer's company, a deficit may not be too serious, but many 'mature' schemes such as ours have funds that almost dwarf the value of the company. Clearly, in these circumstances a shortfall can be very serious. I think it is these thoughts, from which I have certainly not been immune, that is driving the push towards money purchase schemes, although there are increasing signs of employee resistance, and there has even been talk of industrial action to preserve the traditional final salary scheme.

One final word before I leave pensions: the retirement age. Up till 1990 most schemes used the traditional 65 for men and 60 for women, which coincided with the state pension age. Then in May 1990 there was a case in the European Court of Justice in Luxembourg (the *Barber* case) that ruled that not only was it illegal under the Treaty of Rome to discriminate between men and women in wages and salaries, but that this applied to pensions as well. I regard this decision, and subsequent events, as an outstanding example of bad government, caused by our membership of the EU. It is not that I am against equal pensions, but the issues are so complex and potentially expensive that they need careful consideration and any change must be very well planned. But this is precisely what we didn't get. The judges in Luxembourg were not concerned with the practicalities of running pension schemes, but with some political ideal. Their decision caused the whole pensions industry to be in turmoil for no less than five years when some further decisions by the ECJ, and at EU summits, at last clarified the situation. Only then was it decided that equalisation would only be backdated to May 1990 – if not, equalisation would have been not only hardly practical, but ruinously expensive – and schemes such as ours were able to recast their rules. We did what many schemes had done, and equalised retirement ages at 65 (so women could hardly claim to have won any sort of victory). This on its own would have reduced the cost of running our scheme, and to counter-balance this we reduced the age at which there was no actuarial reduction for early retirement to 63. So men got some benefit from the changes, counter-balancing the detriment to women. The whole thing has become very complex, and even now I still have to study our scheme handbook before I can explain to someone exactly what the rules are.

This episode was an outstanding example of bad government. Our own parliament was powerless to do anything to clear the confusion, as it was subject to the over-riding powers of the ECJ, so we had to wait for artificially contrived court cases to be decided in another country before the law was clarified, and no-one can pretend that the final rules were anything other than an unsatisfactory compromise. The best way of governing a country is surely for our own government to make the rules, after due consideration and consultation, and have them vetted by our own democratically elected parliament. But since we joined the EU in 1972 we have subjected ourselves to the various treaties that govern the EU, which are interpreted by the ECJ in Luxembourg. So now any matter that comes under any of the EU treaties (and they now cover almost every aspect of life, particularly as far as business is concerned) is effectively taken away from our own parliament, and decided in Brussels and Luxembourg. Not, in my opinion, the way to govern a country properly.

Finally, it is interesting to speculate how retirement ages might change in future. One thing is indisputable – for any given retiring age, the cost of providing a pension is increasing as life expectancy increases. This why the last government very sensibly increased the state pension age for women to 65 to take effect in a few years' time. This move, possibly because it was announced so far ahead of its implementation, engendered remarkably little comment. This rather marks us as different from the rest of Europe, where the pressure is always to lower retiring ages.

In industries where pension funds, like ours, have done well, the trend has been to allow employees to retire earlier on quite generous pensions. In the financial service industries it is quite usual to retire at 55. In other sectors, such as the police and fire services, it has become very common for employees to seek to retire early on ill-health grounds, often by the age of 50. The cost of pensions in these services has rocketed in recent years because of the cost of early retirement. In Europe, the situation is even worse. Most pensions are paid out of current income, whereas in the UK nearly all private sector pensions are pre-funded. European governments have not been so far-sighted as ours in trying to limit the long term cost of pensions, indeed some are still giving in to demands for earlier pensions. This situation is bound to lead to problems in the long run as pension bills soar, and this is one reason why some people feel we should not join Economic and Monetary Union (EMU), as the UK could be caught up in the need to raise taxes higher and higher to pay the pensions bill.

So I think that the trend towards early retirement is bound to come up against economic reality. Two things could happen – either people will have to remain at work longer to build up a satisfactory pension fund, or when they retire they will have to find new employment to top up their pensions. Although people may raise their eyebrows at the notion of the elderly having to work to make ends meet, it is not so radical an idea. As people live longer, and their health is improved, so they have more and more to contribute to society for longer and longer. A society where everyone over the age of, say, 60, is not economically active will be achieving much less than its economic potential. I am always struck when I go to the USA by how many older people I see working, whether as supermarket assistants, airline stewards, or company executives. I think this is a good thing, and a trend we are sure to see over here sooner or later, and one reason why the US is a richer nation than most of the rest of Europe.

Our Commercial Property
The Aerlec estate that my father describes buying in the 1950s languished for many years with a few tenants and no real improvements, except that two new units, called Unit A and Unit B, were built on vacant land on the the south side of the entrance road. In the 1970s our main tenants were Clements & Street, exhibition contractors, and as they wished to expand we built them a new premises with offices along the front. In the late '80s they needed a expand further, and eventually it was agreed that we would sell them their premises so that they could build the extension themselves. Although this gave a welcome influx of cash, it did result in the fragmentation of the estate, which I later rather regretted. At about the same time we decided to put up for sale some land immediately opposite our factory, adjacent to the Aerlec estate, which was zoned as development land under the Bromsgrove local plan. The successful bidder was Mike Fletcher, who named his new development 'Saxon Park', and which he later extended to include all the land between the road and the PolymerLatex factory in Stoke Works. His development got off to rather a slow start during the recession of the early '90s, but now all the land we originally sold him has been developed, and much of the land further back has also been built on.

Before describing our developments on the Aerlec estate, I should say a little about the zoning of this land in Stoke Prior for industrial development. I am not sure exactly when the land between our factory and what had been the old ICI Salt Works was zoned for development, but I suspect it was done fairly early on in the planning process. The reasons were no doubt that the Brush Works was already built, the Salt Works had long been in existence, and there was also a little development either side of the canal where the B4091 crosses it. The planners no doubt thought it would be sensible to allow industrial infill between these developments, and thus the land, which was to become the Saxon Park and the Harris Industrial Park, was designated for commercial development. However, the planners had not thought it necessary to make any improvements in the local amenities, with the result that it is becoming increasingly clear that what is now quite a large industrial development is very poorly served by local roads. Immediately to the north of the development the B4091 crosses the Worcester

This photo was probably taken around 1960, and shows the Aerlec site, bounded by the Worcester & Birmingham Canal and the B4091 road, as it was purchased by us. An aluminium factory was established here during the war. Across the canal is the Metal & Ores Co that smelted scrap metal and coins for recycling – this has also now been redeveloped as an industrial estate by its owners although the unsightly chimney and old buildings are still there.

and Birmingham Canal, and although this bridge has been strengthened, 18th century canal bridges are hardly suitable for modern lorry traffic. But a short distance further north there is an even more severe restriction which is the bridge taking the main railway line over the road which has a 12 feet 9 inch height restriction. This means that modern full size lorries cannot approach either our factory or the other new developments from the north, but instead have to travel from the M5 motorway junction at Wychbold down to Droitwich town centre, out along the B4090 as far as Hanbury village, then north along the B4091 to Stoke Prior. This is a circuitous route, with a very awkward junction in Droitwich town centre and another dangerous turning in Hanbury.

Similarly with car traffic, access to this industrial area from the north leaves the Bromsgrove by-pass at a set of traffic lights, and the road is twisty and not good. As employment has increased at Stoke Prior so long queues now form at the approach to the Bromsgrove by-pass, and, even worse, lorries have to take the inappropriate route I have described. Our factory alone can account for at least a dozen lorries a day, so the situation at the present time, particularly for the residents of Hanbury and Droitwich, is most unsatisfactory.

In 1999 I was asked to join the newly formed Stoke Prior Business Association by Councillor John Tidmarsh and Dr Henning Bachen who was manager of PolymerLatex. I became Chairman of the association in 2000, and, with the help of the committee I produced a report on the local roads which contained proposals for a new link that would run from a point just south of our factory, along the edge of the Saxon Business Park, past PolymerLatex, across the canal on a new bridge and on to the motorway junction at Wychbold. We did what we could to publicise these proposals, in the course of which we inevitably attracted the opprobrium of the local residents, many of whom were implacably opposed to any further new local developments whatsoever. Dr Bachen's successor, Graham Reed, and I went to see Richard Wiggington of the County Council in 2000, but I am afraid the reception we got was not very positive. It was explained to us that, although it was possible that there may be a few new road schemes allowed in Worcestershire in the coming year or two, these were very limited, and ours was unlikely to be considered unless there were important safety considerations, which at that time seemed to be the main criteria for attracting government support. Graham Reed and I left wondering how on earth Britain had managed to build a transport infrastructure in the first place, and regretting that such negative attitudes towards further investment in roads seemed to rule at the present time. So we are left with the situation which I am afraid is all to common in Britain today – a large new local development, totally inadequately served by local roads.

The Harris Industrial Park from the air before work started on the extension behind, showing Unit 15 added to the left of Unit 12. The premises of Clements & Street, exhibition contractors, are in the centre left.

This was one of the older buildings on the Aerlec Estate – it can be identified in centre of the photo on the previous page. In 1987, following a suggestion from Garth Weaver of Weaver Plc, we completely refurbished this building, together with another unit just visible at the right of the picture, and let them both to new tenants.

Returning to the Aerlec estate, just prior to the sale of the land to Mr Fletcher we had appointed a new agent, Alwyn Davies, who worked for what was then called GA Commercial in Worcester. One of the first things that Alwyn suggested was that the estate be renamed the Harris Industrial Park, and he also encouraged us to demolish some of the older buildings, which were in a very poor state, and build some new units. This seemed a sensible suggestion so in 1988 we approached the well-known local building firm of Weaver Plc, at that time still run by the three Weaver brothers, Roger, Garth and Andrew. We had already worked with Garth Weaver, who was in charge of the 'Design and Build' side of the business refurbishing two of the older buildings on the site in 1987, and he proposed two new blocks comprising six separate units, one backing on to the canal and the other at right angles to it, which we named Units 12 and 14. These were built in 1989 and fairly quickly let to tenants, and throughout the '90s were nearly fully occupied. A few years later one of our tenants, the Lamont Group, whose main operating company was Mercury Climatic, manufacturing large air-conditioning units, asked whether we would build them large new premises, and this we did by extending unit 12 and demolishing the remaining older buildings. This new unit we called unit 15, and has, again, been a successful development for us, on which we continued to work with Weavers.

Behind the Harris Industrial Park was a further field of about ten acres belonging to Bayers, the parent company of PolymerLatex. We conceived the idea that it would be sensible for us to continue development of the Harris Industrial Park into this further area, as we felt it could be a profitable venture for us, and it also had the big advantage that it would enable us to improve the main access into the HIP, which up till then had belonged to Bayers and was in poor condition. So Bayers agreed to sell us this land, and again working with Weavers, we designed an estate road and all the services throughout this area.

Rather than develop the whole area ourselves, which would have been risky and expensive, our plan was to divide it into plots of about 0.5 acres each and offer these for sale, as we were advised that there was a good demand from owner occupiers for land of this type. Alwyn Davies continued to advise us on this development, but because of the size of the project, the total cost of which was going to be about £1.5 million, we decided to appoint joint agents, and after Alwyn and I had interviewed a number of agents from Birmingham firms, we appointed Simon Lloyd from DTZ.

This development was completed in 1999, which was when we started to market the plots. We had also decided to build one speculative building ourselves, if only to make sure there was some "activity" on the site, so later in 1999 we built an office building of about 5,000 square feet which we called 'Hanbury Court' which was again designed by Weavers together with the architect they used, Richard Tranter. Hanbury Court was situated at the entrance of the site and we wanted a building of some distinction. In the end we were pleased with

Units 12 (nearer camera) and 14 beyond, completed in 1988, and originally let to six different tenants. This was our first new development with Weavers.

Unit 15 was built in 1996 as an extension to Unit 12 for Mercury Climatic. The end block has offices, beyond which is factory space.

the result, but for financial reasons before construction had really got under way we decided to sell the development to our pension trustees, so as not to strain our own financial resources too far. The idea was that the pension trustees would let the building, but in the event they received a good offer to buy it from a new hi-tech mapping company called Dotted Eyes.

We had also planned a development of small factory units and offices which was to be called Stoke Court, which would back onto units 12 and 15, but in the end we never went ahead with this development as many of the plot sales were to developers who planned their own similar speculative developments. We were also planning some new buildings on our own site and we did not wish to extend our financial commitments too far. Sale of the plots on the new development went a little more slowly than we had anticipated, but by early 2002 they had all been completed, and our own direct interest in this part of the development ceased when we handed over the roads and other common parts to a new management company. When we launched this new development we decided to call it the Harris Business Park, so today we have the slightly unsatisfactory situation where the older part of our estate is called the Harris Industrial Park, and the newer part behind, the Harris Business Park – I expect one day the whole development will be called the Harris Business Park.

Before finishing this account of our commercial property investment, I should mention that, beyond the ten acre field we bought for the Harris Business Park, there was a further field before the PolymerLatex factory is reached, and we had always told Bayer that, should they offer this for sale, we would like to be considered as possible purchasers. PolymerLatex were against this land being sold as they regarded it as a good 'buffer' around their own site, which contained a small explosion risk. However, Bayer decided they wished to realise the value of this land as well, and late in 1999 I was told it was to be offered for sale and I confirmed our interest. I was rather put out, therefore, when only a few weeks later I was informed that the land had been sold to Mr Fletcher to be added on to Saxon Park without asking any other bidders to tender at all. I never understood why Bayers acted in this way and I did sometimes entertain dark thoughts about underhand dealings. I was particularly apprehensive because Bayers had retained a right of way through the Harris Business Park to this land, and if another developer was to develop it then I had visions of a stream of lorries

A publicity photo of myself and Garth Weaver inside unit 15, prior to handing over to Mercury Climatic. Garth Weaver has since retired from Weaver plc and the company has been subject to a management buy-out, but there is still Weaver family involvement in the new company. Weavers date back to 1865 when it was founded by Garth's great-grandfather.

using our estate road to gain access. However I am pleased to say that Mr Fletcher made the access to this additional land through his existing Saxon Park, so this problem never arose, and, as part of the deal in which we agreed to facilitate the provision of services on the new land, this right of way was extinguished.

As a final note on our property interests, it is intended that by the end of 2002 our remaining interests in the Harris Industrial Park will be vested in a separate company which will be split off from the main trading company. This has been done for tax reasons, as we have been advised that the existence of the property interest in the company might render the shares to be classed as 'non-business assets' which attract far less favourable treatment than 'business assets'.

August 1999 – an aerial view of the Harris Industrial Park and Harris Business Park, with our factory and sports fields at the rear. The Business Park was ready for development at this stage, but we had yet to sell any of the plots. One of the problems with the site was the storm drainage – the culvert under the canal has limited capacity, so a 'balancing pond' had to be built to absorb any excess flow in heavy rain. This can be seen bounded by a fence on three sides. The Saxon Park development is immediately adjacent to the Business Park. The undeveloped field at the bottom right was still owned by Bayer at that stage, and we had some hopes that we might acquire it to add to our development. However, later that year it was announced that it had been bought by the owner of the Saxon Park.

1999 – our joint agents for the sale of plots on the Harris Business Park were Alwyn Davies of Wilkins in Worcester (left), and Simon Lloyd of DTZ who was based in Birmingham.

Our Financial Results 1995 – 2002

In the previous sections I have dealt with the various factors that led to our improved financial performance in the latter half of the 1990s. During this period sales increased substantially as our success with DIY supermarkets continued. From a low of £9.5m in the early '90s, turnover almost reached £20m in 2000, and £25m in 2001/02, something I would never have dreamed of 10 years previously. We have had, of course, sales increases in the past, but the high inflation experienced particularly in the '70s more or less negated these, and if our sales are corrected for inflation then it is only in the 1990s that we have achieved a significant real increase since 1960.

Not only did our sales increase from the mid-90s, but our profits sprang to life as well. By 95/96 we were back in profit, and in the following three years our margin had increased to around 10% of sales, a much higher level than we had enjoyed for some time. So I was very pleased when in 1997/98 our profits hit the £1m mark for the first time, and even more so when two years later they had almost reached £2m. In 2000/01 profits dipped significantly, but the following year they were much improved. Our published profits were always somewhat lower than this, as we had to allow for profit sharing bonus schemes.

The company has never paid any dividends, so all our profits, after the deduction of corporation tax, have been re-invested in the business. Our improved margin therefore allowed for a much bigger programme of investment in new machinery and buildings. As far as machinery was concerned, the main area of investment was in the paint brush factory, and the roller factory. As sales increased, production of paint brushes had had to be increased substantially, and we found we needed extra paint brush head making machines and assembly machines to make sure that our capacity remained ahead of demand. I have always believed that British industry has frequently made the mistake of cutting back capacity that may in the short term be surplus, only to find that when sales pick up they cannot cope. This was one of the factors that led to the rapid increase in the importation of foreign motor cars in the boom of the early '70s – as waiting lists for British models lengthened, buyers turned to more readily available foreign models. Douglas Wride was fond of saying that we should set our stall out to be able to cope with future demand, and I think this has proved a sensible policy over the years. We have often invested in new plant, machinery and buildings before they were strictly necessary, but only on very few occasions have these decisions later proved to be in not our best long term interests.

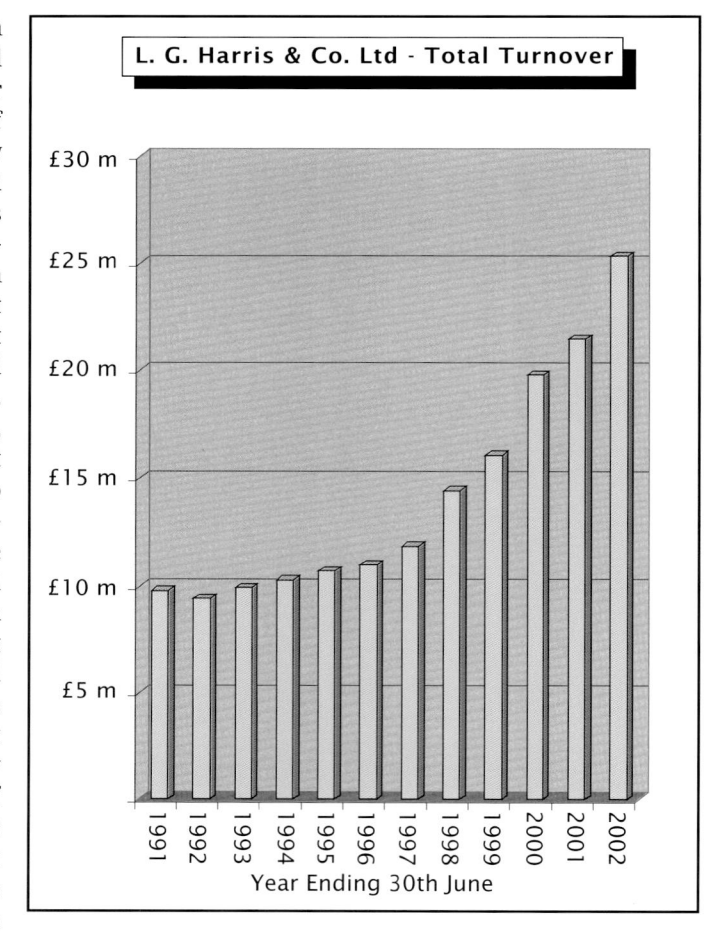

Having made sure that we had sufficient machinery to meet the increased demand, we also found we needed more space. For a brush manufacturer, we have always had quite a large factory, helped, no doubt, by the fact we have a large green-field site. Nevertheless by 1997 we urgently needed more room for

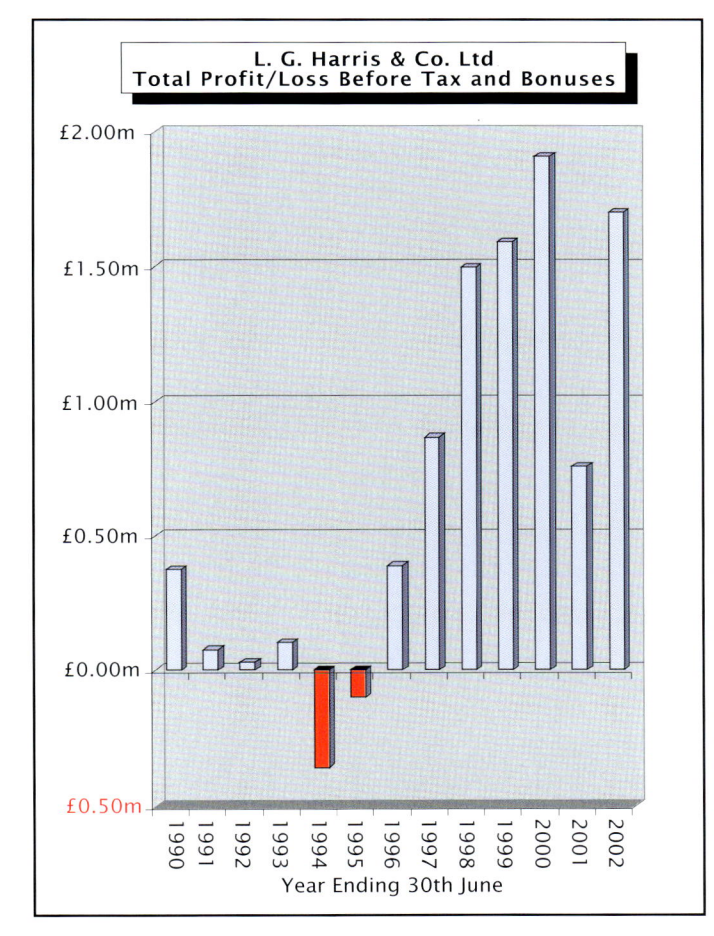

**L. G. Harris & Co. Ltd
Total Profit/Loss Before Tax and Bonuses**

[Bar chart showing annual profit/loss from 1990 to 2002, Year Ending 30th June. Values approximately: 1990 ~£0.35m, 1991 ~£0.05m, 1992 ~£0.02m, 1993 ~£0.10m, 1994 loss ~-£0.35m, 1995 small loss ~-£0.05m, 1996 ~£0.35m, 1997 ~£0.85m, 1998 ~£1.50m, 1999 ~£1.60m, 2000 ~£1.90m, 2001 ~£0.75m, 2002 ~£1.70m.]

our packing department – nearly all the lines we sell have to be individually packaged, and this is usually done after the product is made, in a separate department. We had, in fact, a building available we could use for this purpose, which was the large open sided storage shed of about 40,000 sq ft that my father had built in about 1980 to house our stocks of wooden poles for making brooms. This building had become redundant for this purpose after a few years, since when it has been used for general storage. Encouraged by Garth Weaver, we considered various ways of making use of this building. Our original idea was to make it into four small industrial units to let, but as the project got under way we decided to take about half the building into our own use for packaging, and let the rest. The building was finished in early 1998, and we invited the local MP, Julie Kirkbride, to perform the opening ceremony. Meanwhile, we had found a tenant for the rest of the building – they were Manor Reproductions, who distribute ornamental brassware and other items for domestic use, and they moved in as soon as it was finished. This building has proved most useful for our packaging operations, and it houses our stock of finished but unpacked goods as well as both the hand and the machine packing sections.

Later that year we were awarded substantial extra business from Homebase supplying paint rollers and other products. Paint rollers are very bulky, and again we found ourselves under pressure of space. So we decided to build a new 9,000 sq ft factory unit adjacent to our main brush factory, into which we moved

1998 – an old open sided storage shed was transformed into a modern building, half of which was given over to our own use as a new packing department, and the other half was let out to Manor Reproductions, a company distributing household goods. Our end is that further from the camera.

our paint roller department, including some pallet racking for storing raw materials. Weavers again completed it for us, and it was opened in the presence of Jeremy Bird and Nick Fenner from Wickes in June 1999.

Our third and most ambitious building project to date was a new warehouse. When I first joined the company, our finished goods were stored in rather crudely made wooden bins on two storeys in the old factory. Incoming orders were invoiced every day, and at the end of the invoicing run a 'picking list' was produced showing the totals of each product that had been sold. These goods were then got out of stock, and stacked in a fairly limited area in our despatch department. The orders were packed during the day, at the end of which nothing should be left. If there were a few items left over, an investigation was carried out in an attempt to find the order which was missing the goods.

This was a good system for the limited number of lines that we were selling up to the '60s. But as more and more items were added, and our sales of bulky paint roller sets increased, so we were running out of space, both for bulk storage and for order picking. So we planned a new bulk warehouse with an enlarged order picking and packing area in the early '70s, and the building was opening in 1974. Bulk storage was on pallets, and originally there was space for about 1,500 pallets, on racking four pallets high. Half this new building was given over to new production areas, but in the '80s this was closed down, and the whole building given over to our warehouse and despatch department.

Our new warehouse, opened in 2000. It has space for about 5,500 pallets, but within 12 months of opening we were again running out of space, which led to the construction in 2002 of a second new warehouse capable of storing up to a further 7,000 pallets.

This worked well for many years, but as our business grew in the '90s, and the number of lines we sold increased well beyond the 1,000 mark mainly because of all the special lines produced for our major customers, we again began to run out of space. By this time there was beginning to be a question mark over the future of manufacturing here – brushes were being brought in from China at a fraction of our price, and of increasingly good quality, so I did not consider that investment in any new manufacturing space would be sensible. But the storage and distribution of goods was another matter – however many goods we imported in the future, we would always need to warehouse and distribute them. So I considered the investment in a new warehouse and improved order packing facilities to be a good thing for the long term, and accordingly we started planning a further new building with Weavers in late 1999. The building, as finally conceived, was about 24,000 sq ft, and its main feature was its increased height – 36 feet (11 metres) to the eaves. This enabled us to have racking seven pallets high. We also planned to buy some pallet trucks of a new design that would work in narrower aisles than our old warehouse, only 2 metres as against 3 metres wide. So although the new building was only a little bigger than the old warehouse, we were able to install as many as 5,500 pallet spaces.

The warehouse was finished in summer 2000, and was opened by the then chairman of the Bromsgrove District Council, Mrs Ann Doyle, in September – unfortunately the ceremony was during the 'petrol crisis' week, and the number of guests was rather diminished as a result. The plan then was to reorganise the old warehouse and despatch buildings, to create a new major account order assembly area adjacent to the new lorry loading area, and move the small order picking and packing to the far end of the building, incorporating state-of-the-art 'live racking' for picking. This project was completed at the end of 2001.

This whole warehouse project cost us nearly £1m. The building was the major item, of course, but in addition there were substantial sums spent on re-concreting an area for loading lorries, on widening the south drive approach, on the racking in the building, and the three 'Bendi' pallet trucks.

We were very pleased with the new warehouse, and certainly did not anticipate that we would soon be running out of space again. But by the end of 2001 we found that, although the new warehouse was coping well with our stock of finished goods, we had insufficient room for incoming goods. By the following spring we were having to rent space in a commercial warehouse, and also put 30 containers on our works car park, each with 40 pallets of goods inside. The reasons for this lack of space were two-fold – the business had expanded to more than double the size it had been in the early '90s, and the big increase in imported components and finished goods meant that our stock holdings had to be relatively higher. If we were buying from a local company, then we could afford to keep stocks to a minimum with regular call-offs, but when goods are coming literally from the other side of the world, we have to order them by the container load, and allow for a much longer lead time. Furthermore, our biggest problems in recent years have been to make sure that we can supply all major customers' requirements in full and on time. In the summer and autumn of 2001 we went through a period when we were falling short on the delivery of some of our orders, and at one point we were threatened with a massive 'fine' from B&Q that could have bankrupted us. So again these pressures mean that we tend to keep larger stocks than we might do if some modest out-of-stocks did not matter. When we meet our auditors every year for the annual review, one item we can be sure will be on the agenda is the level of stocks. They always say that we are keeping much bigger stocks than we should do, but over the years we have considered this item again and again, and, although our stocks today in relation to our sales are, if anything, a little less than they were, we still find that if we allow them to run down below a certain level our deliveries start to fall below 100%, which soon has severe consequences.

So towards the end of 2001 we started to discuss with Weavers the building of a further new warehouse. There were a number of alternatives, including the conversion of some of our older factory buildings to warehousing space, but in the end we considered that a purpose built warehouse was the best and most economical answer, so we therefore put in a planning application for a new building on a new site to the south of our south drive of about 30,000 square feet that would, if filled with pallet racking (some of the 'double-deep' type) hold around 7,000 pallets. The proposed building was partly on green belt land, and the planners were accordingly cautious, but after making a strong case that we should be allowed to continue our expansion, permission was granted, and the new project was completed by the end of 2002. Initially we only put racking in one half of the building, but it quickly became apparent that this would soon become uncomfortably full, so we plan to extend this through the whole building in 2003.

As I mentioned earlier, our auditors often comment that we carry too much stock, and as I write this at the end of 2002 it is true that we have over £7.5m tied up in stock, a large amount for a company with a turnover running at £27m. Prior to 1995, when we did most of our own manufacturing, we carried about four months' sales of finished goods in stock, in addition to raw materials and work in progress. Consulting Principals said that by speeding up our response to demand, and running smaller batches with quicker change-over times, we could reduce this quite considerably, which we did. But by the late 1990s we were importing more and more goods, which has had the effect of pushing up our stocks again. When ordering goods from the Far East, one has to allow a manufacturing time of two months or so, then a shipping time of four to six weeks. So we have to order the goods three to four months before they are required, and as we are forecasting a long time ahead, we have to build a safety margin into delivery dates. Inevitably many of these goods arrive a few weeks before they are actually required. Another factor is that we usually have to order in full container loads, which means we are ordering more goods than we might if we were buying them locally. So our stocks of finished goods now (in terms of weeks sales) are nearly back to where they were before 1995, although our raw material stock is much lower.

Although I would not claim that a more efficient management could not get by with lower stocks than we are carrying, after 35 years experience of trying to maintain a balance between keeping stocks down to a reasonable level and avoiding 'out of stocks' (which can be so damaging to our relations with our major customers) I feel that it would be difficult to achieve a major reduction without damaging our customer service. It is one of the 'givens' of British industry that it is wrong to tie up money in stocks, but, like my comments on investing in new machines and buildings, I feel that in our case maintaining high stocks has enhanced our customer service, and has been a positive factor in helping build our turnover with our major customers.

(Next page) An aerial view of our site taken on 12th November 2002, a few days after our new warehouse (green) was handed over by the builders. This was the fourth new building done in co-operation with Weavers, the Bromsgrove builders – the others were the pole-shed conversion (at rear – completed 1998), new roller factory (just behind silo – completed 1999), and new finished goods warehouse (red – built 2000). Our enlarged employees' car park is visible at the top left, but is partly occupied by containers hired to hold stock that we had run out of space for. Once the new warehouse has been fitted out, these will disappear. The road layout is substantially unaltered from the 1940s, but the south (furthest) drive has been widened, as most of our lorry traffic uses this.

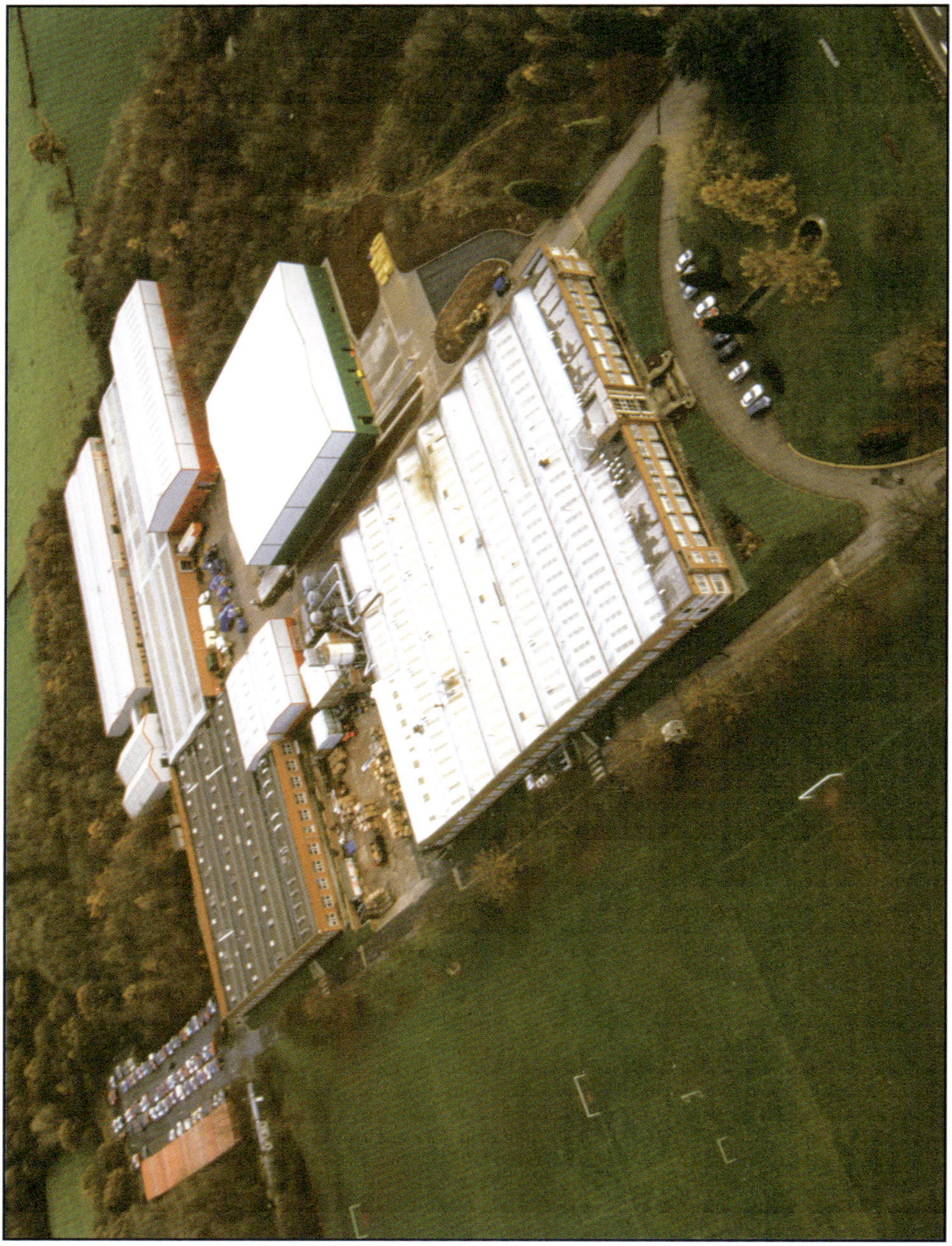

The interior of the new warehouse showing the racking in the process of being installed. This is of the 'double-deep' variety allowing a greater number of pallets to be stored in a given area.

Chapter 4

OUR COMPETITORS

Hamilton Acorn
When I started work in our company, most of the other companies in the brush trade were also family firms, and many went back much further than ours did. The oldest was the Briton Brush Company, which celebrated its 250th anniversary (which my wife and I attended) in 1996. This company has gone through a number of different ownerships, and has merged with many other brushmakers during its history, and at present it is known as Hamilton Acorn. In 1990 Briton was bought by the Lionheart Group (chaired by Paul Lever) which also owned Hamiltons, whose origins dated back to the early 19th century. The Hamilton factory at Harrow was closed, and production concentrated at Attleborough, Norfolk the site of the old Briton factory. At the time of the merger the combined turnover of the two companies was over £15m, and the fact that a few years later it fell to under £10m is hardly an advert for the benefits of mergers, although in fairness it must be said that Hamilton, whose traditional strength lay in supplying top quality brushes to the builders merchant sector, suffered badly in the recession of the early '90s.

At this time Lionheart had financial problems, and Hamilton Acorn in 1996 was subject to a management buyout backed by Close Bros investment bank, and led by Dennis Marrison, the present managing director. This company is still a major competitor of ours, but they have concentrated on their best quality brushes (including the well-known Hamilton Perfection range) which they sell to decorators and builders merchants. They are not very strong in DIY supermarkets or independent shops.

Like all venture capitalists, Close Bros were looking for a way to cash in their investment in Hamilton Acorn after five years. Paul Lever, although no longer associated with them, suggested to me that we might be interested in buying or merging with HA, and I even went as far as attending a meeting with Paul and Neil Murphy of Close in March 1999, at which Neil promised to supply us with further figures. But he never did, which rather mystified and annoyed me, and eventually in 2001 it was announced that the Swedish company Anza had pur-

A photograph taken at the 250th anniversary celebrations of Hamilton Acorn in 1996. (Left) Peter Chadwick, grandson of Sidney who founded the firm that later became Chadwick & Shapcot, bought by Polycell Products in the '60s. The Acorn symbol, still used by Hamilton Acorn, originated with Chadwicks. Later the Reed Group, which had bought Polycell products, bought the Briton Brush Company and merged the two brush companies to form Briton Chadwick. Later they were sold to Williams Holdings, and renamed Acorn Decorating Products. (Second from left) John Cheston, who joined Briton as sales manager in 1963 and was managing director of the group from 1979–1988. Next to him is Douglas MacDonald, finance director of Briton Brush until 1985, and on his left is Dennis Marrison who was appointed managing director of Hamilton Acorn in 1991 (Acorn Decorating Products had merged with Hamiltons in 1990 within the Lionheart Group) and led a management buy-out in 1996. On Dennis's left is Michael Marwood, works manager at the Wymondham factory, and next to him Bob Clarke, who was the last indentured apprentice in the brush industry and retired as technical director of Hamiltons in 1991. On the far right is George Mabbutt, one of a family of very long serving Briton employees. I got to know most of these people through my associations in the brush trade.

chased them. It was also announced that the HA management would be staying on till at least the end of 2002, so this change is unlikely to have any dramatic effect on our business in the short term. Later I learned that Dennis Marrison, Shirley Henderson and Ralph Brindle (the three buy-out investors) would all be leaving in the early part of 2003. In the longer term Anza will have to reconcile the fact that they, like us, are a mid-market DIY company, whereas HA have made a speciality of supplying the professional decorator with top quality goods. It will be interesting to see in what direction they decide to take HA.

Addis

My father mentions the housewares and toothbrush manufacturer Addis, another family company that can trace its origins back to the eighteenth century. They were quite active in the paint brush market for a time, but about the time my father penned his words, they decided to withdraw from the paint brush side of their business and concentrate on their more traditional lines. They have remained strong in the household brush and housewares field, but now belong to a German company, after having gone through yet another management buy-out.

Mosley Stone/Stanley

Our biggest competitor is another company that was a family firm for many years – Mosley Stone. They were the result of a merger between two companies, Stones of Stockport, and Mosleys of Leeds. The former can trace its origins back a long time, whereas the latter was founded before the war by a family of Jewish immigrants. In the 1980s, after the merger, they were managed jointly by Derek Mosley and Raymond Stone, and they ran a very successful business. Derek had the skills and experience in the brush manufacturing side, and Raymond was very good at cultivating relationships with their many large customers. By 1990 their turnover had exceeded £20m (over double our size then), and in 1991 the family owners decided to sell to the Stanley Tool Company of America.

Mosley Stone had their own brand of goods, but this was not very well known to the general public, and much of their production was 'own brand'. The Stanley brand is, of course, very strong, and I fully expected that the new management would re-market their product range under the Stanley brand. But although a Stanley branded range did appear, few other changes were made, and the company continued under the management of Derek and Raymond. Sadly Derek Mosley, who had been a heavy smoker all his life, died within a year of the sale, which

Raymond Stone (left) and Derek Mosley at a trade show before their take-over by Stanley Tools in 1991. Derek died in January the following year, but Raymond continued working with Stanley until his sudden death in 1994.

After his father's death, Henry Stone stayed on at Stanley until he left in 1998 to set up his own company Henry Stone Decorating Products, which mainly imported products from Franpin, the large French brushmaker. In 2001 Henry left to work in the packaging business.

left Raymond Stone and his son Henry running the company (the other members of the Mosley family who had worked in the company left when it was sold). In the meantime Stanley had also bought Freiss, the German paint roller manufacturer, to strengthen their decorating products side.

Mosley Stone continued quite successfully for a time, but Stanley had their own problems world-wide, and made some cut backs, which included amalgamating the two separate brush factories in Leeds and Stockport into a new 30,000 sq ft premises in Leeds. To cope with the output a lot of shift working had to be used, and I should imagine they had some difficulties coping. At about the same time Raymond Stone died suddenly from a heart attack (he was only 65), a few days from the death of labour party leader John Smith for the same reason in 1994. Henry Stone then took over the running of the company, but for whatever reason their fortunes seemed to decline from about the same date. I used to meet Henry fairly often, and he complained that Stanley were not putting in the investment that they should have done. Then some of their senior sales people left, which was rather disruptive. Henry also felt that Stanley, whose headquarters were in the US, sometimes took much too long to give the OK to some urgently needed decision – as a private company, this obviously gave us an advantage. I do remember Henry saying to me once in some frustration "if ever you sell your company, don't sell it to the Americans!".

They lost a lot of business to us from Homebase and other retailers, and I should imagine now that our turnover is much larger than theirs (they don't publish separate accounts as a division of Stanley). Eventually, Stanley issued a rather terse announcement to the effect that Henry Stone was leaving the company "to spend more time with his family" on 1st October 1998. Henry then started his own company in Leeds, 'Henry Stone Decorating Products', whose principal business would be to import products made by the leading French brush manufacturer France Pinceaux. But Henry did not seem to make too much impact with his new company, and early in 2001 it was announced that he would be leaving Franpin UK (as it was now called) to pursue new interests.

Stanley made an approach to us in the early '80s, saying it was a long term ambition of theirs to be in the paint brush market. As with other approaches we turned them down, and as I have related they eventually fulfilled their ambition by buying Mosley Stone. I always found their actions somewhat strange, and I am therefore not altogether surprised that their entry into the paint brush market has not been totally successful. Although it may well have been sensible to leave existing (and successful) management in place when they bought the company, none of us are immortal, and the absence of a long term strategy was exposed on the death of Raymond Stone. What I think they should have done was to have integrated the decorating products more quickly into the Stanley brand and into their mainstream marketing effort. Whether this would have worked is still not certain – brands have a limited span, even well-known ones, and I am doubtful if the Stanley brand would have been as successful on decorating products as on their hand tools. They could also have done a lot more to try and include paint brushes and rollers into their product range all over the world, although again this would not have been easy in view of all the local competition they faced. I think in practice that the Stanley connection gave Mosley Stone very little extra success in export markets – this was evidenced by the fact that the large Stanley stand at the Cologne Fair in 2000 had very few products on it that were recognisably made in Leeds.

Ironically, Stanley had a similar experience in the USA. A few years ago they bought the American Brush Company, and announced their aim was to be the biggest in the brush field. They failed in this objective, and sold the company to Linzler, another US brush company. Although they have said that they intend to remain in the UK market, and have refused to sell the company back to Henry Stone, in 2002 it became known that they had been offering the company for sale (although they refused to give us any details). I later learned that negotiations had been held with Anza, but had broken down on price.

If my remarks in this section seem to indicate a certain scepticism about big companies and take-overs then that would certainly be correct. I remember well what happened after another strong approach that we received from the Duracell battery company in the early '80s. They were creating a new DIY division, and badly wanted to fit our company into it. As they were an internationally respected company, we paid quite a little attention to their interest, and met some of the personnel involved. We eventually turned them down, and a few years later one of their managers rang me to ask whether he could pop in for a chat. I naturally asked how their DIY division was faring; he dismissively replied "Oh, we closed that down some time ago!".

Chapter 5

IMPORTS

The last chapter on 'competitors' leads naturally on to a discussion on our main competitor at the present time – imports. As with so many other industries, we have suffered increasingly in recent years from cheap competition from goods manufactured in third world countries. In our case the main competitor is China. This is because China has long been the main source of the pig bristle used in paint brushes, and as long ago as the 1950s they tried their hand at making British-style paint brushes for sale here. These early efforts didn't come to very much, but by the 1970s there was a regular trade in cheap Chinese brushes, almost exclusively at the cheapest end of the market. For a period in the '80s there was a high anti-dumping duty on Chinese brushes, which had some effect, but this was challenged in the European Court by some German importers, and eventually dropped.

As long as imported brushes were 'cheap and nasty' the more established British manufacturers were able to keep their place in the middle and upper end of the market. What we feared, of course, was that the Chinese would be able to improve their quality, which would pose a much greater threat. In the second half of the '90s there was more and more evidence that that was happening. Chinese prices have always been very low. These have been based on factories using little or no machinery (as I can vouch from my own two visits there in 1978 and 1988) and very low wages – I believe away from the more developed areas, factory operatives are still paid less than £10 per week, although some benefits, such as accommodation and food, are provided at little or no cost. But the problem with hand work is that it is unreliable in quality, and although we have seen some good quality brushes from China, our experience is that it is very difficult to find a totally reliable source. For one thing, if factories get busy, they tend to sub-contract production to other nearby factories, and therefore one never knows whom one is buying from, and quality is never certain. I am sure that China could, and indeed some day will, improve her quality by investing in more machinery, although I think this is bound to push prices in an upwards direction.

Reliable figures are hard to come by, but even in the '70s substantial quantities of Chinese brushes were coming into this country – in 1980 they represented 15% of the total value of brushes sold, but no less than 40% of the numbers sold. Today these figures are much higher. The reaction of our competitors to this threat has varied. Hamilton Acorn, with a reputation for top quality decorators' brushes to defend, believe that nothing coming out of China today can compete with their production, whereas other manufacturers have become largely importers. Mosley Stone announced in 1998 that they would be reducing their manufacturing capacity in Leeds, and sourcing 50% of their production from China.

What are we doing about it? I have always tried to take a pragmatic view of the situation. In some ways I have been surprised how much of the British paint brush industry has survived, when so many other industries, some much more technical than ours, have largely surrendered to foreign imports. To list all the industries that were strong in Britain fifty years ago, and which have now largely disappeared, would take up far too much space, and yet there are still substantial quantities of paint brushes manufactured in this country, even though the number of companies has shrunk drastically. When I started work in the '60s, as well as Harris, there was Mosley Stone, Addis, Beechwood, Briton, Chadwick, Leng Armac, Hamiltons, Halls of Belfast, and Poly, to name just the larger ones, as well as several smaller manufacturers. Now we seem to be the only substantial manufacturer in the middle market, with Hamilton Acorn serving the top end of the trade, and Mosley Stone importing much of their production, as is Halls.

I hope I am realistic enough to see that this situation would probably not last for ever, and the British brush manufacturing would probably decline in the face of cheap Chinese imports at some stage. So I have always felt that if imported goods clearly offered better value than home produced ones, then we should be offering them, as if we didn't then someone else would. Retreating to the top of the market was not an option for us, as the business would not be sufficient to absorb our overheads. On the other hand, it still remains a fact that Chinese quality is unreliable, and their deliveries lengthy, if usually made on time. So I felt we would just have to react to the situation as it developed, without having any pre-conceived ideas one way or the other. Although one's instincts are bound to be to resist a decline in one's own manufactured goods, it is a fact that although we are already importing far more goods than we used to, our level of employment is as high as it has been for a long time. I suppose we are therefore a microcosm of the British economy – employment in manufacturing has been declining for very many years, yet overall employment is now as strong as it has been for 30 years, and the economy still growing. So what does it matter, you can argue, if one sector of the economy declines? A productive workforce, such as that in Britain, will always find something else to turn their hand to if some opportunities are denied them.

Our company has taken advantage of cheap imported sundry items for many years – everything from sandpaper to dustsheets, from trimming knives to masking tape. We have also sold a line of throw-away Chinese brushes since the mid-

2002 – the factory at Zhaoqing, near Guangzhou, which we have leased and where we hope to start production later in 2002.

80s, but it was not until the late '90s that we started to buy more extensively from the Chinese brush industry. This was to satisfy a demand from our export customers for less expensive brushes than we could make (in truth, we have never been very successful in exporting our own paint brushes except in a few special markets), as well as responding to a demand from our major customers for ever cheaper lines. At the time of writing in 2002 it seems that this demand is turning into a flood – in particular, both Homebase and FDIA, who were newly owned by profit-hungry venture capitalists, are seeing a switch to imported goods as the easy way to make more money quickly.

This is against a background of a bigger switch from domestically made to imported consumer goods than I have ever experienced in my working career. In the recession of the early '80s, it was a popular cry amongst Mrs Thatcher's opponents than she was presiding over the dismantling of British industry. It is certainly true that the strength of sterling at that time (brought on by the flow of North Sea oil) did lead to an increase of imports, and was also accompanied by a big rise in unemployment. But although employment has since much improved, the rise in the tide of imports has never abated. Just one example: in the '60s, imported cars accounted for less than 10% of the market. Now, with all Ford's and GM's popular cars being made abroad, the figure is nearly 80%. There was something of a slow-down in imports in the early '90s after the £ was ejected from the exchange rate mechanism and fell sharply, but in 1997 it started rising again, and for the last five years has remained strong, particularly against the Euro. This period happens to coincide with the new Labour government, and I think I can truthfully say that there has been a far greater switch to imported goods generally in that period than there ever was in the early '80s. Pressure on the margins of leading retailers, such as Marks & Spencer, has forced them to look more and more at sourcing their products in low cost countries, and as I write this the price of goods in the shops is actually falling year on year, the first time this has happened since the last war. And no country has been more at the forefront of our new low-cost suppliers than China, and in particular the Pearl River delta area between Hong Kong and Guangzhou (Canton) has become to the world what Birmingham was in the 19th century.

Our Chinese Factory
When we saw the prospects of a big increase in imported brushes, we realised that we would have to improve our contacts with China. My father visited China once, and I went there with parties of brush manufacturers from Europe in 1978 and 1988, but other than that no-one from our company had been there until the late '90s. But since then China has seen a veritable flood of visits from Harris personnel. Nick Evered has been there several times on behalf of our export customers, and several of our home trade personnel had paid visits in 1999 and 2000. In 2001 John Love was made director in charge of sourcing products from China and elsewhere. Then towards the end of 2001 Gary Jordan and Stuart Hobbs proposed that we establish our own manufacturing plant in China. We

In February 2002 we appointed Ken Xu, who had previously worked as a sales manager in a paint roller factory, as the manager of our new Chinese enterprise. This photograph was taken in the White Swan Hotel in Guangzhou, after we had finalised Ken's appointment, with Gary Jordan and Stuart Hobbs.

had, of course, considered this before, but this time Gary and Stuart had a potential general manager in mind. He was Ken Xu, a senior salesman in a company called Mingye situated near Guangzhou, that we were buying paint rollers from. Ken was young and keen to get on and I agreed that perhaps the time had come to start up our own company there. The argument was that it was inevitable that imports from China would go on increasing and our own manufacturing at Stoke Prior would decline. If we continued just to merchant imported brushes, there was a danger that our customers might by-pass us altogether, and buy direct from the Chinese sources. But by having our own factory there, using at least some modern machinery, we could aim to supply a better quality Chinese brush, which was the one area where China was still letting its customers down. Customers, such as B&Q, who have a strong environmental policy also like the idea of dealing direct with a known factory in China, as otherwise checking on the *bona fides* of Chinese factories is difficult at best.

So Gary, Stuart and I met Ken in Guangzhou in February 2002 and, after looking at a number of premises, found somewhere that looked to be ideal in the city of Zhaoqing, about 90 minutes drive west of Guangzhou. Ken was engaged, and production started in our new factory towards the end of 2002.

I have so far only talked about the import of brushes, and I think this will be the main section of our business to be affected. We have always been quite strong in the painters tool market, and in the UK the impact of imports has been relatively small until recently. However, many of the export markets we created with our good value tools in the '60s and '70s have been lost to cheaper products. The first ones that affected us were copies of our tools from Japan, which ate into our markets in Europe in the 1970s. Taiwan took over from Japan as suppliers of mid-quality tools, and we have lost many good markets to that country, including the US and Australia. But they were not cheap enough to compete too strongly in the UK. But there are now signs that China can offer some better quality cheap tools, so it looks as if we might suffer more competition in this field too.

Although we do not import many paint rollers (except mini-rollers, which we have never made), we gave up making the relatively fiddly metal work for rollers in the 1980s, and purchased roller wires and cages from Taiwan, which had tooled up to supply the US on a large scale. As with so many things, Taiwanese entrepreneurs have switched most of their production to China, and we now buy most of our handles and wires from China, although we still wind most of our own roller sleeves, and assemble the finished rollers and sets. These are relatively bulky and low value items, which means that the freight from the Far East is a high proportion of the cost.

Chapter 6

MY COLLEAGUES AT WORK

My father only made passing reference to his fellow directors and colleagues, and, as I feel I owe a great debt to those I have worked with, I would like to mention some of them.

Peter Harrison and Geoff Fox
When I joined the board in 1970 the others were Douglas Wride (production), Henry Wynekin (finance), Peter Harrison (home sales), Dick Deeley (purchasing), Ramsay Eveson (personnel) and Henry Reiner (export sales). They are shown in a photograph at the end of chapter 4. As my father was always very closely involved with factory matters, I worked mainly on sales and marketing in my early years, and therefore had much to do with home and export sales. I got on very well with Peter Harrison, who was my first cousin once removed. In some ways he was very traditional, always addressing the reps as 'Mr', and insisting on good standards of dress ("business suit at all times", new recruits were told), but he had a good sense of humour, and I think the managers and representatives enjoyed working for him. He retired only a little before his 65th birthday, and continued to enjoy his DIY and other hobbies in his retirement. Sadly he lost his wife Diana soon after he retired, but after this he lived on a boat for some time, enjoyed sailing it, and ended his days near his daughter's farm on Anglesey.

When he retired we naturally looked to the sales force for his replacement, and appointed Geoff Fox, who had been an outstandingly successful representative in the Bristol area before being promoted to manager of the west country sales region. The region he led was for many years our most successful one, so his selection to succeed Peter Harrison was not difficult. Geoff and his wife Brenda moved from his native Bristol (where he had been well known as a footballer and cricketer - he turned to golf as he got older) to live in Inkberrow in

My father, Peter Harrison (sales director), and Geoff Fox when manager of West Country Office c. 1960. Geoff later succeeded Peter as sales director on his retirement in 1974.

1974, but they suffered ill fortune soon after when not only did a fireball cause a major fire in their new home, but Geoff suffered a heart attack. But he overcame both of these adversities, and continued to be a successful sales director until he retired at 65, even though he suffered a second heart attack before he finished. Geoff retired in 1989, but sadly died on the golf course on 1st January 1994. It is nice to record that two of his sons have worked for us. Andrew was employed as a representative after he trained as a car mechanic, and was (and remains) very successful. Stephen was a chef and ran our canteen for many years before deciding to leave and buy his own pub.

Glyn Lowe and Gary Jordan
In 1984 we decided for the first time to appoint a national accounts manager at Stoke Prior – before this these accounts had been looked after by our regional managers, or sales director. So we appointed Glyn Lowe, who lived in Sheffield and had been manager of our north east division, to this position, and he and his wife Mary moved to the attractive village of Kempsey near Worcester, very different from his native Yorkshire. Glyn's family had run a newsagents business, but there was not room in the family shop for him when he left school, so he acquired his own which he and Mary ran very successfully for a number of years.

Geoff Fox.

Glyn was ambitious and not afraid of hard work, so he decided to apply for a reps job with us, and in this and his later managerial position he was successful. At Stoke Prior, although he was not so used to working in an office environment, he soon established a good relationship with the major accounts he then had to deal with, and, judging by our later successes, I am sure it was the right decision to base our national accounts team at head office rather than out in the field.

When Geoff Fox retired Glyn was keen to succeed him, which he did, but unfortunately his career was thereafter dogged by health problems. He had a defective heart valve, which began to give problems, and, like Geoff, he suffered a heart attack. I am sure that Glyn would be the first to agree that, partly because of this, he struggled somewhat with the paperwork involved in running a sales force which still consisted of over 50 men – I think Glyn was always happier working as part of a team, or negotiating face to face with a customer, than catching up with paperwork. Eventually Glyn felt he had to accept his doctor's advice and retire early, which he did at the beginning of 1996.

This left us rather unexpectedly having to find a replacement, and again we turned to our own existing staff first. We did consider a number of applications, but we felt one was outstanding – that of Gary Jordan. Unlike his predecessors, Gary had never been out 'in the field', but had joined us straight from school in 1977. His first job was as a stores assistant, but he soon realised he was ambitious to get on, and in 1980 was appointed to a clerical position in the sales office. Then after a few years another, bigger, opportunity came up – that of marketing manager, when the first person to hold that position, George Davies, decided to leave.

Although only 25 at the time, we recognised that Gary had both talent and the capacity for hard work, so he took over the position. To give him a sound grounding in marketing he took the Institute of Marketing exams studying at home, and he soon got on top of his new job. When he was promoted to the board as sales director he had to broaden his skills to include management of people, and, although I think a few people rather resented his rapid rise within the company, he soon became liked and respected by the sales force and the team of national account salesmen he was responsible for.

National Accounts, John Love and Stuart Hobbs

I have already described the importance we attached to our national accounts executives, and when our first, Glyn Lowe, was appointed sales director we appointed two replace-

Glyn Lowe (right) with a retiring representative, Les Monks.

ments. Since then the team has been built up to the present four. Some of our appointments have been very successful, but have moved on. Steve Collinge was appointed straight from Bromsgrove College as a marketing assistant, but after only a short time in this job was promoted to national accounts, where he did very well, looking after the Wickes account till he left to join a bigger company. Ruth Cattel was the only lady in this position, and did well handling the DIA account, and we were sorry to lose her when she decided to start her own consultancy. Two other successful appointments are still with us. John Love was appointed in 1990, and later became the leader of the national accounts team, as well as handling the B&Q account. In this role he started doing deals with suppliers in China and Indonesia for our national account customers, and eventually in 2001 it was decided that he should concentrate on this entirely and become the overseas sourcing director.

Stuart Hobbs joined the national accounts team in 1993, and it was soon obvious that he had exceptional abilities in forming positive relationships with our customers as well as being a good team worker, and it was he, always working closely with Gary Jordan, who built up the Homebase account that was one of the main reasons for the rise in our turnover from 1995 onwards. They also formed a very good relationship with Chris Willmott, who took over the buying

1993 – the DIY exhibition at the NEC. Glyn Lowe (seated left) with Judith Banham (national accounts assistant), Ann McArthur (customer services) and Stuart Hobbs, later National Accounts Director. Standing (left to right) Gary Jordan, Steve Collinge, Carl Dudley and Wayne Hill.

at B&Q in 2000, as a result of which our sales to B&Q have doubled. Stuart was appointed national accounts director in 2001.

Henry Reiner and Derek Starr
In most companies export sales are closely integrated into the sales department, but we have always tended to keep home and export sales separate. I think this was because my father put a lot of emphasis right from the early days on exports, as should be apparent from reading his narrative, and amongst the first directors appointed in 1959 was Henry Reiner, the exports sales director. He retired in 1970 and died in 1991. He was from a well-to-do Austrian family and was born and brought up in Vienna. He came here as a refugee from the Nazi persecution of the Jews. His sister was interned in Auschwitz, but, amazingly,

survived and is still alive in 2002 aged 93. My mother thinks he met my father through his brother-in-law Ron Garman, who was helping to resettle refugees. He was one of a number of men of continental origin who worked for us after the war. Otto Schramm was from Czechoslovakia and ran our accounts department, Roman Bridgewater (his anglicised name) was ex-Polish airforce and ran the canteen, and Richard Schmidl was an ex-German POW who was our production scheduler for many years. Henry Reiner's troubled background did not seem to cloud his life too much when I knew him, and he had a very positive attitude to export selling right up to his retirement. Finding a replacement was not easy, and we made a few unsuccessful appointments from our own sales staff. In the '70s the export office manager was a young man called Derek Starr, and he expressed an interest doing some export selling for us. We were happy to encourage him in this ambition, and he began to be quite successful. Then a tragedy happened that my father does not relate in his book, but I think it should be mentioned in any history of our company.

Due to the many changes of staff after Henry Reiner retired Derek had become the only person who knew all our systems and customers, and was in a considerable position of trust. On 22nd July 1981 (the day after the Royal Wedding), my father called me to his office, where he was in discussion with Brian Middleton, financial director. Something unusual had been reported to Brian. This concerned the commission payments that we made to our agents in different countries. Many of our sales were made to distributors abroad, and so there was no commission involved, but in some countries we still had commission agents who took orders from customers which we supplied direct, and were compensated by a commission payment, usually 10%, and which was paid to them monthly. Strictly speaking, their commission cheques should have been sent to them direct, but some had asked us to credit an account in the UK, sometimes under another name.

What Brian had found out was that commission cheques for several different agents were being paid to the same account in Worcester. He immediately wondered whether these payments were genuine, so after I was briefed in my father's office we asked Derek Starr to join us and explain the payments. As soon as we had told him what we wanted to know, he said without hesitation that everything could be explained – he had written instructions from different agents, and he said he would go downstairs to get the evidence supporting the payments we had queried.

My father, Brian and I waited in the office for Derek to come back… and waited and waited. He didn't come. So we phoned the export office to ask where he was, and we were told that he had left the building. At that moment we knew that he had been guilty of a fraud, and that he would not return to the office, and we informed the other staff.

That same day I was booked to go on holiday to Kenya with my family, and when I left Heathrow that evening I had heard nothing further of the fate of Derek. The first week of our holiday we were on safari, and it was not until we visited our manager in Nairobi, Bill Caleb, that I learned the sequel. It seems that Derek had immediately realised that he had been found out, and had imbibed a large amount of alcohol. He had then gone to a local lake and drowned himself.

Perhaps we should have caught on to what was going on earlier – a few weeks before it happened, I had queried with Derek the amount of commission we were paying, and he breezily put me off a further investigation. But it is easy to be wise after the event. What was happening was that Derek had created some false commission accounts for agents who didn't exist (he kept all these manually at the time) and issued cheques to the credit of an accomplice, whose bank account he used. We never discovered exactly how much money had disappeared, but Brian estimated it was between £10k and £20k – it had been going on for some years. Derek had not appeared to be living above his income, but we found out that his personal life had become rather complicated, and this was where the money was going. We obviously felt very sorry for Derek's family (he had a wife and young child), who were not involved in any way in the fraud, and did what we could to make sure they were not too badly off after Derek's sudden death.

Frank Redfern and his staff

We then had to set about yet again finding a new export sales manager (there had not been a director since Henry Reiner retired). Our next appointment turned out to be longer lived and more successful. He was Frank Redfern, who had recently lost his job when Ronson had suddenly gone into receivership. Frank

The directors in 1996 on the occasion of Frank Redfern's retirement. Next to myself and my wife is Robert Brooks, Frank, Gary Jordan, Paul Chandler and Geoffrey Braithwaite.

had already arranged to take a 6 months course in export marketing, so could not start with us until January 1982, which we accepted. He moved to a pretty cottage near the village of Inkberrow from his native Surrey, and I think he and his wife Janet settled very well here. Frank had wide experience in exports and some language ability, and soon got to grips with the department and our customers. The last 20 years have not been an easy time for British exporters, mainly because of the rise of manufacturing in low-wage countries that compete with us in most export markets, but Frank managed to keep exports growing in line with our general sales throughout the '80s. But during the '90s our exports have stagnated at between £1.5m and £2.0m, which now represents only about half the proportion of our sales that they did previously. Nevertheless, I think we have done fairly well to maintain our sales at a time when many British exporters have had a real struggle to survive. In 1990 we recognised Frank's efforts by appointing him to the board, and he retired in 1996 when he was 61 – a wise decision as world travel is something more suited to the young and fit. Since that time I have taken overall responsibility for export sales, as we didn't want to incur the expense of appointing a new senior manager.

As related in the earlier part of the manuscript, ever since the '70s we have had at least one other export salesman to supplement the export manager. When Frank joined us the export traveller was David Aldridge, but in 1989 he left, and we appointed Christine Davis in his place. When she retired in 2001 Christine had been with us for 13 years, and I have always admired the professionalism and energy she gave to the job, which can be very tiring at times. This is particularly the case with Christine as she chose to try and get us business in South America, a region where we had done very little before. The success of Christine's efforts has been a little spasmodic, but she has never given up travelling to some of the more distant parts of the world. When Frank was approaching retirement he suggested that another appointment be made to give us the right options after he had finished, so we appointed Nick Evered. Since Frank retired Nick and Christine have divided the world between them – Nick doing the right hand side (eastern hemisphere) and Christine the left, an arrangement that has worked well. After Christine retired, Nick Evered took overall control of export sales, and we made two new appointments to join him – Collete Hurdman and John Haynes.

Douglas Wride and Paul Chandler

Douglas Wride was my father's right hand man as far as the factory was concerned, and they would spend an hour or so in conference every day discussing works matters. He was well-versed in a number of management issues, and was very helpful with developing the pension scheme. Douglas was also an active Quaker, and was involved with my father's work with prisoners and ex-prisoners. His service as a Birmingham JP gave him very useful experience, and my father always paid tribute to his calming attitude when others (including my father) got too excited.

Brian Middleton at the time of his retirement in 1993.

Douglas retired in 1984, and sadly died suddenly in 1990. He was succeeded by Paul Chandler, who had joined the company as assistant buyer, before taking over the buying function after Dick Deeley left. Paul therefore already had wide knowledge of the way we operated, even though he had no technical qualifications. Paul is rather like Douglas in being a valuable calming influence, and has embraced 'world class manufacturing' and all that goes with it without any problem, and has been most successful in turning our sometimes rather slowly moving factory ship in the right direction in the 1990s. Paul was not a director when he was purchasing manager, but joined the board in 1985.

Henry Wynekin, Brian Middleton, Geoffrey Braithwaite and David Cooper

Finance is a rather specialist area, and we have had to turn outside to appoint our financial director more than once. In 1965 Herbert Wynekin held this post. He was a very able accountant, but was one of those who talked a lot – I avoided going into his office, as it was usually very difficult to get out! For this reason he did not always get on too well with my father, who sometimes thought he was more talk than action. When Herbert retired in 1972 we appointed Brian Middleton his successor. Brian had joined us in 1952, and had proved himself an able clerk, and so he proved as company secretary and financial director. Although he had previously enjoyed good health, in 1992 Brian rather suddenly found he had a heart problem, and was away sick for several months for this reason. In 1993 he decided he would like to take early retirement. I am happy to say that at the time of writing he is enjoying his retirement, and his health seems to have stabilised.

At the time of his retirement Brian was not yet 60 and we had not planned any succession. But by a coincidence an old friend of the family who had recently retired early was looking for work, and we decided to see him. He was Geoffrey Braithwaite, who had been company secretary at Kalamazoo. We had known him through his father, Morland Braithwaite, who had been a professional photographer and had done much work for our company, including making some company films, and some of the photographs used earlier in this book. Geoffrey was a professional accountant, and had worked for most of his life at Kalamazoo, a company in Northfield, Birmingham, that had very successfully produced office paperwork systems, but that had not been so successful in adapting to the computer age. We decided that Geoffrey's experience would be invaluable to us, and he was appointed on a short term three year contract.

His appointment worked out very well, but in 1996 he was due to retire, and we set about again finding a replacement. After advertising we had several applications, but eventually appointed David Cooper, a 32 year old accountant who had worked for various companies in the Birmingham area and was looking for advancement. In the six years we have known David we have got on with him very well, and he has identified his future with that of the company – he has bought a house in Bromsgrove and in 2001 married, and had his first child the following year. He is presently the youngest member of our board of directors, which has a good balance of ages.

1998 – the opening of our new packing department by Julie Kirkbride, the newly elected MP for Bromsgrove. (Left to right) David Cooper, Paul Chandler, Robert Brooks, my wife and myself.

Dick Deeley and Robert Brooks

Dick Deeley had been with the company since the Birmingham days, and continued to live in Birmingham after the move to Stoke Prior – the same applied to Douglas Wride. Dick seemed to me when I joined to be coping with his sometimes rather stressful job very well. Our purchasing office can often be rather frantic, with the staff having to find urgent spare parts for broken-down machines, check on supplies for the current production programme, bring forward a bought-in line that has suddenly gone out of stock, and devote 15 minutes to seeing a rep who has called, all at the same time. Towards the end of his time with us he had developed a drink problem, and we helped him try and overcome it. But eventually it was agreed that it would be better if he left the company for a less stressful job elsewhere. Sadly he died before he reached retiring age. Paul Chandler took over, and when he was promoted to works director Robert Brooks replaced him as buyer. Robert had worked, like Gary Jordan, as a clerk in sales department, but took to purchasing well, having the ability to retain knowledge of many of the very large number of items he deals with and their suppliers. Robert has remained a bachelor, and was was appointed a director in 1990.

Ramsay Eveson, George Chance and Ethna Harris

Finally, personnel. Again, many companies our size would not have a personnel director, but with our large workforce, which has only once briefly dipped below 250 in 50 years, we have always considered this desirable. Ramsay Eveson had joined the firm when it moved to Stoke Prior before the war, and took a great interest in local affairs, even to the extent of serving on the local Council, although he was politically not of the same persuasion as myself. He retired in 1973 and died in 1988. He lived all his life in a house that he built in Brickhouse Lane, not far from the factory, and his widow Nancy has only recently left it for a residential home.

When we had over 500 employees we had a full time works nurse who was also a valuable help in dealing with personnel problems, and this arrangement continued under Ramsay's successor, George Chance, who had previously been manager of the despatch department. George was another whose service dated back to pre-war days – he joined us straight from school aged 14, and during the war he had served with the RAF, gaining the DFM. He took part in some of the large bombing raids that occurred towards the end of the war, but always thought the immense loss of life these caused was more than it need have been. George was well liked as a personnel director, and continued to organise the long run of successful arts festivals that are referred to earlier. Some time before his retirement he had to cope with the death of our works nurse through illness. As a part time replacement we engaged Ethna Phillips (who later became my second wife), a fully qualified medical sister, and she enjoyed working in a factory environment so much that on George's retirement in 1987 she was appointed in his place. She joined the board in 1991.

The board of directors, December 2001. Left to right (standing) Stuart Hobbs, David Cooper, Robert Brooks, my brother Richard, and John Love. Seated: Gary Jordan, my wife, myself and Paul Chandler. (Next page) – my wife and myself photographed at Christmas 2001.

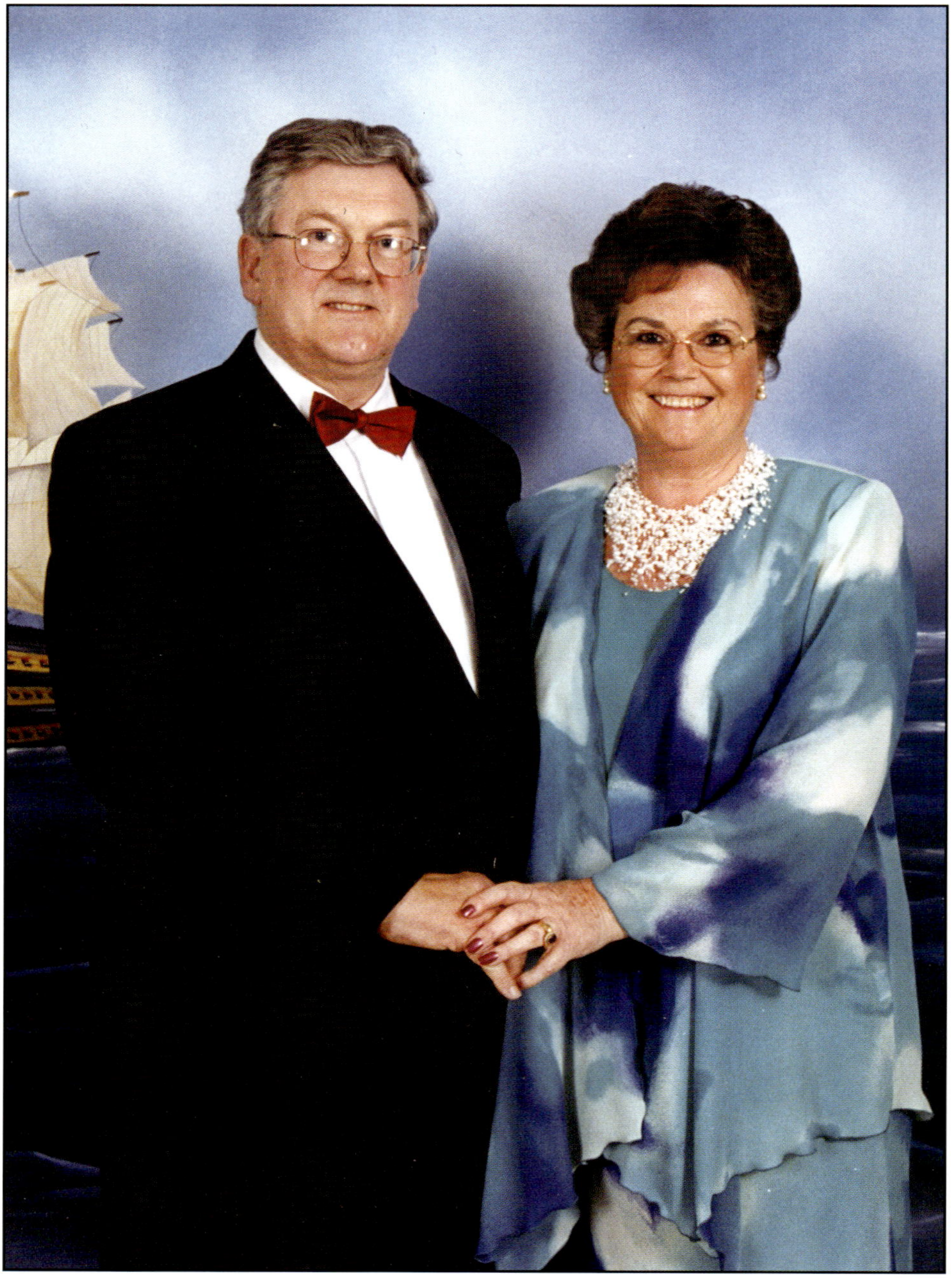